One: Song of Being

Mora McIntyre

True Inspiration Publishing

Copyright © Mora McIntyre 2017

The right of Mora McIntyre to be identified as the author of this work has been asserted by her in accordance with the Copyright, Designs and Patents Act 1988. All rights reserved.

No part of this book may be reproduced, stored in a retrieval system, or transmitted, in any form, or by any means (electronic, mechanical, photocopying, recording or otherwise) without the prior written permission of the author, except in cases of brief quotations embodied in reviews or articles. It may not be edited, lent, resold, hired out, distributed or otherwise circulated without the publisher's written permission.

ISB 978-1-9997006-0-7

First published in paperback and ebook by Ingram Spark for True Inspiration Publishing in 2017

Cover design and illustrative diagrams by Mora McIntyre with professional assistance from Barbara Doherty

Layout by Barbara Doherty
Cover photo © Paul Demuth

To all those wonderful, brave people who have come to seek support in going deeper and finding what is real and true. You have allowed me to see so much and inspired the sharing of this.

LIST OF CONTENTS

Notes 6

Introduction 7

1. Song of the **body-Being** 9
2. Radical Surgery for the **Mind** 26
3. Navigational Skills of the **Heart** 54
4. Exploring the Ground of **Feelings** 82
5. **Intuition** – The Voice of Being 105
6. **Highly Sensitive People** and the Loneliness of an Unshared Reality 131
7. **Body** of the Beloved 148
8. Natural **Aliveness** 170
9. Sacred **Sensuality** 188
10. **Sexual Union** and the Search for the Inner Lover 204
11. A Living **Spirituality** 217
12. Meetings with Remarkable **Teachers** 243
13. **Awakening** through Joy 266
14. The **Politics** of Inner Sense 279
15. Creating a **Community** of One 309
16. **Practical Suggestions** for Coming Free. 341

Epilogue 367

Acknowledgements 370

References 371

NOTES ON READING THIS BOOK

One of the central themes of this book is learning to listen-in and trust your own knowing, so it's important to keep referencing this knowing as to whether what you read feels true. Subtle realities are best alluded to or described tentatively, and all who write are subject to their own influences and potential for misunderstanding or bias. What I am sharing with you is what I am seeing at the moment of writing, and this may change as the seeing deepens. Although I am writing about profound things and part of what I do is teach, I make no claims to any kind of permanent awakening: I simply love to share what I see.

I suggest you don't try to read this book straight through but give yourself time to reflect and digest. This is because whilst the intellect wants to grasp information: to assess, compare, file it and move on; the intuitive heart needs time to receive, discern and digest. Hence the anecdotes, which form part of a deliberate attempt of break the former process, allowing space to relax and lighten up.

NOTES ON EXERCISES

You will find many of the exercises at the end of each chapter include body-based movements, some including words, some with diagrams. They are intended to allow for a progression, so certain exercises are more useful at the beginning whilst others work better further along, when other things have been seen and digested; and some may work better for you than others.

Ultimately, these exercises are guides: your own body-Being may introduce its own, if you can be still and listen, trust and simply follow your body. With all the exercises it is important that you *feel* them as you do them. That way you will be in tune with your own body and *sense* how they work, what they are saying, what they are allowing to be spoken, who is speaking and the integrity of this body-based voice. In allowing Being to speak freely through the body, you come to know the union of body and Being: body-Being. You come to experience your natural state.

INTRODUCTION

I decided to write this book because I wanted to bring together and share different aspects of my work and the experiences outside of this which give it depth. I don't see myself as either an enlightened spiritual teacher, a healer or a psychotherapist. In fact none of the labels we use for people who work with others quite fits. The way I work is unorthodox in that it isn't based on any formal training. Instead, it draws on direct connection with something far greater than this, the essence of life I call 'Being'.

I have been developing this intuitive way of working on many levels for going on forty years. It is here that I have witnessed the essential spirituality of what we call the 'body', itself a hugely under-rated, multi-dimensional organ for apprehending and responding to life. And the primacy of the heart in the midst of all this. The aim of the work has always been the same: to support people in re-connecting with their essence and, over time, to meet and let go of whatever is in the way of living from a place of authentic Being-ness.

This lack of a formal structure based on others' ideas and experiences has in itself been a unique teaching. It has meant there is nothing to hold on to, apart from trust in what I sense it is that actually 'does the work', trust in Being. It has allowed me to see something profound about the nature of life, to have direct experience of intuitive reality without the distortion of the mind. I don't know why I was drawn to simply let go and follow this intuitive process, an essential requirement of which is the letting go of 'me', the egoic mind, which just gets in the way. In this process I have leant that life *knows* if we let ourselves listen and respond. In the end, this is all there is.

It became apparent to me a few years ago, that there was a need for the various ways of seeing and approaching ourselves I have learned through this work, to be made available to a wider public, so for the last few years writing this has been the main focus of my time and attention. I also have a strong interest in what is happening in the world at this time; that whilst we may not always know how to contribute from a place of love and awareness, I sense a powerful longing for the deep values of the heart to emerge and create a different environment. You can call this longing 'spiritual' but you don't need to.

When I started writing this book, some people said to me 'You can't write about all those different things; you should identify your audience and write for them.' I am hoping to prove them wrong, because only in talking about many parts of a whole can something that threads them together be recognised. So whilst writing this is a way of giving back for the amazing grace of this life, it is also an opportunity to keep looking. We are not encouraged to question and dive deep, and that is just what we are going to do here: swing open the gate and pay a call on all those places that are so often shuttered up and out-of-bounds.

It's hard in the writing of such material not to lose any light playfulness when immersed in dark and difficult realms, but there's no way to leave anything out. Because within this book is an attempt to place a lens over life that highlights an intuitive flow, so it can be recognised and lived. To illustrate this, I share with you my own intuitive 'seeing', experiences from my personal life, how this intuitive flow operates in my work with others, and how these strands appear in and impact on all areas of our lives.

I once had a wonderful Irish setter in my life, who regularly took me for walks and reminded me how to play and explore. With her gleaming coat bouncing and eyes shining with delight, she would dig and ferret around, unearthing all kinds of treasures; then she would bow down, front paws-to-elbows on the ground, inviting me to investigate, before leaping up, racing around in circles and tearing off full tilt, turning her head to call me to join her. Every single cell of that beloved creature was fully alive!

This is the kind of invitation I would like to be able to offer you: help in hunting down what is true but often hidden, and tracking this as you rediscover any and all aspects of life that have, for whatever reason, remained unseen, unrecognised and unlived. Questions arise in this process: about why this happens and what can be done about it. In other words, questions about the set-up (because it is a set-up) so you can see what lies beyond the limits most of us have given ourselves about how we live our lives, recognise what creates these and find ways to let them go. And this involves touching into the vast, vital, alive space that we all live within and are part of.

I am calling it 'living intuitive reality' because this is what it is. This space is constantly broadcasting so much magnificence, on so many levels, with no cessation. Its nature is highly responsive, allowing for immediate communication, clear and simple: *this is just not of the mind*. Instead, you are asked to listen inwards and follow a call. It's time to wake up and let go of old defences, insecurities and fears, of false hopes and avoidance strategies; time to risk opening up to experiencing *all* of this reality – including when it feels uncomfortable, even at times painful or scary, and surely not where the mind would choose to go. *Time to apprehend fully what it means to be part of the whole.*

And the prize? The idea of 'spiritual awakening' tempts with promises of freedom from all suffering and a state of endless bliss. But what if letting life live through you is more amazing, more extraordinary, more complete and satisfying than we can begin to imagine? And the union of love and truth, when *known*, its own fulfilment?

Song of the body-Being

'You'll never bump into anything more extraordinary, more amazing, more mysterious than life without your idea about it.' ~ Adyashanti

These eyes have a particular vantage point. They witness Being emerging free from the constraints of a crystallised Ego. They see the evidence. If you want proof you can wait forever – or you can trust what you intuitively know to be true.

The song of the body-Being carries the invitation to listen to the siren song of your heart 'Return... Return... Return...

Living – Intuitive – Reality: wow! Sounds amazing, doesn't it? 'But what does this actually mean?' you might ask. 'I thought intuition was some kind of human attribute *within* reality.' Saying that reality *itself* is intuitive gives it far greater significance. It brings a certain sense of depth and aliveness to reality – a sense of both expansion and inclusion. In fact, the implications are vast. If intuition is the receiving of insight, where does this come *from*? Does this mean that life itself *knows*? Is aware? Can communicate with itself? And if so, how does it do this? Could it be that it does this through *us?* And if through us – then perhaps through everything? You are unlikely to be able to grasp the full significance of what is being said here with an evidence-seeking mind. Where it may be *known* is in the living of what you are: *in your actual experience.*

And here we come to a dilemma: the fact is that many of us have had unusual experiences, experiences that don't fit the parameters of reality we have been given. We may question these parameters, especially when we are young and our view less limited. There is this vague sense of there being more to life, of something important being missing, and yet not knowing how to approach this, how to explore it – even how to talk about it. It all feels too nebulous, too difficult to describe. This is because intuitive reality doesn't lend itself to words or thoughts; it is not of the mind. Rather, it is apprehended through the senses, through feelings and, sometimes, it is just directly *known*. And this being so – if the full range of intuitive reality can be *known* – it raises other questions such as 'What is preventing this happening? What gets in the way? What has happened to humanity that our innate intuitive capacity has become sidelined?' Looking to answer these questions and explore the many realms it touches on – how this intuitive reality can be lived – is what this book is about.

Perhaps you remember when you were a child wondering about life? What it was and how strange it all seemed? You maybe noticed how inexplicable and inconsistent was the behaviour of the adults around you – how this provoked feelings of confusion and doubt. Of not knowing whether to trust your own experience or discount this, because it conflicted with what you were being told? This is a common childhood experience that undermines our delicate sense of connection to a deeper reality: a reality based on knowing who, and what, we are. It interferes with our ability to live *from* this. In response, many of us developed a private, inner world: a world we didn't have to share.

Perhaps one night you had a dream – a dream a bit different to the usual ones – that gave you a deep sense of something profound and magical and somehow *known?* Or maybe while gazing at a star-filled night sky or a clear-as-glass lake, but not necessarily – maybe just gazing into a puddle! Or perhaps it was a sudden sense of immediate and profound peace on smelling the cakes your grandma brought out of the oven, or the way your dog looked up at you, smiling into your eyes or... thank heaven children are not limited by boring old reason and logic, and things having to be proven and explained and justified! They are so open to all kinds of magical events – and magical *interpretations* of events. That is, open to the 90% of reality we have learned to ignore or not truly give value and attention to.

I can remember, as a child, lying in bed and looking out into the branches of a tall oak tree that grew inside our garden, just beside the entrance gates. The angle of the street lamp behind this tree created a dark cross in the branches. And for years – although my family weren't religious – I felt this to be a protection that guarded me from anything malign entering our home. Was there a cross? Was it a *real* cross, or just a trick of the light? And how could a cross protect me anyway? Totally irrelevant questions to a child – because what mattered to me then was my *sense* of safety. And this was not placed in any rational framework. It was my own private property, subject to my own inner longings and fears. A fifteen-foot-high steel fence, topped with razor wire, with a watch tower and armed guards patrolling the perimeter, would not have given me this sense of safety. This was because the things that frightened me weren't tangible, they weren't restricted by the laws of physics – anymore than were the things which drew me in and intrigued and delighted me.

One of the saddest things about the time we live in is the denigration and denial of anything that can't be explained, weighed, measured, proved or justified. Instead, life is reduced to an incredibly narrow, un-nourishing and completely out-of-balance, flat concrete roadway. Everything of mystery is deemed dubious until explained. The sacred that lies in true beauty is unmeasurable, and therefore not addressed. The thrill of listening to a blackbird singing its heart out the same, and so on. And this avoidance and denial has an enormous cost. *We lose the ability to listen to life* – to read the signs and follow the subtle currents. We forget our true nature and what *really* matters. We freeze our capacity for spontaneous response. In so doing, we start to shut down and lose our integrity, our energy, our aliveness – and, along with this – our true humanity.

Cloud gazing and intuition

So what would living intuitively look like? How would it differ from the 'normal' version of reality? How might we approach life in a much more open and fluid way? I have a great love of gazing at clouds, which often seem to inspire a powerful sense of the intuitive. Why should this be so? Let me describe it. Where I live part of my time, in the mountains of Southern Spain, there is a wonderful view of the sky, along with some amazing sunsets. Curiously, we often seem to get unusual shapes amongst the clouds (I am not talking about names given to different types of cloud formation here, but the shapes formed by individual clouds themselves). And it came to me one time, standing utterly absorbed in this spectacle, that perhaps why intuition seems to flourish so well while looking at clouds is because of the *nature* of these shapes. It is easy to project images onto them, to find faces and strange creatures or ships and castles and so on – but then it changes again: *there is no permanency.* One cloud may pass in front of another, perhaps moving at a faster rate, or it may be higher in the sky; but all are subject to the hidden currents in the air, giving the movement a three dimensional aspect.

And – significantly – there are not, *and cannot be*, names for these transient shapes; they can't be captured within the confines of things we humans have learned to identify and give names to, using our mind. As Krishnamurti remarked: 'Once you have been told some winged creature you saw flying across the sky is a bird, you never see it again'. Meaning, once it has a name, you no longer see its true nature, its essence. And so, in looking at these clouds and their constantly changing shapes (or waves moving in the sea, for that matter, or the leaves on a tree blowing in the wind) we are forced to let go of the mind and its concepts. Mind, with its interpretive filter through which we have learned to perceive reality; mind with its attempts to name and classify, and thereby control everything. We have to let go. Then – and only then – do we see *what is actually there!* We see this intuitively: we see actual reality.

How do we know what clouds are doing? What is really going on in the sky? Perhaps some unknown force, some greater being is painting pictures, producing endless shapes and designs that we neither recognise nor appreciate? Who knows what the wind *really* is? A master shape-shifter of clouds of monumental proportion, chasing, sculpting, unfolding and smoothing, teasing and playing in the vast emptiness of the sky; as anyone who has flown through and above so many extraordinary forms can witness. 'What fanciful questions' says a cynical mind! Are they? The wonderful thing about just looking at clouds is it can bring a tremendous relaxation. It acts as a reminder: here is something we don't have to do anything about. We don't need to attempt to control them, to understand them, nor to obey them. What a relief! Here is life, demonstrating its complete disregard for man's puny attempts to do any of this. Life just being itself: revealing itself, as it is. Sharing itself, delighting in itself and allowing us to delight in it too.

For instance, have you noticed how the sunset waits for no one? You have to tune in and be there or you miss out. It can't be rescheduled for our convenience! Once again, all this is another reminder of the vast unknowable nature that we both *are* and exist *within*. It is no wonder so many people love to connect with nature; that this can soothe, heal and inspire. And it doesn't ask to be paid for this, nor that we make an appointment first! The simple truth is that in order to be met and fully related with, all this vastness – pregnant as it is with possibility – this vastness we call life, requires our *intuitive* participation. Nothing less will do. Without this, we shuffle around like blind men and women, separated from so much wonder, so much opportunity, such a feast! Like a beggar too proud to receive the gift, we remain starving – cut off from each other and from ourselves. What a shame.

Has it ever occurred to you to wonder how we come to see the world, and the people and events in our lives, the way we do? What has created this? What may be influencing what we see? And, of course, how this affects us? Because it is curious, isn't it, how people see things so differently, each of us convinced that our view is the right one. Curious, too, how things that don't agree with our view often remain unseen; sometimes for a very long time. And then, one day – for no apparent reason – something different reveals itself. It is as though we are seeing with fresh eyes. We are amazed! How could this be? That something which has always remained unrecognised, suddenly seems so blindingly obvious?

An illustration of this would be when a person assumes that something which is happening to them is unique, that they alone suffer from it. And then – in an instant – *they see through this belief:* they realise that actually it is common, that many other people share their experience. This can bring great relief, but it can also bring a big change in our attitude towards ourselves and others as a result. When insights like this visited to me, I used to wonder, why me? Why is it me who is recognising this? And then I realised: if something is there to be seen, to be recognised, surely anyone can see it? But then I saw that this is not necessarily true. *We can't see things clearly if we are blinded by beliefs:* beliefs that tell us not to trust what we are seeing; it's like a kind of myopia we develop as our conditioning takes hold (by 'conditioning' I am referring to outside influences, something I will elaborate on in the next chapter). For instance, we have all been taught that what has real value can be analysed, explained and validated through the mind, and we start to believe this. Whereas the truth is *nothing* of real value can be understood by the mind. Wow! Hang on a minute – that is quite a statement! I know – the implications are vast. It takes a lot of digesting. And for many people this is simply too unbelievable, too far outside of how they have always believed things to be.

Don't misunderstand me here. The mind is a wonderful, and indeed *essential* mechanism for navigating life on this earth. That is, life in a human body, in the physical, material world: the world of objects. Without this apparent mental function of the brain we would be utterly incapacitated, we would be unable to survive. So yes, we do of course need the mind. And, it's a great day *when we finally recognise mind just has no way to measure true value* – that this is a knowing that belongs to the heart. This capacity for discernment relies on an intuitive connection that is the domain of the heart alone.

Actually, you likely do know about true value. You recognise it, and are most in touch with it perhaps while watching a magnificent sunset or your newborn child sleeping. But – and here lies the rub – we have been taught by the mind to elevate material and moral values. These the mind understands and can manipulate. It can play endlessly in the fields of conceptual reality. Anything deeper, and more in touch with direct, experiential reality – anything beyond its grasp – is subtly excluded, not taken seriously: trivialised. Like feelings and sensings and intuitive knowing: *things that we cannot explain.* (In the following chapter we look at how this whole edifice of beliefs, this mental construct, comes about; and how to address its toxic, life-suppressing influence.)

In my work with people, the most important thing that happens when someone comes for a first session has very much to do with this, and it happens in silence. At the beginning of each session we sit together for a few minutes in silence and a tuning-in happens. In this being still – being present while alert – something is transmitted intuitively. Without any words, the person knows they are truly seen, even if they are not fully conscious of this at the time. Although this deep seeing generally remains constant throughout the session, at the start I can often feel a kind of subtle shock: a shock that ricochets through their entire energy-field. *People are not used to being fully seen and recognised in this way.*

It is this instantaneous, intuitive connection from Being to Being that predicates all that follows. (I will attempt to explain what I mean by the term 'Being' in just a moment, so bear with me.) This connection underpins the capacity to trust: to let go and allow what has always been present to be recognised, however slowly, however long this process of trusting takes. Because it becomes obvious that, within a relatively short space of time, most people start to trust *something,* even if they think it's me and are not aware that it connects with their *own* Being-ness: that the apparent separation between us, on this level, is false. Then, no matter how apparently lost in their minds and emotions, and disconnected from their bodies, something starts to relax and to open – even if this only creates an infinitesimal space: *the lifelong habitual defences developed to survive in this world are breached.* Life, in its pure spiritual form, seeps into our awareness and begins to influence us.

Knowing and knowledge

So now: what *exactly* do I mean by Being? How am I using this word? And here we come to an interesting place – the place where the road divides between knowing and knowledge. In this book you will find little to satisfy a thirst for knowledge; it is *knowing* that is available, so the questions then become 'How do we *receive* knowing?' and 'What is it that receives this?'. We have all been trained to gather information with the intellect. We call this 'knowledge'. But what I am talking about here relies entirely on *knowing,* and both knowing and Being lie essentially beyond the mind's grasp. Mind can only ever have a vague idea about what Being means, no matter how many labels it attempts to harness it with. Mind likes to objectify: to separate and classify, and what I am writing about doesn't allow for this. To know what I am referring to, you will need to access an entirely different capacity from your thinking mind. You will need to invoke your own intuitive knowing, however faint this may seem; your perception of something subtle, that you can sense and feel, that is *there* – like a presence. So it's a kind of experiential form of connecting with something that is already there, but may have been previously unseen.

Mind, on the other hand, behaves very differently. In fact we could liken mind to a giant insect that settles over any written subject matter and proceeds to feed on it. It does this by extracting what it sees as interesting or useful, which it files away for future reference, rejecting the rest as unpalatable. Apart from any natural curiosity, mind likes the idea of expanding its arsenal as it particularly values knowledge for purposes of defence or attack, and generally maintaining control. And because it seeks to complete this process as quickly and efficiently as possible, it loves things like bullet points and spread sheets: lists, diagrams, glossaries, quotes and cross references that appear to verify the material. Above all, mind loves *order*. A spiritual teacher called Adyashanti (whom I quoted at the beginning of this chapter) says something interesting about this difference: *'Very few people will tell us...that we can understand with something other than the mind, that our entire being can understand'.*

So if, instead of struggling to extract the precise meaning of this word 'Being' with the mind, what happens if you approach it differently? If you allow a certain vagueness, at first; and just relax, open and rest in the space of wait-and-see receptivity? If you approach this word tentatively, with patience? What if, instead of demanding it deliver up its exact meaning – instantly – you allow a gradual sense of what this is to clarify itself? Slowly? The meaning of the word can then reveal itself through a kind of distilling process, as if it were seeping through the pages as you read; allowing for a subtle penetration, a recognition even, of what is being said, in different ways and in different contexts. Here repetition can be useful, in the sense of saying various things *about* something, without being specific. This is because the nature of what I am writing about is extremely subtle. It often lies beyond the capacity of a single word or sentence to catch hold of it. This is when what can be perceived from many fingers pointing is more accurate than one hand trying to grab hold of it, all at once.

This very much applies to what I am referring to as Being. Which – much to the mind's frustration – cannot be analysed, explained or understood. Instead, it can be felt, sensed and intuited, and it gets easier to recognise as you become familiar with it. In fact, only as we *ingest* or *absorb* this recognition do we become able to open to what it is pointing to. Then, what is being said can enter your awareness in its own time, in its own way. It can provide a stimulus for questioning, contemplating and responding *to*. This is a very different way of reading words from the way most of us have been taught. It is a more feminine approach, rather than the masculine hunter that seeks to acquire information, store it and move on. This latter approach turns us into information consumers *rather than live beings responding to stimulus*. We listen from a different place in ourselves. And this place can feel familiar: it's the place we listened from at bedtime when we were little. When we were still open and innocent, curious and more fully alive. If I seem to be labouring the point here, it is because what I am saying applies to reading this whole book.

So, about this word 'Being': I can say I am using it as both noun and verb (which makes it different to the words essence or spirit; we don't talk about 'essence-ing' or 'spiriting'), to talk about that which is within everything, that energises everything and that is everywhere – *including the body*. I can say I am using this word to represent that which resides nowhere, yet is never absent (which can really make the mind dizzy)! That which is at first perceived as 'mine' because that is how we have learned to see ourselves: *my* Being, that lives inside *me,* in *my* inner world, inside *my* body. Then, at some moment, Being is perceived for what it is: something that exists everywhere – *including* the sphere of human lives with their apparent individuality. It can't be owned.

Until you have had some experience of this for yourself it is hard to connect with what I am saying. So, if this all seems contradictory and confusing, don't worry: this whole book is about the body-Being. It can sound all a bit esoteric but I will try to keep it – based as it is on my own seeing – as simple as I can. Later on, there will be time to get more of a sense of what I want to convey: not just as you read on, but also if you use the exercises. You may find these help to create more space to *receive* what is being said, to *ingest* rather than understand: to re-remember, recognise and *know*.

Some people prefer words like spirit, essence, or even God (for the sake of brevity I won't include the word Goddess each time I mention this word, as God is surely beyond gender). These words all have different associations for different people. I am choosing Being as the word that, for me, feels most inclusive; referring to that which is both many and one: together. I have seen that it is this sense of connection with Being that allows us to meet and accept, loosen and eventually let go of *whatever* is in the way of residing here: residing in Being. Because sooner or later, we have to meet the place where mind spins illusions that can feel so terribly, painfully real (despite any ideas we may have gleaned from spiritual teachings of its unreality.) This is essential if we are to return to our true nature. There are no spiritual short cuts.

The living of Being

How then, can Being be *lived* in the world? Here we are, having this human experience where events come into our awareness to be experienced and met. We have to deal with a whole range of personal relationships of every kind, and these will challenge our capacity to stay true as we move into intimate connection with ourselves and others, moment to moment. As far as the greater picture is concerned, as we become able to maintain a connection with a deeper sense of ourselves, we see, sense and feel the world more clearly. On one level, we see how there is a natural balance in life and intuitively 'get' that we are way off this. We not only sense this out-of-touch-ness with the essence of life – *we feel it in our bodies*. And this is important, because I am speaking here about our human experience of being in a body. What some spiritual teachers refer to as the 'Relative', in contrast to the vast emptiness they refer to as the 'Absolute', the *ultimate* reality: that which lies beyond the body and our human sense of ourselves. The realm in which everything is just fine, everything is always as it should be: *both are true*.

So looking from this relative, human view, we know that life as we are living it isn't really working out well for almost everyone: there is much suffering and unconsciousness is the norm. From this perspective, it is evident that many of those who have the money, the power – and the privilege this brings – are also the most shut down, out-of-touch and in denial of all of us. That those who believe they are managing okay, are often, in fact, believing a story they have convinced themselves brings them security and stability. We see that these are illusions based in fear: fear of change, fear of the unknown and fear of losing any perceived advantage over others.

For the remaining majority of over-stretched workers or hopeless unemployed, there is often little energy to question or consider alternatives. The young feel the wrongness of all this more than most of us, because it doesn't give them any hope or sense of genuine purpose in their lives: they have no place. It is bewildering and presents no clear course of action to bring about change. They see the dreams they have been encouraged to dream – of higher education, a good job, a house, a future where they can live the good life – receding before their eyes. *And almost no-one suggests we look deeper. Consciousness and the question of who is living this life is not raised.*

Those who are in touch with this disconnect feel the pain and confusion all around: the fear and anger, and a prevailing sense of powerlessness not too far beneath the surface. We see the daily struggles to survive, and witness the numbness and stress resulting from the absurd ways we have devised of living together – ways that stand out in stark denial of life and what it offers. Surely no animal has created a system where they siphon off all the goodies for themselves and leave the rest to scramble and scrimp and starve? Elephants are the largest land mammal, and whales in the sea, and neither take a bigger share of what is available and leave their fellows without; and neither do the carnivores. Everything fits in, and lives on, a part of what is available – leaving the rest to the others, including other species. In fact, there are surprisingly frequent examples of animals helping each other, and working together across species. This co-operation suggests a level of conscious awareness *that is more developed than our own* (undistorted as it is by the demands of ego and a conditioned mind). There is a visible wholeness, a balance – and that in itself brings a sense of the goodness of life.

In taking a clear look at all of this – at how we humans live together and our relationships with each other – it can all seem pretty hopeless. How many couples do you know that are *really* happy together? Deeply fulfilled? You will be lucky to count them on the fingers of one hand. We may keep up appearances – beneath which conflict, frustration, boredom and an almost continuous bickering seem to be common; we learn to put up with it rather than look deeper. And when there are children to include, love can get buried under a mountain of acrimony and misunderstanding. Parents always seem too busy, too preoccupied, too tired. Computer games, Facebook and television replace closeness and real communication. When I sit in cafes or on public transport, as I often do, I am amazed to see how parents are continuously on their mobile phones, inattentive and unavailable to their children. And this just feels so sad. The truth is, no-one is to blame for this – *everyone is doing the best they can under a complete misapprehension of who they are and what life really is.*

On a global level, much unsettling material has been written about things like climate change; about how we are degrading the environment and fouling our nest with destructive policies and processes, driven by our current financial systems. International activist groups like Greenpeace and Avaaz exist, that seek to give people a voice via the internet to remedy this – and it's good that the heart has a place to express its concerns in a global format. But... but, ultimately, it is surely clear that no fundamental change can occur while we continue to function from a conditioned, ego-centred mind. While we continue to believe in the distorted version of reality this presents us with. For a stark example of this distortion, just check out any of the mainstream media outlets. And don't just look or listen to them: *feel* them, *sense* them – *notice what they do to your body and energy.* This is where you will find the truth about what is happening, not in your mind.

What is needed to address this imbalance is actually simple: not necessarily easy, but nonetheless simple. It comes down to acknowledging, investigating and facing the deeper truths of life; looking to see what these are and who, or what, we *really* are. This involves remembering ourselves and our intuitive nature and reconnecting with Being, that knows we are all one. And although, initially, this may all just be an idea in the mind, we have the means to truly *know* it – to intuitively 'grock' (or know by ingesting) this for ourselves. And here the body, with all its many subtle receptors and responses, can be our true friend.

Conscious reconnection

The term 'conscious awareness' is frequently bandied about in spiritual circles. So let's begin by looking at this, and where it is to be found. Starting with the image of a vast primordial swamp, many things apparently took form within this, many life forms became tangible and started to move around and procreate, and (if you believe theories of evolution) develop new species. But as far as we know none of these have conscious awareness. Or do they? Because, by some act of unbelievable hubris, humans have come to believe we are the supreme beings – the only one of God's creatures with the capacity for conscious awareness. But is this actually true?

Watching a film of a woman who engages in telepathic communication with animals, Anna Breytenbach, this belief looks pretty unconvincing. Anna was once a high flyer in the corporate world, a systems analyst, and she doesn't fit the usual stereotype of people engaged in psychic or paranormal activity. She says she transmits and receives information in mental images, silent words that appear in her awareness, emotional feelings and physical sensations. She comments: '*A common misperception about telepathy is that it requires us to waft in the disembodied astral realm or access an induced state of altered consciousness. Even worse, some people believe that some sort of "initiation" into the animal kingdoms or secret mystery schools are needed – some sort of spiritual elitism reserved for the few lucky ones. Nothing could be further from the truth. Telepathic communication is wholly grounded in the here and now. Literally. Feet firmly planted on solid earth and our full attention in the present moment.*'

There is one part of the film where Anna is in silent dialogue with a leopard that has been traumatised, which is especially poignant and dramatic. You can watch the change from vicious would-be killer, to calm, serene dignity during their brief exchange. For the sceptics, she receives verifiable information that is later confirmed – that could not have been known in any other way. And this kind of evidence is repeated, in various instances of communication with other species, throughout the film. It also contains interviews with tribesmen and others who are skilled animal trackers. They describe how they use their *sensing, feeling bodies* to do this – along with intuition and telepathic communication. And they claim this is how animals communicate with each other, including across species.

All this capacity for telepathic communication amongst animals requires not simply intelligence, but in terms of the nature of what is received and projected, a level of conscious awareness *equal to our own.* And this cuts right across a common assumption: that while some creatures are clever, and can do tricks and learn some basic human skills, they are not on an equal footing with us – with humans. How interesting! This is a brilliant illustration of how these assumptions impact on everything in our lives. Because this is all that this actually *is:* it is just an assumption! An assumption based on a *belief* – a belief that we have been taught – *that has nothing to do with direct experience.* In other words a construct of mind.

Witnessing that animals are *also* consciously aware can be a shocking realisation for us humans, so sure are we of our superior intelligence, so sure that our capacity for conscious awareness is unique. It is so disturbing that many will even disbelieve the evidence. They will deny the truth of this, even the possibility, even when incontrovertible proof is offered they will deny it – *they have to;* it's just too confronting to their lifelong belief system. The recognition that not only is everything conscious, but that certain species are perhaps capable of *greater* intelligence than us shatters a crucial part of our thinking structure. The idea of reality we have evolved for ourselves with the mind, based on the belief that man is the crowning glory of evolution (or God's design, according to your preferred belief).

Isn't it amazing? Simply because animals don't communicate in a form that we can understand – like words – because *we* have lost the ability to hear *them,* we believe this. We are surprised when some creature like a crow, with a small brain, demonstrates an ability we had not believed it capable of, or a dog, a horse or some other creature. We look for some other explanation because we assume they are not as capable. This is what prejudice is: sheer arrogance of mind covering ignorance and fear. Because if we recognised this to be the case – that animals are conscious (I would include reptiles, insects and fish here and also plants and, indeed, *all of life)* – we would have to radically alter not just our behaviour, but our whole understanding of life. The implications of this go off the scale. For instance, would you be comfortable killing a pig to eat that could look at you and let you know how it felt about you, and what you were about to do to it?

I am not an ardent animal rights activist, nor am I saying eating animals is wrong. What I am saying is that seeing the *whole* picture when an event is happening is important – it keeps us out of avoidance and denial so we face reality. *And this brings consciousness into alignment across all areas of our lives.* We see that we are no longer the unquestionable top dog, but simply a part of the whole in which our actions have ramifications. A humbling experience for us, true, but an experience that was simply obvious to our so-called 'primitive' ancestors. It's actually not that long ago that humans ceased to recognise the unity of all life and the conscious awareness it contains, and stopped venerating this. Not so long ago that we stopped sharing telepathic and other non-verbal communication with other forms of life. In fact, as we have just seen, some people still practice this today; the telepathic communication with animals used by the hunters of old can still be found. A very ordinary-looking man Anna trained with, Jon Young, of native North American descent, teaches this to those interested in courses he calls 'Intuitive Tracking' in a program called 'Community, Mentoring and Nature Connection' in California. He speaks of the vital need for humans to reconnect with the natural living world – to recognise we are a part of this, and relearn our intuitive abilities so we are able to communicate with it.

Communion with all life

Some years ago now, I had an extraordinary moment of connection with a whale. I was traveling alone in a camper van around the sparsely populated areas of North West Australia. I had picked up two girls who wanted a ride and we had been to watch what was called a 'feeding frenzy.' This is where shoals of anchovy are driven up against the cliffs and gobbled up by sharks and dolphins, accompanied by a few passing whales, and there was a great view of this from the cliffs above. We stopped overnight at a caravan park and I wandered down onto a flat platform of rock that jutted out a few feet above sea level. As I walked out onto it I saw something that my mind could only interpret as the prow of an enormous ship, sticking up vertically out of the sea directly in front of me. It was covered in barnacles and only when it opened an eye and looked at me, did I realise it was an enormous whale!

Everything happened at once. My arms spontaneously lifted up and I found myself singing to it in an explosion of pure joy as I witnessed this deep gaze – a gaze that I experienced as both profoundly wise and compassionate, and also *interested*, demonstrating a clear consciously aware presence: presence of Being. This communion of heart-to-heart probably only lasted a second or two because I felt a tap on my shoulder, turned to see a man standing behind me, and when I turned round again the whale had vanished. (It transpired this man and his wife had been watching me from their caravan and somehow got the idea I might be about to jump off the ledge! And of the two girls, one was busy writing up her journal and the other watching the sunset, so neither had seen the whale.)

The second event was in South Africa, where I was staying on the edge of the Kruger National Park with a friend's parents. They had organised for me to visit a place where they rescued and bred wildlife, and I was being driven around in an open truck with a group of tourists. The driver had been talking about a young lion we passed that had recently been released into the park, and I asked if I could go over and say hello. 'Sure,' he replied, but as I walked over to the lion and sat down beside him, I noticed his ears were pricked, watching something. There, in the distance, were two elephants moving this way. He obviously hadn't noticed my approach because when I reached out to touch him, his head whipped round and I found myself staring directly into a pair of saucer-like eyes: eyeball to eyeball.

I have never felt myself looked at with such intensely focussed conscious awareness! This time it was different, the gaze held intent and interest, but was also more cool and detached. The driver called me back but as we neared the open-truck, with the young lion bounding beside me clearly wanting to play, I realised the group of tourists were all looking pretty alarmed. Afterwards, I wondered about the incident, but at the time it didn't occur to me to be afraid. I guess I thought the keeper must know what he was doing. (Later, I heard they did have occasional 'accidents' but were well covered by their insurance.)

So the capacity for communion – on what I experienced as a wise, heart level – was shown to me with this whale. There was a clear and unarguable depth of *conscious* intelligence. And the lion had an intense *focus* of awareness, which I experienced as far more powerful than most humans. To me, it is clear that *all* life is conscious: I feel it, sense it, know it. Where is the proof? Unlike Anna, I don't have anything to convince the skeptic with, I just have my own experience, so it's rather convenient that others do. These people are collecting the evidence and – sooner or later – this will bridge the defences of our mind-controlled view of ourselves and flood into human awareness in a way that cannot be refuted. If you ask around, or go on You Tube and various social media sites, it's clear there is much interest in communicating with animals. Many of us have had some form of communication with non human forms: with our pets, with plants, trees, rocks, whatever. It's not nearly as rare as we think. The sceptic has no evidence to prove the contrary, *as science can neither isolate nor measure either consciousness or awareness.*

Interesting, isn't it? Because this knowing – *that everything is part of one big conscious whole* – is extremely inconvenient, to put it mildly! It challenges our comfortable assumptions and doesn't fit in with a familiar, secure sense of the world and how it operates, hence the denial. And it is this denial that has limited our understanding in ways that allow us to act totally out of balance with the whole, out of harmony with life itself, with what life really *is*. The vital interconnection that would allow us to rest in a place of knowing who we are lies neglected and overgrown with erroneous beliefs. Here is life playing this magnificent symphony and here we humans are, ruining the performance with our discordant notes!

However, times they are indeed a-changing. I sense that many people hold a memory of this very real connection: it lies just beneath the surface of our consciousness. Just a little more pressure, more shared glimpses (which, thanks to the internet can now pass around the world instantly), and the cracks already appearing in the view of the world we have adopted for these last few centuries, can widen, enabling us to see what lies beneath. The end-of-the-world scenarios of the Mad Max variety don't touch this awakening consciousness. The shift is too big, too subtle, too profound – and way too far beyond our old limited mind-set.

For now, let's stay with this connection between us – the human animals – and the others; because it is fascinating to watch what this presents. When someone is ill, for instance, or suffering from depression or some other mental disability, the presence of animals can bring an impressive improvement. Why should this be so? Could it be that the communication goes beneath our acquired defences to reach directly to the heart? And thus connects us into our very Being-ness? And that this sense of being seen and related to, on this level, brings comfort and release? Because animals see directly – they don't suffer from a conditioned mind that interprets reality according to its prejudices and beliefs. *Animals don't have beliefs,* certainly not in the sense of moral beliefs; they have responses. They watch, and sense, and feel, and recognise *our* responses. Yes, as with the Pavlovian experiments, they can be taught to anticipate an outcome from an action, theirs or others, in simple ways. But that is not the same as holding a belief. They can interpret our actions and intentions, for sure, but they don't *judge* them. They don't sit there going 'What a lazy fucker, he never takes me for walks!'. They don't interpret our actions in terms of morality: good, bad, right, wrong; to be approved or disapproved; they don't play all those complicated mind-games.

And it's the same with nature. When most of us look at nature we relax, because nature isn't judging us and it isn't pretending anything: it is just being itself. A tree isn't judging you, a flower isn't saying to a neighbouring flower 'Look at that woman, how ugly her nose is, she really should get a nose job!'. Yes, it's ridiculous even to say this, isn't it? Yet this lack of judgement, of criticism and blame – this lack of comparison – allows us to feel safe: safe to open up and relax and feel vulnerable in a way that being around other humans often does not. Only when we know we are accepted and loved do we relax in this way. And even then, we have learnt that this can change: even people close to us cannot always be trusted to stay loving and accepting. So we maintain our guard, albeit not consciously. And this takes effort and a tremendous amount of energy to maintain.

As we have noted, both consciousness and awareness lie beyond the mind's understanding – as does *actual* reality. So what is it that the mind cannot understand? What underlies all of this that has been herded into a framework we call the *real world*? This that lies outside the narrow lens of our mind's conditioned interpretation of life? These are the very questions that many children ask, though in simpler terms, that are rarely answered by the adults. Like, for instance, what is a human being? (Being being human?). Where do we come from? What is conception beyond biology, what is birth? What is conceived and what is born? And born into what? And can this be any different to the question of what is death? What dies? What departs? Where do we go?

Most parents scramble for answers from what they have been taught, from either biology or religion. They don't share what they actually *know for themselves*, because in truth we don't know – not in our minds anyway. The real answers to these questions involve us in knowing who and what we ourselves truly *are*, and this is not something that can be put into words. This is not something that schools and universities can teach you, nor can the sources of their knowledge, such as science and academia – and that includes biology, anthropology, psychology, philosophy, even religion. At best, all these can give you are ideas, opinions and beliefs. True, there is much excitement about new discoveries in quantum physics which relate to all this, but ultimately these can only supply speculative concepts and theories in relation to these questions. We are still attempting to understand life through the lens of the thinking mind: trying to catch water in a sieve.

Losing touch with our authentic voice

Within the bland and the fantastical inaccuracies of most people's understanding of life there are fragments of wisdom, and a few people able to teach this. However, they are the exceptions. Both the desire and the intention to access inner wisdom seem to be scarcer than the proverbial hen's teeth. The truth is most of us have learned to doubt ourselves: we don't really trust our direct experience – outside a limited framework we have been conditioned to remain within. Beyond simple, practical experience, *we don't believe we can know for ourselves*. We are taught and believe that we have to learn from others, who – we have repeatedly been told – have access to this knowledge.

When all the time we have been tricked! Innocently, unintentionally, out of ignorance maybe – but still tricked. Tricked into believing we can't know, that others do know; that they know better, they know best. Tricked out of listening to ourselves, out of trusting ourselves. And in so doing, tricked into separation – that is, *into believing we are a separate self*. And who were we to argue? When those closest to us – our family, friends, school, church and the whole society we were brought up in – believed a version of reality that was actually not real, that was alien to us? How could we stand out against this when we were a defenceless infant, utterly dependent on others to take care of us? Later, if we started to question, we were probably gently, or not so gently, corrected. Maybe we were laughed at and put in our place; or patronised and told we were too young to understand these things.

Later, as a teenager, we may have rebelled. But by then we were likely locked into a personal battle for freedom that focussed on getting away from parental control and mixing with our own age group – a battle with its own agendas and fantasies. Or, we may have become isolated and even depressed, rejecting everything we had been taught but not knowing where to turn to find something of our own. This is such a difficult place for anyone, and especially for a young person, to find themselves in: not knowing how to reconnect with our authentic self, yet unable to find the confidence to question and follow our feelings and explore what feels right for *us* – often with no idea of where to find support for this inner journey. This sense of being alone and disconnected is quite common in young people and can be very frightening. And no matter what our age, this is often accompanied by an underlying grieving for what we intuitively know we have lost.

I suspect all of us do know what is real: we know this *intuitively*. How could we not know when this is the essence of who we are? Yet eventually, almost everyone becomes convinced of the mind's version of reality, to the extent that we forget there might be anything beyond this. In fact, this version is believed for so long that it becomes scary to question it. It can make us feel terrifyingly insecure to consider that the world may not be at all the way we have believed it to be. And that *we* may not be who we believe ourselves to be. Our lives have become organised in ways that keep us so busily occupied, especially in our minds, that most of us have little time or space to stop and reconsider. Why go there? Why bother? Isn't life hard enough as it is? But this sense of loss remains in our bodies. It is deeply felt and may emerge in glimpses of angst, anxiety, even depression: a confused sense that all is not as it should be, yet without knowing what this might be. So we keep quiet and distract ourselves, or go to the doctor for some pills or maybe counselling, to help us cope with a sense of reality that is – itself – inherently dysfunctional.

This is often the place where people begin to question and seek a new direction. As we doubt we become more open, more porous; and this can bring a precious opportunity. A gap to discover – by apparent accident or miraculous act of grace, who knows – that there is something present in our lives that we have overlooked, neglected, forgotten: that, quietly waiting in the wings as we play in the theatre of our lives, stands Being. Then, we may begin to discover that most subtle and delicate way of participating in true reality. That is, *listening in* – intuitively. This then allows a spontaneous, intuitive *response,* through the body so Being can start to sing its song.

The Japanese speak of a hollow bamboo: so, when there is no internal clutter, we can simply be played. I feel to say here that the instrument is also the conductor, the musician and the song. In other words, the one Being, living as a unique expression of itself known as you, me, us and them. What I have found is that all the ways of spontaneous, intuitive expression that I describe in this book – whether through touch, movement, use of vocal sounds or colour and shape – all of these require us to listen *in*. And when we are listening in, the mind is tuned *out*. What are we actually listening to? Being: hence the term body-Being. And what I have also found – by way of describing something that is elusive – is that connection to Being gives us an anchor: a place to ground. And this then allows us to spin a web-like silken thread up through our lives, strung with the jewels of insight, to enable us to survive even the most horrendous life circumstances until such time as we are ready and able to meet these, and emerge from our defences, our protective chrysalis, to reveal the true splendour of our body-Being.

Home-play
1. Recognising Being
Ask yourself: is something not already known? Is something not already seen? Not already felt? Already sensed? Despite and beneath the swirling clouds of conditioned thoughts? The mesmerising pull of ego? The sticky attachment of emotions? Listen carefully to your answer.

2. 'All is well'
- Bring the hands, parallel with each other, to within about 2" (5 cm) of the front of the throat, finger tips facing towards the body.
- Breathe in as you allow the hands to descend in a feather-light, stroking-without-touching movement over the heart, gradually widening above the stomach, to unfold, palms upwards, parallel with the lower belly (keep elbows close to body).
- Breathe out as the palms upturn and extend the fingers downwards, saying the words 'All is well' (the final releasing of the fingers expresses a letting go of control, a surrender to Being - acknowledging that Being knows, and is ultimately in charge.

Radical surgery for the mind

'Mind as a slave to consciousness is a beautiful servant. Mind as a master of consciousness is a very dangerous master' ~ Osho

People will write off the clearest, most loving person in the world when he opposes their belief system. They will invalidate him, negate him, obliterate him, prove that he's wrong, he's a fraud, he's dangerous to society, so that they can protect what they really believe is important. They'd rather be right than free.' ~ Byron Katie

'There is nothing good nor bad but thinking makes it so.' ~ William Shakespeare

Humpty Dumpty sat on a wall, Humpty Dumpty had a great fall. All the king's horses and all the king's men couldn't put Humpty together again. Once you see through the illusion of mind there is no way you can reassemble the edifice! In this chapter I will try to make it easy for you to see through this illusion and take account of its impact. Because, like a king in his castle, mind has come to dominate and control everything around it, to the detriment of all the finer feelings and knowings of the heart about what is real and true. In order to dethrone the mind then, and return it to its proper place, we will need to take a good look at what it actually *is,* and how it operates. And this involves putting it in the spotlight so we can see it clearly and identify what is true beneath the illusion. It's a bit of a rough ride as it cuts through everything we have ever been told (and believed) about how reality is – so hold on to your hat! With luck, at the end you will still have your beautiful mind, but without all the tacky embroidery and false claims ego has spun around it while you have been dreaming...

So, what is this mind that I am talking about? And what do I mean by 'conditioning'? How do we become conditioned? Interestingly, *nobody actually knows what mind is* (or thought either) despite our using this term on an everyday basis. It is used to refer to what we suppose must be a function of the brain; a function that deals in concepts and is concerned with interpreting everything that we encounter. (In spiritual circles Buddhists use the term 'mindfulness' to refer to being attentive to the present moment, which is a very different way of referring to mind.) Most people have been taught – *and firmly believe* – that mind is needed to tell us what is real and how to run our lives. It tries to do this by assessing situations using the intellect, with its reason and logic. It uses observation, based on memory of past experiences, and any general information it has gathered and stored. And the mind uses thinking to do all of this.

What is not talked about, however, is that mind *itself* is not free. It is neither open nor objective but already biased. It has been influenced by conclusions it has made *about* information received, by beliefs it has absorbed and by emotions too: all of which colour its perceptions, all of which determine its interpretations – *this is what I mean by conditioning* and it happens very early on in our lives. As the mind functions in a similar way to a computer, one could also say the mind is subject to its programming: that it is *this* which both distorts and limits our version of reality. And as most people remain unconscious of this, we don't see the effect of it, nor the harm it does; and even when we do, when we realise we need to come free from its perennial control, it's not so simple!

One way of talking about this would be to say that mind believes the story it has been told. It believes it needs to remain in control for us to survive and thrive: that this is its job. So in order to come free we have to recognise this and use whatever works for us to stop believing mind's story: *to dis-identify*. Only then are we free to use its amazing capacities in line with the truth of Being.

Mind always knows when it is being undermined and redoubles its efforts to maintain control, believing (as it has been programmed to do) that its central function is to keep us safe until we die. Here I find the term 'coffinitis' useful as a reminder of how mind operates. It attempts to keep us safe by confining us in a cosy, centrally heated coffin, well-stocked with comfort food, protected from the emotional elements, entertained on a comfy sofa in front of the telly – *till we die*. It has then, or so it reasons, fulfilled its role. As it knows nothing about real life and aliveness, this is a very logical tactic.

Plenty of people, especially when their bodies start to run down in later life, are only too happy to follow this option if they can. When you know death is approaching and you may not have much longer to hang out here, there is a tendency to cling to all forms of comfort and security; a kind of ego-driven myopia takes over. But supposing what appears to be a fear of death is, in reality, an intense fear of life? That this is what drives many old people to hole-up in their burrows regardless of anyone else's interests and start to shut down? And the tragic fact is you don't need to be old to begin this process.

When you look at some of the crazy, destructive actions humans are perpetrating, you see that it is often older people who support these. Just as they support war, heavy-duty policing and surveillance methods, and eviction or incarceration of anyone different. Instead of a dignified and open-hearted willingness to help humanity, they retreat. They feel threatened by youth and change, and cling on to what seems safe and predictable. *Of course* I am generalising here and nor is this about blame. But it is invaluable to recognise how this tendency comes about, from having lost connection with ourselves, with Being.

The majority of elderly people, in the West especially, have no sanctuary of wisdom, acceptance and inner peace to rely on, hence there may be little of value to share. So it is perhaps not surprising that they are often neither valued nor respected. This can be seen as a rather sad waste but also as a salient reminder to everyone who seeks true value in their lives. Take your courage: listen to that little voice which is calling you – not tomorrow, not someday soon, but now! Thankfully, there are the exceptions amongst the elderly: those who have not only seen so much but have distilled what they have seen. Then the tendency to discount old-age means we miss out hugely; for someone who has had time to delve deep and learn from life is a store for the most precious diamonds, a mine of true worth.

Connecting with Being

One of the first things that is apparent when someone comes for a session is the dominance of their mind, how much they have learnt to rely on this and not question it. Indeed, we are discouraged from questioning and the most effective tool to do this is ridicule. 'What are you talking about?' or 'Oh do stop being a nuisance, just be quiet and listen to what you are being told!'. At school we are taught to absorb, remember and regurgitate information on demand. Don't question anything beyond the boundaries you are given, the limits of reality you are prescribed. Parents are naturally concerned that their offspring will do well in the world, that they will be successful, financially secure and socially acceptable. They begin this subtle and not-so-subtle pressure on us to believe what we are told and to fit in; and this gets reinforced in school by teachers and often our peer group too. So children learn to keep quiet and, if they continue to question, to keep this to themselves. They may even come to feel there is something wrong with them for questioning anything, or at least feel alienated and alone because of it. We say of these children, 'Oh, she or he is a bit of a loner'.

Many of the people who come to see me have been to counselling or done some form of therapy. Here, they learnt to inquire into their past and they can tell you everything about it backwards. They have talked about it, written about it, analysed it, speculated about it and reacted *to* it. The difficulty with all this is it often leaves them feeling worse: they have all this information and it hasn't changed how they feel. If I know that I hate and fear men because my father was brutal with me...? You have the reasons, the apparent causes, but so what? 'Well, if I make myself forgive him all will be well' – but it's not so simple.

It is true the present carries within it the past, along with our reactions to this. However, what I have seen is that this will emerge in its own time, with a freshness and immediacy that can allow it to be met *in that moment*. When that happens, all this carefully stored information can actually get in the way. We assume we know – been there, done that. And this just gives the mind more ammunition to try to maintain control. Also, timing is not something you can learn about in training; it happens by itself and has its own rhythm. My function is to be fully present: to tune in and follow whatever presents in that moment, *from a sense of intuitive connection*. Without this we are both lost.

And here – in what is rarely attended to in most forms of counselling and therapy – lie the fundamental questions: questions that are not answerable by the mind; questions about who and what we, and life, really *are*. Without this connection or the seeking of what lies beneath and beyond mind, there is nothing to guide what emerges. In my experience this connection with Being – with this that can be sensed but may not be consciously recognised – *this connection is fundamental to coming free from the past*. It brings something to trust in when we feel most vulnerable.

Mind and emotions

How does the mind get in the way? As I have said, the mind is programmed for our survival and much like a computer, it follows these mechanical imperatives. It keeps us breathing and orchestrates our body to keep functioning in millions of ways. It helps us to negotiate our environment, to remember where we left something, how to use something. It allows us to communicate through speech, to take in and store information and it attempts to bring solutions to our everyday needs. Pretty basic stuff: necessary to our continued survival as humans, in bodies, in this world.

The trouble comes when this basic programming gets interfered with: when it is overlaid with beliefs from other people's minds. Beliefs about how best to survive and what is important, along with their beliefs about morality: right and wrong, good and bad; acceptable, unacceptable. We are taught to judge this both in ourselves and in others: what actions to take about it, what to believe about it. Enter the world of 'oughts' and 'shoulds' – and worse – because these beliefs get mixed up with erroneous, but very powerful conclusions we made as a child, often believing, deep down, that whatever went wrong it was somehow our fault.

Where the mind does perform a useful function is in teaching us emotional survival strategies. When a child undergoes experiences that are simply too painful and confusing, the mind goes on overload. Then, if there is no help at hand, it very sensibly learns to repress feelings to defend against hurt: this helps us survive. Children who don't successfully learn to do this may end up harming themselves in one way or another; this may be with drugs or various other forms of self-harm, in order to deaden the pain. They may even commit suicide, or they may end up in a psychiatric ward or out on the streets, acting out some belief of their worthlessness or culpability in activities like prostitution. And some will find ways to ease their pain by inflicting pain on others.

So in a way you could say the mind, in teaching us forms of self-control – like repressing feelings – has been our ally. (This in spite of the negative effects of repression, which we will talk about in a later chapter.) Then, one day, we get a glimpse of freedom! We start to see that these defences no longer serve us; that actually, they deaden our aliveness and limit our capacity to respond and enjoy life. This is often when people choose to look for help. Then, slowly, slowly, these defences can begin to unravel. We discover that we are able – now – to live without them. So then, as we learn to rest in Being, old beliefs can melt away and we can start to relax.

It can be hard: we have all been taught to trust in the mind. At first the reflex to do this is so strong it is challenging for most people to question it, to begin to seek what lies beneath and beyond mind. For some it's easier than others and women usually have greater confidence in their intuition and feelings, even though these are often tangled up with the mind and its conditioned beliefs.

At this point I need to clarify something about words and feelings, because language can be confusing. For the purposes of clarity I am choosing to call emotions those feelings that are controlled by the mind, that is by beliefs and conditioning, and those that aren't – just feelings. I will continue to use the word 'feeling' as a verb, to talk about both feeling a feeling and feeling an emotion, because emoting has quite a different connotation.

A note here about the term 'emotional intelligence' (EI). This has been defined as 'the ability to recognise, understand and manage our own emotions and recognise, understand and influence the emotions of others.' This could be described as an attempt to give value to the feeling realms in a world where intellectual 'intelligence' is given high value. I don't use the term in this book partly because I am using the word 'emotion' in a different way, but also because there is a sense of trying to describe the feeling realms with the mind in order to include these, rather than moving into the greater reality described in this book, where feelings are connectors and the mind a (necessary) separator.

There is a tendency to speak about feelings as if they occupy neat categories labelled sadness, anger, fear and joy, etc., but this is not actually true. Feelings are fluid like a river: constantly moving, changing and combining in subtle ways. And feelings influence each other: they aren't separate commodities that jump the gaps between convenient boxes to fit the storage cabinets of mind. All of this just confuses poor old mind, which needs to separate, categorise and compare, hence the arbitrary labels: once again, we are attempting to sift water with a sieve. And whilst doing this, the subtle information our pure feelings can give us – *the attunement to reality* – is overlooked. So in order to perceive feelings clearly, and to trust these, they need to be disentangled from the mind: de-emotionalised, emptied of beliefs. (How this can happen is something I will elaborate on in the next chapters.)

How do we acquire conditioning?

Conditioning itself is endemic. Is it really so surprising that people find it hard to let go of believing their mind, when – quite apart from the panicky feeling of wondering how we would survive without this to guide us – take a look around you! The world comes at us from all angles with so much information about everything. Has it ever occurred to you that all this information comes from other people's minds? Both living and dead? Spoken or written, via *someone else's* mind? Perhaps elaborated on with photographs, taken by someone else with their own agenda? All, ultimately, coloured by their own attitudes and beliefs?

Most things we learn, we learn from others, from our parents and friends; we learn at school, from what we see on television, read in newspapers, magazines and books or on the Internet. Everyone around us is functioning from this input of other people's 'take' on things, from their subtle and not so subtle prejudices and partialities, ignorance and so forth – in other words *their* version of reality. These ideas clot together and are influenced by various cultural and religious beliefs. All this forms the basis of our conditioning. The mind absorbs this information like blotting paper *but it has no truth filter*.

At this point the mind is no longer an instrument for survival: it has become a means of assessing what is true *but without the capacity to do this*. All of this is unconscious, we almost never question or examine it. It's as though, as small children, we have been put on a conveyor belt and our mind unscrewed and filled with various bits of information until we are considered adult. Then this conditioning is reinforced by these same influences – all originating in the mind. Our parents, our schools, our societies don't teach us about this. They don't teach us about conditioning because most people are unaware of it. *It is so endemic few people realise they live their lives controlled by other people's ideas and beliefs,* let alone that these are mostly filled with untruths, myths, prejudices and distortions that have little bearing on reality. We may have glimpses of truth, but it is hard to hold onto these when everyone around you seems to be colluding with conditioned mind's version of reality.

I remember once, during one of those intense conversations about the meaning of life we have when we are young, speculating with some friends about this. There were a group of us bundled up in sleeping bags on someone's floor. It was during a ban-the-bomb march and after two nights without sleep we didn't need alcohol to loosen us up! Books like Aldous Huxley's *Brave New World* and George Orwell's *Animal Farm* and *Nineteen Eighty-four* were hot topics. There was talk at the time about the Russians brainwashing people, and one boy suggested we could programme people so they wouldn't fight in wars. Sounds good, doesn't it? We could just programme everyone to be good and nice and ... aaah! Can you imagine the terrifying possibilities?

These days, people become anxious about having their personal phone calls and emails intercepted, but that has nothing on this as a potential for us to be controlled – or so it would appear. It is a frightening *concept,* the *idea* that we could be altered in this way. After all, concepts and ideas are what the mind deals in: in this case, ways to control people (and contrasting this with threats of what might happen if we got out of control by presenting emotionalised scenarios of chaos and mayhem, all of which can be used to invoke our deepest fears and persuade us to conform). The effectiveness of forms of persuasion and manipulation, in both degree and duration is not clear. What *is* clear is the need to find ways to recognise and come free from control by a conditioned mind, from beliefs and emotional reactions that have no basis in truth; *to reconnect with a source we can trust.* Because all this brings up the question: if indeed the mind can be controlled, where does true freedom lie? Ah now, *this* is an interesting question!

So how does the process of conditioning originate? Okay: I don't know if this is the ultimate truth but here is one way of looking at this. Suppose we all take form as an apparently separate entity from amorphous Being, via the union of our parent's egg and sperm, at which point we have no conscious sense of identity. In order to develop this we start to respond to what happens to us. We are given a name, and seen, treated as and told in so may ways that we are indeed a separate little 'person'; so, very slowly, we begin to develop a belief in this, a belief that we are separate: that there is a 'me' and other.

But if you had been happily immersed in connection with everything this sense of separation can be not just disorienting, it can actually be terrifying. We are reassured: don't worry, you are safe because *we* know, *we* will teach you, *this* is the way things are. What we are told is reality is described to us in a million ways and we have no means of questioning or refuting this. If we want to be accepted and included we have to go along with it. We imbibe others' version of reality with our milk. Slowly, slowly, we begin to believe we are a separate someone – someone with a name, a body, a gender, an age. Someone with a mother, a father, maybe siblings; we live in a place called home. And all those other beings, that look like us, are other.

As we adapt to what seems to be required of us we absorb conditioning by osmosis, through the pores of our skin. Even before we develop our mind we start to accept others' reality as the truth. We absorb consensus agreements: this is food, this is not food; doing this is okay, doing that is not. These eyes belong to Mother, who is familiar; these to a stranger, who is not. As our senses explore reality we learn those bumps that stick out on 'my' body are called fingers and toes. Later, that that 'over there' is called a table, this a chair. We start to notice that if we cry we get attention, that if we pee on the carpet someone gets upset.

Like the animals we mentioned earlier, an infant learns that if I do this, this happens, so we begin to control our responses. Our feeling senses inform us if this is comfortable and comforting (being picked up by a parent); if this is uncomfortable (being left in a cold, wet nappy). So we start to learn how to respond to manipulate others to get what we want and avoid what we don't want. This thing we call 'Ego' – this imaginary self – *becomes our dominant reality.* But you might say 'How can we survive otherwise?' and it's true, to survive in the world as a human in a body we need a *rudimentary sense of self*. Being able to talk about an 'I' and 'you' has a place. It is when we become fixated and *fully identified* with this 'I' that problems arise, when we believe this 'I' is who we are.

I am aware that what I am speaking about here, this way of looking at things, lies completely outside the usual understanding we are given about ourselves, about what humans are and where we come from. The way I am describing this process may seem quite confronting, even shocking. So if what I have been saying in all this resonates with you, wonderful; if it opens a crack into another view, look into it. And if it seems far-fetched, well, maybe it's just too challenging, too upsetting. Because looking at human beings and what happens to us in this way *can threaten the very fabric on which we have built our secure sense of reality:* our view of the world, of how this operates and our place, as a separate 'person', within this. And this can make us feel very insecure indeed.

However, if it's true that we are all one, as the deeper spiritual teachings all agree, then it must also be true that there can be no *truly* separate 'persons', and that a child born into this world – no matter what its genetic heritage and so forth – is a part *of* this wholeness. So then, at first, this child, this little manifestation of Being, will have no capacity to perceive separation: this is something it has to learn, some say when it is about eighteen months to two years old, which is when the brain starts to develop its thinking capacity.

And herein lies a dilemma: because, as I have said, we need a rudimentary sense of self in order to function. But the mind itself is not designed to go beyond the acquisition of skills to survive in this world, although it can speculate endlessly. The mind is not a 'self', nor does it contain a self. If we use the analogy of a computer again: it is just a marvellous machine. And – *when functioning in the service of Being* – it is truly magnificent. Used in the ways in which it is designed, mind can be not just an essential tool, but a wonderful instrument. It allows us to imagine and transform intuitive insights into practical designs and useful inventions. It helps us repair all kinds of objects and devices, it can open up all kinds of possibilities. It is great at organising: try going shopping without it and you will likely return without half the things you set out to buy! For planning holidays it's wonderful, for working out how to fix the car, terrific; for calculating your taxes, or just gathering information to be stored for future use, it's truly remarkable – *just don't invite it to run your life!*

It appears we have learned to forget ourselves: to forget what we essentially *are*. How did we do this? How did we forget that we are part of a whole? That we are already fully equipped to respond to life in all its full-spectrum glory? Who knows? What is clear is that we have learned to expect the mind to advise us on such things as how to feel, how to express ourselves, how to respond to others, how to behave. How to find a mate, bring up children, where to live; even how to dress! And even more bizarre – what we should believe in and what is the purpose of our lives. How unfair on the mind to ask it to do things it was never designed to do, while we have all these other incredibly useful intuitive capacities that, when we are in our flow, can guide us and inform us, as and when this is needed: in the moment. Of course this means living in a world which is essentially unpredictable, uncontrollable, always fresh and new; and this can seem terrifying to a mind that seeks certainty – even when certainty does not, and cannot, exist!

Social conditioning

The core of our conditioning comes through the family, but social conditioning – that is how we are affected by the world outside of this, especially by our schooling and any religious influences – also has a powerful impact. Attending a private school run on the lines of Summerhill (the original 'free' school, where children were encouraged to follow their interests outside of the usual formal classroom setting), I missed out on much of the conventional programming. Instead, there was a different view of what was acceptable. Nudity was considered an important aspect of freedom and I remember the headmaster's long, pale, bony body shambling around the rose gardens, his willy flapping in the breeze; and his objection to us girls wearing swimsuits at puberty (we might now question his motives). Wearing shorts without underpants (we checked) was *de rigueur*, as were sandals, with socks in winter, and vegetarianism.

I noted his ideas about freedom were all based on what he himself considered important, and was constantly in trouble for challenging these. ('Why do you always have to be so argumentative?' was his constant refrain.) Yet despite this, there existed a very precious support for questioning everything, including authority. We were encouraged to experiment and use our initiative and creativity and allowed to participate in the running of the school. So, for example, the older children were involved in things like choosing classes and deciding punishments for those who bullied others – a process of democratic participation leading to taking responsibility that, as I later found out, is lacking in most conventional schools.

When I was thirteen and many of my friends had left to go to boarding school, I wanted out, I wanted to explore the reality of the masses. My daydreaming and lack of concentration had caused me to be assessed by a psychiatrist. Apparently I had a high IQ., but as I then proceeded to fail the Eleven Plus exam I went to the local comprehensive where, because my arithmetic was so atrocious, they put me in class C. I still remember my first day, noting one of the girls was obviously pregnant, the boys busy rubbing themselves behind their desks, while trying to get the girls' attention to see who had the biggest erection! And quite a few had absent fathers and brothers who were 'doing time'. I found it all rather amazing but, strangely, not at all intimidating despite being teased for calling my mother 'mummy'. *The Daily Mirror* had apparently suggested it was possible to get pregnant through kissing, and because we had sex education at my free school they clustered around wanting to know if this was true. Academically, I learnt virtually nothing but as an education in social conditioning it was without equal.

English conditioning around class is formidable. I was fortunate to live in a house with a sizeable garden, virtually surrounded by woods and open countryside. In that area of Surrey there were rows of semi-detached houses where the middle classes lived. This was commuter land, so the husbands dutifully trotted off to the train station every morning equipped with bowler hat, rolled umbrella and a copy of *The Times* carefully tucked under one arm. The bungalows were more spread out and tended to be occupied by pensioners, and up on the hill were the big houses. Where were the working class? That is, most of the pupils in my schoolroom? Tucked away over a hill with one road that went in, turned around and came out again, like a frying pan, and I found this deliberate planning strategy peculiar.

I would occasionally accompany one of my compatriots to their home and wade through the piles of ironing, ducking the ubiquitous budgie cage, to sit and eat my sandwiches. Sometimes we talked about what we would do on leaving school. I would relate various wild ideas and they would say 'Yeah, that's what I'm gonna do, too!' And I came to see how this would almost never happen. 'What *you*? Do *that*? Come off it! Who do you think you *are*?' Nothing but undermining and ridiculing of any tender aspiration (the school took the girls to see a commercial laundry and a margarine factory, the boys to Dagenham car factory – the lucky ones got apprenticeships). The impact of social conditioning on aspirations was ferocious.

And yet – despite the shouting and the quick hand to wallop someone, I noticed a certain warmth and directness: people talked to each other. Whereas when I got invited to lunch with one of my 'better class' classmates there was this terrible silence. Nothing was said but the atmosphere could be cut with a knife. I remember having a hard time with peas. You were supposed to push a few onto the back of your fork – this was considered polite etiquette. But the peas always fell off, and I had found shovelling them onto the front of the fork to be much more efficient. No one said anything: they just tightened their mouths and the air filled with this oppressive sense of disapproval. I think I realised then the damage this repressing of feelings does to people, especially to growing children.

Later, in my early twenties, I had a boyfriend who went 'up' to Cambridge. Through his friends, I got to witness the terrible repression of feelings amongst the upper class. Those oh-so-fortunate souls whose conditioning involves nannies and the hideous yet unremarked cruelty of sending young children away to boarding school – along with such 'discipline enhancing' procedures as being forced to take freezing cold showers, and the potential for sexual exploitation. I saw how their traditions required of them ludicrous rules of behaviour: like needing to be 'seen' at all the right places, while dismissing their privilege as all 'such a bore, darling'. How, whilst playing with what were then called 'imported birds' from London (of which I was one), they were required to marry the long-nosed, horsy, tweeds-twinset-and-pearls-girls that came with a private estate or money; preferably both.

Of course there were the occasional rebels, but even these seemed to find it hard to shed the conditioned belief in their innate superiority and sense of entitlement. Now, clinging on to old social distinctions in an attempt to ward off the hordes of wealthy middle-class aspirants (especially the more vulgar social-climbers), the inbred remnants are left struggling at the ramparts against a torrent of money-buys-in would-be usurpers. And many of these are not even British dammit! From this background, it's not hard to see why so many of those who get to be 'in charge' appear emotionally dysfunctional.

Whist it may have become more complex, social conditioning hasn't changed that much. An American called Harvey Jackins, whom I met in Australia, developed a form of self-help counselling that was uniquely designed to address this. Within the structure of two people exchanging time listening to each other, Co-counselling was initially based around groups representing various forms of social exclusion such as race, sexual preference *and class*. Of these, the former attract the attention of the public, politicians and the media, but rarely is class mentioned. It's generally ignored or relegated to left-wing politics and is not usually included in mainstream psychology (which tends to be the province of the middle classes.)

Now why should this be? Because it's clearly an issue that causes great suffering and invokes deep feelings of shame, envy, resentment and anger. It's as if within the issue of class lies the last bastion of our conditioned reflex to try to reinforce our own sense of identity and belonging through rejecting others. Yet that's really a way of avoiding our own deep fear of being excluded. And here we touch on the fundamental and acutely painful issue of exclusion from the whole. More specifically, *a sense of exclusion and separation* versus inclusion and belonging – whether this plays out within the family, local community, region or nation, for whatever reason. At bottom and usually unconsciously, we believe ourselves to be unwanted, not accepted and loved. To compensate, we try to find this through connection with others *without ever questioning a lack of connection with who we are*.

This is yet another example of how the mind's tendency to separate life into neat categories – class being one of these – based on superficial differences, gets in the way of seeing the whole picture. Because exclusion is a denial of the wholeness that we are all a part of. It's not just a lie – whether that's based on ignorance or deliberate manipulation – in *actual* reality it's an impossibility. *Which doesn't mean it is not believed*. So then, like other beliefs we act on that are not real, it can lead to the unleashing of violence and cause deep pain. Which is where something extraordinarily powerful may happen. In the letting go into this pain the heart opens so Being can enter. We recognise the truth that what we are can never be excluded, then love can cauterise the wound and bring healing. And for all those trapped in their conditioning, unable to come free, a new breed of younger people is where a still often unconscious recognition of wholeness is surfacing most visibly. And this may prove to be contagious.

Influence of patterns

There are so many sources for our conditioning that all play a big part in how we see life and how we behave. And of course *some* conditioning is necessary in order for us to function in the world with common agreement. This is essential to our survival: it has a practical value. What seriously distorts this basic conditioning – and causes so much harm – are beliefs around morality. Beliefs that we inherit that have their roots in the past, changing the focus of what is, and what is not, acceptable: what is to be encouraged, what condemned; what rewarded and what punished. And naturally this affects our behaviour. Just like a monkey or a dog, we learn to adapt our behaviour to what we anticipate will give us what we want and avoid what we don't want.

The reality is, most people continue living their whole lives with these basic drives controlling them. Of course, most of us learn to be more sophisticated about it, but nonetheless people still develop patterns of behaviour that are intended to serve this ego-based identity. So some learn to please others, to conform; while others learn to fight, to rebel. Some learn to be quiet and not draw attention to themselves; others to demand they are the centre of attention. *But all of these patterns are really the same thing; they are all just different strategies, based on our temperament and our place in the family, to get what we want and avoid what we don't want. From the ego's perspective it really is that simple.*

It's sobering to realise how these patterns of behaviour stifle aliveness, and tremendously freeing when we start to become conscious of them; this bringing the opportunity to witness them so that, with time, they come to have less and less power over us. This drive – to get what we want and avoid what we don't want – is the primary movement of ego and the mind is drawn into service of this. This is what I refer to as egoic mind. As most of us have been conditioned to believe that having such patterns is bad or wrong, even shameful if admitted to, we take great pains to disguise them, especially from ourselves. When, in reality, they are just the natural response of ego: the 'me' that we believe ourselves to be, that has no connection to Being and therefore knows no other way *to* be. It's not wrong or stupid. It's just a disconnect: *an inevitable response to believing something that isn't actually true.*

Having lost our connection with what *is* true – with who we really are – we are wide open to the terrifying belief this loss of connection creates. We conclude that we are all alone in the world. And worse, because this then causes us to take on another fundamental belief: that we are powerless unless we can somehow grasp what we want for ourselves. At this point it can be tricky if we hear some spiritual teacher say that this is all just an illusion, because if you are still convinced the egoic mind is real this just brings confusion. This is where gaps – cracks in the facade of this illusion, called awakenings – are so powerful. Even if only for a moment, they allow a direct glimpse into reality *as it truly is.*

NOTE: By ego, I am referring to the imaginary self we come to believe is who we are. Osho, the spiritual teacher quoted at the beginning of this chapter, comments *'The ego is a puzzle. It is something like darkness – which you can feel, which can obstruct your way but does not exist. It has no positivity. It is simply an absence, an absence of light. The ego does not exist – how can you surrender it? The ego is only an absence of awareness.'*

Domination of the egoic will

Examining the mind and how it functions can make it easier to glimpse the truth of what is *really* happening – beneath the facade; easier to recognise the degree of distortion we live with every day and have come to believe is normal. To quote the spiritual teacher Osho again *'Truth cannot be found by intellectual effort because truth is not a theory, it is an experience.'* Here we return to another important realisation about mind that we touched on before: that the mind has no way of assessing true value. Such as beauty, for instance, which doesn't respond to reason or logic. Beauty cannot be measured or weighed or explained: none of the things mind is so fond of. Even comparison is entirely subjective. You may have been taught that something is to be seen as beautiful – a painting, a statue, a building, a landscape; or a film star, a singer, a model. You may have believed and agreed with this judgement but – ultimately – it depends on a response from within you to verify that this is true. And this response belongs to the heart.

In truth, the mind cannot distinguish genuine beauty or aesthetically pleasing form, things which bring harmony and delight the heart: mind knows nothing of this. It has plenty of *theories*, plenty of learned concepts and abstract ideas; it has endless filing-cabinets full of information. It has methods and formulas and instruments, but when you come down to it *all* this is dependent on judgement. And the egoic mind is seething with judgements: with criticisms and opinions about everything! It likes nothing better than to debate and take a position, and it thrives on argument and discord. With something like beauty, however, it has no way of recognising this. It's not even a matter of programming, because its relatively mechanical processes are limited. And this very limitation can be hard to see – but we overlook it at our peril.

A brutal illustration of this is a cube. Have you ever noticed and wondered why cubic architecture, based as it is on squares, is never truly relaxing? I know some people would disagree with this perception and many architects be outraged (according to Jung's theory of shapes and their meaning, the square represents stillness). So check this out for yourself with your body; there you will find the truth. For a sensitive person, standing in front of the point of a cube – a corner facing you – you can feel the discomfort in the belly. *Forms based on exact squares and perfectly straight lines are almost never found in nature* (Iron Pyrite known as Fool's Gold, a cubic crystal, is a rare exception).

What about circles and curves? The pagans saw the circle as representing equality and eternity and, interestingly, the Earth herself is round, as are the sun and moon, all the planets and stars. Rivers, if left to their own devices, meander in curves. It's not that they follow the existing landscape, for even in flat valleys rivers can change their course. No, it is by moving in curves that water reinvigorates itself. Rudolph Steiner recognised this when he designed a series of ceramic dishes, one below the other, to create a waterfall in which the water formed a spiralling movement. Water forced down straight tubes and pipes loses its vitality; and this, of course, affects all who drink it. Someone I met in Australia had developed a moving spiralled instrument to be placed into a glass of water. He claimed that doing so reinvigorated the water. I have no idea if anyone has followed this up in scientific experiments to 'prove' this, I just know that drinking water out of a pipe and drinking the same water from his glass produced a profoundly different taste. Something in me 'knew' that what he said made sense.

It is this same intuitive sense of knowing that so infuriates the mind, restricted as it is to reason and logic. When you look closely at this, you see that mind and its beliefs – along with so-called 'scientifically proven evidence' – is continually being shown to be wrong. As we have seen, the mind is not an impartial machine. Emotionalised belief blocked vision when, in the 16th century, Copernicus proposed that, contrary to the accepted 'facts' of the time, the Earth went round the sun, and not the other way round. And when Galileo published this, those who claimed authority at the time (the Pope and his minions) found him guilty of heresy and had him put under house arrest for his pains. Not till three centuries later did the Catholic church allow this to be published as fact.

As long ago as 1905, Einstein determined that space and time are not absolutes; rather, they are relative to the position of the observer. In other words, everything that is seen to be so, is subjective: *subject to the perspective of the viewer.* Yet this highly significant observation is routinely ignored in much of mainstream scientific research today. In many ways, science remains limited by its inability to relate to direct, intuitive experience.

Going back to curves, the homes of traditional peoples were almost always circular – from African huts to igloos, teepees to yurts. Ancient formations of stone and wood are almost never square. Women's bodies are full of curves (those ancient figures of goddesses and statues for worship have always been curvaceous). Flower heads and petals are curved, hills are curved (though mountain crags may not be), tree tops are generally curved (though they may be distorted by the wind). Some people even experimented growing plants in circular formations at the Findhorn community in Scotland and found they grew prodigiously – unfortunately so did the weeds!

Even the edges of clouds are curved. Just imagine how it would feel if you looked up in the sky and saw a square sun, with rectangular clouds! Can you even imagine that? Yet manufacturers are developing square tomatoes to make packaging easier, so profits can increase. Most striking of all these examples of circles and curves is the way eyes themselves function: *our vision is circular.* Looking at squares is stressful because we have to extend and contract the view artificially to make it square. So looking at squares can never be truly relaxing. There is a tension from each of the corners which – again, if you are sensitive – can be *felt.* In fact many of these out-of-integrity shapes can be felt in the body. As children we sensed this intuitively, it's just that we have been conditioned to override and ignore these accurate sensing mechanisms of the body.

One time, walking around the streets of London, I found myself passing a small square and I felt this strong pull. As I stood in it I was affected by a beautiful and very powerful sense of stillness and serenity, yet this square was off a busy main road filled with traffic. I noted the formation: there were a group of giant plane trees arranged in a circle and, in the centre, a circular stone structure housing a fountain. It was perfectly clear to me that this was what was giving it this peaceful feeling. Next time, notice how you *feel* when looking at something. With architecture, look at buildings that contain domes and arches. *Feel* the difference in observing an arched window, for instance, instead of the usual square or rectangular shape. Other races like the Arabs, the Berbers, the Persians and the Indians knew about this: hence the Taj Mahal, the Alhambra, the Blue Mosque in Istanbul.

Contrast these with how you feel looking at buildings full of rectangles and straight lines, like all those tower blocks of flats built in the Sixties. Brutalism indeed! I am not saying here that using squares or rectangles is *wrong,* nor advocating avoiding straight lines: this would clearly be absurd. What I am saying is that shapes affect us, often far more than we realise; so it's good to be aware of this, then we can re-value and prioritise and avoid a predominance of such shapes when not absolutely necessary. *Because the shapes we choose reflect our state of consciousness.*

There is about square and rectangular shapes an element of force, of domination typical of mind's wilful obsession. They assert by demanding and distorting natural forms to conform to their *will*. They speak of the kind of power that an ego-driven mind seeks. A direction, like the word 'progress', that can never lead to peace and ease of relationship. This is negative* male power taken to extremes – raw and insensitive, even abusive: *ultimately life-negating and destructive*. An extreme example of this out-of-balance, negative male energy is mining the tar sands and the utter devastation this leaves behind; where areas of outstanding natural beauty – vast tracts of pristine wilderness – are reduced to barren moonscapes by ginormous machines belching fumes.

NOTE: *I am using the term negative here to refer to 'ego-directed', *which can be applied to both genders*; as also can the term positive, which I see as heart-directed. It's worth remembering that both men *and* women contain masculine and feminine energies.

Squares and straight lines are a great symbol for the world we are living in, especially in the West, but now being replicated in all the major cities around the world. (Latterly, a few curved structures, like the phallic 'gherkin' in London, have appeared, but this too has a dominating thrust and the more recent sharp pointed shapes are actually quite aggressive). These structures are most often created using concrete, steel and reinforced glass as building materials. They are very strong, often massive; sometimes crude and – they used to be – absolutely unyielding. Now, in order to survive earthquakes, their structure has had to be modified to give them some degree of flexibility: this being an example of how the natural world has forced man to adapt to *her* will for a change.

All this could be said to represent the unbridled negative masculine, *which is not about blaming men as such.* This out-of-balance macho energy, brilliantly illustrated some years ago in the opening scenes of the film *Avatar*, has it origins in our faith in the egoic mind. This control and aggressive domination mentality is highly visible in the concreting-over of huge areas of land and the cutting of limbs off trees to make them conform to our convenience. Weed-killers are used to exterminate anything that is not considered edible or decorative. Gardens are designed with plants determined as 'architectural' – soft, flowing, wild and disordered tending to be seen as inferior and undesirable. The point being that in all of this, there is neither recognition nor honouring of the feminine, nor of the wild irregularities and flow of nature, of this being the *natural* expression of Being-ness. There is a denial of connection, of relatedness (these being feminine traits) and of the hidden organic impulse of nature. Instead, this is overwhelmed by a blind determination to bring everything under man's control – whatever the cost.

This same force is visible now in all aspects of our lives – from big, multi-national corporations that seek to control the food supply through genetic engineering, to the drive to extract fuels in ever more-destructive forms like fracking, the cutting down of rainforests, polluting of land and rivers and seas: the list is endless, but it all represents the same thing! The rape and pillage of this, our home, our means of survival, *is the inevitable movement of mind-over-matter.* It brings this into high visibility. All is pursued in either ignorance or wilful denial of true worth. The heart is denied. If any other species behaved in this way we would say they had gone insane. Are we insane? Or is insanity simply rampant unconsciousness? Disconnection from the Being that we all are?

Many people feel angry, frightened and helpless in the face of this destruction but it is actually the egoic mind that is insane, *and it is our worship of this mind that brings us to collude in our own destruction.* Which is where a conscious return to intuitive connection with our Being-ness finally gets to be seen as the only solution. For a *truly* intelligent mind is a mind in harmony with consciousness. A mind that functions through the heart, subject to its values and intuitive knowing: a vehicle for Being to manifest. Seeing this, it is clear that a return to sanity requires recognising the conditioned mind and its malfunctioning in our lives; taking our courage to follow that which cannot be proved, explained and justified, but which brings great joy as we realise *what is already here.* As we return our attention to listening to *this,* instead of to the mind, so the heart can guide and restore us to true sanity.

Thinking and beliefs – the structural activities of mind

So what else is it useful to recognise about the mind? What about thinking? Which, by its nature, is abstract. You can't taste, smell or touch a thought, you can only seemingly hear it or see an image, when it registers in your mind. Thinking – that is, thinking *about* something – is what the mind does. We speak about 'thinking something through', and something being not properly 'thought out', but most of our thinking has no purpose. Yes, many of us use thought to explore and create, to plan, strategise and resolve problems, it can be a wonderful medium to play with. But I am referring to all the rest of the thinking-about-something that we do as a matter of habit, a habit that even when we choose to do so, can be hard to break.

We could liken all this thinking activity amongst humans, especially modern, Westernised humans, to a constant barrage of meaningless signals in space, forever circling the world in waves aligned to time zones. In fact, if you could somehow solidify them, there would not be space in all the universes to contain all of humanities thoughts! And all of this thinking takes up a great deal of our energy and focus of attention.

What is really going on here? Why do we spend so much time in our minds, thinking? Have you ever noticed how we use our thoughts to entertain ourselves? Without all that thinking we might have a great, big, empty, unfilled space. Wow! Does that sound terrifying or wonderful to you? If we stop thinking we might have to meet and actually engage with life! On an immediate, intimate basis. And then we would have to deal with all our fears around this, around what might happen, what we might have to feel if we experience life directly.

An analogy we could use for this kind of constant mind activity is a cloud obscuring the sun (representing Being). This cloud is constantly changing shape and form and yet it has no substance. Thoughts can be likened to bubbles that are continuously blown, expanding one upon the other and then bursting, revealing nothing inside. Ego seems to sustain these bubbles and we are taught that we are the one who is blowing the pipe, when actually there is no-one doing this! Still we are captivated – mesmerised by the shiny, multicoloured reflections these bubbles carry. And what about beliefs? Beliefs are like fine sticky threads that wind us up and hold us tight, like flies in a spider's web until they, too, are seen through. And all the thunder and lightning; the icy blizzards and howling gales: these are just feelings turned into emotions, under pressure from thoughts and beliefs that, once this pressure is released, settle back down into the calm, placid – but intensely alive – ocean of life.

The egoic mind loves to take a position and it uses thinking to do this. One day I had this realisation: that it actually makes no difference what my mind thinks about what I am doing or not doing: it is happening anyway! *It is what is happening that counts,* and anything I think about this is, on this deeper level of reality, is irrelevant. I can have a whole range of judgements, opinions, attitudes and positions about an action, I can give these my attention, believe them and create wonderful dramas for myself, especially as these then engage *emotional* reactions. Or, I can simply watch what is happening. I can stay in touch with my feeling, sensing, intuitive responses and notice how these are affecting my body. And I can be aware of where I am coming *from*, in taking any action. For this is key to staying true to myself.

Have you noticed how the mind attempts to solve all our problems with thought? This is what we were taught to do at school. Surely everyone has had the experience of trying to solve something by thinking about it, going round and round without gaining any sense of clarity? Whether the issue is a practical one, like how long it will take us to drive somewhere, or a personal one, like how to resolve an argument with a friend, it can be a frustrating business. Of course there are many kinds of situations where it is useful to have information. With the first issue, it would be helpful to know the mileage, the kinds of roads, the likelihood of traffic build-ups and so on. This is where the mind comes into its own. It is great at assessing, calculating and comparing. But even here we can often get an intuitive 'feel' for the situation: the best time to go, if it will be a difficult journey, if it is a good idea to go at all. Then there is the personal issue, and here the mind really is of no use at all.

So it's odd, isn't it? Because *despite* this, we are trained to attempt to resolve everything, including personal dilemmas, by thinking about them with the mind. True, women are more likely to use empathetic qualities but this is not something that is encouraged or taught in schools. Yet it is precisely through the feeling, sensing, intuitive sensibilities that we resolve personal difficulties; helped by an awareness of our own issues and a willingness to be open and honest and sensitive towards the other.

What about beliefs? (One could write a whole chapter on this!). I once read about a trained psychiatrist, Russell Razzaque, saying *'The more fused we are to our world of thought, the less able we are to see the emotional foundation from which it arose. That's why those with the most strident of opinions are often the ones who will admit least that their views have arisen from emotion.'* What this analysis leaves out is the fundamental part played by belief in this process; as beliefs control both thought and emotion, so it is *beliefs which are the real hook.*

One could say beliefs are a speciality of the mind, and a woman called Byron Katie (whom I quoted at the beginning of this chapter) designed a set of questions to ask yourself that can help in bringing beliefs to light and seeing through them. She calls this 'The Work' and it includes a question that often occurs in my own work, the question 'Is that true?'. This is really useful because, rather like a dog with fleas, the mind is infested with beliefs and these are usually unconscious and rarely turn out to be true. So a central part of helping people unravel themselves involves challenging beliefs.

How do beliefs form themselves? We believe because we have had experiences of the 'If I touch something hot I will burn myself' kind of knowledge, which is based on fact; but there is another form of belief which is purely psychological. And this is where things start to get messy – more than messy, because beliefs can cause real harm. We believe things that are actually erroneous conclusions we have made *about* our experience. So, for example, 'It must be my fault that Mum and Dad split up. If I had been good they wouldn't have. *Therefore* I must be a bad person and should be ashamed of myself' or 'Daddy didn't love me because I wasn't pretty enough, because I was fat. *Therefore* I don't have what it takes to keep someone's love, there is something wrong with me. I can only expect men to reject and abandon me.' Sounds crazy, right? Yet I have seen so many people who concluded exactly these sorts of things out of situations that really had nothing to do with them. These beliefs get buried so deep in the psyche that many people never get to know about them. The tragedy then is that they don't know they are actually being *controlled by these beliefs* and so continue acting them out for the rest of their lives.

We also believe things that we have been told by others, especially our parents when we were young. 'Never mind dear, we can't all be the clever one' or 'You are such a lazybones! If you don't get up in the morning you'll never succeed at anything.' We believe because we have acquired 'knowledge', and this knowledge then blinds us to the fact that something we have been told may not be true. So, for example, we believe that it is not possible to see – quite literally – into the past. We all know this. We do, don't we? Yet the truth is every time you gaze into a star-filled sky you are looking at the light reflected from lumps of minerals and clumps of gases that disintegrated millions of years ago. Right here, right now, you are seeing what no longer exists! Time and space become one.

This is how beliefs – any belief – keep us firmly locked in the past and, by their nature, tend to close us off from reality. As Naomi Klein amusingly puts it when talking about 'climate deniers' in her book *This changes everything*, 'If new information seems to confirm our world view, we welcome it and integrate it easily. If it poses a threat to our belief system, then our brain immediately gets to work producing intellectual antibodies designed to repel the unwanted invasion.' And one last thing about beliefs: they impact on the body; it is affected by and stores *reactions to*, beliefs. So then, as beliefs are seen through and challenged, so the body becomes free to respond and express itself naturally.

The impact of memory

One function of mind that is essential for survival is memory. It would be impossible to do things, like remember where you put something, or remember someone's name, without this. I have a terrible memory but what I notice is that I remember best the things that interest me most: hence I have a very good memory for faces but can never remember a name. Then there is another kind of memory: the remembrance of things that occurred in the past. For some, especially older people, there can be a tendency to dwell on fond memories (perhaps to compensate for current circumstances we didn't choose?) For many others, the past holds sadness and regret and maybe resentment about the way we perceive we have been treated. But memory is a trickster! It can be very informative to ask different people who were all present at the same event what they each saw. So often people have a completely different take on what happened.

Then you begin to see how mind – the great interpreter – colours events according to our beliefs *about* those events. How it selects aspects that resonate with some emotional reaction based on a belief. Yet if we examine this belief, it is usually not true. Then we get to glimpse the shaky nature of this whole edifice and see how we suffer so much by deluding ourselves, by believing things that are simply not true.

The mind has both this highly selective but also extremely tenacious relationship with memories. For instance have you noticed how, when something happens in the present, you can spend so much time thinking about it afterwards? 'I shouldn't have said that, maybe my boss will be angry, but if I hadn't said it no one else would' or 'Maybe if I hadn't gone ... but I promised I would, and mother would have been so disappointed' or 'Why was he so cross? Was he upset with *me* or was he just in a bad mood?' and so on and on. We speculate and ruminate and fulminate and cogitate (wonderful words)! We go over and over situations from the past like a squirrel that has forgotten where it buried a nut.

For so many people, spending a great deal of time with attention locked into a distorted version of events in the past is the norm; even though these events can't be changed we continue to revisit them. It's like scratching a sore spot – we can't seem to leave it alone; telling ourselves stories about how it *should* have been, what we *should* have done or said, how we could have triumphed instead of feeling humiliated, etc., and generally making ourselves miserable. You surely know this experience, and how, all of a sudden, you look up and realise life has carried on happening without you – a glorious sunset has faded, your child has given up trying to get your attention, your coffee grown cold.

The other great distraction is, of course, thinking about the future: 'if' and 'when' land. *If* only ... *then* I'll be happy: 'If only he would look at me', 'If only I could get that promotion', 'If we had a bigger house'; 'If only I could lose weight, start my own business, win the lottery, ...' on and on and on. The mind is like a hall of mirrors: it reflects back to us our wants and desires and secret longings, along with our fears and worries and anxieties, and it never stops! Like a twenty-four-hour cinema, we get to watch the film and participate too. Or... or we don't! The recognition dawns that we have been lost in the mind, and we bring our attention back to what *really* nourishes us, to what can bring interest, curiosity and the possibility of deep satisfaction and contentment into our lives. We re-engage with life as it is happening: this moment, *now*.

Dethroning the mind

All this looking into the mind can be extremely challenging. It can feel quite a marathon, but with it we are laying the foundation for being able to let go of all distortion, which causes so much suffering, so we can see the world with fresh eyes. So, then, how to approach this mind with its solid beliefs riddled with hooks for us to get caught on, with its endemic conditioning and sticky attachments to the past? There are plenty of methods and techniques based on working with the mind to try to change its thought patterns. 'Positive thinking' is one. I remember doing a workshop on this once: we were instructed to write out all these positive affirmations to get our mind working the way we wanted it to. So, for the magic twenty days things seemed to go swimmingly and then – whoops, back came the negative stuff! The law of balance, equal and opposites: where the pendulum has to swing back. Beliefs, it seems, are ultimately stronger and more convincing than any technique designed to banish them!

I am not talking here about awareness, that allows us to choose to move attention from depressing to uplifting things, for example, or focus the good in our lives rather than dwelling on what we don't like; sometimes this just *feels* right and we recognise this. I am referring to techniques based on using the mind to control and override our genuine responses, intended to change our thoughts and beliefs, i.e. 'I used to be a boring/ugly/weak/cowardly person; I am now a wonderful/beautiful/strong/powerful person' – techniques that don't allow our need to see, feel or meet something. When difficult and painful feelings are repressed *these always affect us:* they colour our thinking and affect our energy levels and, eventually, if we refuse to meet them, they can even make us sick.

In this sense the mind has enormous power. However, once you get a glimpse of something deeper than mind, it can start to exert a pull: as with a sudden glimpse of light when you draw back the curtains in a darkened room, what was once not visible begins to reveal itself. Then, by knowing these simple things about feelings and emotions and beliefs and the whole way we operate through our conditioning, how we interpret our world according *to* this conditioning, you begin to see beyond the absurdity of trying to change the mind with the mind! Then – *and only then* – can a deep shift start to happen.

It is here that words can be useful and in perhaps surprising ways they can help unseat the mind from its position of dominance. Mind is accustomed to interpreting thoughts into words. But words are one of man's strangest inventions: they have no colour, no taste, no smell. They are not musical in themselves, nor do they move – they have no sensual reference at all. Usually quite literally, they are black and white with no shades of grey, and even their shape bears no connection to the meanings they carry (Chinese being an exception here). And yet, beyond the brain to translate them, words are utterly dependent on the senses: to be seen by the eyes, heard by the ears, or felt by the finger tips if you are blind. In fact, *without the senses, words have no use at all.*

So in approaching the mind, why use words? Well, actually, one of the most interesting things that words can do is to *touch*. They are invaluable tools in a session. Then – if you are functioning from a clear and present space, and empathically tuned-in to the other – words, with the meanings and questions they carry, can function like lasers. They can shine through a person's defences and beam onto hidden places, and this produces a resonance. What is touched opens up and responds. There is no way you can conduct this fine-tuning or achieve this unerring accuracy with the mind, *but you can use words from a place of intuitive connection with the body-Being to invoke a response.* This response can then loosen the old, fixed patterns of defence and allow things to move and flow, to reorganise and come into awareness. Not only is this extremely powerful, it is recognised by the body-Being of the other that is in full-participation. And the person usually senses this so it can help them relax. One could even say that the body-Being of both relax into the Being-*ness* that is not separate.

One of the most valuable ways of piercing the mind's dominance comes through seeing. Here I need to say something about this word 'seeing', because it is this – that is, looking from awareness – which can cut through the egoic mind's delusion: the false version of reality most of us have got caught up in. This seeing is not of the mind but is awareness itself and it is one of the most powerful abilities we have to penetrate the fog. Seeing allows us to *recognise* what is real. Awareness itself is empty of agendas, of preferences even: it simply sees what *is*. Unlike the mind, it has no judgements, no interpretations of events. It is impartial so it neither attacks nor comes to your defence. It simply witnesses.

So, for instance, in learning the difference between mind and awareness, you can notice how the mind always comments on events; it has a viewpoint, which creates a certain tightness in the body. For example, you have a bad back but you bend over to reach for something anyway. Awareness sees this. *The mind judges your action and comments about this,* that you shouldn't have done that because of your bad back. I use this word 'seeing' a lot in this book precisely because it is such a valuable tool that plays a major role in our coming free from all illusion and able to recognise what is *actually* here.

It is true, recognising the mind and its patterns can seem like hard work but the rewards are infinite! Somewhere deep inside we hanker for freedom: freedom from the narrow limits of a life controlled by a conditioned mind. We know there is more, but we often don't know how to access this. So in reclaiming our freedom to be ourselves, we have to take risks. We have to do something none of us have been trained to do. That is to allow ourselves to rest in a place where *we just don't know* (in the mind). Then, the more we do this, the more we can see just how limiting and distorting of reality this mind-control has been. It tells us so many fairy tales. For instance, do you know what intelligence really *is*? Where it comes from? We are taught that intelligence is somehow produced by the brain. That some people have more of this, some less, according to their genetic makeup and maybe just luck. Parents try to make their children more intelligent with various kinds of early learning processes; we take IQ tests to see who has been more gifted.

Take a fresh look and you may see that intelligence is everywhere! It resides in everything and can't be contained or produced. *Intelligence is not a commodity.* The mind is simply the interpreter: it *receives* intelligence through the filter of our conditioning. Intelligence itself is glorious! Life itself is intelligent – every flower, every rock, every molecule of life contains intelligence, as some of the newer discoveries in physics are starting to recognise. So the joy of coming free is that intelligence can then flood the mind, *without distortion*. Then the mind can return to doing what it is designed to do: to function in service to the heart, as an instrument for Being to express itself. Interpreting in ways that allow us to function as human animals in the physical world, yes, but without altering, limiting or overriding our innate knowing, our connection with Being. Without trying to dominate and control what simply *is*.

In a certain sense the mind is innocent, it is just doing its job. It has been infiltrated by the hidden power of the ego (In other words, by an idea). And one of the things it is very useful to know about the egoic mind is that it thrives on remaining hidden. It does not like exposure and even less, not being taken seriously or even being laughed at. Here, I have found that some of the most effective ways to come free from the dominance of this egoic mind act as a spotlight – they highlight the mind. Then, like a rabbit caught in the headlights, egoic mind does not know which way to run! *And in that precious moment we can recognise the power we have given it through our believing its story* – believing what we have been taught. (Various exercises in the last chapter act in support of this unmasking process.)

The myth of a separate self

There is one area where conditioned mind obstructs a clear view that has great significance. This has to do with how we absorb information – especially if we are not paying full attention – on a subliminal level. Meaning, we often don't notice what we are absorbing and so can't reflect on it, feel into the truth of it or even question it. For instance, using the example of intelligence again, if you ask someone where this comes from they will likely tell you from the brain (as if the brain somehow manufactures it like a machine producing candy floss). They do this because they have learnt to reach for their mind for answers, so it's reflexive. Then, the *reality* – that intelligence is everywhere – is not seen.

Most people are ignorant of the mind's tendency to distort reality; that it interprets, alters and even draws erroneous conclusions about information received *and that it is this that limits and distorts intelligence*. Yet recognising this is crucial. Because if you ask someone who they truly are *they assume they know* and they have never questioned this assumption. They will describe themselves to you by telling you their name, their age, gender, race, job, marital status and so on, to identify themselves. If you ask them *what* they are, they will likely say a person, a human being with a body and brain that *produces* intelligence, that informs them of all this. *They do not know* that the mind has learned, like the good program-receiver that it is, that we are supposed to be a certain thing called a person, with a list of information to describe ourselves with. How would they? Almost nobody talks about this (outside of select spiritual circles). It's beyond taboo.

Here, crucially and fundamentally, lies what the mind cannot tell us. That is, what a person *is,* who we actually *are,* or what lies beneath and beyond this programmed computer that our mind functions as. Whereas intuitive intelligence can reach through the blockade (though not in words and not on demand). Am I confusing you? The reality is intelligence itself does not need thoughts to carry it: *intelligence doesn't need the mind.* That's right. (You may need to take a pause to digest here, as this is certainly not what we have all been taught.) Intelligence can flow through the senses, through feeling, through intuition. Remember: *life* is intelligent. The mind produces thoughts *about* what is perceived; it comments, and with these comments it judges and compares, edits and exaggerates, holds opinions and takes positions. It may applaud, loath or be utterly disgusted; it may agree, disagree, approve, disapprove, like, dislike and so on. So, in order to dis-identify, an interesting question to ask of this perennially commenting mind might be 'And what has this to do with *me*?' (As in, who I really am?)

On this question of who is living this life, try looking for yourself and see what you discover. Can you find a someone? It can be rather shocking to realise we have been raised with no idea of who we really are; to see how this 'person' we have assumed ourselves to be, has been taught to function according to other peoples dictates and, as a result of this, taught to ignore the essential core of our reality. We do our best to fabricate a self, and in the doing convince ourselves and everyone else, that we *are* that self. Those who fail in this usually find themselves in some kind of institution.

In terms of mind and conditioning, this provides a framework to recognise why we are they way we are, and why we behave the way we do. We begin to see that this is where it all starts to get messed up. To quote Osho again, *'Truth is always new and mind is always old. Mind is always of the past, truth is always of the present. That's why mind & truth never meet. Mind is that which you have already known; truth is that which is yet to be known. Mind is the known and truth is the unknowable or the unknown. Mind is just a record of all that has happened. Mind is not an adventure; truth is an adventure.'*

Once we remember who we are – even a glimpse of this – we can immediately see the absurdity of attempting to apply the mind in the ways that we do. It's like expecting a parrot to give a speech just because it has learned to say a few words. *And this is nobody's fault.* What I hope is clear by now is that we humans only try to use the mind in this way, to tell us about reality and truth and how to live, *because we have been taught to.* This was all that was on offer, and now we have learned to take this for granted. Peoples from the distant past (and some still living) would have been amazed by this. They would have thought us weird, or, at the very least, lost and misguided. They may well have even laughed at us! Yet most people see our current understanding of life as progress. Outside of spiritual circles, this whole misapplication of mind rarely gets questioned.

A last note about control and setting boundaries

We use the term 'control freak' as a term of abuse, yet is control always such a bad thing? There are surely times when control is needed for things to function well. It's when we go way beyond this in our attempts to control ourselves, others and situations around us that control can be a real problem. Under the surface, on a level we are rarely conscious of, many people fear others; we fear that without some form of control there would be chaos in our lives; things would happen and people would behave in ways that we really didn't want or feel comfortable with. Hence the attempt to *manage* everything, which comes from the mind: it is fear-driven and survival-orientated. What I have noticed about this is that, yes, there is certainly a need to be able to say 'No' and to set boundaries (by boundaries, I am talking about making clear to others what you are willing and not willing to give or receive from them, especially emotional drama); but beyond this, I have seen that the more I am able to let go and trust – the more I listen in to the intuitive senses and live in this flow – the more life moves harmoniously. Things that need to be done get done, there is time for everything and a beautiful order to the way things happen. People call when I am free, cancel a session if I am tired: somehow my energy is met.

Whereas with mind, there is so often an underlying anxiety: Have I done what I needed to do? Will I get to the airport on time? Is there something I have forgotten? And so on. Or: Was I being mean by saying no to what someone asked of me? And suchlike interpersonal dilemmas. This pressure of mind to control sets up a trap where we can never quite catch up, along with that sense of 'When I have finished what I need to do, *then* I will rest.' Have you noticed how that space somehow never arrives? Mind loves time and order. It's like a watch tower set up to make sure that no matter what, you don't do anything it doesn't know about. It *loves to* understand. Does that sound strange? But then how can you control something if you don't understand it?

Poor old mind. Over these pages it can seem like it's getting a really bad press. But please, don't start to blame your mind. It isn't the enemy, it is just being asked to do what it doesn't know how to do any other way. If you stop asking it and believing it about things it was never designed to know, you might hear a huge sigh of relief! In spiritual circles, where people have heard that the mind is a problem, there is a tendency to fight with it but that doesn't work: it's just mind fighting the mind; and anyway mind loves conflict, it loves nothing better than a good fight! So we try repressing it and it just gets louder and more insistent. What happens if you bring your attention to what is not the mind? And just watch? This is a common instruction in many spiritual circles. At first, crafty old mind will try and do this for you, it will happily become the observer. *So it's immensely valuable if you can come to recognise the difference between mind and awareness* and remember – that which sees the mind is not the mind. In other words, the mind cannot see itself.

As we will explore in the following chapters, there are many ways to tune-in and stay present with yourself, in the body. In fact sometimes – probably more often than we are willing to admit – attempting to sit and 'just watch the mind' can become wearying. But if we are *fully engaged* in something we enjoy, like painting or dancing; gardening, cooking or fixing a motorbike, we *are* present. We are not in the thinking-about-something-else mind. Just walking along the street, sitting on a bus, train or plane or even driving a car, we can discover we can *still be present*.

So, ultimately, conditioned mind doesn't have to be a problem. Through what we are aware of, and what we do with our attention, we can – slowly, slowly – release this bondage. Which is where I find remembering what I love, through the feeling, sensing, intuitive conduits of the heart, opens the way to becoming free. And here is one last question to wonder about: What if there is really only one mind? And all the different conditionings are simply shadow-play in a puppet theatre? Then, the expression 'It's all in the mind' takes on true meaning! Then – like the audience after a good show – we sit up, yawn and stretch, and gently come back to reality.

Home-play
1. Slow shrug, with the words 'I don't need to know'
- Sit with the elbows beside the body, bent to allow the forearms to project frontwards with the hands hanging palm downwards, then slowly lift the shoulders up on the in-breath.
- Turn the hands over, palms uppermost, saying the words 'I don't need to know'.
- Let the shoulders descend (keeping elbows beside body) as you breath out through the mouth, finally opening and extending the fingers as they come to rest (So, if you were holding a ball in the palm of your hand, it would roll off). This last is a gesture by which the body is letting go, saying 'over to you', releasing any tendency to hold on. Trained, as we all have been to know, this exercise can be quite a shock for the mind.

2. Focussing the cradle*
(What I am calling the 'cradle' is a spot immediately above the Mound of Venus in women and the scrotum in men.)
- Breathe down into the cradle, noticing any resistance on the way down, and breathe out from there.
- Now, holding the focus of attention in that spot, ask yourself to think. Notice what happens. In creating an intense focus you will find that thinking is impossible, that this disconnects thought, or at least presses the pause button.

Repeat whenever you feel to.

3. Finger snapping and waving to the mind
- Imitate chattering mind by bringing finger and thumb together, opening and closing in rapid, repeated sequence, or simply wave to it. 'Hello, I see you.' Remember, that which sees mind is not the mind, but pure uninvolved awareness. By recognising it, and personifying and poking fun at it in these ways, you undermine its role of authority, showing it you are not taking it seriously.

4. And here is a playful tongue-twister for a mind that deals in words
'Shedding shoulds shall set you free!'

NOTE: People with a strong addiction to mind (and that's most of us, especially in Westernised society), who have little experience of another place to be that feels safe often find exercises 3 and 4 impossible at first, and may even become angry and strongly resistant. These exercises can bring up feelings of embarrassment and being seen as foolish or even blasphemous! The problem for the egoic mind is that they are supremely effective.

*NOTE ABOUT THE CRADLE: There is one thing that I refer to in other chapters which needs to be included here so you will know what I am talking about. This very personal 'seeing' involves part of the body-energy that I am calling the 'cradle.' I find connecting with this can help in getting a break from a continual and often unwanted input from the mind. So, between the belly and the pelvic floor (just above the Mound of Venus in women and the scrotum in men), is where a still, quiet place can be located, a place that has the power to anchor all the subtle energy centres, even as the Crown chakra can orchestrate them. I sense the cradle as being connected into the vast stillness out of which everything arrises – anchored into infinity, the Absolute, eternity – like some sort of etheric root, if you like, or spiritual umbilical chord. Connecting to this place allows us to rest in Being: it lies outside of time. Once you have established a good connection here you may find this helps create a space from the continual onslaught of thinking.

Other people describe such energy centres differently and this can be confusing. For instance, in many chakra 'systems' the second chakra is seen to be just below the navel. Others, including myself, find this lower down, and some identify both places as being energy centres. Don't worry; none of what I am talking about here needs to be viewed as knowledge. Rather, it may be known directly, in your experience. Just let your intuitive senses 'grock' or ingest what I am saying and check this out for yourself. Then, if we accept that the mind has its limits this doesn't have to be a problem.

Navigational skills of the heart

'It takes a fierce and robust heart to say yes to life, to embrace the entirety of life on its terms, not on our imagined or idealised terms. This requires a connectedness to our spiritual essence, to who we really are.' ~ Adyashanti

'If we do not want to allow the world to sink into chaos, we must release the love which is trapped in the heart of all humans' ~ Nikos Karantzakis

'People say love is blind because they do not know what love is. I say unto you, only love has eyes; other than love, everything is blind' ~ Osho

Life is so beautiful. We have been given so much. We haven't done anything to deserve it, it just is, here – as it is. In truth, is there any place on Earth, no matter how wild, bare or apparently barren that, without man's touch, is *not beautiful*? All that is ugly and destroys this beauty comes from the mistaken belief in an egoic conditioned mind. It's not anybody's fault. Caught in this belief we inflict hurt on ourselves, others, and everything on this earth. When you sit quietly and just look, without judgement, there is beauty everywhere and the heart is full: the rain falling softly on the ground – bringing food to the trees and plants and all of us; the sun shining – bringing warmth and light and allowing everything to grow; the earth, in all its many colours and shapes and textures – providing sustenance. Between them lies a balance, a perfect harmony.

I am fortunate to live both on the edge of a little mountain village and in a city beside the sea. Here I am in the mountains – watching drops of rain splashing up from the tiles on the top terrace, hanging like diamonds under the iron railings. One day the mist is here: hanging in drifts in the valleys, allowing the mountain ridges to be revealed as in a Japanese painting. Then, when the sun and blue skies return, I am watching men and women move out into the fields, if only a few, mostly elderly now. If it's spring it's time for sowing and planting and tilling the soil. In summer the fields are full of life: crops and grass for the animals, wild flowers burgeoning along the edges and pathways between; trees – mostly olive and almond and a few fig – moving in the breeze; rocks everywhere glinting gold and pink, lavender and silver grey.

Then I am in the city – the raindrops still glint on my windows, trees in the gardens sway, small birds flit between them and raucous seagulls stride the chimney pots. There is still beauty everywhere to be seen! On this incredible planet we have deserts where great waves of sand, orange and scarlet and gold, ripple across the horizons. In the northern and southern extremities snow lies crisp and pristine: a white sheet awaiting the pink brush strokes of dawn and sunset. Great forests are filled with the calls of birds and chattering life, hunters silently slinking after prey. Orchards burst into blossom, streams gurgle their way to rivers that meander to the sea. And the seas themselves ever changing, from wild crashing waves to calm flat mirrors. Even the wind, which moves from gentle breeze to the most powerful tornadoes, reminds us that we human animals do not really control life.

Here we are: in the garden of Eden all the time! The apple that Adam bit into is the egoic mind, that takes us out of reality and into believing a dream – a dream that turns into a nightmare. And the only way we can return to paradise is to drop our arrogance and listen *in*: listen to life through the heart that simply *knows*. It's time to drop our learned ideas of ourselves and the world and how to live in it to succeed – all of this given by others. This is the moment for finding the courage to face our demons and go into unknown territory. And this requires trust in something that is not tangible, not visible to the naked eye: that cannot be proved, explained, justified or argued about. The invitation comes to move out of the domain of our conditioned mind, into where the heart lies waiting to welcome us and show us how to express the wisdom already contained in our body-Being.

The time for man to demonstrate his courage by climbing mountains and going to the moon is over. Courage now needs to be used for looking within: for letting go of old habits and beliefs and priorities, and finally letting life live *us – its way*. For we have this extraordinary capacity to serve life: as conscious, fully connected bodies-Being. It is here we find true fulfilment. In letting go of the control of our conditioned mind we discover, sometimes with great surprise, that the heart knows how to respond. Not to react – out of the old fear and insecurity, hiding behind our defences – but to navigate life from within an intuitive flow.

As we slowly start to do this we find moments of unforeseen joy simply bubble to the surface. Gratitude fills us as we relax and let be. How does this process of navigation with the heart differ from the old, learned ways of the mind? It operates through the senses, through feeling (not emotions controlled by mind, remember) and through intuition. This includes all our capacities for touch, taste, smell and spatial awareness. It operates through sound and movement, shape and colour too: all ways that the mind cannot understand and therefore control.

One: Song of Being

The intelligent heart

To many people it's a startling discovery to find the heart has a much bigger role in our lives than we have been told; that it's not just vital to our body's functioning, but plays a major role in enabling our lives to flow harmoniously *on all levels;* that, in fact, in many ways *the heart is more powerful than the brain.* And while some people may feel they know this intuitively, there have been new discoveries in the scientific world, which is slowly beginning to catch up with what the ancients knew so long ago. (Even in 4,000 BC, Aristotle believed the heart was the seat of intelligence, so he obviously had some inkling of its importance).

Did you know that the heart is the first organ to form itself in a growing foetus? There is now growing evidence to show the heart is, in fact, the central, most important organ in the body. For example, new research suggests the heart may actually control the brain *with which it is in constant dialogue*, sending more daily messages *to* it than receiving *from* it, emitting more electrical activity and having a far stronger electromagnetic field. The heart communicates neurologically (via the nervous system), biophysically (via pulse waves), biochemically (via hormones) and energetically (via the electromagnetic field). And, unknown to many, the heart can survive the death of the brain for some time, but not the other way around.

Another interesting 'fact' is that when you bring two hearts together, they synchronise the heart beat. Nothing new to a pair of lovers, but again, this has wide ramifications for our inter-actions with others. It has even been shown how the activity of one person's heart can be measured in the brain of another person, or animal, making clear how we influence each other all of the time. (This affirms why touching is so effective in healing, amongst other things.) Graphs illustrate the different effects of, say, frustration and appreciation on the heart rhythms (a jagged line of peaks and troughs varying in hight and depth versus a pretty regular steady line of up and down movements) so we can see the powerful effect different feeling and emotional responses have on us. Here is where deep, regular breathing helps to keep the heart calm.

Not surprisingly, bringing coherence between heart and mind (through transmitting the loving and appreciative feelings of the heart) has been shown to lower blood pressure and improve the immune system. Conversely, anxious, irritable and other such emotional states interrupt this flow, causing negative effects. There is lots of research about all this for those who wish to study it (for instance there are videos on Youtube by The Institute for Heartmath that have useful graphic illustrations); and although there is much subtle activity that is neither detected nor can be researched in scientific ways, this evidence can be useful in breaking down the barriers of old limited views and resistances to including the vast, largely unknown world of intuitive reality that lies beyond accepted scientific 'fact'. In providing a bridge for the mind, glimpses of the unprovable can soothe, inspire and strengthen our trust in this we call the heart; a word which, as in the phase 'the heart of the matter', signifies this is the true and most vital centre of our lives. Without the heart, without connecting with this primary source of loving intuitive energy, we remain disconnected from what we are, from the presence of Being. Then life can indeed seem bleak.

The intuitive expression of feelings

The heart, with its capacity for empathy and connection, is the centre of our intuitive, feeling nature. With this we can apprehend reality in the most subtle ways. More like the tendrils on a jellyfish reaching out – sensing, feeling and pulsing; touching, exploring and *recognising*. We can *sense* what is really happening, how other people are, where they are coming from; and this can be extended to animals and all of nature. Sometimes I use an exercise to help people explore this sensing capacity. I ask people to close their eyes and imagine they have a delicate, invisible antennae extending out from their forehead, and to touch others in the circle with this: individually, silently, as lightly as a feather. And then to share what they find in terms of colour. It is intriguing to see how often people find the same colour with the same individual!

This exercise can be extended in different ways, but I deliberately don't ask people to look for intuitive or so-called 'psychic' impressions, nor psychological information about other people. This is not the way I prefer to work, as this so often gets interfered with by the unconscious egoic influences of the person practising. In my experience, it's not a good idea to encourage using these abilities in these ways without first getting to know who is using them! A safer way to explore these subtle connections is in the non-human field of nature (more on this in the next chapters). I use these exercises primarily to awaken and affirm people's capacities for these subtle ways of perceiving; to demonstrate how, in varying degrees, these are present in all of us.

One of the regular things I do with people is to ask them to use colour and shape as a means to allow their feelings to express *and communicate*. I don't call this painting or drawing because this invokes ideas: ideas about what this is and how it should look, along with beliefs that we can't do this, or not well enough anyway. When you ask someone how they know this is true they invariably say 'Oh, my teacher told me I was no good' or 'My parents laughed at my attempts to draw' or some 'other' put them off. They tell me they have looked at famous paintings and compared themselves, and it's obvious they can't paint. But this is actually not true: given the materials *everyone* can make shapes and patterns with colours. And what I have seen is that this is *the natural form of communication for feelings:* they don't belong in words. (Hence the absurdity of current art-school practices where they require pupils to explain their art in words; so-called 'conceptual art'.)

In working with colour and shape I ask people to get some materials: preferably large sheets of paper (rolls of wallpaper lining are great) rather than using small, nicely bound drawing pads, to give themselves plenty of room. And not to use restrictive instruments, like felt pens or pencils but things they can get messy with, like paint and pastels. Then I ask them to tune into their feelings (which are often associated with a memory) and let go of all ideas from the mind. That includes all ideas about how to paint, what it should look like and – above all – to let go of *thinking about what to paint*. I ask them not to make a realistic depiction (of a bicycle or a dog, a person or a house) but to simply allow their feelings to express themselves in abstract form. (A well-known psychologist, R. D. Laing, once allowed his patient, a young woman suffering from depression, to express herself using her own faeces to make paintings on the walls of her room, with an apparently successful outcome!)

I suggest people put the resulting images up in some private spot in their home. Then, interestingly, these images can communicate with their feeling self; a conversation begun can be continued. They may keep this to themselves or bring these images to an individual session, in which case I ask them not to tell me anything about them so I can offer intuitive impressions free of input from the mind. And these images are powerful! Looking at a series of images done in sequence, often a pattern, a movement of change becomes apparent. The wonderful thing about doing this in this way is that the mind can't interfere; it simply has no way to understand the content. Even when it tries to interpret, one can feel the *complete absence of intuitive accuracy*: here mind is forced to confront its limitations.

These moments of free expression of feeling are tremendously important. They can open that in us which has been neglected, that often feels frightened and vulnerable: especially to ridicule and not being good enough. Given *permission,* and a medium liberated from interference from the mind, the feeling realm can start to move and express itself freely. What joy! What a relief! No matter how terrible or painful the feeling content may be, just the space to do this has enormously underrated value. This doing something in a way in which the mind cannot participate makes it easier for the presence of – and hence connection with – Being to be *felt*. This brings space and a quality of stillness which underpins the whole process. There is an intensity, yet within a relaxation of control: a flow, however transient, which is felt; a loosening occurs as we unconsciously recognise something that cannot be put into words. During this whole process we are living and breathing and being simply *what we are.*

Something else I have seen to be powerful is the use of movement. Many people now go to Yoga, Tia Chi or a dance class, or they practice some other kind of movement-based form. Here they are told 'how to' – how to move, what positions to take, when to change these, when to relax, patterns to form. We are once again in the realm of learning from others. Yet what I have found to be so extraordinarily powerful, while also so very simple, is *listening to ourselves* and allowing our body to move according to this listening. You would be amazed by just how hard people find it to do this! We are so conditioned to being told what to do and how to do it, to learning a method and to getting it right: to achieving and succeeding.

Coming loose from this we again enter a territory where the mind cannot follow. It can be surprising what the body may do once we allow this, once we let go of our inhibitions: it may tremble and shake, twitch, wriggle and jerk; it may, oh-so-tentatively, reach out a finger; it may leap up and stretch out, whirl and shimmy; it may roll on the floor and kick and throw itself about or curl up into a ball. Anything becomes possible and – more importantly – *everything becomes acceptable*.

Before giving your body the time it needs to move in these ways, it makes sense to clear a space. As with all these processes: take the phone off the hook, switch off the mobile, put a note on the door and choose a time when your family or house-mates and neighbours are out: whatever you need to do to feel safe and free to express. Having a rug and a few cushions about can help to ensure you don't hurt your body. (By the way, you don't need to spend hours giving time to your feelings in this way, even a few minutes can be wonderfully freeing.) When you watch trees moving, or grass or corn, has it ever occurred to you that they couldn't move without the wind? This allows them to dance. We human creatures also have our dances. Then (in a manner of speaking) Being can blow through our bodies allowing *us* to move.

Many years ago I attended a workshop given by a lovely man called Richard Moss, who has written books about his way of seeing. Here he got people to stand in small circles, each with one person in the middle; that person would then either dance or sing, with the focussed attention of everyone else in the circle around them, *until they became the dance or the song*. All tribal people know and knew the power of song and dance and used these regularly. We have forgotten how to let our bodies be free *to simply move by themselves*. This is not only healing, it brings us back into the field of intuitive reality: of listening *in*.

So many people have been made to feel foolish about how they move, so they make great efforts to move in ways others will approve of, or avoid such situations altogether. Only with alcohol or drugs can most people start to let go and even then there often remains a self-consciousness, a fear of attracting derision. But look at nature – does a willow tree look ridiculous when it dances in the wind? Only humans, through our constantly judging and comparing minds, have learned these inhibitions. So moving freely takes a while to get used to and in general is likely to be easier without the pressure of others looking on.

The third means I suggest to express and communicate in this intuitively guided way, where the feeling-body can express itself freely, is through the voice. 'Oh, but I can't sing!' people say. 'I am out of tune, I have a dreadful voice!' Who is judging? Having a 'good' voice has nothing to do with being able to express yourself through sound. The body has a myriad different sounds that can express feeling, *if only it is permitted to do so:* from whimpers to wails, from growling to roaring; from high notes to low notes, hard notes to soft notes, even in whispers – *all voices are capable of expression*. So, once again, it is a case of regaining spontaneity by moving beyond inhibition. And this coming free has the blessing of reconnecting us with Being: through the body and its capacities we merge and blend and remember our natural flow.

Workshops and individual sessions

I want to add a word here about workshops that offer a place where people can go to express their feelings. These can be extremely useful in providing a space to do what most of us can't do, either in our homes or out in the world. If you live in a flat, or even a house, there are the neighbours: you can't really let go knowing that if a scream erupts, or you find yourself having a tantrum and jumping on the floor, you are likely to provoke an unwelcome response. Even in the shower with the radio full blast, it's hard to feel safe to be spontaneous. Few people have experienced this kind of letting go – letting go of all control, that is – with an agreement that you don't hurt yourself or others.

When I had time and energy for this, I used to hire venues and run workshops just for this purpose, to give space for free expression; providing mattresses and lots of cushions, using intuitive, connected breathing to facilitate this connection with, and expression of, feelings and emotions. This form of release definitely has a time and place and this is sadly lacking in most people's busy, often excessively controlled, mind-focussed lives. So it's good to monitor a need for this, but also to be aware that continued catharting (expressing strong feelings and emotions) on a regular basis *can* become a kind of indulgence.

At weekend workshops, people get to let their hair down, which can raise the energy and feel good, while on a deeper level something may be missed. So it's important to remember that however amazing the experience, however much energy is released, *workshops are no substitute for taking space to be alone to just sit with your feelings*; they can even be a way of avoiding of this. It's nice to meet like-minded others, to feel accepted and included as part of a group; to talk about ourselves and our glitches. Just be alert to what may be happening within this on a subliminal level, in the context of your life as a whole, and make sure to *also* take time out to be with yourself, alone.

Where individual sessions are very different to groups or workshops is that they allow for a fine level of *tuning in*, moment-to-moment, between the two of you. This means that when an intuitive connection between the practitioner and client is established – a connection that invites Being to take charge, as it were – the energy just naturally flows towards whatever is in the way. (By 'in the way' I mean of that person functioning from their true inner authority, connected with their body-Being: that is, living in total aliveness, able to respond naturally).

The truth is one-on-one meetings can be very intense, and for some people this is just too much, they feel safer in groups. This is why establishing trust early on is so crucial. But what I have seen is this: that it is in these individual sessions that – over time – the most profound movements take place. And the idea of a so-called 'breakthrough', which can feel so powerful and look so dramatic, is actually false. In fact, we function more like a mole, which tunnels away unseen underground for some time and then pops its head up out into the open air. The evidence of what is actually *an ongoing internal movement towards coming free* becomes suddenly visible. This may take the form of a powerful insight or revelation, it may be accompanied by an outburst of energy: Impossible to predict, but it's actually no big deal.

It is not my job to monitor this process. In fact, my part in this unfolding is not what people sometimes imagine. It involves simply being there and responding: staying alert to any interference coming from mind so I can be fully present – *present and responsive in each moment*. Then (odd as this may sound) 'I' am not responsible for what happens. 'I' have no *idea* about what is happening. 'I' have no *notion* of what the other needs. In fact, this 'I' is no use at all! My intention is always the same: to simply allow innate, intuitive capacities and skills, developed over time, to be in the service of Being – that is, in service to this movement towards total aliveness. That's it!

I know this can seem a strange way of looking at things. Am I avoiding responsibility, the mind asks? But as this 'I' (the egoic mind) has no means of understanding what is happening, it can't know the answer. Not only does this lie beyond its grasp: *it was never intended for this purpose*. In its absence, the body-Being uses *intuitive intelligence* to get on with the job: knowing – as it does – exactly how, what, where and when. When to stay back, when to intervene; when to use words, when to stay silent; when to touch or when to invoke a different form of expression. Over the years I have learnt that this is absolutely to be trusted. There is nothing else: *it is all that there is*.

As we have seen, the thinking process is so full of conditioning, so burdened with old beliefs and emotionally linked reactions that, despite the best of intentions, it just gets in the way. I have watched how, when the 'I' doesn't interfere, this process of intuitive response is automatic. It is a direct response between this body-Being and that of the other; it follows its own pattern, its own current. *I have no idea what I am doing* and, at the same time, *I know exactly what to do:* both of these are true. This is the difference between the heart and the mind.

This capacity to know from the heart is present in all of us, even if it is lying dormant. But if we don't allow ourselves to recognise this, we can't live it. And even for those of us who can, it isn't usually continuous; it gets fragmented and forgotten again once we are 'out in the world', dealing with whatever threatens our sense of ourselves. For most of us, the pull of distorted reality – ego-land – is just too strong. So, then, the crucial difference between me and the client 'other' during the session is our roles: the focus is held on *them*. This is the agreement, this is what they are paying for; this is what they can choose to come back for, or not.

A word of caution here: although I am virtually untrained, I am not recommending that people just sail out and start practising what I am describing in this book. Hypocritical as that may sound, some things were already there. Not just a complete trust in Being, but a clear sense of how the thinking mind can interfere – along with some awareness of my own patterns and consequent potential agendas. I was aware of how the egoic mind will use anything, and how being involved in some kind of supposedly 'helping' or 'healing' role invites unconscious motivations. A common example of this would be a need to feel useful, to be helping *others*; to feel special, important and so on. Or to focus 'the problem' on someone else and then try to fix it.

There was an insight about the difference between working intuitively and psychic practices (which I go into in the chapter on intuition). This, together with a *knowing* that I needed to be present in my body and grounded: not just for the people who came, but for my own protection. (I use the word 'knowing' here deliberately, as in inner knowing, because I rarely *thought* about any of this, hence there was no room for knowledge from the mind.) Perhaps most importantly, I began with the body, with massage, which is relatively simple and safe. Everything else developed on from this organically, over time, and by itself. I can't imagine how the depth and wide-ranging flow of the work, as it is now, could have happened in the early days.

Have you ever had the experience of feeling truly *seen*? Recognised, and held in that space? This is quite something in itself, and for many people this experience is new. One can *feel* how this creates a resonance, and how this resonance then creates safety. In an incredibly subtle and often unconscious way, the Being-ness of the other starts to sing – starts to vibrate and participate. Much as when you are in a room full of stringed instruments, if you play on one the others will respond: a resonance of mutual recognition forming a synchronicity is created. At least this is the nearest I can come in words to describing what I sense is happening.

So for me this time is sacred. There is so much joy and deep gratitude in being able to witness this movement in others: from being caught in pain and fear, doubt and illusion, to slowly beginning to trust and let go: ultimately, to emerge into clarity and love – whatever that looks like, whatever form that takes. It is tremendously reassuring of this being the true nature of things; profoundly reaffirming of what we apparent humans really *are*. What a privilege! I still find it moves me to see how – asked a few leading questions, given a gentle poke while offered support and encouragement – the movement towards recognising who we really are appears to quicken. For this *time* is needed: as in years, usually (I say 'usually' in case there really *are* exceptions!). But then who knows what is really going on with someone else? Or even with ourselves? Drop assessment-loving mind and how can anyone know for certain where another is at? On this seeming journey of moving into total aliveness, total awakeness, how ready they are? How willing and able to perceive and live as part of true reality?

Distinguishing feeling from emotion

Whenever there is an intention to find how to live from the heart, learning to distinguish feelings from emotions becomes invaluable. There is a predominantly male view that emotions are no guide as to how to run your life. And I would agree! *Emotions* are a terrible guide – which only highlights the need to distinguish genuine feelings from emotions. Yes, the heart is the centre of feelings, but unless we can make this distinction, the heart cannot be trusted and then nothing really flows. And this is especially true in the area of relationships (after all, even a hermit has to relate with something, if that's only her or himself!). However, in order to look more deeply into this distinction, and as this is such a crucial part of coming free, we will need to use labels. So please remember: labels applied to feelings can only ever be loose approximations.

This heart I am speaking about is actually far more than the centre for feelings. I use this word to refer to the whole realm of intuitive, feeling, sensing *intelligence*: an intelligence that corresponds directly with Being. This intelligence of the heart extends way beyond the limits of mind and has a major role to play in our lives. And the wonderful thing about this is that when the heart is anchored into the silent depth of the lower belly, what I call the 'cradle' – that is, when it has its foundations in place and is grounded – *it can be trusted to guide us in all the deeper matters of life*. This is enormously significant, and feelings are very much part of this navigational process. However, there is something that can interfere with this connection and this is activity in the Solar Plexus (see note at the end of this paragraph about energy centres). This centre, which is situated between the lower belly and the heart, acts in tandem with the Throat *and is highly reactive to emotions*. And because unconscious reaction to emotion is habitual, this reactivity has come to be considered 'normal' behaviour.

So we can see that using the heart instead of the head to tell us what is real and true can only work if we can see through interference from an emotionalised mind, which impacts the Solar Plexus; if we can identity this interference and not believe it. This is vital. In fact, we come to realise that listening to the heart is not just a means to connect with ourselves and live in harmony with everything: *it is a necessity for the continued survival of our species.*

NOTE: the body has, according to most sources, seven main energy centres, or chakras as the Indians call them. These are known, from the lowest, as the Base, Sacral, Solar Plexus, Heart, Throat, Third Eye and Crown. (See the diagram at the end of this chapter.)

After a while, something you begin to notice is how getting feelings mixed up with emotions leads to endless drama. How this in turn can lead to a form of dishonesty, where we (women especially) use this to manipulate others. This is when listening to your body and what is going on with the different energy centres can really help. Take the example of feeling sad. This is a basic *feeling,* which may be a response to something that is happening now – for instance, your beloved dog has just died; or it may be triggered by a film you are watching now that puts you in touch with *old* feelings of sadness: feelings about something that happened in the past that are stored in your body, so then a sad memory may surface; or sadness may simply come upon you with no apparent cause.

So far, no problem – you are just being visited by sadness and this will pass. The body may move, it may adopt certain positions and perhaps make sounds in reflection of this feeling: for instance we may sob, shake, shudder or sigh; we may lie down or curl up, rock and hug ourselves, tears may come. But whatever happens *it lies within this letting go into the simple feeling of sadness itself.* There is no external interference or pollution of this pure feeling with thought.

Then conditioned mind steps in with its *interpretation* of the feeling, and all its insistent voices about what this *means*. So the dog dies: 'If only I hadn't gone away for the week-end' (blaming oneself); 'My bloody flatmate! If only he had checked up on him like he said he would' (blaming someone else); 'I never want another pet, they just lead to heartbreak' (strategy to avoid future pain); 'I shouldn't feel so sad, it's only a dog' (avoiding a feeling by rationalising it). All of the 'if onlys' and 'I shouldn't haves: erroneous conclusions and unnecessary strategies to avoid pain. *All these are invoked by mind* instead of a simple response of sadness to an event, in this case a loss. So we see the messiness of getting caught up with guilt and blame, and what the mind does with this.

This whole sequence can happen with an *old* feeling of sadness, too, triggered by something happening now, or just a memory surfacing: the thought comes 'They shouldn't have done that' (blaming others, again); 'It wasn't fair' (self-justification); 'Why do horrible things always happen to me?' (self-pity); 'I will never be happy', get it right, succeed, be loved, etc. These are all ways to cover the pain and console and justify ourselves. And, more subtly, 'I can't bear that there is so much suffering in the world' (*displacing* our feeling of sorrow onto an external situation).

We can see how endlessly recycled thoughts, turned into conclusions and gelled into beliefs by the mind, get tangled up with our simple feeling of sadness and grief. These are the underlying beliefs that can lead to endless self-recrimination: 'It's all my fault', as the mind replays these. One could extend these examples endlessly but you see the pattern. The point here is to *recognise interference from mind when you have a feeling;* then you are truly mining diamonds!

So what might the heart tell you about this feeling of sadness? Who knows? In taking time to simply sit with the feeling, whatever wants to present itself can do so, in its own time. Then – sooner or later – you will find out. It may be that this specific incident has associations with something that occurred in your past; it may open up deeper sadness to be felt; it may be that something changes, or drops away: you can't predict or control this process when you are surrendered to the heart. Or, you may find yourself walking to a spot you regularly visited with this animal and building a cairn of stones – you can have no idea. And the seeing is *that it doesn't matter*.

There can be a sense of sweetness about sadness – a kind of nostalgia, a melancholy, a recognition of touching into the vast collective sadness that is part of the human experience. And there may come a feeling of resting in something that simply *is*: you know these feelings may change, but right now you are willing to give them your time. There comes a sense of rightness about this, a certain gentleness towards yourself. We are not talking indulgence here: no hippopotamus wallowing in the mud of self-pity (i.e. mind interfering with its story of 'poor me'). If you just stay present and don't pay attention to the mind you can trust that the heart, the connector to Being, will take care of it.

Some differences between women and men

Have you noticed how differently men and women tend to operate here? Of course there will always be exceptions depending on the balance of feminine and masculine energy and conditioning received but nevertheless, (most) women trust feelings and emotions before thought. It's also evident that (most) men are far less fluent with their feelings and emotions than women: they tend to trust their head before the heart. Hence a man's tendency to attach importance to thinking about something, using acquired knowledge and reason over more empathetic, intuitive ways of knowing and perceiving. Russell Razzaque, the psychiatrist we mentioned earlier, commented *'We see emotion as the unreliable and, often, undesirable facet of human nature. Particularly in the West, many would rather reject the fuzziness of emotion wholesale, in favour of a world in which we are rooted solely in the solid ground of reason.'* which I would say illustrates this male tendency well.

However, what is often not seen is that men's thinking may be heavily influenced by emotion – especially when they are talking to other men. You can *feel* the emotional content between men arguing their position: whether it's a need to be right, to know best, to be deferred to; a need to feel superior, to stand out from the crowd or just not be talked over and ignored, there is usually an emotional undercurrent driving the conversation, however hidden from clear view. A competitive element is present about who is top dog *that has emotions firmly embedded*. And because (most) men lack (most) women's familiarity with, continual referencing of, reflection on, and deftness in, the use of feelings and emotions, this can lead to acts of violence; even, ultimately, to war.

We women, on the other hand, not only recognise and trust our feelings *and* our emotions, we tend to check these to know what is real and how to respond. So if we haven't learnt to distinguish between these, we are vulnerable to believing a reaction rather than a true response of the heart. You might think a woman's tendency to be more trusting of her intuition would help here. But this, too, can also be misrepresented by mind, it can be distorted by ego for it's own purposes. (Something we will look at in the next chapter.)

It is when women fail to distinguish between feelings, emotions and intuition that things can get very messy. We try to justify the unjustifiable: 'But I had this *feeling* that I should do this...' or 'I just *intuitively* knew he was wrong...', etc. Without seeing how devious egoic mind can be, we may use what we claim are feelings and intuition to manipulate others; and whilst men may use physical violence, women are particularly skilled in the use of *emotional* violence. What is emotional violence? Saying and doing things that are intended to hurt: to provoke, put down, undermine, humiliate and punish the other.

The freedom to respond instead of react

Remember how one of the things mind loves to do is to *think about* feelings? And tell us stories about these? What they mean? And how this produces reaction? 'That woman is such a snooty bitch, she just ignored me' or 'Look at that man throwing his weight around – typical man!', etc. The real underlying *feelings* are not recognised: rather, we are captured by the emotionalised thought. What is really going on here? If we examine this we may spot it. Ah yes! There it is! It's *emotion* that is triggering these judgements – that is, *old feelings enmeshed with beliefs*. So, in the first instance (about feeling ignored), we can see a defensive response to perceived attack; the person *believes* they have been snubbed so they *react* by making the perceived attacker wrong. It doesn't even matter whether this apparent snub is true or not: the actions of the other are *interpreted through the lens of our own issues;* our own beliefs about others and ourselves, largely based on our childhood experiences. Unconsciously, a story is believed and this story hooks us in.

A true response to this belief might be an internal 'Ouch!' and even when we can't *feel* this, we can still notice that we feel anxious and uncomfortable when we are not acknowledged. Then, rather than attempting to deflect the uncomfortable feeling by lashing out at the other, this awareness gives us a chance to connect with the *underlying feelings* – which might be anger and hurt and sadness – and to let the emotion, with its *story about* what happened and what this means, go. The same applies to the woman's reaction towards the man. This is also likely to have been triggered by an old unmet hurt of her own around men. By blindly reacting to this, she misses out on an opportunity for recognising this old hurt and attending to it: in other words, acting *consciously.*

From these examples it becomes clear where this whole edifice of interpreting, judging, criticising and condemning, comes from. We can identify all this resisting and reacting as just the defence mechanism of egoic mind. Here, it is interesting to note that none of these defensive responses would be activated *if we felt secure*. These are activated because of an underlying insecurity. True, this may be based on a conclusion we reached somewhere in our past – that we are not good enough, we are somehow wrong or deficient – but the point is the ego, as a construct, *is itself inherently insecure.* How can a construct feel secure?

Only when you know you are part of the whole are you free from this, which is where clear seeing helps us *recognise and own* what is really happening. Then this whole edifice crumbles as we touch base, back home in our body-Being where we belong, with no interest in being enticed back into the drama – thank you *very* much! It is such a relief when we finally realise that the more we are able to just be with all of our feelings, the less we need to defend against a surprise attack opening up an old wound. The dark dungeon of our secret fears loses its ability to frighten us. Slowly, we begin to lose our vulnerability to others' judgements as we are able to be present and at ease with ourselves. We no longer need to pick these up as belonging to us: *we stop taking others' reactions personally.*

At this point one could say – as Advaita non-dual spiritual teachings do – that there is no-one there to be hurt by anyone because individual lives are an illusion. So hey, why bother with all this nonsense about feelings? However, whilst this may be true on an *ultimate* level, it becomes a dangerous misunderstanding if applied by a conceptual mind. Because like so many of the deeper teachings its *real* meaning is beyond translation. (More on this ultimate, or what Advaitists call the 'Absolute' in the chapter on spirituality.) Then, as a *concept,* it can actually interfere with acting consciously! We are deceived into believing something that may lead us to acts we later regret: the egoic mind has snuck in under cover of a 'spiritual' dictum.

In my own seeing, how we relate to our feelings is not just an important part of our spirituality, *it is an essential part*. It is this familiarity and comfortability with our feeling nature that allows us not just to see through emotionalised mind, but to actually connect with the truth that is felt *in the body*. Even after an awakening a fear of feeling our feelings can recur, along with an egoic drive to avoid them – we may even become a 'spiritual escape-artist'! And what I have seen here, over and over, is that *the willingness to be present to our deepest feelings eventually frees us.* In this simple act we allow our deeper nature, Being, to take the helm. Then, fear fades as we accept that anything that is being avoided has, sooner or later, to be met.

The beautiful gift in all this is that, as we untangle these reactionary and defensive associations of the egoic mind around pure feeling, so we come free to simply respond: spontaneously, from the heart, as an uninterrupted expression of Being. What joy, even if the feeling itself is painful. Pain isn't saying 'WARNING! Stay away!'. Pain is saying: 'Stop avoiding me! *Feel* me! *Open* to me! Let me in! Only then can I move on.' It is saying 'Let me go! Set me free! I am a part of life too. I have a right to exist!' What glues pain and sadness to us is *fear of them*, fear of feeling them. Same with anger which is often a defence: a defence against perceived attack maybe, but also *against feeling our pain*.

I am talking about all this not to turn this book into some kind of handy, psychological self-help manual for the mind, but because everything I am saying can – and needs to be – *felt*. Ultimately, these things are best discovered freshly, for yourself, in the exploring of them. Because this is all about us becoming conscious, so it is vitally important that we learn to distinguish heart from mind. How else can we recognise when we are lost in unconsciousness again? Without developing this capacity to see, we remain like a hamster in a hamster wheel: endlessly acting out our stories with reactive emotions until, hopefully – *finally* – this is seen; seen for what it is: just a fabrication of mind.

Here is a another quote from that wonderfully clear teacher, Adyashanti: *'Live in the gap between the mind's stories, and the mind will come to see that being in harmony with life is far easier and more benevolent than living in opposition to it.'* In fact, it is rather amazing the way eventually, by some act of grace, there comes a moment when an emotion is pulling us to act out, and we catch sight of it. This emotional pull can be *felt*: it has an insistent, wilful, sticky quality about it. We start to learn that every time we act of our emotions this just causes drama, that it invites *reaction*. Yet even when we know this, like a recovering alcoholic, sometimes the old pull is just too strong. Only afterwards do we have space to see how what we already knew came about; we just got lost in the drama. Then, we may regret our action and perhaps feel to make amends. Whatever we do, it's important not to get caught up in blame here, in attacking ourselves.

Because, remember, *it is in the seeing of this whole game playing out that we at last begin to come free.*

If I seem to be emphasising the point about feeling our feelings it is because this understanding is a game changer. I am aware too that, for many of us, separating feelings from emotion may seem foreign; we haven't been taught about this, it wasn't part of the school curriculum. Yet this insight is pure gold! Its value in allowing us to live our lives from a sane, authentic, connected-to-Being base, inestimable. Clearing away the nettles and thorns around the heart to allow the princess to come free – as in the old fairy tale – is not just about being able to have more loving and intimate relationships either, although this is certainly a great benefit. Once we start to look into our emotionalised feelings and see they are not real, that they are not to be trusted, *everything* changes: an important part of the veil of illusion is pierced, and this has deeply spiritual implications. *We are building the foundations to sustain our ability to be true to ourselves and live in the world as it actually is.* And this has to include letting others be, too.

So when these reactive emotions can be recognised for the fabrication that they are – that they are based in insecurity, woven out of our beliefs and fantasies, bound up with old wounds we have neither healed nor let go of – we come free from their bondage. In the very doing of this we create a strong platform for Being to express through the heart: a ground for resolving the source of so much conflict, both our own and that of others. A base is created for reflecting the light of our newly-fledged ability to see clearly out into the world around us. *And this holds true power*!

It is only as this capacity for seeing is honed, this capacity for recognising when we are reacting from emotionalised mind, that the heart can be restored to its real domain. Then, free from mental and emotional domination, the pure feeling, sensing, intuiting, discriminating and knowing heart becomes our true friend: our source of wisdom and wise action. And, ultimately, an overflowing fountain of unconditional love.

Emotions and morality – guilt

Some people have speculated that morality originated out of the needs for co-operation within societies, but is this really true? *Because rules of behaviour are not the same as morality.* Morality, which is based on mental concepts (also learned from others) involves making value judgements *about the person* whose actions obey or disobey the rules. It allocates meaning to these actions. Many of these judgements come from interpretations of religious texts by various faiths, notably Christianity. Which is where it's good to remember that not all religion is spiritual, and that morality has nothing to do with spirituality.

So Paganism, for instance, which existed prior to Christianity and has it's own rules, does not contain *moral* judgements, such as a person being a 'good' or 'bad' *person*, invoking guilt for which absolution may be offered. Certain actions are understood by a culture to be incorrect, or 'not done', not acceptable – say hitting a child or taking something that belongs to someone else; but this in itself doesn't require a value judgement about the *meaning* of the action, with labels such as 'greedy', 'vain' or 'selfish' applied to the person doing them. And it is these moral judgements that are instrumental in creating both damaging beliefs about, and emotional reactions to, a variety of thoughts, actions and behaviours. *All of which interfere with a direct response of Being.*

Let's take a look at some of the difficult emotions these *moral concepts* provoke, because, remember, it is in the looking that we develop this invaluable ability to see clearly. Not only is this freeing, it creates space for lighter, more uplifting feelings to emerge. It's a bit like diving to the bottom of a muddy pond to retrieve the diamond ring you dropped – worth a bit of temporary discomfort. So let's start by examining this most pervasive and toxic of emotions: guilt.

Guilt is one of the heaviest and most destructive of all the emotions. It has a powerful, life-suppressing impact and is not a true feeling at all. That is, it is not a simple response to something from the heart. Instead, it is a *learned response* to a judgement of the mind. Perhaps you can feel that? How it's dominated by the mind? Guilt relies on judgement and depends for its existence on both fear and belief. Guilt says you have done something (deemed to be) wrong. It is action-dependent and implies fault and a threat of punishment. The idea is that without guilt to control us we might do things that are not acceptable to others, to society, so guilt is instilled in children from an early age. But what if children could simply be informed that something is not acceptable – like taking another child's toy – and that was the end of it? A simple, practical teaching *that distinguishes the action from the child*. So the reprimand is underpinned with a sense that the child who is taking the toy is, *itself*, totally accepted and loved?

This is where the introduction of moral concepts such as 'bad' and 'wrong' combined with the fear of retribution, can be seen to be so damaging. And this includes a word commonly used with children, 'naughty': as in 'Naughty boy! Don't do that.' The implication is the same, *the child* is made wrong. These words not only cause confusion and make us feel bad about ourselves but – significantly – they disconnect us from listening in; they block our connection to Being informed by our own loving heart; we are persuaded to trust the judging mind rather than the loving heart. Then, an essential learning for the child gets overlooked. That is, that the loving heart can also say 'No', to oneself or to others: however, *it does this with acceptance and without blame.*

All of us have been taught morality, that is moral *concepts,* even if we didn't have a religious upbringing – children absorb morality through the pores of their skin. Everyone has an *idea* of right and wrong (unless they are pathologically disabled); *belief* in guilt is found everywhere (certainly in countries or communities with a strong Christian base, though whether Jesus himself condoned guilt is another matter). Notice the old familiar language of mind here: *concepts, ideas* and *beliefs.* Guilt is used to make us conform to others' ideas about acceptable behaviour, and also their desires for power and control. And the tragedy is people then learn to suppress their natural, spontaneous responses. Out of fear of being wrong, we lose our autonomy – we learn to dissemble and stop listening to what is true. In other words, we cut off from the heart and more, because guilt is mightily tyrannical. It saps our life-force and continually makes us feel bad about ourselves. (Which is an excellent example of how egoic mind uses emotions for its own ends: that is, to control.)

It's not hard to recognise what I am saying here in your own experience, is it? What may be harder to spot is how guilt confuses genuine feelings, so we often don't know what these are; how, in acting either out of – *or to avoid* – guilt, we lose touch with our innate knowing. Also, we may perceive another as 'making us' feel guilty, then unconscious resentment can fester and provoke a negative reaction. Examples of this are passive aggression and cruelty to others, including predatory sexual behaviour and violence. What is really going on here? Essentially, we have closed off from the heart. When this happens people lose touch with their inner guide, with Being. Then, rudderless, cut adrift amidst conflicting emotions, with empathy and compassion disconnected, they are capable of anything – we all are. This disconnect allows people to do things they would not otherwise do. We could say *the ego wants and fears and is utterly heart-less, whereas the heart aches and loves and is guided by truth.* So, in it's wisdom, the heart knows that to hurt another is to hurt itself.

But surely (the question arises) we all need to learn control? Imagine the consequences if everyone acted out their spontaneous desires! Is this true? Certainly, if we are operating out of egoic mind, then yes. As we noted in the previous chapter, control has a place. The real question here is, 'Is guilt *necessary* to stop us from hurting each other?' And that's a hard one, because egoic mind responds to threats and incentives. So, perhaps during any transition into conscious connection with Being via the heart, all we can do is remember *the true heart needs neither control nor incentive,* and bring our attention to learning to distinguish: to listening to and trusting this true heart and encouraging our children to do the same.

And one more thing: remember how the intuitive, discerning heart is itself able to feel *a sense of wrongness or rightness*? This is *felt* and *known* (both these being capacities the mind lacks). Here we see that the heart is not subject to the judgements, rules and commandments about morality devised and taught by religion and society and held in place by the belief structures of a conditioned mind: it has no need.

Regret, remorse and shame

Both regret and remorse, which would seem to be related to guilt, are interesting to look at here. While regret can be just a simple realisation – that something we did, we wished we hadn't done – remorse tends to involve a sense of the heaviness that comes from blaming ourselves: we not only regret our action, it has a story behind it, a belief of wrongdoing that is closer to guilt. However, with guilt, it is the *action which is judged to be wrong* (by ourselves or others) *whether we regret it or its consequences, or not*. Whereas regret is a simple response that stands open to both heart and mind. The egoic mind may co-opt it for its own reasons (for example, we can regret doing something because the outcome goes against our own interests.) Or regret may connect us with the heart, and include a genuine *feeling* response *about* what we did. As with remorse, this response derives from a feeling of sorrow, for having done something that maybe had consequences we didn't intend. We see this now, and perhaps we didn't see it at the time. So regret can open our heart towards the other. We can *feel* sorry – feel it and mean it and say it: 'I am *so* sorry.' (More on this when we come to look at sorrow and grief in the next chapter.)

When I look back on my life I can see so many occasions when I acted out of ignorance, fuelled by arrogance – an over-confidence in my own ability to know. This left me ignorant of my ignorance until life showed me the truth and I was able to recognise this. This is where becoming conscious can be painful but also, where sincere regret can help us see the value of this; because only when we are aware of something can we choose to stop causing harm.

Guilt, on the other hand, closes us off: we shrink back as mind tells us we have done something wrong, with recriminating thoughts like 'I shouldn't have done that'. Egoic mind loves guilt! It is its favourite means of control (as religious institutions know so well). So if guilt is in the ascendency there is no space to feel regret. Fear has taken over: fear of being wrong, of being *seen* to be wrong and judged for this, and fear of being punished. You can *feel* the difference, can't you? One is clean and can be let go of, the other is sticky and dark and heavy, and tends to hang on and coagulate with all past sensations of guilt. As children grow they are profoundly affected by this, as most parents and teachers use guilt to control their behaviour. And so the cycle is perpetuated.

What about shame? Shame is another toxic experience we speak of as a feeling. However, once again, when you examine this you realise – hey, hang on a minute, shame is not a pure feeling either! It is a sensation *yet again* dependent on a belief: this time the belief that *I* am wrong. It differs from guilt in that guilt says I have *done* something wrong. Guilt is action-dependent (even if it is feeling guilty because of a thought, or because you can't make yourself love someone, for instance) and often carries the threat of punishment; whereas shame says *I* am wrong, *me*. Phrases like 'I am ashamed of you' and 'You should be ashamed of yourself' invite a sense of hopelessness. With guilt there is the possibility to confess and be forgiven (especially if you are a Catholic). But shame burrows deep into the psyche destroying our dignity, we feel bad without any redress. Even confessing doesn't remove the sense of our being less-than, tarnished, somehow rotten at our core.

And it is the deadliest of wounds to the Ego. (Strange, isn't it? The egoic mind uses these moral concepts to control, and ends up attacking itself!) Shame is related to another excruciating emotion: humiliation. But with humiliation, someone or some situation invokes this – we *believe* we have been shamed. Then, as with guilt, there often comes resentment or even hatred towards the person who humiliated us, and this brings a desire to get even or to humiliate someone else in return. The deadly thing about shame is it tends to *remain,* under whatever facade we erect to survive, along with an unconscious belief that there is no escape, we are doomed, with the possibility of forgiving ourselves (especially for children) out of reach.

How we use language here is important if we are to distinguish these subtle and delicate areas of feeling and emotion. In other words, what belongs to the heart and what to the mind. It's such a mix-up – not helped by a tendency amongst men to describe feelings as thoughts, and women to describe thoughts as feelings. Here, shame and guilt are just the tip of the iceberg in calling belief-referencing, emotional reactions 'feelings'. To these we could add: annoyance, antagonism, anxiety, arrogance, avarice, boredom*, competitiveness, conceit, cowardice, depression*, despair, disappointment, disdain, disgust, envy, fascination, failure, frustration, greed, hate, hope*, hubris, humiliation, inadequacy, irritation, jealousy, loneliness, lust, misery, nostalgia, pity, pride, resentment, scorn, sentimentality, smugness, spite, superiority, unworthiness, vanity, vengefulness – add on your own. (*It is worth mentioning here that neither boredom nor depression are really emotions. They are more accurately described as energetic states, often disguising true but threatening feelings. Hope is more complex and we will look at this further on.)

Why are the emotions listed above not true feelings? Take spite or resentment: *you can't feel these without a story behind them*. The mind believes a thought attached to a feeling, perhaps of being humiliated by someone, for instance. The thought might be something like 'It wasn't fair, they shouldn't have done that' or 'They were just being horrible to me' followed by the emotion 'I hate them, I want to get back at them,' etc. This is the story. The truth about all this is that children are born innocent (despite the Christian teaching of original sin) and can, initially, only feel simple, basic feelings and sensations such as joy, anger and fear. In order to develop emotions they need a mind, which then turns simple *responses* into *reactions*.

And so the whole process of emotionalising feelings begins. In fact, all of these emotions are responses to *beliefs* about oneself, others and the world, compounded by old stored hopes, hurts and fears. Although these emotions often get projected out onto others, they have their roots buried deep in our unconscious attitude towards ourselves. Which means that when something triggers these *we believe it to be true*. We are no longer responding to reality – we are reacting to unconscious beliefs. Our view of reality is now coloured by reaction, which means we will project this onto everything around us.

This is precisely why emotions are potentially dangerous. They not only disconnect us from reality, they drive our actions and can, as a result, cause vast amounts of harm. An emotionalised crowd can be terrifying; there are echoes of this in the roar at a football match or the screaming at a pop concert. Whenever people get together in large numbers, there can be this sense of an entity that is capable of anything, a sense of this lacking all accountability, so that, as emotions spread these could override any feeling for our fellows: in other words, rampant unconsciousness in action. We can all think of examples of this, so it's good to be aware how *emotion can allow us to act – and justify our actions – in ways that the heart would never condone.*

Here we can see how concepts of morality can act like adding petrol to a smouldering fire, stoking fear and anger into acts of hatred and persecution, with self-righteous judgements and justifications. *'They'* are deemed bad, wicked, lazy, unclean, deserving of whatever horrible fate we bring to them... as the provocative words of current figureheads like Donald Trump illustrate so powerfully. It becomes even more pressing that we re-connect with the heart and use whatever ways we can find to free ourselves from this whole toxic mix.

What about unworthiness?

Without morality there would be no concept of sin and unworthiness, the idea that we are somehow worthy or not worthy. This is the single basic emotion that interferes most profoundly with our ability to relax and let be. Why? With its powerful judgement of us as being less-than it provokes deep feelings of pain and distress: we are condemned and this is debilitating. There is a sense of being rejected, unwanted, helpless and forever unable to achieve happiness and contentment. It brings the unconscious belief that we have to somehow prove that we *are* worthy. It is this that drives super-competitiveness, that keeps us anxious and afraid. We fear exposure and feelings of unworthiness are the last thing most people would want to acknowledge, yet so many feel this at their core. Cut off from connection to Being, we have no recourse to an inner knowing of oneness that can sustain us.

The following is an illustration of how this can play out. It shows how we trap ourselves and points to how we can come free. It is a typical example so you can see just how crazy this gets. It is *not* intended as some kind of four-step process! It is both simplified and abbreviated, and I hesitate in including it precisely because of the danger that mind will try to turn it into a 'how to' recipe, when it is just intended as a way of looking into what happens. So please, just allow it to give you a glimpse of something, don't let grasping mind get its teeth into it and start analysing, judging, comparing and turning it into some kind of concrete method. It isn't and it can't be. *Life is not a method*. My suggestion is to just open to receiving an impression, then let it go.

So, the example:

1. *What happened:*

Subject: 'My parents were unable to give me the love I needed' (there may even have been abuse and neglect).

2. *The conclusion they reached about this:*

'This is somehow my fault, there must be something wrong with *me*.' (This became their *primary belief* underlying everything about how they relate to themselves and others, and how they live their lives generally.)

3. *An interpretation*: (one of many possible interpretations)

'I must suppress my own feelings and needs and take care of my parents' feelings, so they will not get upset or feel guilty, then one day they might love me.'

4. *Some things that may help now:* (in no particular order)

a) Tell the truth to yourself about what happened (point 1) and breathe this into the body (essential). (This can only happen if and when we are able to let ourselves know what is true – so, no pushing here.)

b) Question if the beliefs about this are true (points 2 and 3).

c) Allow any feelings to be felt in the body, and keep breathing!

d) Open to reconnecting with Being. *(*This is fundamental and ongoing and, as already described, involves intuition, the senses, feelings and the body, and periods of silence can help.)

There will be lots of other factors involved, like the parents themselves not receiving the love *they* needed plus possible abuse or neglect, so this isn't about blame. The degree of love and care or abuse and neglect received by someone will vary from marginal to extreme. However, what I have seen is that the degree does not necessarily affect the conclusion we came to, the beliefs about this nor the ability to come free: it very much depends on the child.

Children are often extraordinarily empathetic (*sensing* their parents' feelings), they don't use reason or logic, so this example is typical. The child draws erroneous conclusions *because it has already lost connection with who and what it really is*; this destroys its sense of security as being part of a loving whole, leaving it with no basis to affirm itself. As the sense of separation develops the (belief in) ego grows to fill this void – along with fear and doubt which then distort the child's ability to recognise the truth. And even if they begin to see something amiss, children can't afford to hold their parents accountable; at least while they are young they are forced to deny and pretend. In fact, a striking aspect that reveals itself in all this is just how often the child will not only blame him or herself, but will attempt to take responsibility for its parents too (those who, even as quite small children, 'parented' their parents are not uncommon).

I have chosen to include this example because it illustrates a fundamental dilemma that emerges in so many people's childhood once they start to really look beneath the surface. Despite the best of intentions, it seems few of us are able to devote our full loving hearts to caring for our children without some interference from old unconscious baggage.

Acceptance and resistance

In using the intuitive skills of the heart to navigate, listening *in* is essential. So I want to mention something here about acceptance and resistance, openness and closed-ness; because these very much affect this process. A powerful spiritual teacher, John de Ruiter, used to speak about how we really only ever have one choice – to open or to close to life; that we can notice when we are closed, and choose to let go and open again. Another way of putting that is to become aware of our resistance and learn to let go of it. As we have already mentioned, this process is not so simple, so it makes a huge difference if we can approach life with *conscious awareness of our resistance*.

For example noticing how, when we are in resistance, the body tightens up, the breath shortens and so on; reminding ourselves that with acceptance the flow will return. There is always a certain tension with resistance, whereas with acceptance the body relaxes, so remember: acceptance releases, resistance clings on: this is a fundamental insight. Try it: notice what happens to your body and you will see for yourself.

There seems to be a certain confusion around this word 'acceptance': many people think it means saying yes to everything, including things the heart has a clear 'No' to – it doesn't! It means accepting our 'Yes' *and* accepting our 'No'. And – most useful and enlightening of all – accepting what simply *is*, as it arrives (whatever your response to it, *whether you like it or not)*. This is the most confusing bit, the part most people get stuck on; the mind can't grasp this, the heart has no such problem. Because this is such a valuable insight, I will risk repeating myself as I want to make it really clear. Seeing what is already here, in all its is-ness*, does not have to preclude moving to change this*; within this movement to change something, acceptance of what is can also be present. In other words, there is no need to dissolve into an apathetic puddle of non-resistance in order to accept something!

And, it's not easy. It's one thing to say 'just accept life in its reality as it is' and 'whether you like it or not changes nothing.' It is quite something else to really *get* what this means and live it. And what, in my experience, is extremely tricky and requires awareness, practise and skill, is this saying 'Yes' to your 'No', *without either letting go of your 'No' or moving into resistance*. And – once again – you can find this in the body. Resistance here carries a quality of pushing against the *fact* of something: it carries wilfulness of mind. 'No. I don't accept that this is happening, because I don't feel that it *should* be.' The body tightens and tenses, unlike its opposite, acceptance, where it relaxes and opens. Then we might say 'I have this knowing that something is not okay *and* I fully accept that it is happening.'

Can you feel this, this that can hold both 'No' *and* 'Yes'? 'No' to what doesn't feel okay and 'Yes' to the reality that it is happening, *nonetheless*? Mind can't do this, only the heart can. So *'Yes* that woman did just hit her child *and* that felt wrong to me – as in out-of-true: I had a 'No' to what she did.' There is an *inner, intuitive knowing* about this, a 'No' that cannot be moved or altered in any way. There is a quiet stillness about it – unlike the insistent quality that goes with resistance, that rejects on an energetic level that it happened and goes into the resistant energy of 'She shouldn't have done that', with all the attendant thoughts of the mind judging and criticising and blaming the woman. There is, instead, an acceptance of whatever outcome happens that, on the greater level on which life plays out, it is okay. Can you see this? It keeps the mind out of what happens and relies on the discernment of the intuitive heart. Whether or not this leads to action is not the point here. This inner 'No' carries an unshakeable integrity.

Many years ago, during the Nicaragua crisis I think it was, I read about mothers being forced to watch their babies being tortured, and I remember thinking this had to be my very worst fear; I wondered just how I would hold up under this kind of torture, not betraying my loved ones. More recently I have come to see how, *even in spite of* our inability to endure physical or psychological pain – no matter what we might be forced to say and do – *this inner 'No' can remain constant and true*. Because it is alive and living in the greater intuitive reality, that has no place for mind beyond a tool for survival and play.

Let's use a concrete example: an evangelist arrives at your door and you don't want to speak to him, you don't want him to be there. You can pretend he's not there, or you can resent him and get angry about his being there; you can tell him to go away or invite him in. You can get in a panic and hide under the bed (and feel terrible afterwards); you can swing open the door and sock him one (and feel terrible afterwards). But, whatever you do, and whatever you feel, and whatever you think about it, *the fact is he is there at your door*. You can complain to your friends that evangelists shouldn't be allowed to call at people's homes:

he still came to your door. You can convince yourself that he had no right to be there: he still *was* there.

What is happening here is that a great deal of energy is being spent on trying to change or avoid reality – we are in resistance to what is. Almost all of us do this, instead of letting ourselves accept the reality of what is happening, *and* the reality of our response to this. So, fact: an evangelist came to your door. Fact: you had a response (to that fact) and took action or not. The 'story' here is what we tell ourselves *about* his coming and *about* our response, and any other bits of information we embroider this with. Thoughts like 'he has no right to be there' and 'I don't want to have to speak to him', tangled up with feelings like anger and fear, make a meal out of what is, essentially, a simple situation. Don't lose sight of the fact that we are talking about letting go or holding on here. Reality remains reality, whether we accept it or resist it. And, most often, by resisting what is we create suffering.

There is something so lovely and freeing about this word 'acceptance' and the heart's capacity to embody this. It implies acceptance of ourselves as we are; acceptance of others as *they* are; acceptance that things are as they *are.* And – significantly – acceptance that some things are not okay with us: acceptance when something in us moves to redress what doesn't feel right, honouring an intuitively-felt recognition of wrongness, something out of alignment with truth: in other words, accepting our 'No'. Because this beautiful, discerning heart speaks to us! And it really does seem we have a choice: to listen, or not. Here is another quote from Adyashanti that speaks directly (as he so often does) to the heart: *'True sacrifice is to sacrifice resisting what is, and embrace the moment with love and wisdom.'*

In the next chapter we explore feelings themselves in greater depth. In the meantime, it can help to remember that we were all born with these navigational skills of the heart. We lost them when we began to believe in the supremacy of the mind, we were not told that the mind was designed to serve the heart; so it is just a matter of recognising this and returning to live guided by what we know and love: in line with life, in touch with Being. What could be more truly intelligent?

Home-play
1. Bringing the energy up from cradle to heart
- First, make sure you are grounded with feet on the floor and pelvis erect, with buttocks firmly planted on a seat.
- Next, breath down into the cradle.
- Having established a strong sense of connection here, slowly move your awareness up into the heart (maintaining the connection with the cradle while you do this). This gives the heart a sense of being supported. With this

support established it is easier to feel, and be present to, whatever you find in the heart.

2. Bathing the mind in love
- Follow the first exercise.
- Now, keeping the connection steady with the cradle, feel the love emanating from the heart and direct this upwards, imagining filling the mind with love and blessing it, releasing it from all erroneous programming, so it can be fresh and new and come into service of the heart and Being.

You may see something subtle as you do this, such as a delicate pink colour, a mist or vapour, but whatever you see or don't see, stay focussed on the pure feeling quality, which may bring a soft, gentle, melting sensation. The more you do this the more you will recognise it.

3. Appreciation as a practice
Wherever you are, wherever you go, make it your practice to connect with the heart and open to what is around you with appreciation: this may be visual, as with a magnificent tree or a tiny ant; it may be just the colour of a scarf someone is wearing, or the way the sun highlights the silver on the spoon you are using to stir your coffee. It may be a smell, like newly-mown grass, or the sound of rain pattering on the roof of your car. A taste, even just your everyday porridge, toast or whatever you are eating; take a moment to savour this and connect with where it came from, appreciating the process it went through to arrive on your plate. Or it could be the soft feel of the velvet cushion you are sitting on, the smooth feel of the skin on your own arm. (This exercise is so simple, yet it can revolutionise your life!)

4. And here are some 400-odd words that relate to the heart to play with
Just reading through these can give you a real uplift when you are feeling down.

~ *acceptance, accessible, accommodating, accompany, in accord, aching, admiration, adoration, affecting, affectionate, aflame, alchemy, alert, aliveness, all-embracing, all-including, allowing, all-seeing, altruistic, amazing, anointing, appreciation, approachable, assisting, assurance, astonishing, attentiveness, available, aware, awe;*

~ *balance, balm, beauty, being, belonging, beloved, beneficial, benevolence, benign, blessedness, blessing, bliss, blissful, brilliancy, boundless, bountiful, bracing;*

~ *calm, careful, caress, caring, celebrating, chuckles, closeness, communion, community, compassion, concern, connected, considerate, consolation, constancy, co-operation, courage;*

~ *dancing, dear, deep, deep listening, delicacy, delight, demonstrative, de-*

pendable, depth, devotion, discernment, dissolving, distinctive, divine, divinity;
- ~ earnestness, ease, ecstasy, elevated, embracing, empathy, empower, enable, enamoured, enchanting, encouraging, endurance, enfolding, engaging, enlivening, enraptured, enriching, eternal, everlasting, exceptional, exhilaration, exquisite, extraordinary, exuberance;
- ~ faith, faithfulness, fathomless, fearlessness, feeling, fierceness of heart, fineness, fine-tuned, fluid, fond, foolishness, forever, forgiveness, fortitude, found, fragrance, freedom, fresh, fulfilment, fullness;
- ~ generosity, gentleness, glorious, glory, given recognition, giving, giving back; grace, graciousness, gratefulness, gratitude, grieving, guarding, guidance;
- ~ harmony, harmonious, healing, helping, holding, holy, holiness, honesty, honouring, hospitality, humble, humility, humour, hurting;
- ~ inclusive, incorruptible, inimitable, innocence, inherent worth, insight, inspiration, integrity, intensity, interconnected, interrelated, interested, intimacy, intoxicating, intriguing, intuition, in tune, invaluable, invigorating, inviting, involved;
- ~ joined, joy, joyfulness, juicy;
- ~ keen, kindness, kindred, knowing;
- ~ letting be, letting in, letting go, lightness, lilting, listening, longing, limitless, loving;
- ~ magical, magnificence, majesty, making way, meeting, melting, miraculous, mischievousness, moved by, music, mysterious, mystical;
- ~ natural, nesting, never-ending, non-invasive, nurturing;
- ~ obedience to truth, obedience to the heart, offering, on fire, openness, openheartedness, overcoming, overflowing, overwhelming love;
- ~ patience, participation, passionate, paying attention, peaceful, penetrating or piercing the heart, permeable, permission, perseverance, playfulness, prayer, preciousness, preservation, profound, promising, protecting;
- ~ quality, questing, quietness;
- ~ rapture, reachable, reaching out, reassuring, receiving, recognition, refreshing, regret, rejoicing, rejuvenating, relaxation, releasing, reliability, relinquishing, remarkable, remembrance, renewing, resilience, resolving, respect, resourcefulness, response-ability, responsiveness, resting, restoring, returning, revealing, revelation, reverence, richness, risking exposure, ruthless devotion to truth;
- ~ sacredness, sacrificing, safekeeping, salve, sanctity, sanctuary, satisfaction, selflessness, sensibility, sensing, sensitivity, sensuous, serenity, service, setting free, sharing, sheltering, shining, significance, silence, silliness, simplicity, sincerity, singing, smoothing-over, soaring, softness, solace, sorrow, soothing, sovereignty, specialness, spiritual, splendour, spontaneity, spontaneous laughter, steadfastness, stillness, strength, stroking, sublime,

subtlety, succour, sufficiency, support, sureness, surrendering, sustaining, sweetness;

~ tenderness, thankfulness, tickled pink, timelessness, togetherness, totality, touching, tranquility, transformation, transmission, transmutation, transparent, transporting, treasuring, true, truthfulness, trusting, trustworthy, tuning in;

~ uncovering, undefended, undivided, unending, ungraspable, unguardedness, unhurried, unique, unity, upholding, uplifting, unassuming, uncompromising, unified, unpretentious;

~ valuing, vigilant, visionary, vulnerable;

~ waiting, warmth, welcoming, willingness, wisdom, wonder, wonderful, worshiping, wounded;

~ yearning, yielding.

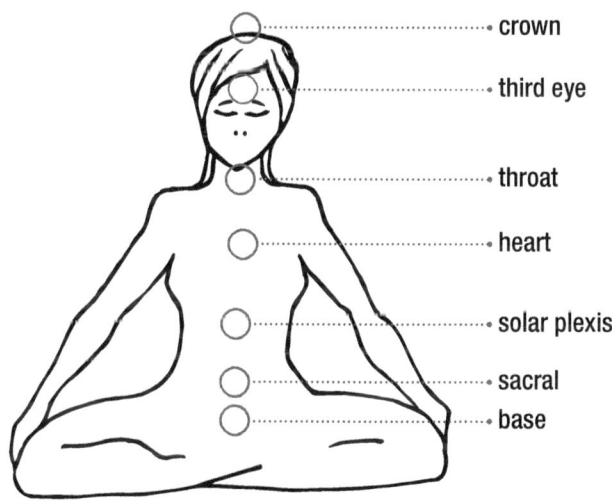

Diagram of the Chakras

Exploring the ground of feelings

'How much the world needs tenderness today!' ~ Pope Frances, Christmas Eve, 2014

'Anger is not the opposite of love, for the opposite of love is indifference. To be angry is to care tremendously. It is a signal that your caring extends beyond polite conversation, and that you are willing to risk a confrontation to share how you feel' ~ Doris Moreland Jones, God's Gift of Anger

'Sorrow prepares you for joy. It violently sweeps everything out of your house, so that new joy can find space to enter. It shakes the yellow leaves from the bough of your heart, so that fresh, green leaves can grow in their place. It pulls up the rotten roots, so that new roots hidden beneath have room to grow. Whatever sorrow shakes your heart, far better things will take their place' ~ Rumi

What would our lives be like without the capacity to feel? Can you even imagine it? What amazing depth and breadth of responsiveness would be missing! To remain unmoved by music or poetry, by the glance of your lover or the spontaneous chuckle of a baby. To be unable to empathise or share another's sorrow or delight. To live as automatons with nothing to do but to plod on and scheme. For those sad souls who have suffered greatly and closed off as a result, life is reduced to a monochrome.

So let's take a closer look at feelings themselves: because feelings, *when not emotionalised,* play a big part in being fully alive, with their subtle ability to receive and respond to everything around us. In our culture, and especially in the West, feelings are often dismissed as unimportant and there is confusion around both what they are and how they operate. So now we have seen how they differ from emotion, it should be easier to identify pure feelings themselves. Feelings – as I am using the term – are called emotions by psychologists, who divide them up into five basic categories: sadness, anger, fear, interest and joy. Yet these are each qualitatively different! Let's start with one of the most misunderstood: anger.

Anger has a place

Anger is so often given a bad press yet anger, in its raw, unpolluted nature, *is simply a call to action: to attack or defend.* Partly because this is often their role, men tend to feel anger more easily than women and may resist deeper, underlying feelings – feelings like sadness or fear, that can make them feel more vulnerable and thereby undermine a need to act. And some people, especially in spiritual circles, see anger as wrong and are afraid of it – in fact many people are afraid of anger: we associate it with violence. True, for some this is based on their actual experience but for others it's anticipation about where it might lead; but either way, it's not something we are usually comfortable with. But is anger *always* violent? Or can it be simply an appropriate response (not a reaction) that prepares us for action? Is there such a thing as *conscious* anger? Let's take a look.

The feeling of anger has a natural, outward movement that, with practice, may be contained and focussed; it carries a potential for bold, fierce, incisive action, and can be a wonderful help in such ordinary, everyday situations as needing to stand up for ourselves, or for others. As a journalist called Jeb Lund expressed it *'Anger has a clarity all its own. It renders most detail extraneous, and it animates like nothing else.'* It relates to a sense of heat that is felt in the body: we speak of red-hot anger. When it is fresh, in the moment, anger is an intensely alive feeling, and gives courage to actions that we might otherwise be too fearful to take. So in some situations, like confronting a bully or rescuing someone or in war, anger can produce acts of heroism.

We need to be reminded that anger can have a useful function, that it's not all bad news. However, when it is suppressed, *and especially when this suppression has been going on for years,* it becomes toxic. Like old meat past its sell-by date, it has a bad smell and is potentially dangerous. It can quickly become inflamed into rage, producing acts we may later regret, or it turns into *an all-pervasive emotion*, felt as an underlying sense of frustration or irritation; a vague grumpiness that makes us tense. And this works away on the immune system and our general health and sense of well-being.

Most of us are pretty ignorant about our anger, this is often something we are reprimanded for without any support for learning about it or permission to fully experience this feeling. For instance, I notice how people coming for a first session may deny feeling any anger at all. They will admit to all it's milder expressions, such as frustration or irritability, and are surprised to connect these with anger. They don't know that the fire of a toxic-because-repressed *feeling* of anger, is stoked by the mind with thoughts. Thoughts such as 'My boss is an idiot, I could do the job in half the time!' or 'It's not fair! How could my wife do that to me?' or 'Nobody treats me like that, I'll get even with them!' Resentment and petty spite bubble away under the surface and the beliefs that underlie these thoughts such as 'Everyone is out to get me!' and 'I have to look out for number one, because no-one else will!' remain as the unconscious drivers that can turn simple feelings of anger into an internal hell realm. As we have noted, repressing feelings takes an enormous amount of energy so it's not really surprisingly that, under pressure from these negative beliefs, our energy levels get drained and we may start to feel bitter and depressed.

When feelings of anger fester, this provides fertile ground for indignation, and a sense of injustice and victimhood – all of this usually remaining unconscious. There may be a sense of wanting to hurt someone, to show them up or vanquish them; to punish and get revenge. Thoughts apportioning blame, that say *they* were in the wrong, *they* did something bad to *me,* eventually become poisonous. And not just towards others, but towards ourselves, because they keep us locked into a repetitive fantasy; we are lost to reality – *then we become the victim of our mind.* If sat on too well for too long, feelings of anger can erupt into senseless acts of violence; we become so enraged we lose control.

I once knew a woman who taught Art to 'lifers' in a maximum security prison in Sydney, Australia. There she met an old man who was the personification of kindness and gentleness. He had never expressed anger in his life, and everyone saw him as mild and meek. Then, one day, he had become so incensed by something his wife said that in a moment of blind rage he stabbed her with the carving knife. Terrified, he buried her in their garden – where he was later found, beside himself with grief. This poor man had never learned to connect with, own and express his natural feelings of anger in a safe way.

The irony is that many of us are taught anger is somehow not acceptable, even wrong. It is uncouth, it indicates we are out of control and will inevitably lead to violence or trouble of some sort. It is especially not acceptable in women: we are called 'nags', 'slags', 'fishwives' and 'old cows/crones/bats/bitches' and worse, when in reality anger can be wonderful! – *when it is free from egoic drives.* Anger is pure fire: terrifying images arise of raging volcanoes, roaring forest fires and blazing furnaces; down to gentle sparks lighting up the night sky from a bonfire in the garden; flames flickering against the orange and red of glowing coals in the fireplace, logs crackling and snapping as the heat consumes them; or a simple candle flame burning in a darkened room. Fire can warm us and comfort us and, it can also cut through the crap, bringing courage to speak our truth and act on this. Jesus was hardly feeling friendly when he kicked over the tables of the money lenders. So undoubtedly fire has great power: which is why it is often used in ceremonies to purify.

We were all taught that water puts out fire, were we not? So I remember being amazed to see images on film, of molten lava from an erupting volcano actually tunnelling under the sea! Quite extraordinary, and an illustration of the potentially unquenchable power of fire. So it's good to be aware that while both fire and anger can be enormously destructive – *it all depends where we are coming from.* Caught up in the beliefs of mind, the fire of anger is absolutely not to be trusted. Emanating from a fierce heart it has a place. Perhaps that is the real meaning of the phrase 'righteous anger.'

In talking about inhibitions concerned with expressing anger, I am reminded of an incident when I was working in a cafe/bar in the commune of the spiritual teacher Osho, in India. There was a big German fellow with enormous sandalled feet behind the narrow bar with me, and he kept bumping into me and treading on my toes. Eventually, I lost it and found myself shouting at him until I stopped, suddenly feeling embarrassed – what were all the customers thinking? There was a Frenchman leaning on the counter with his coffee, and he smiled at me and said 'Ma,' (they called women that in the commune) 'your anger is so *beautiful!*' in that lovely French accent – and I was taken aback. What? My anger beautiful?

It's hard not to be affected by other people's attitudes and reactions, especially when we are growing up. In Christian circles, most people stress the gentle and mild nature of Jesus, and often look uncomfortable if you remind them about what happened in the temple with the money lenders. There is a reluctance to admit that Jesus – the good guy – got angry and acted this out. But it's not anger itself that is the problem. The unwillingness to admit our ignorance about our feeling nature and to address this, especially concerning such crucial aspects as the beliefs (moral and otherwise) of mind, and how conditioning operates, leaves all of us wide open to prejudice and misunderstanding.

Sadness and grief

Sadness and sorrow have quite a different feel to them from anger, don't they? There is a sense of collapsing, of being brought down by these. The movement is inward and this can overwhelm us, it can close us off from what is going on around us; it can also keep us locked in the past. But sorrow can also empty us, opening us up to letting in – to receiving the flow of life. It has a strong connection with water and the way this can dilute, dissolve, nourish and refresh. Our tears themselves are liquid: we speak of 'dissolving into tears', of 'crying rivers', of our eyes 'streaming'; of a 'deep well' of sadness, of sadness 'welling up'. Perhaps surprisingly, sorrow – which has its root deep in the heart – can also be beautiful in its own way: that is, *when we can let go into embracing it*. It has its own dignity. Perhaps you have felt that? Here it is interesting to note that the degree to which we can *feel* our pain shows us just how open we really are. Then, if a sharp pain comes suddenly, you can feel it piercing the heart. If this happens don't be afraid and close off. Allow it to be fully felt, knowing that the more we are open, the more effortlessly pain can simply flow through us: it is our resistance that keeps it clinging on. The heart has endless depths, it can embrace everything; *and somehow this embrace is needed before we can truly let something go.*

The main part of grieving, sorrowing, allows us to feel the depth of our connection. It allows the wrench of separation to be felt, the loss of a loved one to be mourned. And sometimes it helps to do this together. Then the expression of sound, in the form of wailing or keening, expresses this in perfect synchronicity with the heart (dogs and wolves know all about this!). In rural Mexico they celebrate the 'Day of the Dead' like nowhere else. A woman called Ali Alvarez comments on the degree of comfort provided by this. *'It's a really amazing tradition – one day of the year that you talk about people who passed away, build an altar, bring up stories. You're not left alone in your grief and in your memory of a person. Everyone in your neighbourhood comes together to tend to the graves and you'd see little kids and dogs and aunties running around the cemetery.'*

If we are willing to sit with sadness, it can bring great healing and release: it has a very positive potential. We can move into a deep state of surrender and acceptance of what is that holds the wisdom of Being; we are held and comforted, we can let go, in our own time. There was a very simple song we sang with Osho that went 'I bless what comes, and I bless what goes.' Can you feel how this honours life's passing? When we lock sorrow up inside of us it can create an underlying state of misery that fosters bitterness and resentment, especially towards others who seem cheerful and happy. Once again victimhood invites us, through the mind, into endless pools of self-pity, resignation – even martyrdom. We close off from life with thoughts like 'I don't deserve this' and beliefs like 'Life is just endless suffering.' And so we wallow. believing self-pity's false promise of comfort and justification for our sorrows. And, of course, our energy levels plummet, we attract sickness and pain, and we fulfil our belief. Invited in, hopelessness and despair enfold us: we are locked in the past.

And this is where it can get interesting! Because it is precisely at this time that, instead of subtly holding on, we just may actually give up: we may, finally, let go. Then it can be seen that – like a desperate sailor clinging to the rock of his beliefs – only once we let go can we enter the ocean (of our sorrow, of our true feelings) and there discover the truth. Life itself raises us up and our pain washes us back onto clean, dry sand. We find ourselves back on the shore in the sunshine, naked and new – remade. There are the famous stories of the Buddha who, after all that time sitting under the Bodhi tree, finally gave up – and then he awakened! And other contemporary spiritual teachers speak of similar experiences.

It's as if when we give up and let go, we let *in*: we become truly receptive to life: *to what is already here*. We stop demanding that life give us what *we* want (even and *especially* if this is awakening), on *our* terms. So, in the everyday living of our lives, the more we can let go, the easier the flow – and sorrow can be both helper and teacher here. Have you ever held a small child that is crying?

At first, it may yell and scream and go red in the face, with tears in full flow. After a while the crying gets quieter, until there are just a few snuffles, a deep sigh, and there it is – sound asleep! With all the soft, clear innocence of one who is completely unconcerned about the past: even five minutes ago. Infants are born knowing how to let go.

A further word about grief here which is not, in itself, simply a feeling but rather sorrow connected with loss. One of the greatest causes of humanity's angst is a sense of loss – a loss of connection to something vital, that we intuitively grieve for. As we have noted, most people in the world today suffer from a profound state of disconnection: disconnection from the essence of life, from Being: that is, from who we truly are. This underlies so much doubt, anxiety and confusion and it is not simply personal. There is a collective sense of grieving for all the discord, all the pain we have both caused and suffered, throughout our history.

There is a powerful film called *Griefwalker* (made by Tim Wilson). In this film, a man called Stephen Jenkinson talks about what he learnt as head of the palliative care counselling team at Toronto's Mount Sinai Hospital, sitting at the deathbed of well over 1,000 people. There, quotes the narrator describing Jenkinson's experiences, 'what he sees over and over, he says, is "a wretched anxiety and an existential terror" *even when there is no pain.*' Because of this, Jenkinson rejects the practice of palliative care and, drawing on insights from native traditions, 'has made it his life's mission to change the way we die. To turn the act of dying from denying and resistance into an essential part of life.' In the doing of this, grief is returned to its proper domain – not simply as the heart's way of bringing love and healing but, in so doing, weaving life and death together, *as an inseparable whole*. So unless we truly grieve, this opportunity stays out of reach.

Grieving may connect with regret. A sorrowing of the heart for actions taken or not taken. As we noted earlier, guilt is the mind's way of trying to make us conform to a given set of moral behaviours. It shuts us in and drains our energy, whereas regret can open us up to our pain, so that *when felt,* this includes grief. As such, *the act of grieving* becomes a powerful healing process that can transform pain by acknowledging and accepting our part in something. There is a felt sense of rightness about this: we *feel* the truth of it, deeply – *it is this coming into alignment with truth that heals*.

This is the true meaning of the word 'repentance.' Then, we don't need to hold on to it to punish ourselves – the anti-life approach of the mind. This is where certain spiritual teachings, that can become beliefs, can be harmful. Teaching people that there is no-one there to be responsible for their actions can encourage a leapfrogging of an inner knowing, and dislocate us from our true response, and from our ability to heal through this alignment with truth. Knowing this, we are reminded to listen our heart, not a learned spiritual concept of the mind.

Is fear a feeling?

So what about fear? This most powerful of drivers, we call fear a feeling, don't we? And certainly, it can provoke a wide range of both reactions and sensations, all over the body: we tremble and shake, cry out and scream, feel nauseous – we may even curl up into a ball in sheer terror. We get goose bumps and the hair on our body stands up; our heart rate speeds up, we may hold our breath, or just breath shallowly; we may even faint. Our eyes may go round and, as the expression goes, 'start out of our head'. Certainly, our whole body will be taught and tense. We speak of being gripped by fear, frozen by fear: we can't act, which means we can neither escape nor defend ourselves. And have you noticed how fear seems to move around in the body? So sometimes it's felt in the thymus area, between the throat and the heart; at other times in the solar plexus or just above; or even right down in the gut? It doesn't have just one location.

It's interesting too to note how, if the threat is immediate, this can bring us right into the present moment – *this is pure fear*. Then, however scary, whatever the source, we are right there with it; even though the mind is telling us to run away or trying to pull us into a fantasy, in that moment we confront our fear. So the response of our body in pumping adrenalin, giving us extra energy right when we need it, means we can choose to stay and face it or try to escape. This is healthy fear: it lets us know about danger and prepares us to act.

Then there is another kind of fear: *the fear of something happening*. This is future-based fear predicated on 'if' and 'when'. This might be based on something that happened in the past that we fear repeating, but this is still future-based and, as such, it can only be a product of the mind. We are, once again, in thrall to our emotions and beliefs, which act like sparks to ignite our imagination. So perhaps, for instance, we fell over trying to ride a bicycle. The memory of falling over tells us to beware, we may fall over again. This memory may be accompanied by a sense of humiliation and fear of hurting ourselves. Then, when we are about to remount the bicycle – *now, in this moment* – we are filled with dread. Or perhaps we failed our driving test. And now, when we are about to take it again, the fear of failure returns and makes us nervous, thereby increasing our chances of repeating our failure.

This is learned fear, and you can see how this impacts the body, keeping us tense. As fear operates through our nervous system, if we don't release this fear of what *may* happen, it goes to ground. Then it keeps us in a perpetual state of nervous anticipation. The underlying belief here is that life is not to be trusted, it is not safe; *we* are not safe and we must, therefore, always be on our guard, like a dog with one ear cocked against an unknown threat. Once again, this uses up vast amounts of energy and impacts our health and well-being.

But fear of a future event does something more: it essentially disconnects us from being fully p*resent:* here, *now.* It keeps us locked into a cycle where we believe the mind and distrust our intuitive, sensual body-Being. Fear is both the natural, underlying movement of the egoic mind – that is afraid of losing control (and, therefore, of being unable to get what it wants or avoid what it doesn't want) – and the *means* by which it attempts to persuade and control us.

Yet another kind of fear is the *fear of* someone or something; this is a fear we can cultivate by *thinking about* something that inspires fear in us. We are all familiar with the great taboo: the fear of death? With how this plays out in different ways, in different cultures? So in some cultures there are great rituals around it, even celebrations, while for others it is taboo: they scrupulously avoid all mention of it. And some (like the Spanish, for instance, with their tradition of bullfighting) seem to derive a greater sense of life by including the reality of death. Whatever the response, everyone knows about the fear of death. However, what few people seem to be aware of *is the fear of life*. Which is rather a shame as we have no control over death: we can be certain it will happen to all of us! Whereas with life we are given the opportunity to shed the constraints of our conditioning, to come free to fully engage with it, *because the fear of life is all about conditioning*, all about the stories we tell ourselves about what happens to us, and what we choose to believe – and hold on to. (In the chapter on aliveness we will look more deeply into this.)

So it becomes clear that beyond a simple need to defend us from an immediate and present threat, fear has no useful protective function – quite the reverse. As we have seen, when a threat is anticipated and we think about and fear someone or something *in the future* – then we can know ego, disguised as fear, is playing phantom! That it is conditioned mind that is ringing the alarm bell. We come to recognise the signs 'Oh, oh! Here we go again!' Once we see that any ideas about the future belong to mind, we are able to detect the old pattern of interference that hooks us into unreality.

In fact it is this trait of mind as much as any other that causes humans so much suffering (unlike animals, which don't worry about the future); because this kind of fear, fear of the future, carries a high cost. This is not simply in terms of time thinking about a future that hasn't yet happened – taking us away from the present – it also creates a level of nervous tension and tightness in the body. And this, if we start to live with habitual anxiety, or even dread, can do terrible damage to our whole body, weakening our immune system, with cancers, heart problems, strokes and all kinds of illnesses and diseases following on.

'Hang on a minute,' (you might say), 'that's all very well, but what about real situations that *make* us fear for the future, even fear for our lives? Like war? Or terrorism? Or an outbreak of a contagious disease, a pandemic? What about when you know a threat is imminent? Like climate change? Or, on a more personal level, the imminent loss of your job? Your home? A loved one? To be clear, *I am not saying you should be fearless*; that would be absurd. Nor even that you *should* be free from egoic mind's influence. Knowing there is a threat is a call to be alert, which may lead us to take action or not. But this is not the same as remaining in a constant state of nervous anticipation. If fear is present this needs to be *met,* and a wise heart knows this.

Living in constant fear of something that has not yet happened is not only debilitating, *it is actually not needed* in order to meet that threat, in order to be able to act; instead, it just drains our resources. Yet this is precisely what the mind encourages us to do: to worry and remain anxious, *in case*. There is a delusion here that is believed: that worrying protects us, that if we stop we will be caught unawares. So when these deceptions of the mind can be seen through, from a place that is anchored in Being, this allows for the possibility of becoming so fully immersed in the present that the future has no power over us. Then fear can return to its natural place.

Interestingly, the true heart is fear*less*, as I discovered for myself after a potentially fatal car accident in my early twenties. As a result of the hospital staff not being able to do an X-ray for possible head injuries over the weekend, the nurses couldn't touch my head, so they hadn't washed the blood out of my matted hair. My face was covered in cuts and stitches and heavy bruising: with scarlet eyeballs, I did indeed look like something out of a horror movie! So they carefully removed all mirrors, and I clearly remember what happened on my finding one, accidentally, in a toilet – looking with both interest and great curiosity at this unfamiliar and distorted apparition in front of me. Because – despite other people's concerns – *I felt no fear whatsoever*, just a warm acceptance, along with a strong animalistic instinct to eat, sleep and recover.

It was an interesting learning experience that left me with a strong, intuitive sense that fear does not belong to the heart. That it is not so much a feeling, but more a subtle, instinctual, nervous *agitation:* a chemical reaction, activated by an alarm system in the body to warn us of danger. And it is when the mind interferes with this system that fear spreads beyond its natural domain.

Have you ever watched rabbits in the wild? I have a favourite spot in a field I like to visit that contains a warren: it is a lovely place to just sit and contemplate the view or take a nap. The rabbits have their burrows under the bank where I sit and I have found that, as long as I stay calm and still, they ignore me. It's fun to watch them coming out to feed and play, yet this inevitably puts them at risk. But despite stopping every now and then to sit up and twitch their ears, they seem so at ease and relaxed – hopping around, touching noses, munching and just generally enjoying life. Then there comes a direct threat in the form of a sound, a movement, the shadow of a raptor overhead and they are gone – instantly, just like that, not a whisker in sight. Clearly rabbits know there is danger but they don't let that interfere with them leading their lives. So how come we humans, with our assumed-to-be vastly superior intelligence, can't manage this? This might sound absurd, but really: are we inferior to a rabbit?

Love, interest and joy – our natural state of being?

So what about interest and joy? I would suggest that possibly both of these are simply our natural state of being. I find it puzzling that psychologists include interest in their list of five basic 'emotions', because interest isn't really either a feeling or an emotion: *interest is the normal bodily response to being fully engaged with life;* hence disinterest (and depression) indicate a shutdown of this engagement. For how can life not be interesting if you are fully alive? Even when it is difficult or painful? Most children know all about this.

As for joy, this is something we *feel,* certainly. But my experience is a little different here. As I have said, the more we are able to stop listening to the mind and believing its content, the easier it is to connect with the heart. Then, as we become more open and available to life from this place, *joy is what is naturally felt as life percolates through us.* In other words, joy not only emanates from the heart – it is a *felt sense* of the spontaneous response to life itself. What I am saying here is very subtle and, like so much in this book, is best 'proved' in your own experience. I am saying that being alive is, *by its nature*, both interesting and, potentially, full of joy. If we were birds we would sing, as cats we would purr! Lacking this last amazing response-ability we can only express our joy in other ways. True, humans can also sing – we can laugh, dance and make love – and we can celebrate and feel joy in every fibre of our being as we do so.

What gets in the way of feeling our joy is being caught up in the conditioned mind, and this includes emotionalised feelings. Also, if we are occupied with genuine feelings, like anger or sadness, we are likely to temporarily lose touch with our joy. So it is helpful to recognise how – when they are not repressed – feelings are transitory. Whereas my experience is that joy *remains present, at our core*, to be felt when we are free from feelings that override it. Joy remains to be experienced when we are fully alive and available to all of our feelings. That is, to all the many other true, undistorted feeling responses that can arise in this body-Being: *feelings* such as affection and delight, reverence and thankfulness.

And fear and pain? Hard to connect with joy when these are blotting out everything else; *but you can still know joy is there – a constant presence waiting to surface and be felt when it can be.* Sadly, we are not taught this at home or in school, nor by most religions. In fact, anyone even suggesting this might be our natural state is likely to be met with a cynical 'Who are you kidding? Get real!' The crushing affect of this on a tender young aspirant is not seen. Even a disdainful smirk or gleam in the eye can be a deadly wound to a vulnerable heart. (In the chapter on awakening through joy we explore this further.)

So what about the prime feeling we all associate with the heart: love? Is this a true feeling? Or is it, once again, just our natural state? The natural movement of the heart? What we *call* love certainly appears to stir people up and gets us to do some pretty wild things! But is this really love? So much nonsense gets spoken using this word. It's been so distorted and clichéd and trivialised that it has lost much of its potency – from schmaltzy puppy love, to idealised romantic love; from sexual attraction, to emotional dependency, to till-death-do-us-part endurance marathons. Maybe, like the deepest of mysteries, love is something that cannot be encapsulated by words? Easier to look at what it is not. For instance, we speak of unconditional love – but how can genuine love possibly be conditional?

Actually, there *is* something that we do know about that demonstrates real love, for all but the most damaged parents love their children. Here we see a love that is instinctive and intuitive: that stretches far beyond convenience and carries a quality of such choice-less surrender that you know a parent would give everything for this precious child. We also see acts of great love and courage out in the world, especially during extreme times, like war and famine. It is in attempting to capture love's essence between two people that things get tricky – I think I'll leave that to the poets! And there is one other form of love that isn't really a *form* at all: the love of life, of God, of the 'all-that-is'. Adyashanti comments *'Love calls each of us to a deep and profound participation in the act of being, so that we become a loving presence in the world'*. And something I have noticed is that the questions 'Who are you?' or 'What are you?' don't touch me, don't reach me, as deeply as the question 'What is it that you love?' This question seems to open something that allows a depthless knowing of what I love, an absolute certainly, a recognition that lies beyond description..

Here is a marvellous story that brings into focus the unknown nature of love and who or what it is that loves. A four-year-old girl playing in her garden accidentally dropped some crumbs from a biscuit she was eating and a crow picked them up, so she then deliberately began to scatter bread and soon a whole platoon appeared. Over time, these crows began to follow her to the school bus stop in the mornings and then gathered to wait at the stop when her bus was due to bring her home. Noticing all this her mother built a bird-table in the garden and the next time the girl went to put food out, she found various tiny, beak-sized objects starting to appear. She began collecting these in boxes, labelled with dates and marking her favourites.

So what did these objects represent? Could it be that the crows were responding to love with love? The mind tends to resist this, dismissing it as sentimental nonsense that anthropomorphises animals, and it comes up with all sorts of complicated theories to exclude this. The heart *already knows.* Because the crows weren't being rewarded, they were already getting fed. It is known that various birds, such as magpies and the Australian Bower bird, collect bright objects; the latter using them to decorate its nest to attract a mate. So it's clear these birds value and respond to these objects. More to the point is why so many people assume that no other creature – in this instance a crow – is capable of appreciating gifts and repaying generosity?

In other words, why this resistance to accepting *all* sentient beings are capable of feeling love and responding from the heart? It just may not fit with *our ideas* about what love is. There are many inexplicable sightings of animals helping and even rescuing other animals, across species, apparently showing compassion. We assume this must have some survival value. But could it not be that humans, in our current state of supreme ignorance, are deliberately avoiding seeing such acts as demonstrating love, are even subconsciously afraid in case it's true and what this would mean? Because if animals experience what some call 'higher' feelings like love and compassion, then, as we noted in the first chapter, this totally upends the belief in our supremacy.

True compassion

Compassion is one of the most powerful and distinguishing responses of the heart. I am including it here, even though it is not exactly a feeling like anger, sadness or joy – in the sense that these are feelings that affect us, that change our mood – *but more a felt empathetic response to the feelings of others*. Nevertheless, in examining this quality of the heart we see how it depends on the capacity for deep feeling for its existence. The expression 'heart-less' is used to mean lacking in compassion. But the heart can also be fierce! For, remember, the true heart discerns – it has the capacity to see through the trivia and deceptions and convoluted emotional ploys of mind with a ruthless accuracy.

One way of expressing this capacity would be to say the heart has eyes: eyes that see, clearly, without distortion (in that sense, we could say the mind suffers from glaucoma!). When Jesus said 'Forgive them for they know not what they do' this demonstrates enormous compassion: compassion towards the very people who were intent on killing him, and in a very painful way. It also speaks powerfully to the reality in the world today; to so many thoughts and actions carried out with neither conscious awareness nor connection to the compassionate heart.

The heart is the source of empathy, which allows for the tuning-in to the heart of another. And this is very different to pity. You may have wondered, in the earlier chapter, why I put pity in the list of emotions? This is because cunning old ego-mind, with its conditioning around morality, while presenting pity as a noble sentiment, masks the true motivation. That is, elevating oneself above the pitied: feeling superior and, in the process, subtly putting them down. Pity comes mind-manufactured and is separating, whereas *empathy,* on the other hand, essentially connects us and levels us. With empathy we *feel* how the other is feeling, we empathise *with* them directly – we tune in. With compassion we feel *for* them, we feel for the pain of others: hence empathy and compassion go together.

And sympathy? This is altogether more complicated. Although we speak of being 'in sympathy' with someone or something, which suggests a *feeling,* sympathy often has a sense of subtle separation from the sympathised-with. It implies that we *imagine* how it must be for the other, referencing our own feelings with the mind to do this. So then, in the imagining, there is scope for a whole menagerie of distortion: from our own experiences being quite different to theirs, to inaccurate projections of what the other may be feeling (which is likely to be coloured by our own beliefs, patterns and agendas).

This means sympathy is open to error as it is dependent on the mind, and therefore can be influenced by egoic drives. For instance, we may be responding out of a desire to impress, to be *seen* as kind and compassionate, or to be liked; or even from just wanting the other to shut up and stop complaining! Whatever our motivation, *it is coloured by what we want for ourselves*: in other words ego-tainted. Instead of genuine empathy with someone else's pain and distress, it can be just mushy sentimentality of the 'oh, you poor, poor thing!' variety. And this has no connection with a true feeling.

It is useful to recognise here how both empathy and compassion require *connection*. So people who are autistic and lack the ability to empathise (and thus feel compassion) can find things hard: being unable to relate to others' feelings in this way means that forming and maintaining close relationships with others gets tricky. There is growing evidence of this autistic tendency becoming more frequent, including amongst people who have learnt to repress their feelings. Yet despite this, in our current society – where the qualities of the heart are generally not prioritised by those who make decisions affecting others (with the exception of some religious bodies) – empathy is radically under-valued. And this affects all of us. (Remember here, that in making any distinction we are talking about words, and these may carry different meanings for different people.)

There is an interesting tale about compassion that I first heard from a wonderful woman called Joanna Macy who, it is clear from the nature of her work, is very much motivated by compassion. I first met Joanna, who is quietly Buddhist, in Australia where she was involved in the Deep Ecology movement founded by John Seed and the late Arne Ness. She was teaching workshops called *The Great Turning*, designed to help people help each other through the pain and difficulties of living in the times that we do, with so much destruction of the environment and horrific tools of war.

Joanna talks of how, in the Tibetan tradition, there is a prophesy about an army of warriors called Shambhala, who have neither uniform nor supply line, but wander alone each carrying two swords. One of the swords represents compassion and the other 'insight into the radical interconnectedness of all phenomena.' Both are needed as where compassion represents the warmth of fire, insight has a cool quality, so they balance each other. Compassion brings the fuel, the motive force, but that is not sufficient. It is the *insight* that allows one to not be afraid of the suffering of the world. I remember hearing another version of this tale in which the second sword represents ruthlessness. The teaching here is that ruthlessness without compassion harbours cruelty, but *compassion without ruthlessness can become mushy sentimentality* – both are needed. And this is something that is not taught in Christianity, where there is an emphasis on charitable acts; nor have I heard it much talked about in western Buddhist circles, where practising loving kindness is emphasised. And this touches on the deepest mystery of the heart and of what love really is, and how it moves.

The greatest challenge for us humans seems to be in living with, and relating to, our fellow humans. Here, as we have seen, is where the conditioned egoic mind creates the most havoc and seemingly perpetual conflict. So in navigating this whole area we absolutely need empathy and the discerning heart: from bringing up children, to establishing a harmonious relationship with a partner, to taking care of the elderly; in relating to our friends, neighbours, workmates and the man in the street, we need to know *in our experience* the true nature of love. This is not to be found in study nor even observing, because our personal conditioning will distort what we see.

The truth is that in order to be able to *really* love another – that is to include and accept them, yet still respect our differences – we need all the qualities and skills of the heart. And, *essentially,* we need to be able to say 'No'. Some people have called this 'tough love', and this is something that is seen more clearly around children, where issues around power, authority and dependence play out most visibly. This being able to recognise that true compassion can say both 'Yes' *and* 'No' is of great significance. Then, in order to discern our *actual* response to others – to *feel into* what is true for *us* – we have to listen *in* (something which applies to all of our feelings).

This means that to listen in accurately, we need to be consciously aware of how mind operates (interpreting everything through judgement), and such things as interference coming from our conditioning, from patterns and beliefs, and the difference between feelings and emotion. And, for the vast majority of people trying to live together on this planet, this is still new news! (If you feel I have been labouring the point about the conditioned mind, this is why.) So perhaps in reading about feelings in this way you will feel inspired to seek professional help to explore this most delicate and precious of areas? If so, here are some comments and suggestions.

Finding help to explore our inner world

The feeling realm can seem such deep and difficult terrain to explore by ourselves so you might want to find help, at least for a while. But where to begin? Some people try their doctor, who may prescribe some kind of pills or put them on a seemingly endless waiting list for counselling. Or a friend may recommend someone, you chance to see a card in a shop window, someone at work mentions something; life coaching perhaps, as a way of achieving your goals – it can all get pretty confusing. I don't advertise, the people who come to see me do so through someone's recommendation and this feels the best way to start if you can. It's easier to take this step if you have heard something about the practitioner. (I am using the word 'practitioner' here as a kind of catchall shorthand for all people working in the so-called 'helping professions').

My suggestion would be that you start with some kind of gentle body-energy work, perhaps cranio-sacral therapy, for instance, which is very safe, subtle and relies on listening to the body for its direction; or massage, which is a good place to practise receiving and getting in touch with your body. Look for someone who is not technique-oriented and is able to be present. In fact, any non-verbal process carries less potential for the mind to play its games. In talking therapies finding someone can be trickier and this very much depends on where the practitioner is coming from; there are so many forms but they all depend for their efficacy on an ability to tune-in, to listen deeply and be fully present; and not to interfere from a personal agenda. You will find people in all areas who can do this, even if this takes you a while. In other words, in my experience, it's the individual not the form or qualifications that is paramount. In all approaches there are people able to go beyond any limits of their training and use their intuition.

I am aware that the way I work is not suitable for everyone. It goes deep and can be very challenging, and to meet this a great deal of trust is needed. And this is not what the majority of people want and that's fine. It seems to be so much a matter of timing and readiness. After all, why should it matter how we approach ourselves as long as it feels right for us? *As long as it is respectful.* If you get persuaded into something that doesn't feel right or you fail to connect with the practitioner, use it to practise your capacity for saying 'No thanks' and learning to trust yourself. Or you may work with someone in a particular way for some time and then take a break, or try something different. I am not writing about how I work because I see this as the only way to help people reconnect. I am sharing this to give you a sense of possibilities and an insight into something you may find different, that may be useful and, ultimately, because this is what I know and love.

What can you expect will happen in an individual session? I have talked about the non-verbal processes in previous chapters. In watching presence in action in the talking part, I have seen how it uses everything and anything – especially questions – to suggest, teach, direct, challenge, provoke, expose and reveal; to soothe, support, invite, encourage, affirm, validate and inspire. Questions like 'Is that true?' or 'Does that feel true to you?', reminds the person to check what has been said *for themselves* and so is particularly useful.

Whatever comes up to be seen, sensed or felt, it is vital that sessions are grounded in respect and acknowledgment for who you really are – beneath and beyond what you are presenting. Then, in working from this place of presence, spontaneous responses to deep listening and tuning-in to the energy in the moment can be followed. You can't know what will happen. The energy moves to unpack each of us in its own way. I love just watching what happens in sessions, and the people I work with seem to thrive *as they come to recognise it has nothing to do with giving away their power* but is all about helping them find the place of their own true authority. So as you allow yourself to know what is real, and what you *really want,* life, in its true richness, starts to become available to you. What that looks like you will find out!

And working in groups? This prospect can seem quite scary and there is, in my experience, good reason to be cautious. What I have found is that in group work *safety is paramount* and going deep is done best with an experienced leader whom you trust. If there is no ground of trust – and the sensitivity and skill needed to create this – people won't take risks. With a degree of maturity and an intention to maintain permission and respect, un-led groups can offer a place to share in a supportive environment. However, I have known some where people are invited to give 'feedback' and witnessed the damage this can do, as everyone projects their judgements and criticism, or what they see as helpful advice, onto others. Or they try to get a 'fix' on the other and practise their intuitive skills willy-nilly. Ouch! Not only can this be painfully re-wounding, it destroys the safety that encourages people to open up.

Keeping things both open to movement and risk-taking and yet safe in a group requires delicacy, as well as clear-sightedness, and an ability to *feel* energy. Here I see some kind of control as essential. Control has had a bad press but control itself is neither good nor bad: as we have seen so often now it depends entirely on *where it is coming from.* I actually like control in groups when it is coming from a clear source, from someone who is able to attend to the needs of both the individual and the whole. Because it can be scary to open up in a group. It takes great trust, and as the connection with the body-Being gets stronger this gets easier. Then you are not simply trusting the group leader, you are trusting the ground on which all this is happening.

I have seen how working in groups can bring a unique opportunity for exposure unavailable in individual sessions. Working individually, trust is established with one person; in groups this can be far more challenging: here people get to see their defences and learn to go beyond these – and they see others doing the same. Participants get to witness others' patterns and difficulties; they see movement and change and this gives them confidence that they too can do this. For example, when someone is challenged to do something *they believe they can't do*, within a space of trust and support, they almost always find themselves doing it anyway, and the others get to watch this. Indeed, there are so many learnings and seeings that can be shared within a group of people who trust one another to be present and not to interfere with their own agenda.

One of the most powerful learnings in the groups I work with is how to listen deeply, which is dependent upon being fully present. People learn to watch without judging or trying to work anything out, and quickly get to see there is no need or place for the old ways of competing and defending around others. A sense of trust is established that – whilst allowing participants to go deep – maintains a level of individual responsibility, and this helps keep the group safe from projections. Once someone is able to allow space for others' needs, then I find working in small groups *in addition to individual work* can be really valuable (by 'allow space', I mean able to contain whatever is going on for them in order to give their full attention to another).

It takes vigilance and practice to stay aware and not get caught up in powerful projections: which is why it is so incredibly useful to recognise that no matter what the external provocation *this is all about us,* and thus release ourselves from victim-blame roles. Then attitudes like seeing others as a 'worthy opponent' and situations as a 'free workshop' help keep us in awareness and out of the mind (more on this in the last chapter). We both witness others *and* participate in the unravelling process itself, whilst developing a simple seeing, sensing, intuiting, body-based focus on what is true.

I guess you could say I am a stickler for setting clear boundaries. For instance, I ask participants not to socialise with each other nor introduce other group members to their friends and family. This might seem excessive, but what this does is create a deep bond of safety. There is an agreement for participants to meet to exchange half an hour each of alternating sharing and deep listening, with a different group member each time. As this is outside of the group itself, and they often do this sharing in their homes, these boundaries help keep everything clean, especially so if they live somewhere like a small town where people tend to know each other. If you are sharing intimate details about yourself and others, especially those close to you, this allows for confidentiality to be securely maintained.

Then, one of the most valuable experiences people get from these groups and relating together in this way, is a learning around the meaning of unconditional love: an opportunity is provided to experience this. As they share deeply together participants become close, but in a way that is quite different to the usual relating, where our patterns and reactive emotionalised mind, our needs and insecurities come into play. In these groups there is no scope for dependency on others.

So many of our friendships are based on levels of dependency that involve unconscious dealing: 'I will say and do whatever makes you feel good and not confront you with anything you don't want to hear if you will like me and be my friend' is one. And how many times, when we listen to the other, are we just waiting for our turn to talk? Or we play roles, like one person gets to feel good by dominating the attention and the other gets to feel needed by giving it, and so on. It is rare in our society for relationships to be clean – in other words free from ego – even when we are genuinely fond of one another. So here in these groups one can taste how it might be to relate freely: *to care without strings*.

I want to emphasise that confidentiality and clear boundaries *are essential* to supporting others in opening up into deep and painful material, because I have seen what can happen when these are not prioritised. This seems so obvious, doesn't it? Unfortunately ego can be just as active (and can even get inflated) in group leaders, causing them to ignore or override these safeguards. The truth is that respecting boundaries not only provides much-needed safety but it is a way of practising love.

When I first started working with groups, I realised how much I had learned over the years from participating in other people's workshops, where I saw a few pretty messy examples of leaders taking advantage of vulnerable participants. This seemed to be especially evident with well-known and charismatic leaders, usually men. But don't let this put you off going to a workshop. There are so many ways of moving energy: we are all different composites and workshops, as I mentioned in the previous chapter, can offer valuable experiences that help with opening-up, and being with, what presents itself. There are many responsible and sensitive leaders out there and most people recover from a bad experience; it's like life – nothing is gained without taking risks. And it's a good opportunity to learn to trust your own sense about someone.

What is rather sad to see is just how impressionable people are, how easily we forgo our own inner sense about groups and leaders because someone has a big name; and how timid people are around confronting those leaders who exploit their participants. Which is, of course, not only how most of us have been raised, but also what allows these people to get away with it. Anyone in a position of authority can attract and exploit people's projections: for instance, by becoming the 'good daddy' and then, following the law of group dynamics, if someone confronts them the rest of the group will close ranks against the critic, and people sense this and are afraid. So trust yourself, stay connected with your own gut feelings and responses, and let your sincere heart guide you towards places and people where you can find true support – support for this tremendously significant work of opening-up, meeting what is there, letting go of what is neither true nor needed, and, like a lotus flower with its roots deep in the mud, allowing yourself to flower naturally, in your own time, in all your true uniqueness.

Misunderstanding mental illness

Lastly, a warning: whatever happens, whatever extreme space you find yourself in, however difficult – unless you completely lose all touch with reality – in which case you are unlikely to have a choice – don't go near a psychiatrist! I am not entirely joking because, unfortunately, their training and attitude too often demonstrates one of the biggest mistakes those who put their faith in the mind make: treating people as problems to be solved (and using the mind to do this). A largely male profession, many psychiatrists suffer from an extreme form of denial and disconnection from the intuitive reality we are talking about in this book. As this is unconscious and an attitude supported by society at large, this makes it difficult to address.

When someone is confused and unable to resolve inner conflicts, when they are acting these out in destructive and frightening ways, the last thing they need is to be analysed, categorised, treated like an idiot and have all their dignity stripped away. *Of course* there are times when pacifying drugs may be necessary, temporarily, especially given the way we tend to live in big, largely anonymous, unaccountable societies. *But what everyone going through troubled times needs is a place where they feel safe to feel their feelings, where they are treated with respect and their basic needs are provided.*

What are these needs? There are beautiful stories of how the Tibetans met these situations in wise ways, understanding real needs perhaps better than most; certainly better than we in the West. They provided a quiet space with soft lights, low sound levels, *and minimal interference;* a space where a person could be left alone to rest quietly and settle by themselves; somewhere with access to fresh air, simple, healthy food (not loads of greasy, sugary, canned and processed foods), herbal remedies, plants and the natural world, including animals and, if appropriate, children. Touch, as a direct means of connection, in the form of massage or simply being held – *if the person concerned wants this –* is profoundly helpful as it can reassure and include. And people with a strongly developed feminine energy (which is not necessarily women) are often better at providing this kind of support.

The masculine tendency is to be solution-orientated, using the mind to study, analyse, label, categorise, make comparisons and reach conclusions. Chemical treatments are seen as useful for suppressing feelings and emotions that produce behaviour deemed undesirable or unacceptable. All is underpinned with a strong need for control. In other words, nothing is known about the heart and true healing, because central to most difficulties labelled 'mental' are a person's *sense of exclusion*, of feeling lost and unable to connect – with themselves as well as with others. Unable to tolerate being in their body, the energy gets lost in the mind.

In the past, before we handed all authority to the mind, humans knew about this. It is remembered in cultures who remain connected with the intuitive, healing flow (although in these cultures the egoic drive towards power may operate through exploiting beliefs in helpful or harmful spirits). Here in the West, where we claim to be free of such beliefs, and where man has strayed so far from his intuitive roots, the same egoic drive towards power nonetheless finds its way by seducing with fantasies of conquering everything with the mind.

Thankfully, there have been changes to the way we approach 'mental illness'. More women have entered the field and attitudes widened to include a more empathetic approach. A psychiatrist based in the UK, Russell Razzaque (whom I mentioned earlier) in his book *Breaking Down is Waking Up: The Connection Between Psychological Distress and Spiritual Awakening*, brings his own glimpses of awakening into his work with his patients, using mindfulness meditation, what I would call "deep listening' and being fully present in the here and now, to address the deeper meaning of mental illness and how this can be supported rather than misunderstood. He praises 'Open Dialogue', a process which affirms participants experience of reality, no matter how bizarre this may appear to others, in a communal context (this being based on the long-known fact that non-Western societies, like Africa for instance, have a far higher rate of success though engaging the whole community.

The hidden power of feelings

Before ending this chapter, I want to point out something that too easily goes unseen: which is that *feelings contain a hidden power that rarely gets recognised*. Many people regard feelings as rather troublesome phenomenon that need to be carefully controlled, or else as a great source of passion and emotional drama to be indulged. But feelings are so much more than this! And because of the mind's overriding tendency to seek to control, their value often goes unseen. I say this because they have a unique function: for feelings – *true feelings that is* – allow us, even force us at times, to open to life, *to connect*.

The powerful relationship between feelings and spirituality (and also sensuality) is demonstrated in the work of Nobuyuki Kabayashi, who creates extraordinary photographs that seek to capture the spiritual aspect of nature. He says 'I feel as if I am taking portraits of the gods' (referring to the Shinto belief that everything in nature contains a god) 'I feel I am not the one who finds places to shoot but am led there by places'. The Japanese word 'yûbi' signifies both 'gentle' and beautiful', and also 'excellent': excellent in it's beauty, which is something he says he feels intuitively. Using a printing technique known as Platinum palladium and paper used in ancient times, Hosokawa 'washi' – that takes up to 5 years to be ready – he seeks to give his work a Japanese identity.

Listening to him talk, he continually uses words like 'feeling' and how he can't work if that is not there, how he needs his emotions to come alive in him in order to connect with what it is he is photographing. Looking at his work, you feel his reverence and deep penetration into what is *actually there*, through this intuitive feeling connection. (There is a beautiful video *Portraits of Nature – Myriads of*

Gods on Platinum Palladium Prints.) He uses the word to 'capture' (which I would prefer to call reveal) the essence, the Being-ness he is not merely witnessing, but through this feeling connection is actually present with, open to and part of.

Feelings and openness are intimately connected. Do you remember I said we would look at the word 'hope' further on? This is something that carries a powerful potential for opening us to life. Of course you could say that hope is more of an emotion than a true feeling, as it relates to the future. And it's true: hope *can be* just a desire to be rescued from something we don't like or want, and given something we do; to be lifted out of a painful, frightening or uncomfortable feelings perhaps. In other words, an egoic desire to escape or control life, to control the future. However, in its true form *hope is an opener*. What do I mean by this? What do we open to? We open to trusting in life itself: instead of shrinking and closing off out of fear, becoming depressed and apathetic, hope allows us to open *despite* whatever we are facing – to reconnect with the intimate vastness of Being. (Don't worry if that sounds paradoxical to the mind, can you feel how the intuitive receiver in you *knows* what this means?) So here is another example of how something, in this case hope, depends for its meaning on where we are coming from.

For instance, there can be an element in depression that is not just resistance but a wilful refusal to play life's game *on its terms:* a child-like insistence that life must play by *our* rules. We are fighting with existence; God, the 'all and everything', which is at fault, has got it all wrong and isn't doing what *we* want. So we contract and refuse to participate, 'cutting off our nose to spite our face'; *whereas hope that stems from our heart,* from our love and trust in Being, opens us into an expanded place where life and lightness can enter again: a kind of absolution takes place. Ultimately, there is no need even for trust because once you recognise what life truly *is* there is no possibility of wanting anything to be different; but for most of us, reaching a place where we can both hope *and* let go is pretty amazing. From here, to use a challenging example, even when a friend is dying of cancer, we can both hope for their recovery and accept that they may not.

When the heart is fully open gratitude is simply there. Is gratitude a feeling? Absolutely! This is one of the most freeing and nourishing of feelings: freeing because it helps us let go of blame, nourishing because it connects us with the heart, the essence of Being. Gratitude could *also* be called a natural state of being fully conscious and fully alive. There are many other feeling sensations, states and experiences that we could mention. There are so many words that resonate with the heart: such as contentment, satisfaction and pleasure; devotion, adoration and bliss; wonder, curiosity and appreciation; peace, tranquillity, serenity and so on. We could say that all of these are a natural, organic response to living life from the heart.

But the purpose of writing this is not for the mind to make neat lists and categories; it is to encourage you to feel and sense and explore for yourself – *to verify what I am talking about within your own experience*. It is not possible to make totally accurate distinctions; what I am sharing here are ways of looking at feelings that fit more closely with intuitive reality. Much of what I am speaking about is already known, intuitively. It is simply that we are living in a time when so much of real value gets overlooked and discarded, so even if you have seen this for yourself, it's easy to forget, and then it can help to be reminded. And now, a bit like one of those strange machines that people walk around with on the beach, hovering over the sand or pebbles looking for buried treasures, we can uncover (or *re*cover) and enjoy and share these nuggets – and in the doing of this redeem our true nature.

Because the wonderful thing about playing in the field of feelings is we regain our precious power to discern and respond, authentically: be this with delicacy and tenderness or wild passion; all is acceptable because in this field there are no fences, no feeling is unacceptable or off limits: we can rest as ourselves. Then – finally – as the heart starts to open, there can be a miraculous turn around. The way we see things starts to change, the way we see other people changes. We no longer see them as separate: as potential threats, enemies or competition, or as pathetic rejects. Instead, we see them as truly amazing beings, each with their own flame inside (however apparently dim or buried); each unfolding in their own totally unique way, in their own time. Then, with all the situations that present themselves to us, we become able to watch and simply ask 'I wonder what will happen next?', without fear or resistance 'I wonder what I will do?' or 'What I will find myself doing?'; perhaps with curiosity, certainly with interest *we discover the heart has no agenda*. Our vision is transformed: from the smallest raindrop to the wildest storm everything becomes a gift – a source of endless curiosity and appreciation.

Sitting on my terrace in the mountains, I watch a host of tiny droplets twinkle in the sun; a small bird I cannot see starts to sing – I am entranced. True, this being enraptured is often easier in nature full, as it is, of things happening without interference from a distorting mind. But even in the cities rain still sparkles on the window pane; a small spider weaves a web inside my window, like an immensely delicate, uniquely graceful offering; a pigeon coos and another answers; a small yellow dandelion shouts out from a crack in the wall; street lights provide a reflection upon gleaming pavements: there is no end to this magnificence if we are willing to notice it and receive it! And each time this occurs – each time we give recognition to what is actually *here* – this moment of connection and wonderment is like a prayer. The heart expands with a sigh of contentment for being part of this continuously unfolding landscape: a landscape that can be *felt* – Aaah!

Home-play

1. Vulnerability to feelings: opening the heart slowly
- Place both hands over the heart and breathe in, allowing a deep sense of connection, settling into the heart as you breathe out.
- Now, moving slower than a snail, lift a finger away from the body (reminding yourself that you can close up again at any time by lowering this finger back onto the heart). You may notice an actual, physical pain in the heart as you do this.
- You can continue, *but only if you feel safe to do so,* raising another finger and another, stopping frequently to check how safe you are feeling, until all fingers are fully extended (including thumb), leaving an open, unprotected space over the heart. (Don't attempt to extend the arms fully open, even if this seems easy). Stay open to any sensations and let yourself replace the hands over the heart whenever it feels right to do so.
- Then sit quietly just being present with this centre. Give space to any feelings that may come up.

This exercise is extremely subtle and will lose all value if you try to hurry it. It requires a tender, delicate attention and must not be forced, rushed or coerced from any sense of 'should' or need to achieve something. You are not being cowardly if you don't feel safe to open. Time is often needed, sometimes a great deal of time. This is your body's wisdom: trust it, honour it. Remember the story of the hare and the tortoise (the slower one got there first)!

2. Welcoming pain
- Next time something happens that feels painful, just sit quietly and, literally, open your arms wide to receive it. *Feel* it with a sense that, no matter how deep, it is welcome. Notice what occurs.

3. Nourishing the heart
- Sit somewhere or with something you find beautiful. This might be in the countryside, in a garden, or simply with a flower in a pot; or it could be with a stone, a crystal, a painting, a scarf with beautiful colours; or a photo of a baby, a pet, your lover; whatever works for you.
- Now allow yourself to relax, open and *breathe in* this beauty. Notice a sense of connection with the radiant energy or life-force of this place or plant or whatever you choose to focus on. Feel your heart expanding and let this in. Feel the simplicity of this: the love and gratitude. Do this frequently.

This is what churches were intended to invoke, and for some people they still work. Many people have a 'special' place, a special tree perhaps, or they make some kind of altar in their home. In which case it is important to make time to just be with this.

Intuition – the voice of Being

'Cease trying to work everything out with your minds. It will get you nowhere. Live by intuition and inspiration and let your whole life be Revelation.' ~ Eileen Caddy, co-founder of the Findhorn Foundation

'My grandmother could look up at the sky and read the clouds to tell you what time it would rain that day.' ~ Rastafarian poet, Benjamin Zephaniah

'The intuitive mind is a sacred gift and the rational mind a faithful servant. We have created lives that honours the servant and has forgotten the gift.' ~ Albert Einstein

How many of us *really* know what is meant by this word 'intuition'? It may intrigue us and arouse our curiosity, or it may provoke suspicion and distrust. Few recognise its essentiality and what it truly is. The fact is most people have insights that seem to appear from nowhere; inexplicable knowings, sensations and 'gut feelings' that we recognise but don't know how to explain. We may not listen to these, but that doesn't mean they didn't occur.

Throughout this book I am writing about intuitive reality and how this appears in many diverse areas of our lives.

So now, in this chapter, I want to invite you to take a deeper look at intuition itself, because this is such an important link between the heart and Being: it gives us a way to *know,* and this includes direct access to knowing about the deep and important things of life. And, of course, *it can only be trusted to do this if we can recognise it and are aware of what gets in the way of this.* Then, the wonderful reality is that – when undistorted by the mind – intuition brings an accuracy about many things that goes way beyond anything the mind itself can present us with. This being so, it might surprise you that there is a dearth of meaningful information about intuition; a significant gap in the way this gets looked at and talked about. For instance, of the earlier books written, most focus either on developing intuition (an impossibility – although you can certainly improve your receptivity and recognition, and learn to trust this) or they leave a hazy view that just reinforces the idea that intuition is somehow flighty and unreliable, belonging to believers in New Age philosophies.

More recently, many books have been written from the standpoint of how to use intuition to your advantage, to 'corporatise' it, rather than looking at what intuition actually *is*. Perhaps this is not so surprising because in many ways intuition defies definition. So I will attempt to clarify a few things by sharing my own experience and looking at what intuition is *not*, but often gets mistaken for. As I have said, this whole realm is not subject to the mind's ways of understanding. What is there – what is always there – *is the opportunity to explore your own direct experience as a means of finding out what is true;* and finding out what is true is not the same as getting it 'right'! Hence, I am not interested in an academic approach to capturing and defining intuition: I liken that to sticking a beautiful but very dead butterfly onto a board to form a collection. This is an approach that kills the aliveness of this, our most precious gift: a gift that can function through all parts of our sensing, feeling body but not, in my sense of it, through the mind.

Did you notice that Einstein calls it 'the intuitive *mind*'? and another man, Johann Kasper Lavater, a 17th century Swiss poet, philosopher and theologian refers to a *concept 'Intuition is the clear conception of the whole at once';* you see how difficult people find it to talk about intuition without referencing the mind. Here are some dictionary definitions. 'Direct perception of truth, fact, etc., independent of any reasoning process' (interesting they separate truth from fact); 'Immediate apprehension' (not sure why this needs to be intuitive); 'A keen or quick insight' (yes...); 'An immediate cognition of an object not inferred or determined by a previous cognition of the same object' (not sure about that one, sounds a bit helplessly lost in the turgid); 'Pure, untaught, non-inferential knowledge' (this is closer, but you can feel the mind struggling, can't you?).

Where intuition is concerned, I find the word *'knowing'* useful. It is more accurate here than the word 'knowledge', which suggests something that can be taught and stored away for later use; whereas knowing infers a quality of direct connection with what is known, in that moment: in that sense it is *personal*, there is nothing abstract about this word. I would add that receptivity, the feminine principle which is also essentially *personal*, is a key part of using intuition. There is no place for the distancing possible with mind (could that be why some people find it threatening?), nor any apparent objectivity, for intuition is neither subjective nor objective. It *is* impartial, in that it is neither controlled by mind nor emotion. It could be described as life speaking to itself: truth or reality being transmitted, Being in continuous conversation with itself.

An illustration of this might be a vast web of inter-connections which, when you touch it with your presence, resonates across the whole web to bring a response to you. In other words, *intuition accesses the whole to know;* whereas mind searches through it's endless filing cabinets of stored knowledge, and works away on this with it's reason and logic trying to find answers. Hence intuition is rooted in truth, the mind (as with any programmed computer) is not. Interestingly, intuition is frequently used, and hunches valued, in such practical fields as police work, while science quietly relies on it for many new discoveries. Also not much talked about in the public domain is the part played by intuition in the business world, and in the design, development and marketing of all kinds of things. And yet... *and yet it is still not recognised as an essential guide to apprehending and responding to everything in our lives:* a whole and natural way of living.

My own sense from using intuition as the primary source of guidance in my work over all these years is that what we call intuition is actually Being speaking to us, directly – *intuition as direct knowing connected to the source*. Which means that because everything is interconnected, everything that is occurring is available to us at all times. It is as if *life itself* is this vast store cupboard, and by opening to intuitive input we open to receiving direct knowing out of this. Then, what we intuitively *know* is that which connects with our particular part of this whole; perhaps in a similar way to listening to someone talk, where we may pick up what affects us and tune out the rest? I see this as a kind of co-operation between the individual body and Being.

The mind thinks knowledge belongs to it, and treats it as a commodity accordingly. But once you have learned to pay attention to the *immediate, alive freshness* of intuitive insight, you see a clear difference. Then, everything the mind seeks to hold on to as knowledge has this slightly ponderous, almost stale quality in comparison – like listening to one of those televised game shows, where everyone is so intent on locating the right answer there is no space for wonder and awe. Another interesting factor is that this intuitive input of knowing can neither be demanded nor sought by the mind. It is either available – to be seen, sensed or felt – or it isn't. In fact, we have no control over what is there, nor whether anything appears at all. We simply have a choice to bring our attention to this. The great orchestrator, Being (God, spirit, the universe – your word preference) is ultimately a mystery. And for that I am very thankful. Imagine what would happen if the egoic mind could get its sticky paws on intuition and control it!

Intuitive perception is referred to as insight: in-sight or inner sight – implying seeing something within. In one sense this is true, but it can also be misleading as intuition does not have a position, inner or outer; it has no location, it is simply perceived: one moment it is not known, the next it is. Intuition – or direct knowing – is received through any facet or none (at least none that we know about) of our sensing apparatus. It may be apprehended in the form of sounds, images, feelings and the other senses or it may simply *be known*. What I have noticed here, what I am aware *of*, is a constantly moving flow of intuitive knowing – a knowing that I have learned to follow and, essentially, to navigate by. *And I never question this.* Something is known, in the moment, and then it is gone again, leaving space for the next insight to arrive. It's like a continuous sense of receiving, responding and letting go, with no separation between these. As nothing is grasped or fixed, this flow of knowing simply occurs in the present moment.

When I am working with people I open to this flow: I let go and follow this process. Outside of this it is different. I am not always paying attention: I may be distracted or engaged in my mind, there may be interference in the form of thoughts or emotions (conscious or not), especially during interactions with other people. So a word of caution here: although I have always received intuitive knowings, I am careful about how I use these in my everyday life. This is because I have seen how easily this pure, direct knowing gets interfered with and overlaid by input from a conditioned and emotionalised mind. Without the capacity to know when this interference is happening, we are all vulnerable to deluding ourselves. And this applies to intuition as much as anything else (we will look into this in more depth further on in this chapter).

In one way of looking at the role of intuition in our lives, we could say that mankind has been involved in a dangerous experiment: disconnecting from the voice of the One, that knows what we need to know, when we need to know it. And that the results of this disconnect are evident in every aspect of our lives. *No other creature on the planet lives without this connection*, it is how everything is able to live with balance and harmony. If we recognise this voice we call intuition to be our connector, we can see how it is as vital to our survival as the blood coursing through our veins and that instead of this, we are living enslaved by a conditioned mind, bound up in fixed beliefs and weighed down by repressed emotions, only able to perceive a fraction of the magnificent reality of which we are an integral part.

In recognising the truth of this, we are enabled to seek ways to reconnect: ways to see through the illusion and expand into fully engaging with life with love and sanity. The invitation – life's invitation – is to dive into the apparent darkness of the unknown to connect with an unquenchable, underground river of joy. With profound simplicity and a willingness to question and look into; to see, sense, feel, touch and be touched by everything we come across, life itself opens up; then we can recognise not just who and what we are, but also where: in the silent heart of the one Being, as a unique expression of this limitless, ever-changing, living intuitive reality.

Using intuition to work with others

Here, I want to share a little about using intuition to work with others, whether you are a would-be or actual 'practitioner', a client or both, or just interested. Because this experience can offer glimpses of how this intuitive connection with Being functions. In working through just being present in this intuitive, inter-active way with people, I had no idea that it seems to be unusual. I am not only speaking about its total reliance on an intuitive connection with Being, but also its *inclusiveness*. Most approaches stay within one modality – whether that's talking, bodywork, movement, sound or art therapy, whatever ' (amongst the exceptions being Karuna-trained therapists, who include body-work in the form of

Cranio Sacral therapy). Nothing wrong with that either, I just found that I couldn't contain what happened within any one or even two of these modalities. It was just what I knew to do and it evolved by itself. I didn't really choose it, I had no burning desire to be a healer or spiritual teacher or some kind of therapist, it just arrived in my lap and I went along with it.

I knew I felt comfortable with touch, and I knew I could access my intuitive knowing easily. Sometimes others would affirm this and call me a 'sensitive', but I have always been allergic to labels: sensitive, okay; 'a sensitive', no thanks – no boxes please! The process is such a fine, delicate, subtle one, it's not easily put into words. From the first I received clear inner guidance that, instead of training to follow someone else's understanding and way of working, I allow life to speak directly through *this* body-Being, with its many subtle languages; and *especially* through its feeling, sensing, touching and responding capacity: anchored in presence of Being. It is this last that allows moving from stillness – this is something I feel and recognise and know, even though the truth of what this *is* can't be captured in words.

There was always a clear knowing that the most important thing was not to allow interference from thoughts and emotions during this time: in fact, not to go there at all. I don't know how I knew this but I followed it. I found myself in a place within myself where the thinking mind – with all its judgements, beliefs and conditioning – held no interest. It received no conscious attention, and this left my attention free to move as directed by something else, something I have chosen to call Being. There is a fresh, unplanned, unknown-before-it-happens quality to this movement. I didn't *try* to trust it, or feel I *should* trust in some deeper place: it was happening without my thinking about it. I had no *idea* (and still don't) what to do in a session: what to expect, what will happen. I wasn't concerned. It didn't matter at all because Being took care of this. There was nothing for 'me' – as the egoic mind – to do. And yet, at the same time, *something knew precisely what to do*. Can you feel a sense of this? This that sounds so paradoxical to the mind? There was no doubt with any of this, no fear of getting it wrong. In that receptive, intuitive space there was nothing for the *'me'* to get caught up in. I simply responded and trusted the response would be appropriate.

What did I trust? I am not even sure 'trust' is the right word. I *knew* that if I stayed fully present, without interfering, Being would get on with it. Being would facilitate whatever was needing to happen – in that moment. This kind of intuitive knowing doesn't lend itself to being rationalised: you either feel it or you don't. Was this faith? It feels more like simply a resumption of connection. Or, another way of putting that, a cessation of the urge to separate, *of the belief in separation*. What became clear to me is this: that the content and direction of intuitive work *is already contained within this moment*. And this gives it a certain freshness: it can't be planned or considered or anticipated. Then, anything that is in the way – in the way of someone being fully present, fully alive, inhabiting their unique Being-ness – will, sooner or later, call attention to itself; then, if not interfered with by mind, this unfolds organically.

I somehow knew this 'I' had no need to try to control this. I could feel (and have witnessed) that what happens in a session has very much to do with this coming fully alive. Being resonates and pulses with aliveness – *it is aliveness:* both aliveness and that from which aliveness arises. (Don't worry, this apparent paradox, like all paradoxes, is something the mind cannot grasp: it's not its territory.) And more: because aliveness itself is intelligent! So in using intuition as the guide, what I see to be happening is that as we surrender to this knowing, *we open a channel to the direct receiving of truth:* only then can Being assume (or resume?) control.

This connection with Being is paramount because it grounds intuition in a reliable source. Without this connection other input can interfere, such as fantasy, fixed notions, or just wishful-thinking from the mind; or it may be psychic input, which can be equally distorted without this anchor in truth. No matter what medium is used, it needs to allow this connection to Being to unfold in its natural, powerful, but extremely subtle way. This then allows the process of unravelling to happen in its own time and its own way, each person being unique in this. Then, ultimately, what remains is what was always here: the essence – or essential Being-ness – of what everyone actually *is*. The burden of what we are not is released: that is, *what was believed but was never true*. People then come free to just be themselves; to sing their song, free from any desire to control what that is, what it will look like, how it will respond.

What this means is that any form of help without this intuitive connection with Being is going to have a limit; it may even be unhelpful. And this applies to so-called 'spiritual' teachings, to shamanic or other healing practices or, indeed, to any form of conventional or alternative therapy. The more predicated it is on the belief structures of mind, the more it re-enforces these – however unintended this may be. We are deceived into believing the mind can unravel itself. But why would it, when it has been programmed to help us survive in the only ways it understands?

I have come to trust this intuitive flow in my work space because I have learned to detect interference. I now know that when I remain fully present this interference rarely enters. One way of describing this might be to say it feels as though 'I' exist in an island of stillness, of silence, though this 'I' is not really present in the usual sense: *it is as though presence subsumes the sense of 'I'.* Interference with being fully present (and thus connected with Being) only seems to happen when the attention is on, or referencing, this 'I' (in other words, focussed on oneself). When this referencing is disconnected – when the attention is focussed on the other, and for a specific length of time – this seems to work to keep interference at bay.

However, it is important to note here that *this is within the session space itself;* outside of this anything can happen! The egoic mind can regain attention, hooking us into some drama, some anxiety about something, invoking reactive emotions. But... but we can know that we will meet whatever happens as best we can, in that moment, and that this is enough. This helps keep things relaxed. Then, as we return awareness to the stillness of Being, we have this secure sense of knowing that *no matter how things may appear,* all is well.

Recognising intuition

Is there anything we can say about intuition that distinguishes it from other forms of perception? Yes. Intuition itself – as direct knowing – *has no interest in what is received*, no agenda, any more than a telephone has an interest in what is being said. Unlike egoic mind, intuition has no interest in gaining or avoiding anything. Something is known, but there is actually no-one who knows it (we will talk more about this 'no-one' later on in this book). What is known does not belong to anyone: it is simply there, whether it is felt, sensed or simply just *known*. Nor is intuition the instrument of some kindly being, angel or good fairy, just waiting to fulfil our desires and protect us from our fears – this is just infantile delusion. Something is simply known, or rather (an even more challenging way of looking at this that fits with my own experience) *what is in the way of a constant stream of knowing moves aside or is seen through*. We may well have a *reaction* to what is known; however, this reaction is always later (if only milliseconds), after the instant of recognition, coming from a fear-and-excitement-based mind. So, for example, if you receive an intuitive impression that your life is about to change, you may become fearful. Here, the conditioned mind is reacting to an *idea* about what this may mean.

How we react will depend, as always, on our conditioning: according to our patterns and beliefs. But the reaction itself does not mean that what we 'knew' was not intuition. And this is where things can get tricky. Here, there is no way out other than taking a moment, when you feel calm and connected again, to be present with yourself and to listen *in*: listen to your body, your senses, your feelings; and remember what you know about the conditioned, emotionalised mind. Then, as in casting a stone into a pond, whatever is there to be seen will ripple to the surface and present itself *all in its own good time* (or not), and just being quiet can help this. You don't have to be physically still, you can go for a walk or move your body in some way; you can allow your gaze to wander or just look at something, anything.

What you *can* do to interfere with this subtle process of opening to intuition, to what you know, is to *think* about it: to try to get it back and worry at it, like a terrier after a rat, or become agitated and stress out. These are sure ways to confuse yourself. It doesn't work to employ your male energy to play the hunter and try to find out. The feminine, receptive, is where you need to rest. And remember: whatever you saw, whatever you momentarily knew, it's all okay – *always*. All that stops you from recognising this are associations of the mind *about* what you saw: yours to listen to and believe, or not.

So what about other drives and experiences that get mistaken for intuition? An example of this would be instinct. Instinct appears to be a function of the brain, an inbuilt program for survival and procreation. What can be confusing here is that people speak of both instinct and intuition in terms of a 'gut feeling.' The movement away from danger – to pull back when a big lorry is passing on the street, for example – is reflexive: this is instinctual. We talk about 'sensing danger', referring to this instinctive capacity. We feel hunger and thirst and move to assuage these; or cold or excessive heat, and move towards shelter or some other form of relief from these. We respond to a look, a touch, an image or (usually less consciously) a smell, or even the timbre of a voice, with desire for sex, for example. Although this desire may be repressed it is still an instinctive desire.

All of these responses are instinctual rather than intuitive. As such they have no particular relationship to truth, *which may require us to act against our instinct*. Surely Jesus would have known, instinctively, that getting hung on a cross would be both painful and end his life? Yet intuitively, he knew to let this happen. When he asked God to let him off, this might have been an instinctual response, but when he said 'Forgive them, for they know not what they do', this implies he had accepted his fate: his intuitive calling to live the truth of himself as God (Christians would say the *son* of God) – *regardless of any instinct for survival*. So intuition is an instant knowing about something that lies beyond the basic urge to survive. And this is a significant distinction: intuition connects us with truth. So we can see that, while the urge to survive serves the experience of continuing to live in a human body, it is not our ultimate guide: as in 'guide to living what we are, beyond this embodied experience. Whether we can and do follow this intuitive knowing is something else.

Another trait that gets confused with intuition is impulse, but impulse is not the same as intuition. Impulse relates to the word *im*pulsive, so has a connection to the word *com*pulsive: one is a whim, the other a desire that has a sense of *must* about it; one feels free, the other caught. With impulse there is a momentary wanting, an attraction towards something: whether this is towards a person, an event, or just to eat an ice cream! Or it can be a desire to get away from something, to avoid. Although it is felt in the moment, it is still subject to the law of attraction and repulsion: it exists in the world of mind, in duality. And here lies the crux of much misunderstanding because intuition exists in a realm beyond duality, it has a quality of wholeness about it (more on this later). Children are impulsive: one moment it's 'I want this' then 'I want that' or 'I don't want this' then 'I don't want that.'

This momentary *attraction* or *repulsion* has nothing to do with intuition. It's like a radar antenna that constantly swivels around looking for something of interest. Impulse has no connection with Being. It comes from a desire for gratification or avoidance. And this, we come to see, is of the ego: a desire to fill a sense of lack or to avoid a perceived threat. During the hippy era, being impulsive was seen by many as the highest pinnacle of freedom: the 'I don't feel like taking care of my kids today. I will go hang out with my Guru and let the community take care of them' sort of idea. I remember once, when I was walking around an outdoor country market, watching a naked, filthy infant crawling amongst a group of young hippies; they were lying around smoking dope and playing guitars and there was no sense of anyone caring for this child. It felt so sad because, clearly, everyone there *believed* they were demonstrating freedom and spontaneity. Delusion can be very appealing!

Distinguishing psychic from intuitive reality

How to describe psychic reality? In my experience, psychic occurrences exist in a field that most of us have learnt to exclude from our visual or other sensory information sources. In other words they are a *natural* part of life, a part which certain people are more open to perceiving than others. People who don't have this experience may well be sceptical, whereas those who do won't be, though they may be afraid and deny them. What is important here is to just be open to the extraordinary nature of life, that is so much more mysterious than is generally recognised. People talk about 'keeping an open mind', so if you can suspend *disbelief,* life can then open up for you in many and sometimes surprising ways. You may start to have your own experiences that confirm psychic reality for you; then, what anyone else says will be irrelevant.

It's curious, isn't it, why we would want to exclude anything that lies outside of what are considered to be the limits of 'normal' sensory input: that is, *outside of a proscribed version of consensus reality*, a version that is almost universally believed amongst 'developed' Westernised societies. (Although almost nowhere else, be it Africa, Asia, Russia, India, South America, or indeed native cultures anywhere.) Hence we have developed the terms 'extra'-sensory, 'super'-natural, 'para'-psychological and the label 'phenomena' itself, which all serve to reinforce this view of the psychic as lying outside an acceptable norm.

Well for most people that is, because there are always those who would seek to exploit the psychic and, whereas the intuitive exists beyond the influence and understanding of the mind (and therefore cannot be controlled or manipulated), the world of the psychic is more of a grey area. So for example, it offers hidden scope for use in espionage and covert programmes of surveillance, which is why most of the research is paid for by the CIA and its Russian equivalent. In the revised edition of their 1970's classic *Psychic Discoveries Behind the Iron Curtain,* Sheila Ostrander and Lyn Schroeder show how Russian scientists advised Pentagon officials on controlling the thoughts of David Koresh during the 1993 Waco standoff. And then there is the whole at times murky world of selling psychic abilities, which we will look at in a moment.

One way intuition, as direct knowing, differs from psychic perception is that it doesn't *depend* on either thought or any of the senses to make itself known (even though it may be apprehended through these). With intuition, there may be no images, voices, smells or other sensory input to be questioned, doubted, ridiculed or denied (making it even harder to define). Another clear distinction is intuitions' essential spontaneity: as mentioned earlier, intuitive knowing comes by itself – whether you want it to or not! All you can do is try to ignore it, or overlay it with doubts and refuse to listen.

Psychic material, on the other hand, whilst it *may* arrive spontaneously *can also be sought* and, with practice, frequently obtained; people can be trained, or train themselves, to do this. However, unlike intuition, its accuracy will vary, as may the (apparent) source. The person receiving psychic material (which may be mixed with intuitive input) often relies on an intermediary such as tarot cards, a crystal ball or what they believe to be a discarnate entity: someone who has died and is communicating from 'the other side'. They may see the spirit of a powerful being from another time – a Native American in full regalia, for instance. They may hear voices and 'channel' information from what they believe to be other sources, such as aliens living in another galaxy.

Is this real? Depends what you mean by 'real'. It is tempting to say 'Is anything the mind conjures up real?'. But that would be to confuse the *form* in which input appears to be received with the input itself. Who knows how the mind and the world of psychic activity interact? A more useful question to ask might be 'Is anything really separate?'. Why are we so convinced information can only be received through certain vehicles? Via our physical body, like our eyes and ears? Only able to be recognised by the mind? As if information is itself a commodity, when the reality seems to be different. I don't know how what we call the 'psychic' fits in, any more than I know what part dreams play in our lives; all I can say for sure is that they are both a natural part of life.

In fact, the truth is, *there is no such thing as 'super'-natural'!* This is a figment of mind's imagination, a fig-leaf to cover its ignorance and impotency. So responding to any input, psychic or otherwise, is simply our nature; and the fact that this input is not explicable to the mind need not be problem, because whatever we call it makes no difference to our response. Beyond that, as we will see, it is important to stay connected with Being so we can recognise what is true. This is where intuition differs radically from psychic input. It not only brings us into direct relationship with Being, *but this connection can then become both the foundation and the means by which we navigate our lives.* Then, through this very practical application of intuition we are enabled to re-orientate our lives around truth.

'Is it really necessary, or even feasible, to make a hard and fast distinction?', you might ask. Both 'Intuition' and 'psychic' are, after all, just words, and words can be used in different ways. It depends what you want. If the focus is on receiving what is true, then it can be very useful indeed because, in my experience, intuitive input can be trusted, whereas psychic input is – or can be – subject to the demands of the egoic mind. I would suggest this distinction is best made *through your own experience*. I can share my experience with you (though others may see things differently), but what soon becomes apparent is the sheer hopelessness of trying to categorise these differences with the mind. Hence the value of trusting direct experience, as any distinctions are something best *felt, sensed* and *recognised* for oneself. You may well be familiar with either intuitive or psychic experiences but even if you are not, you can still get a feel for what I am saying here.

So to repeat, I am using the word 'intuition' to refer to the direct reception of truth: something that is simply, directly known, *with no regard to what we want or how we feel about this input*. And, in a manner of speaking which can never be entirely accurate, I see Being – the essence of life, of intuitive reality – as both the container and transmitter of truth. Whereas I notice that what we call 'psychic' experiences are often directed towards something we *want* (such as love, money, to help, harm or have power over others, finding something or someone, or contact with the dead) or something we *fear* (such as ghosts, spirits or others having power to harm us) or something we are intrigued by (which might also be ghosts, spirits or contact with the dead).

In fact, it is almost impossible to talk about the psychic without including the dark underbelly that holds the three 'f's': fear, fantasy and fascination. Yet if you look closely, you will see that these are all associations of the egoic mind. The so-called psychic itself is an extremely delicate, subtle *and interactive* aspect of reality and as such it can be easily imprinted – unlike intuition, it is in a sense absorbent. Out of this arises the whole ungrounded world of selling psychic 'services', and along with it the media's self-serving parody and creation of programmes that feed on people's fear and fascination. Abased and abused in this way, the extraordinary *natural* world – of which the psychic is an integral part – becomes distorted by the egoic mind's need to exploit, within its complete ignorance of true value. What a waste. And worth remembering that when you shine the light of consciousness into such places the darkness dissolves; so then, like the sunshine after rain, it leaves a bright, sparkling, fresh reality. Here, silently, is where intuition informs the psychic – a bit like the elusive nightingale: we hear the song but with no glimpse of its source.

The following is an example of what happens when the egoic mind becomes fascinated by the psychic and loses all connection with truth and reality. Some while ago, someone I knew said they were going to a 'psychic evening' and invited me along. There, I found two groups of people seated in two circles, outer and inner, with each person facing the one opposite them. The idea was that the people in the inner circle had picked up unwanted 'entities' and the people in the outer circle were going to free them. This they did by addressing the entity residing in the person opposite and talking them over to 'the other side'. So a conversation might go 'Come on now, this is not where you belong! It's time for you to go on to the next world' and so on – a mixture of cajoling and threat. After a while, I began to notice that as soon as someone was apparently freed, another entity would jump in and take up occupancy, and the whole process would need to be repeated: a bit like being infested with fleas!

Afterwards we all had dinner together and then went home and I left feeling glad I had been able to witness the sheer absurdity of this procedure, which cured me of any desire to be part of such a scene again. Another time, I visited the College of Psychic Studies in London (this must have been in the late Seventies or early Eighties and it may well have changed by now). The whole building was painted dark grey, with shiny black windows and doors. Inside everything felt musty and oppressive, full of old books and dark furniture, with what I felt (or possibly projected) to be a shadowy ambience that was strongly reminiscent of the stuck, unconscious spaces of the mind, and I couldn't wait to leave!

Repression of the intuitive

As you may have noticed, there is a kind of invisible wall between what we, as children, often knew as a sense of vibrant possibility and the narrow path we are trained to walk along: rather like the dray horses of old, which wore leather pads beside their eyes called 'blinkers', designed to keep them on the straight and narrow and prevent them from seeing anything that might frighten, interest or otherwise distract them from pulling their load. *Full, intuitive reality is a threat to established order.* In truth, neither psychic experiences *nor* intuitive insight fit comfortably into the view of the world we have adopted since the Enlightenment. This was when rational thought managed to gain the upper hand over anything non-rational (much to the chagrin of the church with its investment in maintaining power through faith), and we might question why the history surrounding this event tends to be left out of school curriculums.

So first you have the tribes, with their interpretation of both the intuitive and psychic as being an integral, even essential, part of their world view, which continued, in its various forms, for many thousands of years. Then – comparatively recently – you have the emergence of religions like Christianity, that sought to increase their hold over people through morality and by denying and persecuting anything even remotely psychic or intuitive. And then, *barely a few hundred years ago,* the trouncing of this by rational argument, logic and the scientific view of life – in other words, mind and the intellect gained dominance. And this has its own agenda around control.

In recent years, the denial of both the psychic and the intuitive has taken the form of ignoring, dismissing, trivialising or ridiculing anything that cannot be 'proved', argued, justified or explained. Currently, we see Western medicine and the big pharmaceutical companies doing this too, along with seeking to control a growing interest in 'alternatives'. These all stand to gain by excluding any unorthodox, non-corporate ways of approaching health problems, including the selling of herbal remedies. In fact, we see the same attitude and intent extended into all areas where people were once unregulated and free to practice intuitive skills as they chose. Why? Why this fear and the subsequent need to control?

This isn't just about a threat to profits, though that is part of it*; using intuition helps people know what they need for themselves, hence reducing dependency on others* (in other words, coming out of nappies). And this is not helpful to those who wish to control or exploit others, for whatever reason. In connecting with the truth of Being comes a sense of profound Inner security, and along with this the means to help ourselves and so function independently. Then people can neither be deceived nor commodified. And clearly, it is not in the interests of big corporations to have people wake up and take charge of their lives. Yet in a collective movement for change (that we explore in the chapter on politics) this is an emerging trend – especially amongst young people.

If this all sounds like it's getting political that's because it *is* political! The ego itself is political. Why do we assume that politics and the more personal and spiritual aspects of life can be separated? If you look deeply enough into all of this, something starts to become visible. You start to see that, inherent in the denial and suppression of both intuition and the psychic, and underlying any external desire for power and control – *regardless* of whether this is by the church, science, academia; by power-hungry despots or commercial interests – *lie the desires of the egoic mind*. Naturally, if it could employ these intuitive capacities it would do so. And when it can't? When it fails? Then it has to deny them, *especially intuition,* because access to direct knowing is a threat to its power.

As we have seen, mind controls through manipulating information *and emotional reaction to this information,* based on beliefs. Direct access to what is true undermines this control, so of course intuition is a threat. Which means that anything in this current narrow, tightly regulated, materialist version of reality most people are living in – anything that doesn't fit this – *has to be dismissed as mere fantasy.* This is essential in order to maintain this same egoic mindset, a mindset that we imbibed with our mother's milk.

Interestingly, this very dismissal has an unintended consequence: people are drawn towards the psychic and intuitive *precisely because these offer a glimpse into a part of life that is denied us,* that is usually hidden. There is a growing hunger for something deeper, something that lies just out of reach (or so it would appear). That this hunger may get fed with glamorous images of other worlds, other times, is unfortunate, because this breeds fascination. Then the ego takes over in areas such as past lives, where everyone seems to have been Cleopatra or Napoleon or Genghis Khan and no-one just a housewife or a humble street cleaner. Here anyone claiming psychic or intuitive abilities who can present a convincing image can score; with little to prevent imposters it can be a lucrative trade. Of course there are many sincere and honest people too, it's just that those who exploit this psychic arena play into the hands of those who want to deny and condemn the genuine. It confuses people seeking something real and distracts them from going deeper.

Knowing all this it should come as no surprise to see that, from the conditioned mind's point of view, intuition is an irritating interference with its organisational role of command. Intuition can't be subdued, so both intuitive *and* psychic input create a problem for the mind. No matter how much it seeks to exclude them from its version of 'reality' – even when it enlists respected bodies to deny their validity – they can never be satisfactorily eradicated. All the mind can do then is to poor scorn on them, while distorting their impact and attempting to exploit them in any way it can. Does this sound strange? Because it's perfectly logical. To anyone who has an investment in the supremacy of the mind an open, intuitive way of looking at things is naturally threatening; as it is to anyone who benefits from *the belief* in the minds' exclusive authority, or who is simply too far entangled in their own beliefs and emotional reactions to be able to extricate themselves.

The point here though, is not to make anyone or anything wrong. It is, rather, a call to wake up from the illusion of the narrow, circumscribed version of reality we inhabit. It is a call to drop fear and prejudice and vested interests, and embrace what is – and always has been – one great, big, largely unknown (and even unknowable) existence: to participate in a flow that delights in connection with the whole of life, through both what we call the psychic and the intuitive. In fact, *without this recognition* we appear doomed to extinguish ourselves, having failed to metamorphose into claiming our true nature as part of this totally amazing, ungraspable, full-spectrum intuitive reality.

Magic and mystery

In clear contrast with all the cynicism and scepticism directed towards both the intuitive and psychic realms, lies the world of children, with their love of magic and mystery. This is a vital and fascinating part of their world: *at least if they are allowed to enjoy it*. So many children now are stuck at home and in nurseries in front of 'entertainment' like *Teletubbies* and, later, anthropomorphised animals in mindless, full-volume, action-packed cartoons – at least until they get into computer games, and are made to knuckle down and study. Magic and mystery are not available to so many children and that is truly sad. And the results start to show, with children growing up with few inner resources and little sense of a world beyond the realm of their home, their schoolyard, the cinema complex and shopping mall. An obsession with violent computer games, horror movies and escapist drugs seems a predictable continuation of this living in a fantasy world. Here emotions are provoked, *but not fully lived*. We get to experience a sense of aliveness through the adrenaline rush, rather than engaging with life itself.

However, as the *Harry Potter* sales proved, there is a huge reservoir of enthusiasm for magic and mystery amongst both children and adults alike. Look at a young child's face when it is watching a magician using the most simple of tricks – they are entranced! Or when you tell them stories of fairies and witches and dragons; when you take them out walking and point out an elf's home in the bole of a tree, or generally regale them with tales of things outside their daily experience. You can see, especially if they are sensitive (as so many small children are), how their whole being lights up with interest as they open to absorbing new possibilities. The way they ask questions, their emotional responses to what they hear – often verging on the edge of excitement and fear: they are so open to extending their horizons. Then their world can become so much bigger, richer and more rewarding.

What does the word 'mystery' mean? Mystery means something that is not yet known, not fully revealed. It invites curiosity and wonder and is the essence of aliveness. Many years ago a man called Eden Phillpotts wrote in his book *A shadow passes*, '*The universe is full of magical things patiently waiting for our wits to grow sharper.*' So it is no less than tragic when others around them, both older children and adults, start to rubbish a child's innocent enthusiasm and make them feel silly and gullible (and in so doing, repeat the whole anti-life mantra they themselves got caught up in, projecting out their own denial and fear of the unknown). Children are naturally inquisitive, so exploring and adventure are not only part of a healthy child's development, *they are essential to this*. As is an interest in all things of mystery – such as tunnels and caves, castles and ruins; empty houses, abandoned lots and overgrown gardens.

Television and films bring us *fear without risk;* without the opportunity to test our courage by meeting the fear, gaining strength and confidence as a result. And most children's and young people's activities are focussed around *physical or mental* challenges. There is something quite different about confronting situations that are unknown and unpredictable on many different levels; situations that call on more subtle resources that can extend one's perception of reality. Here, support for imagination and investigation is important, as is validating a child's capacity to tune into all kinds of experiences that lie outside of the mundane world. Children are naturally intuitive, so let them know that it's good to be sensitive, to develop and trust their sensing, feeling, intuitive experiences, and help them to feel at ease with themselves *just as they are*. This is such a precious gift!

Healing and the veneration of all life

In this time, we absolutely need to be open to recovering and experiencing a sense of awe towards the extraordinary phenomenon we call 'life'. Then, feelings like veneration and reverence are a natural response of the heart, as we receive and communicate *through intuition* with this greater reality, with the whole of life. (Even when we don't necessarily know – in our mind, anyway – what is being said.) These *feelings*, that come through the heart, can connect us with Being. And, they can also be misplaced. People revere idols and venerate anything from false Gods to movie and music stars. So the feelings themselves are no guarantee of what you are connecting *with*.

Here, there is a stark difference between psychic activity and intuition. As I have said, intuition allows for a direct connection with truth, so aligned with this, these feelings can be trusted. Whereas the psychic world has no such anchor and when infiltrated by ego can be used to exploit. And this can be confusing. For instance, the version of psychic activity focussed on talking to the dead would appear to entirely lack a connection with the heart. And yet, *it may well hold a connection with grief*, which is itself of the heart, indicating a need for the person seeking contact with the dead to allow this grieving to take place – in natural ways, in touch with themselves, open and available to genuine feelings: in other words, in connection with the heart. It is here where healing takes place.

Elephants are known to connect in some way with dead relatives through communing with their bones. We don't know exactly what they are doing but, from their behaviour, it would seem to include both grieving and honouring. Indeed, there is wonder to be experienced in psychic connections. Something I have seen here is how intuition can help keep these connections clean, because intuition pierces through the distortion-prone mechanisms of mind. Then, anchored in Being, no matter what the mind's response, no matter what it tries to do with psychic material or how it *interprets* this, intuition – as direct knowing – is, and remains, unsullied.

I want to take a quick look, in passing, at an area that often gets linked in with the psychic and that is the misty world of healing and its beliefs, whether called psychic or not. Here, people make claims about certain streams of energy and teach others how to 'heal' using these. However, in my experience, what this often seems to entail is freeing people from *the belief* that they can't already do this! So it's interesting to ask: 'What is healing?'. What does this word really mean? And who, or what, is doing the 'healing?'. For how can a person operating from their unconscious, conditioned mind heal anyone? Which is not to say they can't be a *conduit*. Some of the greatest healing has happened through very ordinary, unassuming individuals. However, as with the whole psychic realm, this word 'healing' is loaded with beliefs that have little to do with what is true. Healing suggests that someone cures someone else by taking away their illness. After all, Jesus healed the sick, didn't he? But maybe he did this in the hope that people would listen to what he was *actually teaching,* and when he realised this wasn't happening he stopped?

In other words, sickness brings a gift that only the sick person can receive – the gift of using sickness to become conscious, in whatever ways this wants to happen. Because, as I have come to see it, *life brings us everything, in each moment, that we need to become conscious*; to come free from the dominance of the egoic mind. So to be passively healed in itself has no spiritual value (although it may make life more comfortable in a body). In fact, it's interesting to watch how disease often recurs if that person continues along the path they were on without making any changes. I remember hearing about a woman whose body was totally contorted. She received Rolfing (a form of extremely painful body-manipulation) for six months, after which her body was remarkably upright, free and well-adjusted. Six months later, her body had returned to its former contortion. During the whole of this time, this woman had done no inner work at all, be it called psychological, emotional or spiritual.

In offering to support others in any way the same rules apply – whether this involves individuals or groups that may be intending to heal other species or particular places, or even the world itself. Here, the expression 'healer heal thyself' can be translated to mean 'become conscious'! Become aware of your own patterns and tendencies and how the egoic mind operates, so you can spot any hidden agendas. What is your true intention? Can you let go of any ideas about *how to* heal? Any *trying* to heal or control anything? And, instead, simply let Being get on with it? Sort of plug into Being? For I have found this to be the great powerhouse that can amplify and bring accurate focus to creating apparent 'miracles' (a miracle simply being something the mind cannot understand).

After all, where do we imagine figureheads like Christ and the Buddha found their courage, conviction and inspiration? Their capacity to know and live the truth? Clearly, this world and everything in it needs our love and care; *as do we ourselves.* And, it can be extraordinarily revitalising when we reconnect with our source; reconnect with the love that we all actually *are.* Then just watch what can happen! What lies way outside the beliefs of a conditioned mind about what is possible, without any need to control this. Then we are letting life live itself, unencumbered by an imaginary ego.

Personal experiences

For me, and others who share my experience of intuitive reality, there is no problem with things that are unexplainable by the rational mind; incidents that would be labelled bizarre by others, or simply unbelievable. An example: one day, when I was sole manager of a small art gallery in Wimbledon, it came to lunchtime and I fancied a boiled egg, but I couldn't leave the gallery unattended. A young man who worked next door passed by and I called out to ask him if he would get me some eggs. 'Sure' he replied and off he went. A while later a couple drove up and came in to look at the paintings. As they left, the man opened the boot of his car, took something out – and without saying a word – put a box of eggs on my desk and drove away. When the young man reappeared I thanked him, thinking he must somehow have passed the eggs to this man. The young man (who thought I was being sarcastic) said, 'Oh God, I'm sorry. I completely forgot!'.

An example of a different kind of incident was when I received what turned out to be prophetic information, in the form of images. This was in Australia and I was sitting with my then lover high up on an escarpment with a breathtaking view out over the surrounding countryside; there was a sense of enormous space. Quite suddenly – out of the blue – I felt these small tugs in my belly area and three images unfolded, one after the other. The first was of a place of domes and ornamental roofs, in pinks and golds and earthy, dusty, creamy colours, that felt hot and dry. The second image was cool and fresh, with deep blues and turquoise and white, and a sense of water and sky. The third (which was less distinct) contained scarlet and white and yellow; this time there was a Spanish or Mexican flavour.

As I shared these images with my friend I realised I had no idea what they were about; *only as each fulfilled itself did I have a context to put them in.* Shortly after this experience I had to leave Australia and I travelled to India, to visit the commune of Osho. There I recognised the first image in the shapes and colours all around me. A few months after this I spent almost a year living in the village of Findhorn in Scotland, where the second image came quite breathtakingly clear. It was fourteen years before the third image showed itself, when I found myself called to the high mountains of southern Spain.

Another intriguing experience occurred shortly after this, when I was about to leave Australia. After eight years, which included an appeal, my application for permanent residency had finally been rejected, and I was pretty upset about this at the time. I had been living by totally trusting my intuition and couldn't understand why I had to leave Australia which, by then, felt like my home. A German woman I knew who was into channelling (where that person believes they are receiving messages from someone else) and whose English wasn't that great, was helping me pack.

After a while, I noticed she had gone rather quiet and then she came over and handed me four small sheets of paper. In *perfect* English – but with odd, quaint phrasing – there were these pages of rather poor poetry. This talked about my soul, and how it was necessary for me to let go and leave at this time – that there were new friends and new experiences waiting for me elsewhere; it included general words of comfort and reassurance and the last page was signed 'all of us'. What struck me as strange about this was not so much the content, nor even where it came from, but how it could have been written, given my friend's very poor and absolutely not 'quaint' grasp of English! It did indeed appear to have been dictated, and I still have this letter with no idea of how it came to be written.

In looking at these examples, it is clear that all three of these incidents lie outside what is considered to be 'normal' experience. Whereas the reality is that things like that – with absolutely no rational explanation – are not so unusual. I know myself to be amongst many others for whom unexplainable incidents are relatively frequent. Just how common these are is not known as people don't talk about them, fearing they may be seen as weird or unbalanced. Not all such incidents feel intuitive, either; as in the first instance, this could have been a form of telepathy: something categorised as belonging to the psychic world. It certainly seemed to contain no obvious 'spiritual' message, no connection with anything profound. It didn't affect me, in the sense that I wasn't touched by it: I was just surprised and curious (and I ate every one of those eggs!).

With the second incident, people seeking to label psychic abilities would claim this to be precognition. But here the distinctions between intuitive and psychic get hazy, because intuitive reality has a timeless dimension and to me it felt like a direct knowing, *even though I could not place this at the time*. It had a vibrancy and sense of connection that I associate with intuitive input, so I would call it intuitive: it was directly *known:* to me. Whereas the third incident, although I was both moved and grateful to receive it, was not my own, direct knowing: it came as a message via someone else so I would call this psychic rather than intuitive.

In fact, instances of channelling are common in the psychic world – it happens, even if the source of this remains unclear. This could be a separate entity, as claimed; it could also be from the channeller's own mind, perhaps in some kind of telepathic link; it could even be a link in this person's mind to a group mind. Who knows? Maybe this allows for a sort of cross-pollination of thoughts and information? If so, it is not clear how these mix and affect each other. Either way, as with so much in the psychic realm, this is simply speculation: we really don't know. I can only share that, for me, so-called 'psychic' input of this kind has a vague sense of mind about it. Whereas I recognise intuition as being direct reception of Being; perception of what is real and true: with no channel needed.

Intuition in daily life

Before I end this chapter I want to include something about how we use intuition around others in our personal lives. And this applies to psychic perception too. I touched on it briefly earlier and, because this doesn't seem to be much talked about, it feels important to include it here. So, to repeat, *in using intuition in any situation we absolutely need to know about egoic interference:* I can't stress this enough. Otherwise, the tendency to exploit the intuitive connection to our own advantage will continuously get in the way of maintaining harmonious relationships. It can be *so* uncomfortable to acknowledge this tendency, yet this can be – and usually is – entirely unconscious. Remember how ego uses everything? It will naturally attempt to exploit access to direct knowing to manipulate others in some way. Which is precisely why intuition can be, and can be seen to be, a threat. So it is not only vital to be aware of this, but to realise that there is no such thing as a reformed ego! It's just that some operate more skilfully and persuasively than others.

Take the ubiquitous need to be right. Here the egoic drive can so easily burrow in amongst our intuitive insights, often with devastating effects. Then, not surprisingly, others will react to this and may feel undermined or threatened. It's the 'I am right' that brings with it the 'and therefore you are wrong' agenda: the quintessential dynamic of power. Pretty well everyone has issues around power and control, this is central to human interactions; in any relationship there exists a power dynamic. So, if not seen through, the ego will use any resource in its drive to dominate. Then, exploiting intuitive insights is no different to exploiting intellectual information for the same ends (or any other aspect of the mind, feelings or body, come to that). So vigilance is needed because, as we have seen so often now, *everything depends on where we are coming from.*

One thing I learned in working with people 'professionally' is that boundaries are essential. These need to be both clear and consistent. Obviously, therapist/client relationships have to be one-way focussed if they are to be safe. I have seen some extremely messy situations where boundaries were not respected: this destroys trust and can be hard to clean up. Anyone whose work involves supporting people as they open into deep and painful material needs to know this if they are to be worthy of trust and not get entangled with their clients' issues. What changes – and I see this change as radical – is outside this agreement, in one's everyday life: *it is here where things can get really tricky.* So it's good to develop not just a strong sense of boundaries, but an awareness of permission too, or lack of this – and even then, to beware. Otherwise, it is all too easy to be unintentionally invasive, to make comments the other person may neither wish nor be ready to hear.

Once again, it can be helpful to distinguish the *motive* for any comment, where this is really coming from, to see if you can sense the shadow of ego hiding behind the impulse to share something. For example, you have probably met someone at a party or somewhere, who gazed into your eyes and told you something unsolicited and personal about you and your life: perhaps doing this with a sense of pronouncing your fate, with this air of 'I can see into you', 'I sense things about people' and (just under the surface), 'aren't I special!'. (Note the number of 'I's!) All kinds of silly and potentially hurtful power games get played out, so it's best to watch out and stay clear of looking into other people's business. And this, in my experience, is easier said than done – especially if they ask you questions. Therefore it makes sense to stay alert and be prepared to deflect or, if that doesn't work, smile and refuse to be drawn.

I remember one time during a romantic holiday in Greece, lying on an idyllic beach beside a glittering turquoise sea with my current boyfriend, feeling totally relaxed and at peace with the world. I found myself saying idly, 'Shall we go for a swim?' and he looked startled, saying 'I was just thinking that!'. An obvious coincidence you might think, but my saying what he was thinking continued until it got quite scary; then it stopped. I hadn't intended it and I didn't do anything to make it stop, other than become concerned because he was clearly shaken. These kind of incidents, where I spoke other people's thoughts, happened quite frequently, especially with people I was close to. Another boy got so freaked out he became quite angry, and I realised he thought I was doing it deliberately! I usually avoid talking about this because people can start to feel uncomfortable around you.

The fact is that outside my workspace, this capacity to pick up on other people's thoughts and feelings can be a real nuisance. I have never intentionally *sought* to know what another is thinking or feeling in this way. But to the person who is being 'received' this can feel really intrusive: as though I am in their head. They start to think I know what is going on with them when I don't, and nor do I wish to. Just imagine how complicated and disorienting it would be if you could always know what other people are thinking! Not to mention the potential for power games. And in terms of feeling what other people are feeling, this can get even more convoluted; especially when the person themselves doesn't know what they are feeling, or worse, doesn't want you – or anyone else – to know this is what they are feeling!

From all this you can get a sense of just how problematical unsolicited information can be, can't you? Both for the person receiving it and the one imparting this to another, whether it has an intuitive or psychic dimension (because technically, according to the labels anyway, perceiving the thoughts of others would be called telepathy rather than intuitive knowing). But whatever the source, the same rules apply and the distinctions are not always clear. As Anna Breytenbach (the woman who communicates with animals) pointed out, she receives information on many levels: thoughts, images, feelings and sensations in her body. And so do I. And if you too are someone who has had experiences of this kind (and there are likely many more people than we know about) it can be invaluable to find ways to live with these that don't invite trouble.

What I have found to be helpful in difficult situations is to keep one's energy grounded and focussed in the present, bringing attention to the breath and body; and sometimes taking 'gaps' to escape and be alone for a few moments (even if that has to be in the toilet) can help. Where I find it hardest is trapped somewhere – like in a car or around a dinner table – with other people's expectations; when I am asked questions and generally expected to join in the conversation and behave a certain way. It takes practice not to make an intuitive response, *not* to say what you are perceiving and to substitute something else. You can't be spontaneous and this can be tiring and not really much fun; especially if you are drawn to being real with yourself and others instead of playing the usual social games.

For instance, it can be acutely uncomfortable to be around people who are clearly feeling one thing but saying another. The more sensitive you are to energy, the more you may find this disturbing. So sometimes it's just easier to stay away from social gatherings altogether. If you find this happening, don't make yourself wrong. Respect your nature, take care of your gift, and save it for where it can be used safely. Because, as I have discovered for myself, if you are foolish enough to let yourself get drawn into letting slip some insight, you may cause unintended hurt and attract anger. You are perceived, albeit unconsciously, as a threat *and maybe you are!* People tend to gravitate to others who share a comfort zone in terms of behavioural norms. And that means people – many people – may not share your comfort zone. By which I mean the ambience, focus of interest, degree of openness and depth that feels most natural to you: where you feel you can be yourself. After all, why should they share this? So, if you find yourself in a place that feels difficult, stay alert; watch how you respond to it and if it gets rough, take time to be with yourself afterwards.

Whenever you feel you've messed up, or come away bruised from an encounter with others that didn't go well, come back to yourself; be there for yourself. By that I mean give attention to the small, insecure or hurting part – *but don't turn what happened into a story.* We are so used, and so conditioned, to blame either ourselves or others. So just rest in the presence of Being: breathe, relax your body and, if the feeling of discomfort falls away, wonderful; if it remains, let that be okay, too. Maybe it is bringing something to your attention to look at; something to see, to learn from, to let go of. Perhaps the situation revived an old hurt and you took something personally that really had nothing to do with you. Either way, all you can do is retain *the intention* to be consciously aware, to not get caught up in mind games – beyond that life does what it does.

For me, the most difficult people to be around are not strangers in the street or simple exchanges with ordinary folk. It is being around those who have strong and usually unconscious rules of behaviour. (The middle classes of Southern

England are especially ripe with these: for instance, nothing is ever said directly). It can be hard work to spend time around those who have a strong need to keep up appearances and defend a self-image (which same traits can be found amongst those involved in 'personal growth' and spiritual aspiration, too)! The truth is we are *all* fallible, which is where a degree of conscious awareness can make such a difference. I remember one time staying with a friend and her partner in the house of some friends of theirs. The house was full of distracting objects, including a huge television blaring away in the background that no-one was watching. I wanted to be able to listen to what people were saying so asked my host if he would mind turning it off. Whereupon my friend's partner gave me a steely look and said, 'You *don't* ask someone to turn off the television in their own house!'

Living intuitively

'So how can I become intuitive?' the mind wants to know. What do I need to do? The real answer to this is *nothing*. If you wish to receive intuitive input it may help to be relaxed, but intuition can arrive anywhere, at any time. In a sense it's like a wild creature giving birth: all you can be sure of is that you can neither induce it, nor control it. What can help overcome a doubting mind is to recognise that everyone has this intuitive capacity: *it is our nature*. It is only mind, with its conditioned beliefs and emotionalised reactions, that can block this flow. This may be at least partly why I, and many others too, often receive intuitive impressions while our attention is already engaged: perhaps watching a flock of birds wheeling around the sky or water flowing over some rocks; or looking into the flames of an open fire, or even just a candle flame. Maybe while listening to music, stirring food on the stove, digging the garden – anything that doesn't involve concentrating on *thinking*. Here, Adyashanti says something interesting *'Our capacity for insight depends on the quality of our listening'*. He is, of course, referring to listening *in,* for which a moment not dominated by thought is needed.

Although I don't ask for intuitive input, there is nothing wrong with seeing if something wants to appear and just sitting quietly in a receptive space. What is important here is that you don't move into *trying:* trying to make something happen, wanting to achieve a result. So if nothing appears let that be okay. Remember, there is nothing to do: *receiving intuitive insights is not a goal to be achieved*. In truth, it doesn't matter in the least if you receive an intuitive response in this time of being receptive and inviting. You may find this happens later, unsought, in which case you can simply recognise this, without fuss. What is interesting to ask here is 'Who is it that wants to get something? That fears failing to get it?'

It must surely be clear by now that in order to be able to fully live intuitive reality, without distortion, conscious awareness is needed; and perhaps a degree of awakeness that few of us are yet able to maintain? By which I mean the ability to not get the 'I' in the way, thus allowing transmission of what *is* simply to flow, undistorted. What grace! However, in the meantime, all of us can bring our attention to this interference; we can choose to refocus attention away from the mind and towards the heart and body-Being. What would it be like, for instance, if, instead of *thinking* about it, we *felt* and *sensed* and *intuited* our way into what is happening: into reality? We are so used to *thinking* our way through our lives. We wake up first thing in the morning and start thinking: thinking about what we are going to do that day, worrying about something we did yesterday, planning what to say to someone tomorrow; or just trying to decide what clothes to put on!

There is usually an emotional undercurrent attached to these thoughts, such as anxiety, and sometimes it's hard to know which comes first – are we anxious because we started thinking about something problematical? Or was the anxiety there, just looking for a cause to attach itself to? Either way, we are not fully present; we have abandoned ourselves, disconnected from our bodies, our feelings and sensations and what is happening all around us – the dawn chorus singing away outside the window goes unheard; the reflections of light and shadow on the curtains unseen; breakfast smells of coffee and toast somewhere, unnoticed. Reality is happening all around us and we have absented ourselves.

Imagine what it would be like if you could – literally – watch yourself; watch your body lying there on the bed whilst your attention is worlds away? You would see this body, puppet-like, being constantly jerked around by thoughts and feelings and emotions. You would see it responding with varying levels of tension and tightness – brow furrowed, frowning; clenching the hands or teeth or buttocks; tightening the mouth, shoulders hunching, leg trembling, breath held or jerky and uneven. All kinds of responses are happening that we normally remain unaware of. And all the while there is a very different way of being! A way that not only brings so much to be seen and felt, sensed and intuited, but that keeps us connected with our body: firmly awake in reality – *fully alive.* Living this intuitive reality.

This is very different to the behaviour of thought. Have you noticed how thoughts are continuously dividing and branching off? Getting caught up in the past and the future, and then returning again? Especially if there is a strong emotion attached that acts like a magnet? When two people are talking together there can be a whole host of agendas playing out beyond what you hear them say: for instance, what you think about what they are saying, what you think *about them* for saying this, how you want to respond, how this makes you feel, what *you* want to talk about, what you want them to know about *you*, what impression you want to make, what you think they may be thinking about you, on and on and on. Engaging in this way, like an army general, the mind is busily occupied with assessment and defensive manoeuvring. *And all the while there is another way of relating.*

The thinking mind tends to assess the world primarily through *visual input*, which keeps things safely at a distance, with sound playing a lesser part. So just imagine if you were dumb and blind, how different this interchange would be. You would have to rely on your subtle senses far more to sense other people's energy and where they are coming from; listening to the inflections and timbre of their voice would have far greater importance, along with noticing subtle smells, like fear. Your finger tips could reach out and trace shapes, feel textures; notice moisture or dryness and generally explore the other: with time given to these subtle impressions. All of this is actually a far more direct and immediate form of engagement: one in which the whole gamut of learned defensive procedures has no place. It is intimate, open to connection and, as such, it has a certain innocence.

Can you imagine how it might be to extend this into exploring life with your intuitive 'white stick'? Feeling your way, searching for clues, sensing where to go; when to move, to reach out; when to pause and simply wait – open and trusting? In my experience, this is what living with intuitive reality is like. There is an openness to delicate, subtle impressions: impressions that arise and invite and inform. The whole movement is one of flow: you always know when you are on the right track because of this flow. There is a sense of extra buoyancy, extra vibrancy, extra vitality. Watery words like 'flowing', 'fluid', 'flexible', 'floating' and 'free' describe this well – as does 'sublime': *because when this flow is happening it can feel utterly sublime.* Unlike the tight, controlling or excitable energy of mind, this way of being allows for relaxation of the body, as we let go of trying to understand and just let life be: let be what will be. Like that old Doris Day song *Qué Será, Será, Whatever Will Be, Will Be.* Then, following this intuitive flow is like following a perfume: we can't see it but we are drawn to it; we recognise its fragrance, its significance, its beauty and preciousness. Like the Pied Piper, it calls us with a tune: a tune we remember we already know.

Home-play
1. Opening to intuition
This exercise involves just quietly being: idling if you like, rather than concentrating on getting something done (having taken whatever steps you can to ensure you will not be disturbed) and breathing gently into the cradle. It doesn't matter what position the body is in (as long as it is comfortable) or if it is moving or still.
- Allow yourself to relax and let go of any expectation: remind yourself that it really does not matter if you receive an intuitive impression or not.
- Now, from this still place, allow your attention to focus something that is unclear to you. Feel into this, *sense* if it wants to tell you anything about this

situation (or, more accurately, if something is not *already* known about this). Maybe there is a feeling response, which could be very soft and delicate, or quite clear and strong. It may appear as an image, a colour, a sound; or in words, as a sensation; or it is simply *known*.
- Notice any interference from thought (like doubts), or emotion (like anxiety). Simply watch these responses and then return your attention to resting.

2. Pay attention to the fleeting glimpses

You may find that, as you do this, this gets easier and happens more frequently. Don't make a meal out of them, just notice what is perceived. If these are images, they may appear at the periphery of your vision. And sometimes intuition can be surprisingly quirky: like a comical image or a flow of letters that make up a word. Accept that you don't know how you knew what you know: it simply is there. Remember, intuition is the knowing itself, rather than any vehicle used for its delivery.

3. Learn to distinguish intuition

- Start to notice the difference between intuition, and mind and emotion; between instinct and impulse; you may even find you can distinguish psychic input, too. Distinguishing simple feelings and sensations that are not intuitive is also useful.

And remember: all of these *input sources* can respond or react to what the intuition brings, and this may seem confusing and distracting, especially when there is a reaction of fear or doubt, or an egoic drive *to use what is seen*. Learn to trust what you know to be true, without any need for explanation and don't worry if you make mistakes along the way.

Highly sensitive people and the loneliness of an unshared reality

'Our fact-based culture is so terrified by anything mysterious or inexplicable. Being curious outside the set cosmology is still something of a sin. And it's hard for those people to be faced by mockery and lies, to diminish the question. Life is so much more beautiful and indefinable than our culture seems to admit to.' ~ Mark Rylance, Shakespearian actor

'I remember feeling very shy when I was little and feeling more comfortable with animals and nature than with people. I also remember being very small and looking at the adults when they would get agitated and wondering what the problem was. Then growing up, I found out why they were all so worried. They thought they had to run life and carry it and defend it.' ~ Pamela Wilson

'Highly sensitive people are too often perceived as weaklings or damaged goods. To feel intensely is not a symptom of weakness, it is the trademark of the truly alive and compassionate. It is not the empath who is broken, it is society that has become dysfunctional and emotionally disabled.' ~ Anthon St Maarten

We live in a time where there is very little appreciation or understanding of either subtle energies or heightened sensitivity, nor of how these constantly affect us. So if you are one of a minority for whom awareness of these is part of your everyday life, aspects that lie *outside of the consensus reality*, it can be very confusing, even hurtful. Maybe you had experiences as a child, and still do, of not feeling really seen or heard? Not truly: not as you are, as you experience yourself to be? I suspect this is common for many of us. Even when it's noticed, we don't talk about it: it feels too deep and too personal. Yet this can bring with it an acute sense of isolation, even alienation, as we feel unable to share our most profound experience of ourselves. For those people with greater sensitivity, and the extended perception of reality this brings, this can be excruciating. It creates self-doubt and can undermines our confidence in a big way, and yet this is not something generally recognised.

Because we don't talk about it most people remain unaware of it, and so children grow up feeling there is something wrong with them. Even when we allow ourselves to recognise it, it is not something easily communicated. So for those of us who have been born with certain abilities – abilities that lie outside the common frame of reference for 'normal' – this can be troubling. This has been my own experience, and it often presents in the people I work with as a deep and unmet source of distress. One of the chief difficulties such people experience is how to express this difference in ways that can be heard without judgement. To say to someone 'I am just highly sensitive, so I have certain needs and experiences most people don't share' is to invite a negative response of the 'Oh my God, she's wacko!' or at least 'She's so *precious* about herself' or 'Is she saying I am *not* sensitive too?' variety.

Many of the people I work with are not just highly sensitive, they may have, or develop, an awareness of subtle realities – realities the general public has little if any awareness of, and therefore interest in. To many people this is just not part of the 'real' world they inhabit – which is hardly surprising, given prevailing attitudes. Because so many people are unable to trust their own experience, attitudes tend to be formed by those claiming authority: that is science, academia and sometimes religion; often via mainstream media outlets where most people receive their information. But as those who claim to know tend to share a strongly allergic reaction to these subtle realities – in fact to anything mystical or 'alternative' – this creates a bias.

These same dominant sources of opinion seem hell-bent on informing people that this is all baloney, fantasy and fraud; good material for a send-up so stay well clear! And this not only cuts out a huge chunk of reality, but the fact that for a considerable number of perfectly sane people this wider perception is a normal part of their lives, gets ignored or trampled over. And, of course, there is widespread fear of the unknown. To feel unseen, unvalued and have no place to share one's experience or to use one's abilities is not a comfortable place for anyone to be, so seeing intuitive abilities and 'extra'-sensory perception rubbished and denied can be painful and frustrating. Again, as we have noted, in days gone by people with certain exceptional qualities were valued members of their community; they were allocated certain roles, like that of shaman or healer; artist, songwriter, storyteller or poet. This was their function and they were respected for it; others were good at other things.

What then happened, historically, has had an enormous impact on people's attitudes towards all this. In large part thanks to the determination of the various religious bodies to gain power over the people, those with these kinds of abilities have been persecuted and often killed. Mainly women but not always, they were named as witches when most of them were simply herbalists, healers and midwives. With no recourse to justice, these people were subjected to the most horrific forms of torture and often burnt at the stake: in their thousands, all across Europe and into America. Indeed, Arthur Miller's book *The*

Crucible (which was made into a film), documents these 'witch trials' at Salem in America in 1692.

At that time, local people were encouraged to denounce their fellows and even rewarded for this, which would have given anyone with a grievance or simply petty spite against their neighbour, an opportunity for revenge. So we can imagine what it must have been like living in those days for anyone with heightened sensitivity, with any kind of pronounced intuitive or psychic talent. Who knows whether past lives are real or not? Or if these are simply ways we dip into the collective unconscious? But I have known people who have had clear recall of events they attribute to a past time, experiences that don't fit with their current lives, and not a few of these – especially amongst women – involve memories of these horrific events. Maybe these kinds of traumatic experiences live on in the collective unconscious of humanity? No one can say for certain but what has been left, like a sticky residue, is a great fear around all of this – fear and a certain fascination.

Today, because of current attitudes of scepticism and denial, there is neither mainstream support nor training in how to live with these abilities and perhaps use them to benefit others. So it's hardly surprising that people get confused and even delusional. Even in the alternative field it can be hard to find real help. It's easy to get lost in the shadowy worlds of psychic 'phenomena' (as we talked about in the previous chapter) this bringing experiences that can be very un-grounding – fertile territory for unconscious egoic drives like self aggrandisement or just the need to feel special (and who doesn't have this somewhere buried in their psyche?). So many opportunities for talents to be exploited for personal gain. None of this is about morality, right and wrong; it's about finding integrity and avoiding messes: your own and others. *And that means getting very clear about what it is that you want*, along with awareness of unconscious patterns that can interfere with a genuine movement of the heart towards supporting others.

If you open to using these sensibilities you need to know who or what is using them. And here, as we have seen, what so often complicates things is the psychological area. Remember how the influences of the egoic, conditioned mind can distort everything we perceive? Along with what we do with this input? So then, knowing this it is clear that highly sensitive people, *perhaps more than anyone*, need to take responsibility for their nature. And that means finding ways to come into the body and maintain contact with the earth, staying anchored in the intuitive reality found in the presence of Being: *firmly focussed on what is true*. And all of this is made harder by the hostile attitudes of society intruding into what could otherwise be a genuine experience of the vast richness of life.

Special needs

I have said that many of the people who come to see me are highly sensitive, so what exactly do I mean by this? I am referring to a heightened awareness of subtle signals and sensory input generally, with a latent capacity for receiving intuitive and psychic information that is finer and more developed than in the average person (which doesn't mean such people are not capable of gross insensitivity on occasions, too, especially when they are stressed and go on over-load). These are people who just happen to be more open and sensitive in these ways. Does this make them superior to everyone else? Absolutely not! As with any speciality, some of us are better at some things, others at others: we can all serve a useful function. However, in many ways – and in this society – these abilities can actually be a handicap. If you have particular needs that no one seems to recognise or respect, it can be hard. And the tendency amongst society at large to put these sensitivities down, to scorn, trivialise and discount, means highly sensitive people may even try to hide or deny them. 'She's weird!, flaky, a bit touched' and 'Who does she think she *is*? Has she got a hot-line to God or something?' are common responses.

Journalists in particular seem to be offended by the very idea of these abilities being real and evince a compulsive need to deride them. So if someone is unwise enough to reveal these traits, this can attract a vitriolic response: in other words, the response of someone feeling threatened, a response grounded in fear. And this is not just a fear of difference, but that this difference may give that person access to information that we don't have (and it might be about me!) – a potential threat around power and control. These abilities may even bring envy and, amongst certain kinds of people, unwarranted adulation. All of this speaks to the suppression of the intuitive and the veneration of the limited concrete 'realities' of the material world that we have been talking about throughout this book. And this naturally makes it difficult for highly sensitive individuals to relax and be themselves in an environment where they feel safe and accepted.

Such sensitivities can be especially hard for men, in a society where they are supposed to prove their virility either in the world of sport or through some other form of competitive achievement out in the marketplace. In reality, playing macho man requires blocking or shutting down sensitivity in order to survive in a tough world, and men who do this often believe this will bring them status as 'real' men. Perhaps for this reason, highly sensitive men often have lots of women friends but few male ones. Women appreciate their tendency to be more open, gentle and caring, to empathise and be good listeners. Some people equate sensitivity with being homosexual (which these men may or may not be) and sensitive men are generally more vulnerable to being teased and bullied at school.

It may be that highly sensitive men are more feminine, but I prefer not to attach these labels because, like homosexuality, they tend to attract assumptions and prejudice. We could say they are more open and receptive maybe, and more in touch with their feelings and intuition; but where women are more likely to find friends and places to share their intuitive nature, for men it can be a lot more challenging and there is some visible damage amongst those with less inner strength to survive. So one of the lovely aspects about working with men like this is seeing how, as they begin to open up and trust their true nature – as they are both supported and validated and start to make a deeper connection with their body-Being – so they come to rest in a more balanced and functional place. They become more able to be there for themselves too, an essential part of this process.

An American psychologist, Elaine Aron, wrote a book called *The Highly Sensitive Person* and what she goes on to describe fits all this perfectly. She talks about how, in both humans and animals, some percentage of the population are highly sensitive. So, in herds of wild horses for example, this applies to about 25%, *and these animals serve a particular and very useful function*: they tend to stay on the periphery of the herd as they pick up signals of danger before the rest. So with humans too, there is a certain percentage of the population that are highly sensitive and, as we noted, these would have served a useful function amongst earlier peoples who recognised their value. It is only now – and particularly in the West – that there is no recognition of this, and therefore almost no respected roles to play. Many of the people who gravitate to the fringes of society and participate in New Age and older traditions like Wicca are drawn because here they feel more at home: they are accepted and appreciated.

And yet, here we are – living in a time where the world is entering a highly precarious state; where the continuation of all life, including human life, is under threat. It could well be that people with this kind of sensitivity have a valuable contribution to make, even if the form this takes is not yet clear. In which case, it is imperative that everyone takes a good look at their unconscious fears around all of this so that attitudes can change. It takes courage to acknowledge prejudices that are based in fear, and real honesty. So here is something ordinary people (that is, people who are not necessarily in positions of power) *can* do, in the midst of a general sense of powerlessness. Questioning, challenging and opening up to the vastness we are all a part of changes everything. Then, in addressing this fear, we free everyone to expand into living their unique potential as vehicles for the intuitive expression of the heart: that is, *living Being-ness*.

What is it like living with acute sensitivity?

Highly sensitive people are amplifiers: by that, I mean that whatever is going on around them in the world of the senses is amplified. So, for a person of regular sensitivity, the world is a relatively comfortable place to be. For the extra sensitive it can be excruciating, especially with things such as discordant sounds, harsh lights and clashing colours. Many are supersensitive to energy, some more than others, so being immersed in certain colours can feel draining; as can loud noises that others easily screen out. This can be a real problem: walking through a giant supermarket with its fluorescent lights and sounds of crashing metal baskets can be anything from uncomfortable to a nightmare. And not only is no-one else aware of this but, as I have said, it's often hard to explain and to be understood. Here again, the response of someone who doesn't feel this, of the 'Don't be such a pathetic moaner!' variety, can be hurtful, because this is not something we choose; nor is it something we can change.

A while ago I was riding in a car with some people I knew, heading off to see an art installation about two hours' drive away. The driver had a CD playing Shostakovich full blast: one of those chaotic, fast-moving pieces with lots of 'plinkety-plonks' followed by crashes. For me, this was an exact replica of neurosis, madness of the mind, which directly interfered with my sense of ease, making it impossible for me to relax and enjoy myself. Clearly, he was loving it and it was his car so I chose to keep quiet and endure as best I could. Another time, I found myself having to pack up and leave a peaceful campsite in the middle of the night when a flock of teenagers descended and proceeded to play Metallica full blast late into the night. Okay, many people might be bothered by that, but I had no choice. I simply could not tolerate it.

It is not just noise that is a problem for sensitive people, who go on sensory overload more quickly than others, but other input too. For instance, we often perceive the distress signals of other forms of life more forcefully. A social animal like a dog, that is chained up and deprived of all company, for instance, or walking through a zoo, where other animals – especially large primates like gorillas and chimps or bears, lions and tigers – are held captive. I find it hard to pass trees that have been brutally lopped, shawn of all beauty and dignity, often for no other reason than convenience, without feeling a painful response. This isn't a thought, like 'they shouldn't do that' (though it may induce this), it's much closer and I feel this in the belly area of my body. This might sound like an absurd over-reaction. You might want to say 'But why can't you just accept what is happening? Why make such a fuss?'. In other words, why pay attention to what your body is telling you? To which I would say, whatever way you choose to meet these feelings and sensations, it is important to acknowledge their validity; not to close off and ignore something because it's inconvenient and you may not be able to change it. I see the ability to respond in this way as an important aspect of being fully alive. It's a part of our energetic makeup that informs us of what is really happening, what is true.

There are many subtle ways we can receive information that we have learned to ignore. For instance: if you pay close attention you can notice that music with a beat just faster than the heart rate keeps your heart racing (it can even be fatal for someone with a weak heart) but many people are completely unaware of this. It's popular with young people because it gets the adrenaline moving; if your energy is flat or sluggish, it gives the illusion of being more alive: the world can seem suddenly more exciting – similar to a caffeine rush. Which means that for anyone with high sensitivity this can be a real problem. With something like epilepsy, it is known that flash photography can trigger an episode, but very little is known about how and why people's responses differ to various stimuli and the impact this has.

I remember reading about a bunch of highly sensitive people in America who went to live in the Arizona desert to avoid this input of disturbing sensory 'pollution'. The phrase 'noise pollution' indicates a growing awareness of the difficulty of getting away from noise, and 'light pollution' too is now more widely recognised, as people become aware of the potentially harmful effects of both of these on health and peace of mind. And yes, I do have ear plugs and a sleeping mask, but these also intrude and can separate us from sensory input in an unpleasant way (apart from cutting off any warning sounds of danger) and anyway, who wants to sleep like a mummy!

In the next chapter we will look at something known as the 'subtle energy-field' or 'Aura', within which our *physical* body exists. For now, I just want to draw attention to how this can affect sensitivity. Most people are unaware of how the quality and vibration of this energy-field reflects our state of mind, which maybe anything from irritable or aggressive; excited, tense, nervous or needy to calm, relaxed, warm and welcoming, and so on. So the more you are aware of this the more it affects you. Some people's energy-field is closely focussed around the body, which makes this energy dense and less porous – hence less sensitive – but keeps them well protected, while others extend their energy outwards towards others. These people – who tend to be highly sensitive – rely on perceiving the energy of the other to keep themselves safe. They 'read' this at a distance, but this very extension works two ways: it allows us to know something of what the other is bringing and, at the same time, we are vulnerable to the energy of others affecting us, even draining us.

As the way people's energy moves, between extension and contraction, is different for different people, so some HSP's find ways to screen themselves. I once heard a spiritual teacher say about this that we can come to a place where we don't need to close off or defend, as everything passes through us. However, if you are not in that totally clear place some kind of protective measure makes sense, along with finding simple ways to clean and maintain your energy field (see the exercise the end of this chapter). However, it's worth remembering that sometimes we can become too good at withdrawing and protecting ourselves, at shutting others out; because in closing off the heart becomes unavailable and we can unconsciously perform small acts of cruelty as others sense our rejection, encouraging a climate of distrust.

For highly sensitive people, learning how to take care of your energy just makes so much sense. Don't expect other people to understand and empathise when you suddenly get up and run out of the room, supermarket, stadium, whatever, or refuse to travel on the underground: just be grateful when they do. People who care about you may be able to give you space to be the way that you are and may even support this, but others are unlikely to do so. If they don't have these sensibilities – or to such an intense degree – it's difficult for them to share your experience, even to imagine what you might be feeling. Then, it's hard to interpret your behaviour as anything other than you being difficult. And yet it's a fact: you do need more space to yourself; time to be quiet and rest and not have to respond to other people or interact with their energy all of the time. This isn't about being precious or selfish, it's about knowing you own makeup and taking care of it, learning how to manage your energy; accepting how you are wired up so you can be there for yourself when others can't be.

I once had a conversation with someone that went like this:

Them 'I've been trying to get hold of you all afternoon. Why didn't you answer your phone?'

Me 'I have been working all morning and have a group tonight. I needed a space.'

Them 'I left three messages on your phone.'

Me 'I don't look at messages on my mobile. I prefer to check my landline when I get home.'

Them 'But how am I supposed to get hold of you?'

Me 'I don't want to be available twenty-four seven.'

Them 'But that's what mobiles are for!'

People are shocked when I tell them I only use a clunky old mobile sporadically, for friends and family to make arrangements on the day, and don't use it for emails; that I am not on Facebook, don't do Twitter or LinkedIn, and don't always check my emails when I am away. They look astounded and somehow affronted too, as if I am being deliberately obstructive and choosing to live in the Dark Ages. But this is an important part of me taking care of my needs for space (apart from avoiding the radiation). So take time to sit and just be; get out and move your energy, preferably by walking as this literally keeps your feet on the ground. Touch your body or get it touched, frequently; find out what foods work best for you and avoid those that don't and cherish this that you are.

The value of solitude

What is of utmost importance for a highly sensitive person is to learn to be alone. What I mean by this is to know the difference between aloneness and loneliness, and to be able to access the former. In this place we can rest and rejuvenate – especially necessary for someone who has to be out in the world of work, perhaps surrounded by other people, maybe squashed onto busy public transport and dealing with the many stresses of modern life. Being immersed in a general level of unconsciousness, where the egoic mind acts out its dramas – the world most of us live in – can be exhausting (not that highly sensitive people don't have their own baggage!). In contrast, the wonderful thing about nature is that it is entirely conscious, it doesn't do ego-games. Perhaps you have heard how, in the days of the shamans and such people, this need to be alone was accepted and respected, and they tended to live a little apart from the main group? So make sure you get out into nature regularly – whether it's your garden, a park or wherever. And don't forget cemeteries: these can offer a rare sanctuary, a place of peace and quiet to just be in the midst of the general buzz of a town or city.

Looking back, I realise I was incredibly blessed as a child to live amidst acres of beautiful countryside in which I spent a lot of my free time, often alone. There were these gigantic old oak trees in a wood just across the road that I had an intimate relationship with, and we had a largish garden with an orchard and chickens at the bottom. So sitting up one tree or another was normal for me – a natural place to be. I drew much solace from the company of trees; with birds and wild creatures all around me hours passed, while I sat just watching or daydreaming, without a sense of needing anything. Not that I didn't have a few encounters with the damaged people who always seem to haunt empty places, and some were scary, but I survived. The presence of animals was important: we had a family cat, I kept a series of rabbits, guinea pigs, mice and tortoise and brought home flee-ridden hedgehogs, wounded squirrels and birds, and at ten, I was finally allowed to have a dog.

The seasons were marked by looking for tadpoles and birds' nests in spring, which was always exciting; summer meant swimming in rivers (looking out for crayfish hiding under the banks that would nip your toes!) or lying under a tree, watching the play of light and shade and the clouds forming patterns in the sky. Sometimes we children slept out in the garden and the sense of enormous space, filled with stars and the very occasional lights of a plane passing over, was magical. Autumn brought giant stag beetles that rustled amongst the piles of leaves, and so much everywhere to see and smell, to examine and wonder about: big swathes of wispy Old Man's Beard hanging off the mellow brick walls, Lords and Ladies with their scarlet berries hiding underneath; gathering rose-hips and blackberries, hunting for mushrooms in the early morning mist before someone else got there. And in winter, finding the first snowdrop quivering in the frosty morning always felt profoundly moving.

For me, growing up in a world without all the technological developments we have now, meant there was time for scheming and dreaming and wondering about the meaning of life – I don't ever remember being bored. I drew pictures, composed stories and we sang around the piano; and whatever the weather my dog had to be walked. As a highly sensitive child and a late reader (I was mildly dyslexic and didn't learn to read till I was nine), this gave me plenty of space to simply be. I remember spending hours just gazing into the fire on those long, dark, winter nights, watching the shapes forming and colours flaring, and I found the sounds of the odd shifting and crackling wonderfully soothing. Somehow the doing of this – being present in this way – opened a space within me in which intuitive impressions thrived.

Living in what might be termed the 'outer suburbs', I have no memories of connecting with people as part of a community. In fact I regarded the social surroundings as an alien world (neither my school nor my schoolfriend's houses were local). I was vaguely aware, on the occasional contact, of stilted codes of socially-accepted behaviour, while at the same time being pretty much immune to a degree of hostility and suspicion: we were definitely 'oddities'; which, while bothering my sister, just encouraged my tendency to go off alone. How fortunate I was to be able to access the gentle solace of nature. For children growing up now it's so much harder, with the constant seductive presence of television, computer games and the ubiquitous 'I'pad. For city kids, walking along concrete pavements or through local parks can be both grim and unsafe. Sitting alone in your room is better than nothing, but this doesn't offer the same sense of connection with a reality vibrant with the aliveness found in nature. Books can be wonderful and enriching, but they can also be used as an escape that disconnects us from the here and now.

Social pressure on children to relate can be intense. The general interpretation of being alone a lot as meaning we lack friends, are unwanted or somehow not 'normal' (signifying something is wrong) can be hard for highly sensitive youngsters. Without someone who understands a child's need for time alone, this can create a feeling of self-doubt that persists into adulthood. Then when we do spend time alone – even if we give ourselves permission to do this – the mind tends to get busy with thoughts, so we may turn to some form of meditation. However even a simple activity like sewing, carving wood or fixing something that is broken has a way of helping us to sit quietly without thought: this is what followers of Zen Buddhism refer to as 'carrying water, chopping wood.' In fact, walking can be a meditation in itself. True, sometimes it can feel like an effort to get outdoors, especially in winter, but remember how you often feel so glad you did, afterwards? It's truly good for the soul if you are well wrapped up and can get warm and cosy once you get back indoors again.

Remember, for highly sensitive people taking time to be alone allows your energy to regenerate in a way social interactions generally don't. Some men do this solitude thing in sheds, where they can escape the pressures of family life for 'a bit of peace and quiet' but for women it's less usual, kitchens being places where everyone comes and goes. But you can always find somewhere if you really want to, *if you put value on this time to be alone.* It's a question of priorities, of making this important.

But it's not just about being alone but also about finding your alone*ness,* your sense of being present with yourself *even in a crowd*, and this can be challenging. I am not talking about cutting off and pretending you don't need anyone – this is just a form of defence against *experiencing loneliness,* or rejection. Rather, if loneliness comes then try sitting with it and, perhaps surprisingly, you may discover it has changed. You know how sometimes you just feel full, complete and at ease, for no particular reason? A sense of being filled with something that is both still and yet very alive? Surrounded by a kind of dense but invisible presence? There comes a sense of inner calm and even contentment. These times are precious. This is when you know you don't need anything or anyone: *there is no hole that needs filling.* This is what I mean by aloneness. You could say this is your reward; this is what is waiting for you when you value it and give it your attention: so especially if you are used to always being around people, you can discover you actually enjoy being alone.

I am absolutely not suggesting here that highly sensitive people should become hermits! It's a very natural human tendency to want company, at least some of the time; to want to share, our pain and laughter, to play and share things you enjoy (and most forms of play are more fun around others). You don't have to become all serious and restrict connections; but just be aware so that – unless you experience a genuine feeling to connect – you don't put expectations on yourself to do so or allow others to pressure you into this. For instance, have you noticed how, when someone calls to ask if you are free, unless you have something already arranged (or it's someone you really don't want to see) the usual response is 'Yes'? We are not used to valuing this time alone. So how would it be if you first checked in with yourself and then maybe said something like 'Sorry, I need some time alone with myself tonight'? And maybe even marked out specific times in your diary for this?

We are not trained to listen to ourselves in this way: to listen to our bodies, our energy – just the opposite. Yet for highly sensitive people this is even more important. Feelings of tiredness, even exhaustion; headaches, upset tummies, irritability, anxiety, restlessness and what people call 'nerves': these can all be symptoms of needing space. There is a kind of unease we feel when we override this need to be alone, to be quiet. So it's up to us not to betray this inner need. This is an important part of cherishing what we are and what we have been given. If I seem to be going on about this it's because the world we live in can often be likened to a travelator: we have to make a conscious decision to step off.

The danger of becoming too self-focussed

One danger highly sensitive people face can come from living too much inside our own reality. In spending a lot of time alone, and this is something only-children often suffer from, we can become too focussed on our own feelings and needs. We aren't used to sharing and adapting and fitting in. We may lack the awareness of others that comes with being part of a group – whether that's a big family or part of the wider community. This lack of awareness isn't intentional. If parents and teachers and those around us fail to attend to this, in whatever ways they can, we simply remain ignorant, oblivious. And something I only became aware of many years later was how this affects our parenting skills.

For instance, my mother lived very much as an only-child. She had two elder brothers but they usually went off without her. Her mother preferred to take care of the cooking and housework herself and she was not allowed to play with the village children, who were seen as 'too rough'. This meant not only did she spend a lot of time alone, but she had very little practice at relating with others, especially those outside the family. Her shyness, which was only partly a result of her sensitivity, remained with her for the rest of her life, limiting her experiences of the laughter and gaiety she could actually enjoy. She lacked confidence about how to participate and, I suspect, compensated for this by staying a little aloof. I had glimpses of this lively spark occasionally, but when I had a boyfriend who really brought this out in her, I was both delighted and amazed. And of course, I carried this through in my own parenting where, despite my sincere intention, I could later see how I had failed to take care of some of my children's important needs: I had been blind.

So we see how a lack of social interaction can also be a disadvantage. Especially given a sensitive child's tendency to avoid this. Which is where parents need to be especially vigilant and find ways to include and encourage that enhance the child's social skills: their confidence and enjoyment of relating with others. Ways that help them be aware of the feelings and needs of others, whilst teaching them how to take care of their own needs – teaching them they are not weird, but that engaging and sharing with others can be fun.

Synesthesia and the potential value of high sensitivity for our survival

It's tricky describing all this, for which I have to use labels, because in the defining of some people as highly sensitive (or HSPs as Elaine Aron calls them) this can make them feel separate and others excluded. And of course mind loves labels! It loves to separate and categorise. So what to do? Here, in another example of labelling we find the word 'synesthesia' (which can also be spelled synaesthesia, from the Ancient Greek *syn*, 'together' and *aisthesis*, 'sensation'). Those who study the brain talk about how the senses are separated out into smell, taste, touch and so on; but for some people (and I am one of them) these senses are mixed up, or crossed over: they call us 'synesthetes'. So sometimes (but not always), I *see* sounds. This is especially so, I have discovered, with live music, when I had my first vivid experience of this at a concert given by the Cream many years ago. I also realised I can feel external movements of others *in my own body*. Again, I noticed this most strongly during a live dance performance, when I became aware of this response to the dancers movements. Eventually I came to see how all the senses are interconnected: *they are all ways of receiving information that connect us in with the whole.*

A relatively recent occasion illustrates the complexity of this experience. One hot August night in a village in Southern Spain I attended the annual Flamenco festival, which was held outdoors. Tomatino is perhaps the most superb Flamenco guitarist alive and as soon as he started to play I began to 'see' these incredible colours forming shapes; shapes that were constantly changing – moving and reforming and then disappearing – a bit like flames, and I *sensed* their energy. The nearest I can come to describing this might sound fanciful but it felt real enough to me at the time; it was as if these notes *came alive*, as entities, as if they were creatures of *a different species,* who could only live in the moment of playing by this amazing guitarist who acted as a catalyst for their brief existence. To anyone who has taken drugs this may sound somewhat familiar but I hadn't. In fact, in order to fully experience what was happening I found myself spontaneously opening up on all levels, energetically I mean.

At the same time *my physical reality* was that I was packed in amongst hundreds of heaving, sweating bodies in an enormous crowd, including some who had been drinking and were laughing and shouting across to each other throughout. And every now and then a sometimes vast body would push its way through the lines of plastic chairs perched precariously on the rocks, in search of more beer.

It's hard to describe how an experience like this affects you unless you have been there yourself, but for me this *dividing of attention between co-existing but extreme realities,* this intense surrender while constantly being distracted, felt like being energetically pulled apart on a rack, or tossed about in boat on a wild sea – sublime, excruciating, disorienting and exhausting all at the same time. And all of it entirely outside my control. I was aware that something unique and extraordinary was happening but could neither fully meet this nor protect myself from what I experienced as the sometimes gross energy around me: I couldn't reconcile the two. To add to the internal turmoil, I found it painful to witness what seemed to me such disrespect for these great musicians who come back and offer their skills every year at this free event. So perhaps from this, you may get a taste of both the difficulties of living with this kind of sensitivity and it's extraordinary, unknown potential?

To quote a man called Norman Diodge, who has studied what he calls the 'neuroplasticity' of the brain and its ability to heal itself *'There are no lights, colours, smells or sounds inside the brain. There are patterns of electrical information and our sense receptors; our retinas, the cochlea of the ear are, in energy terms, transducers.'* Meaning that what they do is translate one form of energy – sound, light, heat – into another; which suggests that perhaps within the brain there is a function that can either separate or link, overlap or cross-pollinate these various sensory signals? And possibly this keeping separate has been useful in order to navigate in the physical world? Surely if we were to be constantly bombarded by this cocktail of sensory input we would go on overload and become completely dysfunctional.

This would seem to suggest that the parts of the brain that perform this filtering process are essential to our wellbeing. (Indeed, one way of looking at certain kinds of 'madness', would be to say it is caused by this filtering function not working properly.) Yet dolphins can reportedly 'see' inside bodies, producing sonar images to assess the health of another for instance, using vibrations, and I remember reading in the 70's, how the Russians had trained children to 'see' through their elbows (Sheila Ostrander and Lyn Schroeder again). Only recently, experiments found Octopus can see with their skin, through a light-sensitive pigment called Opsin; which 'seeing', through what are called 'chromatophores', *may be controlled without using the brain.* Opsin may also detect vibrations, suggesting it is present in other senses apart from vision. From all this it becomes clear how little we know of this amazing organism called a body!

The truth is this mixing-up of our senses contains a potential for participating in a greater reality. Take hunter-gatherers living by their ability to track animals, for instance. You can imagine how useful it would be if you could *feel* an animal's movement in your body and not have to depend on hearing them. Or if you could *see* the sounds they make; this could amplify the ability to know what is making the sound and where it is coming from. *And this is, in fact, precisely what these people do!* The people who are most able to track animals skilfully are descended from tribal peoples, like the San, the African Kalahari 'bushmen' and native Australian and North and South Americans; people whose ancestors lived in a time when these abilities were not only seen as natural – taken for granted even – but were recognised for their value. In that sense, we could say that these people have an ability to relate to life in a deeper way, on a far broader scale than we do, because of their understanding that they themselves are part of the whole of life. They don't separate life as we have learned to do, into nature and us. Nor do they rely on their mind to tell them what life is about and how to live it. *And this is a radical difference*.

Seen from the perspective of our so-called 'evolution', the tribal view of life is usually dismissed as based on ignorance and superstition. Once again, we have learned to deny so much of this greater reality because it can't be grasped (and thereby explained and exploited) by the mind. Yet in doing this, we have opened up the possibility of atrophy: that is, that these abilities – if not attended to – may die out (disappear from the collective gene pool perhaps?) or, at the very least remain unused, leaving us with a very lopsided way of perceiving and responding to life.

What *this* implies is that the whole way we have come to see life, in terms of 'evolution' and 'progress' may be at fault. Rather than a forward progression it may be that useful, *if not essential* abilities are being lost; that, as we develop and come to rely on one aspect, so we lose another. Could it be that by overusing the intellect and our mental abilities, we are damaging or even destroying other essential human qualities? I guess we will find out. In the meantime there are some good people out there, like Jon Young, the man who teaches intuitive tracking skills, that give space to re-claiming, developing and preserving – and hence re-valuing – these marvellous abilities.

Coming back to this term 'synesthesia', the tricky thing about it is what it implies: that it is not normal, but rather the result of a (presumed) fault in the wiring of the brain. We think that our senses *should be* perceived separately, that this separation is how things need to be. But again, is this actually true? Or is it yet one more way in which the separating mind disconnects us from the whole? Because words, used as labels, define and separate, whereas life itself is an open invitation to recognise the wholeness inherent in everything *and to participate in this recognition through connection*. Not only is the mind ignorant of this but, in most Western cultures anyway (as we saw in the second chapter) the mind is venerated. We worship the mind as we once worshipped God. Mind demands our full attention – *it demands that it is believed before anything else*. Everything else is labelled ignorance, fantasy, wishful thinking or superstition.

In the seeing of the intuitive body-Being *as a multifaceted organ of perception that can reveal truth*, this whole belief structure is challenged. We start to realise that in making a separation between the senses there is a danger of losing sight of their true function: *this being as a source of connection through which direct reception and transmission of reality takes place, both within and as part of, the whole*. And here is where highly sensitive people can serve a useful function as transmitters. From the periphery of humanity's world view, sensitives can more easily tune in to what lies beyond the mind's idea of the 'real' world, the material world. Such people may function as an early warning system about threats to our survival, like the highly sensitive horses.

Even more interesting and profound: we may serve an as yet unclear role in connecting, opening to and possibly bridging an unfolding of consciousness – an awakening if you like – on a greater scale than is currently apparent or even imagined. Who knows? But there is a sense that this capacity for a high degree of sensitivity has a far deeper and more radical application; implying that – *to the extent that the ego is seen through* – so highly sensitive people can serve a valuable function.

It may even be that these intuitive senses offer the only true way of relating directly with the mystery of existence – of life itself. And while the mind is busy trying to abstract, separate and define reality on *its* terms; interpreting according to its programming and trying to squeeze reality into concepts (so it can think about and talk about them), it may be that all the while a quiet shift is taking place: a re-alignment of focus following an inner direction that is beyond the mind's grasp. This is because, to re-use the analogy of trying to catch water in a sieve, reality escapes definition.

If life and reality were only a giant jigsaw puzzle or a game of chess, mind would be happy. It could order and sort, compare and classify; scheme, calculate, manoeuvre and do what it was designed to do, and do it well. However reality, the domain of Being, cannot be defined in any way at all. In the seeing of this, in the recognition our intuitive senses can bring to us, lies freedom: freedom from so much unnecessary suffering, freedom to live what we are as fully responsive body-Beings playing in the field of form, which itself lies within the form*less*. Then, sensitivity can be applied to receiving and sharing this deeper reality which lies beyond words, which needs neither explanation nor justification because – when illusion is finally seen through – this reality simply *is. Then we see that it has been here all along, present: just waiting to be realised.*

Home-play
1. Cleaning the Aura or Subtle-energy field (See diagram)
- Standing with the feet planted comfortably on the floor, about the same distance apart as the pelvis, bring the arms up (elbows parallel) placing palms of the hands flat on top of the head (see fig1).
- Now, draw palms down over the face and neck (maintaining contact the whole time, especially when passing under the throat) down the body to the feet and let palms rest on the ground.
- Next bring the right arm across the throat placing palm onto the back of the neck. Bring this hand down over the shoulder and arm, bringing the thumb onto the inside, so it cleans palm. Shake out this hand (see fig2).
- Repeat with left hand on right side (see fig3).
- Lastly, reach up as high as is comfortable on the back and bring the hands down to the feet with palms resting on the ground (see fig4).

Highly sensitive people and the loneliness of an unshared reality

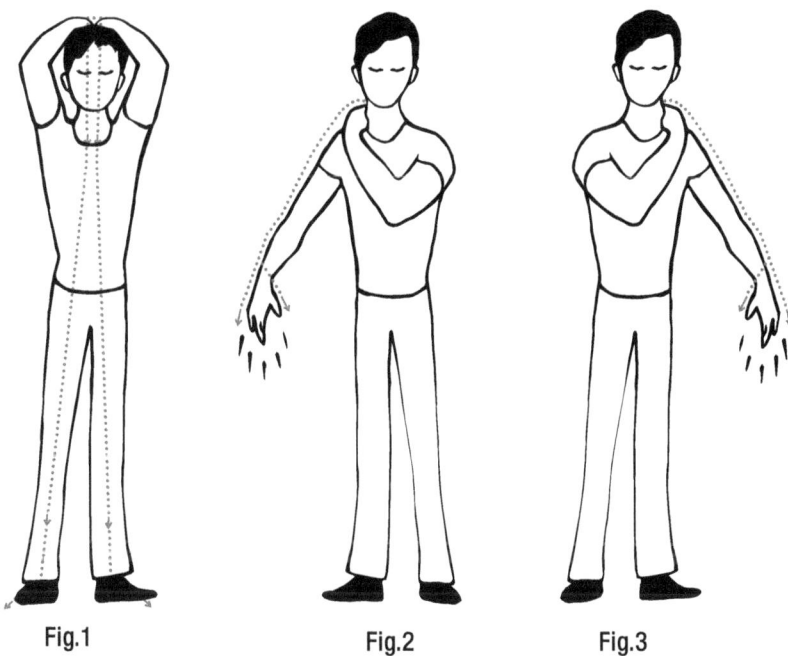

Fig.1   Fig.2   Fig.3

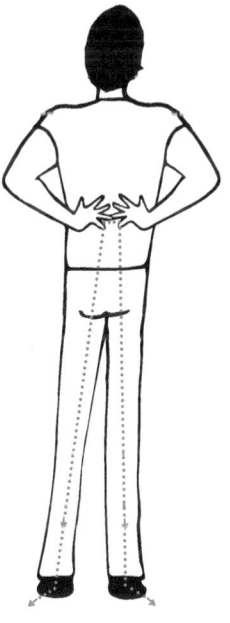

Fig.4

Do these movements slowly. Each time you make contact with the ground, or shake out your hands, feel a sense of the earth sucking up the negative energy. Imagine your palms as being like the nozzles on a vacuum cleaner and visualise your aura as covered in a sticky, negative residue you have picked up, including other people's thoughts, feelings and energy; that these nozzles can suck this up, and the earth is a vast compost heap for processing this.

The best time to do this exercise is after an argument or confrontation, after being in a crowded place, and last thing at night before you go to bed. (If you are in a public place you can always do this in a toilet). Make it a habit, like cleaning your teeth.

Body of the beloved

'If anything is sacred, the human body is sacred' ~ Walt Whitman, Leaves of Grass

'The physical body knows how to come to rest. Allow the activity of mind to respond to the body by settling down towards the earth, following a thread of grounding' ~ Mukti

'Walk as if you were kissing the earth with your feet' ~ Thích Nhät Hanh

We have all learned to take the body for granted. But still the question remains: what exactly is a body, really? What is its purpose, beyond our biological, psychological and scientific understanding? Coming from the perspective of limited mind, it is not really surprising that we assume and accept and believe that this is all it is – just a vehicle to allow us to operate and survive in the world. But what if this is not what the body is at all? Even though it contains these abilities? *What if the body is actually the instrument through which spirit expresses itself in form?* From this deeper recognition, the body is seen as sacred: a sacred channel that allows Being (spirit, God, reality, life, whatever term you prefer) to converse with itself; to explore, experiment and express through all the many senses.

There are so many forms to play with, such as dance, singing, sex and, of course, a whole repertoire of feelings and sensations. I can say that the body is indeed our temple. So listen to it, nurture it, worship within its many capacities to receive, engage with and celebrate the truth. Because it is through the body, through *form,* that truth can be expressed; can express itself. So it is completely natural to love and honour this body, to cherish this that allows us to experience life. And even when it is time to leave we can be grateful for all it has made possible.

The body is not only a wondrous instrument; when we listen to it we can rediscover the rhythm of life. For a species that has lost touch with so much of its innate potential, this is powerful stuff *because it is through the body that we come fully alive.* This means able to respond, to take part in the conversation; and not only that, but to do so in a way that is in harmony with the whole instead of reacting against this flow. I remember once asking a spiritual teacher about responsibility, which I was finding confusing. It felt like a concept loaded with a sense of heaviness and burden, related to duty and obligation, inducing feelings of guilt when not obeyed. The answer I received was this: 'Response-ability is simply the ability to respond' and I found this wonderfully freeing.

If you don't grasp what is being said here it's easy to see it as just a clever play on words – or worse, to use it to override inner promptings, feelings about something you are doing or not doing that doesn't *feel* right. What the ability to respond freely is pointing to is actually profound. It means being able to respond *without distortion,* able to act from a spontaneous pull of Being. As most people not only can't do this, but are unaware of this possibility, acting with true responsibility often isn't an option: hence the introduction of morality and the murky areas of 'conscience' and guilt which the mind uses to enforce this. And yes, an intention to take care and act with consideration towards others – *in the absence of this ability for true response* – is a really great idea! Imagine living together as we do, the even worse messes we could get into without this.

So it makes absolute sense to get to know the body; to get to know how it functions on the many subtle and often hidden levels it operates on, and to make a practice of listening in. It can be surprising to realise just what a rich variety of responses a body is capable of: an instance of this being the reflex to hold on, to tighten up and close off. I mention this because once you become aware of these responses, they become useful indicators of your true emotional state – and hence your real inner response – enabling you to stay in touch with yourself. This is what is meant by being 'consciously' aware. Also, these responses can greatly affect your health, so becoming conscious of them brings the opportunity to change them. For instance, instead of tightening up, to relax and let go, to open *and take a breath!* And beyond all of this to let *in,* to *receive;* because the body is a receptacle.

When it is open and flowing, without impediment from a conditioned mind, the body expresses spirit naturally. This is its nature, this is the body-Being. The body is not really separate from spirit – nothing ever is or can be – from the perspective of the deepest truth: it just appears to be when we see it as only a biological phenomenon. The reality is that without a perception of separateness (from other bodies and everything we see as being 'outside' these) we wouldn't be able to function at all. The problem arises when we extend this sense of separation to include *our essence*; because it is this essence, or wholeness, that extends beyond the physical appearance: this essence is what I call Being. And Being permeates life and can be heard and felt through the body – hence the term body-Being. It is the body that allows the illusion of separation to be acted out. *Without a body, there would be no sense of self:* nothing to do or not do; and also, nothing to lose or gain. Ego would have no playground!

When I speak of the 'body beloved', this wholeness is what I am referring to. When this is *seen,* there is no possibility of discounting this miraculous phenomenon as 'just a biological entity'. Indeed, it gives us the means by which we can express spirit freely, once we have seen through the illusion of ego and the distortions of a conditioned mind: then we can simply *be.* Sadly, for many people, the way we relate to our body is tangled up with egoic wants and needs;

becoming something we want to look a certain way in order to feel good about ourselves: it has be a certain shape with muscles bulging here or curves there, and no fat please! The truth is, we pay most attention to it when it fails in this, or gets sick and starts to collapse. Which is why, for many older people, it becomes the main source of their attention, and often their conversation as a result. Then doctors and hospitals, pills and cures, aches and pains become the main topics – that so much of this suffering is caused through disconnection from our Being-ness is not seen. So the body gets abused and neglected, blamed when it goes wrong and forgotten about when it's performing okay. What a shame! And this disconnection starts so young.

There are many people in the spiritual world who like to emphasise that we are not the body. Spiritual traditions like Advaita state clearly 'you are not the mind, nor the feelings, nor the body.' What they are talking about here is *identification* – believing that the mind, feelings and physical body is *who you are*. So at certain times, for certain people, this may help them to dis-identify. However, for the vast majority this approach can be profoundly unhelpful (especially for Westerners, who so often live disconnected from their body anyway). This is because this teaching is often interpreted to mean the body is in the way of spiritual 'development', and of course this is totally false. In reality we are everything, so how can we *not* be the body? Over the years of my practice, I have seen just how incredibly valuable the body is, providing a form through which we can reconnect with true reality. And what is spirituality if not reality? Not the reality of a conditioned mind, as in the expression 'the real world', but the reality of what is *really* here, of everything that we truly are.

It is through the body, with its capacity to sense, feel, listen and intuit, that we have perhaps the most direct access to what is real. Especially when just sitting silently, *we have the capacity to be in touch with the deep current of life that flows through everything*; and the physical body, along with its subtle energy-field, is a potential transmitter *of* this reality (it's very subtle what I am alluding to here). This transmission is subject to blockages and distortion by (you guessed it!) the conditioned mind. And this is where the supreme value of *seeing* comes in – seeing as awareness. Learning to trust this seeing so we can see through these blockages and distortions. In later chapters we will look at this further, but for now I want to talk about how these capacities of the body for connecting and transmitting intuitive reality can be accessed and used to permeate and dissolve these distortions.

The primacy of touch

Firstly, I want to talk about touch, because this is hugely underrated and massively misunderstood in our culture. *Touch has extraordinary power.* It has a direct, subtle and far deeper capacity to open and help us receive, to move and connect us with the body-Being in direct communion, *than almost any other approach*. Much of this book is written with reference to touch, but not simply the physical kind. We think of touch as being what we do when we touch something or someone *physically,* but the word 'touch' carries a much wider meaning. We touch and are touched by words and what they evoke, as in poetry – we are touched internally. We are touched by shapes and colours – and not only in the form of what we call art. We are touched by sounds – what we call 'music' is just a part of this sonar repertoire, an arrangement of sounds made by instruments, including voices. We are touched by movement, and here again what we call 'dance' is just one form of movement, a word used to describe this particular form. We can even be touched by smells and tastes, strange as that may sound, and also spaces; and by light and shade, warmth and coolness and so on. All these forms of touch have a subtle, feeling dimension: they connect with the heart. *And the interesting thing about this is that all and any of these can pierce beneath our habitual defences.*

I have seen how Being comes into form most powerfully through physical touch. In fact – and I can't stress this enough – touch is one of the most valuable forms of communication. We have forgotten the importance of this yet it is such a powerful way of speaking. Above all it says 'Here you are and here I am, and we are meeting together'; it *includes* and reminds us of our connection with one another, of our belonging, and it can give a sense of reassurance, caring, affection and love. Touch communicates directly with Being *and it does not lie*. We know when someone touches us whether they are sincere, what they really feel: so touch is a powerful truth-teller. And people suffer greatly from the lack of it, especially in our society.

I once met a woman back in the Seventies called Jean Liedloff who had written a book called *The Continuum Concept*. She had been out in the rainforests of South America amongst remote tribal people and found their lives to be very harmonious and contented. She noticed how, whenever they were together, they always chose to sit close to someone, how they were always touching each other. Unlike much of Western society where, if you enter a public place with other people in it – be it a cafe, cinema, bus or train, people often choose to sit as far from each other as possible. Touching is not acceptable, unless there is no choice because of the crowds (the exception being when people drink alcohol in a communal space, maybe a pub or club, where their inhibitions get released).

Anyway, when I met the author I was surprised to see this very tall woman, in a black trouser suit with glamorous long blonde hair who, I found out, had once been a model. I don't know what I expected – someone in khaki shorts, looking tough like a man? She wrote about the importance of touch and her book was eagerly snapped up by people who seemed to be amazed by this revelation: that touch is actually good for you, even a necessary condition for a healthy life!

Most of us experience some degree of touching others in our daily life, accidental or intentional, wanted or unwanted – unless we live as a hermit. We use it or avoid it but rarely do we consider what is happening when we touch, the fine levels of communication it allows for. We may touch spontaneously: nationalities like the French, for example, touch a lot. I once had a French boyfriend and found it amazing and wonderful how easily and naturally he used touch – so very different to the English!

In fact, if you look around the world you see each country has its own customs around touching that may be linked to religious attitudes, as in cultures where men only touch men and women only women, except within marriage or the family. Outside of these cultural barriers, those who live in warm climates tend to use touch more frequently than those from Northern and colder countries, and the effects of this frequency of touch are visible; there is a *comfortability* with touch that is evident in the ease with which they move around each other and the relaxation of their bodies. Most people use touch freely with children or lovers; here we allow ourselves to follow our impulses and we usually cuddle our offspring, at least when they are small – this is seen as normal and therefore acceptable behaviour. Yet even here some cultures evince inhibitions.

Standing outside a bar in a little mountain village in Southern Spain, I was struck one day by a group of men and boys, of varying ages, all gathered around a baby in a pram. No matter how young or how old, they were *all engaged*, all interested and openly showing this. In the country of my birth, England, few young boys or men show interest in babies until they have their own and if I – even as a woman – gaze into a strangers' pushchair, I sometimes encounter an instinctively hostile response from the mother. This is sad but also understandable, with cases of child abduction or abuse so frequently reported in the papers. We live in societies where many are divorced from their bodies and where, in extreme cases, natural sexuality has become distorted, creating actions that have led to touch being seen as a threat. Then anger and fear and revulsion are provoked by all kinds of inappropriate forms of behaviour, from minor to extremes of deviance, where tangled and desperate desires and addictions override any concern for others. This is such an indictment of a deep disconnect in society, something we barely notice let alone question. And yet it doesn't have to be like this, because touch is a powerful means of bringing healing and even transformation.

Do you remember the words I quoted of pope Frances? 'How much the world needs tenderness today'? It is so true: *everyone needs to receive tenderness and to feel accepted*. When we hear this it feels so obvious, doesn't it? Yet it rarely gets said. This is enormously healing and through the hands this can be given and received, even from the hands of a stranger. It transcends all barriers of our apparent differences: we don't need to be a parent, or even a friend, to give through touch. Touch has such great power. Perhaps you have experienced a situation where touch worked to calm someone or to alleviate pain, where nothing else could? It can be very moving to witness how a simple gesture can soothe or lessen anxiety where words cannot; and when someone dies and another is grieving, touch provides the most profound source of solace.

Indeed, touch can be used in so many ways: to pacify, to reassure, to lower fear and aggression. Most precious of all, it reminds us that we all *belong*, we are all part of one Being-ness, there really is no separation; so then our body can not only relax, it can become a receptacle for this knowing, this acknowledgement. Reaching beneath all defences, touch makes us permeable; we imbibe the truth even though this may not be recognised by the conscious mind. Love is present, is transmitted, and with this comes a resurrection – *a felt sense of something beyond daily experience*. No need for embarrassment; on this level of profound unspoken communion we are one, something is remembered, affirmed, verified.

Using touch as a means of communication you can tell someone they are accepted, forgiven, desired and loved far more powerfully than by using words. Words can be so clumsy, and words can also deceive and betray. Look at the advertising industry: that's what it does. People train in psychology in order to earn a living through learning how to manipulate others, by evoking their dreams and promising things that will never deliver. Through this, we are betrayed and we betray ourselves, over and over again: trust is broken, our weaknesses exploited. If you just had *that*, you would then feel *this*. Maybe, for a few moments – and then? Then you need something else.

The pleasure in getting what we hoped would do it for us wears off and we are left somewhere unconsciously shamed and bereft. And this speaks to our need to discover who it is that wants, and what it is that remains unsatisfied when we got it. With touch there are no lies: even if it's someone hitting someone or hurting someone – as not all touch is wanted or pleasant. Children pinch and poke each other, partners may hit one another, of course touch can be violent; but I am talking here about using touch to bring us closer, to dive beneath the plethora of words to where reality is simply known, felt, recognised.

Using touch in a session (what is called 'massage')

I used to teach a class I called *Intuitive Massage,* but it was really about touch itself and accessing the heart and Being through touch. Because fingers not only touch, *they can listen*; they receive subtle information – as indeed does the skin all over the body. Through touch the body has a magnificent capacity for communication. So, a light pressure, a deep stroke, a pause: all this becomes the language of communication through touch, through the skin. Attention is on what happens when we touch another and, above all, on how being fully present *and listening when we touch* allows our hands to move from a space of communion.

It can become a kind of sacrament: we are creating a sacred space together that includes the spiritual and invites Being to take charge.

The intention in these classes was to include subtle, intuitive knowing, so the hands could interpret this guidance spontaneously. When people aren't taught methods and techniques, they experience for themselves how the power of giving and receiving touch from this source allows others to move into all kinds of spaces: spaces that are often new, opening and sometimes even confronting. This is because the more present we are the deeper the touch goes, and this brings a state of vulnerability and openness *where trust is absolutely essential*. However, trust cannot be relied upon unless the giver is aware of any ego-needs that want to interfere with this simple act of communion. So bringing conscious awareness into touch is itself a learning; not a learning about getting it 'right' or 'wrong', just about holding a loving *intention*: following this and then seeing, sensing and feeling what happens. Because in using touch in this way, what takes place can be far more than simply 'giving a massage' in the accepted use of this phrase.

Over the years I have seen how many people, even those using touch every day in their work, remain unaware of the most important aspect of any form of using touch, and that is *connection*. Without this, there is no way to listen to and follow what the receiver – as a unique being and in that particular moment – needs, as they need it. This connection happens right at the start and I find beginning in silence is paramount. So first, take a moment to be present with yourself, and then allow the other to 'feel you out' before you touch them. This may sound strange but animals do this all the time. They do it instinctively and they do it *consciously*; it is an important part of their intelligence so they use it; whereas most of us Westernised human animals have forgotten or blocked this ability consequently, if we do it at all, we do it unconsciously.

Clothes are a form of protection and before getting on the bench the receiver is required to remove most of these, thus exposing their body in a way that puts them in a position of vulnerability; and even before touching, the energy fields of both giver and receiver are interconnecting. As everyone has defences these will limit the amount we can receive, so taking time at the beginning is essential. Here words may be useful to help the person let go and relax: reminding them there is nothing they need do except relax and receive whatever is needed in the moment; reassuring them by telling them to say if something doesn't feel okay and to ask if they want something. I usually suggest they tell their thinking mind to take a walk on the beach, and to just stay as present as they can to their own bodily experience, and following my hands can help with this.

This issue of trust is paramount. It is surprising how we can receive a massage, especially if it is focussed on muscular release or uses lots of technique, and still maintain our defences. Nothing wrong with that if it is what you want, but for people who are seeking to go deeper then these learned defences just get in the way. So time is needed and the slower the touch, the deeper it goes. Have you ever stopped to appreciate how precious this letting-in process can be? Who it is you are going to touch? It's like entering any private space. Would you just walk into a stranger's house without asking permission? Let alone enter their bedroom? So even if they themselves are not fully aware of it, it is still a sacred trust.

It may help to imagine your client as a small defenceless child, or someone you know and love. Then you will intuitively *feel* the value of bringing your hands down slowly, making contact very lightly and gently, like a butterfly landing on a flower, before increasing the pressure. Here, once again, waiting a moment with your hands still for this checking-out process to complete and the connection to be made: because people know intuitively how present you are and where you are coming from. If they sense a disconnect, they simply withhold, *even if this is unconscious*; so we are talking about a very fine process of tuning-in here. And this can only happen to the extent that you are relaxed within yourself. Like anything else, touch can be a doing, or it can simply happen – a spontaneous movement of Being which is subtle, intuitive and requires the full attention of your senses *and has no place for the mind.*

Then touching is like a conversation: we simply respond to what is there. So pauses happen, pressure is increased and decreased, patterns of movement occur and may be repeated. The mind cannot help in this because it doesn't have the ability to tune in in this way: this requires *empathy*, the domain of the heart. If I try to think of what to do when I am working I am lost. Once again, I have no idea what I am doing but I know exactly how to do it! (Rather like a mantra, just saying these words can allow something profound to penetrate and you can explore the meaning of this directly.)

For most people, using touch with another in some form of massage or bodywork feels too scary without some kind of instruction to hold on to, so they learn methods and techniques to use as guidance. The problem here is this listening to the mind inhibits the capacity to listen to something else. We are once again involved in doing things the way others have taught us: back in school with rules and procedures that ignore this tuning-in. Then – because most of us have learned to reference the mind and may feel very insecure without this – we override our own intuitive capacity; and in so doing affirm that we are not capable of this, it cannot be trusted, the mind knows best. Our conditioning once again gets in the way. It is true, it can be very challenging to just sit with a body and see what happens, to allow ourselves to explore and experiment. Obviously this is best practised first in a workshop situation or somewhere where the receiver feels safe and willing to offer their body for this process of experimentation.

What I discovered from following these intuitive movements is that I would do something with no idea as to *why*, and only afterwards could I see this. For example, I noticed that I felt drawn to work on the back first and then turn the receiver over to work on their front. Later, I realised this was because people feel most vulnerable with their belly exposed, so it came as a result of an empathetic intuiting about safety and trust. Then I noticed at the end of a session how I always found myself folding the receiver's hands over their belly. I realised later that *this was a way of giving them back to themselves*; that after spending a length of time in intimate communion, in which they allowed me access to their body, trusted me and received what was given, I was withdrawing from the conversation if you like; the session was completed and their body and energy field once again inviolably their own.

Something else I noticed was that most strokes ended on a downward movement and that at the end of a session I was moved to hold their feet. Once again, I realised only later that this was about grounding, as most people are so caught up in their heads they have difficulty with this. In all of these instances this was a *felt* realisation, as was the knowing that, as at the beginning of a touch session, the conclusion also needs to be made with clarity, love and sensitivity. In fact, this whole moving into and out of someone else's territory in this way requires not only their unspoken permission, *but the integrity that comes from being fully present*.

Techniques have teachable rules. Swedish massage for instance, teaches that all strokes must be brought towards the heart as that is where the blood flows (and someone once mentioned that a person might suffer a heart attack if you don't do this). Is this true? It is certainly *believed* and this belief comes from a place of mind, of fear, and this interferes with the knowing of Being. I am not saying here that all strokes must go downward: *the truth is there are no rules*. The lovely thing about working in this way is that if you are fully present, you can just surrender and allow the hands to move as they wish.

There is something of great significance that can happen through the use of touch during this time of focussing attention on the body with someone, when both physical and non-physical aspects of the body are included, and this is *integration*. Sadly, this aspect too often goes unrecognised. For people who use words this means that to whatever has been opened up, moved, seen and so on, *touch can bring a time and place to integrate this in the body, along with its energy field*. For myself, I only experience a session as complete when touch is included; I find this fundamental to integration. This is not to say other ways of working are not useful; obviously they are, and in some situations touch can't be included for a variety of reasons; some people simply aren't drawn to using touch and others are resistant to receiving it.

In practical terms, more time is needed and a bench, with space for it. I find I need an hour and a half for a session (nearly double the fifty minutes of the usual talking session) of which a third is spent on the bench. So is this maybe – at least partly – why so few people seem to combine talking 'therapies' with touch? Yet the principal obstacle to opening up with another is our defences and here establishing trust through touch can be such a powerful way in. The irony is that, in this very process of defence, many people retreat into their minds and become so disconnected and out of touch with their bodies that they actually fear touch – on the one hand we long for closeness, but on the other we are resistant, especially to the touch of strangers. So clearly there is value in combining both talking and touch in one session, as a help in establishing trust and safety. In fact when I thought about it, I realised I have only ever done one or two sessions without touch and when I did, I noticed a sense of a lack of completion; what had been aroused had not been fully grounded in the body-Being: almost as though the body and its energy-field felt left out!

For me, everything began with touch: initially, this was how I knew to connect with people in a way they might find useful. I had received the inner knowing to just put my hands on someone's body and see what happened. I had done a weekend course in Esalen massage and this provided a familiarity with the body without imposing strict forms of 'how to' touch. In those days this, combined with a short crammer course in anatomy and physiology, allowed us to obtain an ITEC certificate (which I have never needed to use). Things are more complicated today and some countries don't allow people to practise any form of bodywork without some kind of recognised accreditation, so it can be hard to avoid learning techniques. The important thing is not to get caught up in these and ideally, if you can find a course of some kind of intuitive massage where presence is focussed and there is permission to explore and experiment, you can, in your own time, learn to trust Being.

I want to say a word here about Anne Parks, a woman who played a significant part in all this. Although I have said I have not been trained, I did receive much inspiration from this wonderful woman and her very fine and intuitive work. I met her through a dear friend who functioned as an important catalyst in my life at that time. This was the late Seventies, when London was full of people offering all kinds of alternative ways of getting to know and express what was on the inside. One day I mentioned I had an interest in colour and he suggested I explore colour healing with this exceptionally gifted woman from California. Next thing I knew, I found myself booked into an advanced healing workshop through a misunderstanding. In walked this elfin woman with a cap of fine silvery-blonde hair, slanting, catlike eyes and wearing a long purple dress. After staring at me for a moment she said 'Well you are here now so you might as well stay!'

Later, during an individual session, she told me that I did indeed have a remarkably powerful intuitive gift and it was absolutely useless until I did some work on myself, as I was hopelessly ungrounded and my emotions were all over the place. What a gift! She sent me off for weekly counselling (where I talked the therapist round in circles and failed to move deeper), weekly intuitive massage (which was wonderful and taught me a lot about what I liked to receive) and I had subtle energy sessions with Anne herself every six weeks. I also joined her group for a year and later on attended a few classes with her teacher, Bob Moore, a true master of subtle energy. A little while after this a gifted healer, Andrew Watson, said to me 'You can wait forever to be ready to work with others. Why don't you just begin and see what happens?' So I did.

Some exceptional experiences using touch

When I first started working with touch, various individuals came along who brought me some quite strange and challenging experiences. One day, when I was working alone at home, a youngish man arrived and when I looked at him I saw this terrible black, lumpy shadow completely distorting one side of his face. I had no idea what this was but it felt scary. I was nervous about working with him but didn't know how to refuse, so I asked him to lie on the bench. During the session I felt quite frightened but there was nothing to do but stay present and trust. At the end, standing holding his feet, I felt something dark slither down my legs and disappear earthwards. I have no idea what it was. Negative energy? A malign entity? Anybody's guess, but he certainly looked much lighter and brighter when he left and, as he didn't come back, I have no way of knowing how this affected him in the longer term. I washed my hands, cleansed my aura and felt totally fine, unaffected, not drained at all – and nothing like that has happened since.

Another time an unremarkable little man, perhaps in his fifties, who told me he worked as a cleaner and lived alone, walked in. As we exchanged a few words it became apparent he was hoping for something else, some kind of sexual relief. I said I was sorry but that wasn't the kind of work I did and offered to let him leave without paying. He apologised profusely and said he would like to try my kind of massage anyway. At the end of this he sat up looking like a new born baby, his grey, wispy hair sticking up all round his head, and beaming at me said '*That* was what I really wanted, a caring touch. I just didn't know where to go to find it!' On another occasion a man in his late sixties turned up and told me a bit about himself. He lived in a room in a men's hostel where they were not allowed to have women in their rooms or visitors after 10 pm. He had no living family and had never been in a relationship. In his childhood he had spent *ten months in a wardrobe*, hiding from the Gestapo in Holland during the war. He got up on the bench and as soon as I touched him he broke into great shattering sobs.

Then there was the day one of the ugliest young men I have ever seen laid himself down. He had eyebrows like black spiders, his skin was sallow and he was covered from head to toe in spots and pimples. As I worked, I noticed how all my reactions to his body just fell away; I not only found myself feeling comfortable working with him, I got to see how meaningless this judging of the outer appearances of people is. In fact, I felt a great tenderness, recognising that he must have incurred so much rejection because of the way he looked. Over the years I have had some stunningly beautiful people, of both sexes, come for sessions, and noticed that what makes them attractive to work with has little to do with their outer appearance; it has to do with whether their body is occupied or not. If they are living in their minds – as so many do – the body often lacks a sense of vitality. Then slowly, as it is worked with, the body begins to wake up; it radiates a sense of aliveness and you can feel a gradual wholeness and harmony as the different aspects come into balance (this is true for the subtle energy-field too).

All of these sessions I mention were challenging, in different ways, and it seemed as if these people came to teach *me* – I even wondered if I should give them their money back! There were other kinds of challenges in the initial years, but later on, most of the people who came seemed to be increasingly ready and able to open, let go and move deeper. The way it seems to work, as far as I can see, is that people tend to come according to where you are in yourself. Which means that, as we move deeper, able to be more clear and present, so the people who come are mostly those who are ready and able to take advantage of this.

The subtle energy-field

In speaking about subtle energy we are again venturing into the land of no boxes, no real need for labels. Having acknowledged the reality of psychic experience and how this differs from intuitive in a previous chapter, I prefer not to clutter direct experience with expectations from the mind, coming from labels attached to different kinds of psychic activity. This leaves us free to explore *what is actually here* – but often goes unseen – for ourselves. I have said that life or Being-ness resides everywhere and that there is a world of subtle energy that emanates from all living things; that this is responsive and can communicate and not only be *heard* or *felt,* but also *touched.*

Remember what we said about synesthesia? There is a universal common language which does not restrict itself to just one sense, such as hearing sounds. Nor does it need to come through the mind as thought. So when mind asks 'How do you know all this is so?', as I have just said, *it can be directly apprehended through the psychic and intuitive senses.* That doesn't mean I can offer a tidy explanation that will satisfy a sceptical mind, obsessed by a need for 'scientific evidence' before it can include something in its limited version of reality. In this vast, intuitive reality I am writing about we can sense many things: including subtle energy, but also a presence *or even presence itself* (we will talk about presence in the chapter on spirituality) in ways that the mind has no clue about. Even the word 'sense' itself has so many connotations and barely-glimpsed mysteries, as does the word 'energy' – whether we describe it as subtle or not.

That said, there are some interesting new discoveries in the interface between conventional science and alternative approaches to using energy to heal. For instance, in his book *The Genie in Your Genes – Epigenetic Medicine and the New Biology of Intention,* Dawson Church talks about the body's connective tissue system as a giant liquid crystal semiconductor, which insight he attributes to James Oschman and his book *Energy Medicine in Therapeutics and Performance*; and there are many others exploring this field of 'energy medicine'. In fact science is beginning to recognise the value of including more intuitive, less-structured approaches and it is not my intention to dismiss such investigations. I would simply point out that they are based on a need for factual evidence that can be proven and is acceptable within a mind-based discipline. And this is different to the focus of this book.

There have been individuals 'working with' various forms of energy since time immemorial. What is perhaps more common now is people seeking to use their experience to become conscious and connected into a deeper mystery, what I am calling Being. And this is something which these approaches cannot touch. So while physics struggles to understand and define, Osho has this to say about the world of energy: *'The universe is an expansion of energy, and life is the crystallisation of this energy. What we see as matter, what we see as stone, is also energy. What is seen as life, what is experienced as thought, what is felt like consciousness is also a transformation of energy. The whole cosmos – whether it is the waves of the sea or the pine trees of the forest or the grains of sand or the stars in the skies or that which is within us – all are manifestations of the same energy in infinite forms and ways (...) If you search correctly you will find that the centre of life is everywhere and it is expanding everywhere. But to know it, to experience it, it is essential that we ourselves become energy that is tremendously alive.'*

To keep it simple, the physical body is constructed within a field of subtle energy, and another powerful way of working with touch involves interacting *with* this energy, which I find happens during the time set aside for physical bodywork, on the bench. Each body has a series of distinct, egg-shaped layers of subtle energy, one within the other (like one of those Russian dolls), that radiate out to varying distances. Now the mind will look for maps and instructions here, but in working with this subtle energy, I soon realised that nothing is fixed. I find things change, not just from person to person but moment to moment, so I have learnt to just let the hands do what they do and to trust that, when intuitively guided by Being, they will do what is needed.

If you want more information there are plenty of books written about this so-called Aura, subtle or electromagnetic energy-field. Many of these were written in the late nineteenth and early part of the twentieth century, and what I find delightful is the way they frequently contradict each other! They differ as to the position of the energy centres, or chakras, as to their number, colour and so on. There are many systems and instructions about how to work with these if you want to study them. But as I keep saying, if you can let yourself explore free from concepts you open yourself to direct experience. And this then allows for a deep, intuitive response grounded in the moment of contact. Unencumbered with thought, Being can enter.

During this time of subtle energy work, I often 'see' colours and sometimes images; I may register sounds or, very occasionally, words, and sometimes I sense presences. These may include people, animals or various scenes, some seemingly set in the past. When described, these may be recognised to be a much loved pet, or someone the person had a strong loving and perhaps guiding relationship with, often a grandparent. I never ask for these experiences, nor do I probe for 'information' about them, or attempt to explain or classify them in any way. I simply notice they tend to offer comfort and support, especially to those who received little of this elsewhere in their childhood; or they may invoke a memory or a response of some kind. Sometimes people say things like 'When you were touching my head, I felt another pair of hands touching my feet.' Again, I have no idea – *and no interest* – in questioning who or what this may be; it's not my business. Am I aware of it? Sometimes, but it's not where I put my attention. Some people believe an entity – like the archangel Gabriel for instance – has come along to lend a hand. This seems to me just another invitation to mind to enter where it has no place so 'Who is it who wants to know?' is a useful question to ask here.

At times I ask people if they themselves can also see colours or experience a variety of sensations while I am working with their subtle energy. Why do I do this? Because I feel it is important to encourage and validate what we *all* have a latent capacity to perceive. Here again we meet our conditioning and its effects, because most people hold a strong belief that *they can't do this*, even if they are open to others being able to. So what often happens when I ask is that they *try* to see, they make an effort with the mind, and this never works. You have to relax your vision and allow *what is already present to become visible,* to reveal itself. It's like a deer in the forest standing in the shadows: you only see it when you stop hunting for it.

As I said earlier, what I find over and over is that most people have learnt to ignore these subtle impressions of colours and so on. I have heard it repeated so often about how, as a child, when we noticed things like colours around other people, if we talked about this it was either denied or discounted, or we were laughed at and ridiculed, and how that left a wound. There is a fear from parents that their children may be strange and different from others, and children often take this on board. We become anxious and learn to not pay attention to what our eyes are showing us. We may even deny what we see because we have convinced ourselves that we can't see anything! Crazy, isn't it?

Because this 'seeing' is subtle and happens on the periphery of our vision, it is easy to ignore it and stay safely focussed on what we are accustomed to look for. That is, to stay within our usual mode of seeing, the mode we have learned, that is definable by a conditioned mind and therefore safe and acceptable. This is a great pity and it is only one example of how we do this. Then, in narrowing our focus on to what is seen as 'normal', we edit out a whole field of life and aliveness and, along with this, connection with Being. *We have all been trained in self-censorship* and – as long as this remains unconscious – we remain cut off from seeing what is true. We can no longer distinguish, and this means the door is left open for the vast quagmire of pseudo-psychic illusion to move in; we are ripe for those who wish to exploit the gullible or decry the validity of the genuine. And then of course, ego has a feast! Which is why encouraging people to recover their ability to see and sense subtle energy, and other such subtle realities, in a safe, grounded environment, can help them trust their own experience and expand into what is everyone's birth-right.

Spatial awareness

While talking about bodies and their ability to sense and feel, something else that we rarely notice or talk about is *spatial awareness* – that is, the effect on us of our physical relationship to the space we are in and people we are with. In fact our bodies are continuously responding to these subtle awarenesses, as I mentioned in an earlier chapter about the shapes of buildings. Perhaps you have noticed for yourself how different spaces affect you? For instance, take a large supermarket that maybe has a flat ceiling and is divided into long, rigid straight isles with rows of horizontal shelving.

Contrast this with how you feel inside a typical church, with its lofty arched ceiling, tall curved windows, round pulpit and empty space before the alter. Can you feel how one keeps you tense and the other inspires peacefulness? I remember reading in a book on geodesic domes by a man called Keith Critchlow (these were originally designed by the famous architect Buckminster Fuller), about how these domes create what he called 'psychological space'. And I could *feel* what he meant in my body, how the empty dome above us creates a sensation of freedom to expand energetically – what some people call 'soul space'.

Interestingly, our bodies don't just respond to spaces created by inanimate physical objects, but also to space between people, each with their subtle energy field. For example, at one time I had a boyfriend with a sports car which had bucket seats. We used to drive off somewhere together and without fail, within half an hour, we would be having an argument. Then one weekend, we hired a van for a workshop that had a long bench seat in the front and we didn't argue once! The difference? With the bucket seats we were locked into a rigid spatial relationship to one another, unable to alter this. With the bench seat, whoever was not driving could adjust the distance, could move away or move closer (this was in the days before seat belts became compulsory). And this flexibility makes a subtle but nonetheless significant difference to how we feel.

In some countries they have closer boundaries around people than others. Visiting Holland, for instance, I was struck by how physically close the Dutch come when they are with you, even complete strangers, whereas the English like to keep a good distance at all times! Unless it is friends or family, coming too close can be felt as intrusive or perceived as a threat. Obviously, if someone is being aggressive and looking for a fight, we may choose to move away and keep a distance. Conversely, if someone is upset we may move closer to comfort them.

So spatial awareness seems to be an instinctual awareness that can be affected by learned codes of behaviour. And yet, although the ability to alter this relationship of distance and closeness, to be able to regulate it, is an important part of maintaining comfortable, relaxed connections, too often this is not made possible. Modern life provides so many situations – like work for instance, or school – where people sit in rigid, fixed relationship with one another. Tension builds, we may start to feel stressed and irritable, or we may get a headache or even a migraine, but rarely do people recognise how this spatial constraint affects them on a daily basis. And this is a pity as, with awareness, much of this could be changed.

Crystals, candles, incense, music and plants

How do you respond to these being used in a session? For some people they represent airy-fairy mumbo jumbo and wacky New Age practices, while for others it is natural to include different life-forms that can enhance sensitivity and provide support. Ask the mind, and it immediately starts rummaging through all kinds of conceptual information and beliefs, so our view will depend on our conditioning; whereas if you directly *feel* and *sense* what these are bringing to a session there is no need to try to justify anything, the contribution is obvious.

Take crystals, for instance: it can be amazing what you find if you just stay open to what they can teach you, through direct attunement. I see the crystals I use as a family – they each have a different energy and, once again, if 'I' don't interfere, they get picked up and placed on someone's body as *they* choose (usually at the end of a session on the bench). I have learnt they like best to be cleaned in sea water and dried in sunlight, but this is not essential. And that's it. Why would I need to know more? Like what they have been named? Or other people's theories about their particular impact? (Which, as with auras, anyway differs.)

As I said earlier in talking about touch, there is an immediate intuitive response, which I can elaborate on afterwards with various insights. So with candles, I like to have one burning during a session. Why? I can say it gives a warm, friendly glow to the room, that it includes the element of fire, that it feels cleansing and that the flame is symbolic for the flame inside each of us. But deeper than all of this, their presence fulfils a *felt sense* of appropriateness. With incense, it too can be cleansing (that's why they burn it in churches) but also – why should dogs be the only ones who get to enjoy a life of smells? And plants bring their very own delicate contribution with their vitality, their colours and shapes. I sometimes use relaxing sounds too, but these are a particular combination attuned to what feels supportive for me as well as the client.

You know when you visit the dentist and there is some kind of irritating noise yammering away in the background? Telling you the latest things to want or to worry about? Wouldn't it be great if they too cottoned on to the value of soothing sounds to relax their patients? The reality for me is that whilst working I am in direct sensory and energetic relationship with all of these elements and this is so clearly beneficial that I don't question it. I am just grateful.

How bodies talk

Quoting Osho again: *'I can't speak without my hands. If you tie my hands I cannot speak a single word, because it is not only that a part of me is speaking, it is my whole being that is involved in it. My eyes, my hands, my whole body is involved, My whole body is saying something, is supporting what I am saying in words'.* One of the things I love about the body is its ability to express feelings in the most clear yet subtle ways.

In groups, I often use an exercise near the beginning where I ask each person in the circle in turn to express their feelings, using a particular part of the body *without any words*, while the others look on and 'listen' to what these movements are saying. I might ask them to do this with their hands or feet at first, as this is easier and more familiar, but any part of the body that moves independently can be used: the arms, the knees, the head, even the nose for instance. It can be fun to use the bottom, for which I ask people to stand up, and within the safety of an all-women group even the breasts can surprise you with what they have to say about how that person is feeling!

I ask people afterwards not to go into words to describe what they felt, or witnessed. I just point out how immediate and direct these expressions are; to notice how they can allow a more exact communication than words, which are so clumsy around feelings. I also use a similar exercise asking people to express their feelings using sounds. And because people are unused to doing these kind of things – especially with others watching them – they often feel awkward and embarrassed at first. So with gentle prompting, this can allow for a whole new area of discovery about ourselves and our feeling-bodies to open up, at the same time challenging inhibitions and fears of inadequacy.

The body plays an essential part in individual sessions and not just on the bench. Frequently my own body will suggest a movement for the client to make directly; and sometimes I suggest they repeat this at home later. (This is how the exercises at the end of each chapter arrived.) There is no thought involved in this, I simply follow what is happening and watch how this movement allows something to relax, open up and start to come free. And the client usually feels this, without necessarily needing to put anything into words. This movement often provokes deep feelings and it works with a powerful, intuitive accuracy of its own, grounded in the connection with Being. The problem with books and trainings, especially if these teach a method or technique to be followed, is that what may work for one person at one time may not work for another or at another time; it may even have the effect of further locking things up. So listening to the body becomes an integral part of any loosening, reorganising and emerging of whatever has been constrained. Along with trusting this, of course.

Most people are familiar with the term 'body language': we use it to describe how the body expresses our inner feelings and thoughts. We are constantly giving and receiving these signals although, I would suggest, these are actually far more subtle, complex and interconnected than is generally recognised. Indeed the body, with all its capacities, is a truly miraculous phenomenon! So it is no less than tragic to witness all the constraints, distortion and actual deformity evident around us, as bodies are forced to carry so much repressed emotion under the influence of a whole gamut of conditioned beliefs. If you just stop for a moment on a busy street and watch the people walking by, you notice after a while that it is quite unusual to see someone truly relaxed and comfortable in their body, and this lack seems more evident the older we get.

Simple body-awareness can make an enormous difference to how we move, how we feel, our energy levels: so much is affected by this. So just be willing to return the attention to what the body is telling you, quietly – or noisily, if you won't listen. Remember, the body knows better than any book, website or anything else, what it needs in the moment. (I am not talking about serious medical issues that need professional help; though here too, if you can find someone who can use their intuition to really listen in, it makes a big difference.) By simply listening to it, and giving it permission to move in any way that it wants, the body can largely attend to itself; *and it loves your touch*.

I used to teach a deeply focussed form of self-massage, including a cleansing ritual, as part of a silent day of inner work. Spending a whole day in silence, giving your full attention to the body: touching, pressing, stroking, rubbing, caressing different parts – or the whole if you have time – *from a place of presence* is very powerful. It's giving and receiving combined, a wonderful form of meditation, meditating on the body, and it's deeply nourishing.

Taking care of this body-beloved

Isn't it remarkable how so few people have learnt such a simple thing as taking care of their body? Not even in the most basic ways? Yes, we wash it and comb our hair and trim our nails; we weigh it and decorate it and even take it to yoga or the gym, but most of us don't really give it *our attention*. We don't relate with it and ask what it needs because we don't see it for what it is – our most precious gift! We don't realise it has a voice. But then, as we become more sensitive, we start to listen in and *feel* what it needs, as in the food we eat for instance (I am not talking vitamin pills and diets fads here, that is the mind speaking). As you awaken your body and its sensitivities, you may notice a *natural* tendency to want to eat more fresh, unpolluted food; probably more vegetables and fruit, certainly less heavy, greasy and sugary food. You may find yourself drawn to juices and teas instead of sugar-laden fizzy drinks and the old milk and caffeine latte. I notice I get a strong urge for miso soup whenever I have been travelling with a limited choice of food available. (I once asked an air steward on a cheap airline if they had anything without pork; he first offered bacon sandwiches, then ham.) Is it so surprising that bodies don't enjoy being bombarded with guilt trips and obsessions about food? They like to relax while they digest – so leave your mind with its 'should' and 'shouldn't' out of your stomach! Take *time*, chewing slowly: these are things we find ourselves doing naturally as we allow the body to speak.

What about 'exercise'? This word we use for moving the body is loaded with *ideas* about what this means. So once again, if we leave the 'shoulds' alone we may find ourselves avoiding artificial environments that can be harsh and punishing, like gymnasiums and the motorway lanes of our local swimming pool – instead seeking places where our body can relate with the elements and *play!* Like cats, bodies like lots of time to stretch and relax, and they like to be given good, comfortable support, too, so maybe you'll find yourself prioritising a good mattress, and weeding out synthetics (I recently indulged in an organic silk duvet and my body absolutely loves it. It snuggles around you when it's cold and wicks away excess heat when it's hot).

Watch out for computers, which have a nasty tendency to override the body's messages to give it a break. Don't forget the body loves good smells too; and soft, furry, silky things to touch; certain colours on certain days, etc. It doesn't have to cost the earth to take care of it and give it a sensory feast. *And what about play?* Maybe you have grown older, but the body can still respond like a child (discounting a bit of stiffness, a few aches and pains, less energy and other general tendencies as we age). It loves to be let off the lead and allowed to do silly things, like bouncing up and down on a trampoline, immersing itself in warm mud, rolling down a grassy slope. Don't go all proper and into your dignity with it: there is a wild child inside all of us so give it a chance!

We tend to forget that our body is responding to gravity 24/7 (the force that anchors us to this ball we call the Earth, hurtling through space) so the more sensitive you get, the more you can feel this connection with the earth, and how good it feels. Why? *Because the Earth herself has an energy-field that we need to be connected with*; it helps maintain our individual energy levels and supports our immune system. What disconnects us? Synthetic materials and composites of these; for instance, the earth's energy can travel through bricks made of earth but gets blocked by concrete, plastic, PVC and other man-made materials. We get disconnected in all kinds of ways: travelling with rubber tyres between us and the earth (that's cars, buses and yes, even bicycles) walking on synthetic surfaces and so on.

There is plenty of information about this on the web but even better, you can learn to *feel* this for yourself. For example, try standing with bare feet, one on stone and the other on concrete, or on wooden versus plastic flooring. Can you feel the difference energetically? One feels alive, the other dead, inert. So a simple way you can help yourself stay connected with the earth is by wearing leather or rope-soled footwear and walking, sitting or lying on natural surfaces – the important thing is that we *maintain* this connection with the earth, especially when we are sleeping and recharging our batteries (you can even buy special 'earthing' sheets and pads). As most kinds of modern technology such as wi-fi, computers, 'smart' meters and mobile phones connect us to varying levels of harmful radiation, it's quite a challenge to keep the body healthy and happy in this modern technological age!

Often, it's not so much what as *how* we do something that makes a difference. So, for instance, instead of turning something into a series of 'shoulds', what happens if you change one letter and tell yourself 'I *could*'; or, even better, *invite* yourself to do something and notice the change in your energy; notice how resistance can move into acceptance, surprise yourself by finding you actually *want* to do something and can enjoy it! Over the years I have become ever more grateful to this awesome creation we call a body. It has and does give me so much pleasure and delight, even now – despite a few saggy bits and wrinkles. I have come to recognise how thankfulness and pleasure *belong together*, hand in hand. So it's good to remember how the attitude we have towards our body affects it on all levels. If we don't bully it and make demands it has to struggle to meet, and choose instead to cherish it and listen to it – to be tender and considerate as we would be with a lover – we have a friend for life!

Lastly, there is the one thing that really impacts the body and that is our conditioned mind, with all its heavy, emotionalised beliefs. So focussing on becoming consciously aware can make an enormous difference to our vitality levels and to how our body can maintain itself; the rewards for this are huge. In fact, it is profoundly moving when we get a sense and feel and intuition of what this body *truly is:* for without it there would be nothing to experience, God's playground would not exist! So as we learn to come back down out of our minds and into our body and fully reside here, consciously, we come to see that in this life – in our human experience – *this is where we belong:* in reverent and joyful union with this beloved body.

Home-play

1. Make conscious contact with your body often and every day

Spend time focussing on your body: touch it, sense into it. Does it want to express something? Tell you something? What does it need? Know it as a sacred portal to Being, and let your heart open with gratitude for its beloved support.

2. Grounding

(Before you start this exercise, try lifting one foot off the ground, which should be light and easy to do. Then try again afterwards, and you may find your foot now feels heavy and reluctant to lift off the ground.)
- Breathe in through the soles of the feet, up the legs as far as the belly.
- Breathe out again down the legs and out through the soles of the feet, down into the ground. (If you can't have your bare feet on the earth, you can still imagine the earth beneath you with earthworms, gas pipes, whatever makes it real for you.)
- Simply jumping on the ground and feeling the impact as you come down onto the earth each time, particularly in the base chakra and cradle, is also helpful.

3. Explore the difference in the body between making ourselves and inviting ourselves to do something
- Use your body to express making yourself do something; exaggerate this and examine how the body feels doing this and what effect it has on it, including on breathing. This might include: restricting the breath, tightening of arms against your sides and the balling of hands into fists, or whatever your body chooses.
- Now use your body to express inviting yourself to do something: letting yourself in. Once again, notice how this affects the body - feel it and experience the difference in your energy. At first, it can help to pretend you are welcoming a beloved (which you are, just not an outer, visible one).

These exercises are especially helpful with things that we are trying to get ourselves to do (usually because we *think* they will be good for us), a process that cuts us off from any actual desire to do them.

4. Take a moment to touch something each day with reverence
- Sense it as you touch it, give it your full attention; feel your appreciation for its existence.
- Receive anything that comes from this connection through touch.

5. Touching the beloved
Feel into your loving heart and then reach out and touch someone, recognising the beloved both in you and in them as you do so. (You don't need to tell them what you are doing.)

Natural aliveness

'That unchanging aliveness, that spark within you, is the light of the world. That's the light that allows everything to come into being.' ~ Adyashanti

'The real question is not whether life exists after death. The real question is whether you are alive before death.' ~ Osho

'He was mastered by the sheer surging life, the tidal wave of being, the perfect joy of each separate muscle, joint, sinew in that it was everything that was not death, that it was aglow and rampant, expressing itself in movement, flying exultantly under the stars' ~ Jack London, The Call of the Wild

'Alive-ness': this carries an association with vigour and vibrancy, indeed it's quite a juicy word! Aliveness is something we *feel*. Like a river it surges and streams through us, bringing vitality, health and gladness of heart. Everything is perceived to be alive and, as such, *of interest and potential relationship*: nothing is left out. So it's one of life's greatest tragedies, the way we tend to squash and squeeze the aliveness out of our children. It's usually so unconscious and unintentional that we simply don't recognise what we are doing. By aliveness, I mean our energy and sense of interest in and connection with everything around us. When this is uninhibited we humans are naturally curious and spontaneously joyful; everything holds a sense of wonder about it. When we say something is wonder*ful* we are perceiving it as *full of wonder,* and this is how children start their journey into life.

When you are in touch with the vast array of experiences a child can have – on multiple levels – and you see the lively curiosity and interest, the excitement and delight they are capable of, the pressure to suppress this is painful to watch. It starts with birth, which by its nature can be traumatic for the infant. And this is often intensified by bright lights, loud noises, harsh disinfectant smells, sometimes rough handling and general levels of pressure and brisk, impersonal efficiency amongst hospital staff (unless you have a home-birth, of course). Then comes the influence of parents, who are generally unconscious subjects of their own childhood conditioning, and the patterns they inherited and developed that inevitably get acted out on their children. And this happens despite the best of intentions; because both parents and the extended family, along with neighbours and friends, all are likely to be suffering from some degree of inhibited aliveness themselves.

Then comes school. If I liken school to a concentration camp you may be appalled; that sounds pretty drastic doesn't it? After all, many children enjoy school, at least some parts of it. There are teachers who really care about their pupils and try to engage them and make the curriculum interesting, especially in their earlier years. And children can enjoy just being around other children – or not, of course, because for those who suffer bullying, school can be pure hell. However, one way or another, what happens to most children in school *is a process of intense conditioning.* They act like a pressure cooker – slowly but surely the conditioning children receive begins to disconnect them from their bodies, their authentic feeling, sensing selves, *and their own intuitive authority.*

Schools instil a slow but steady dampening down of their natural aliveness (and in boarding schools the demands to conform are even greater). There is constant pressure to submit to and trust others' authority before their own. Anyone who rebels becomes the target of the teachers' anger and blame, usually resulting in some form of punishment and perhaps exclusion from their fellows. And yet – ironically – it can be the good, hardworking, conformist child who, in the relentless pursuit of intellectual achievement, becomes the most shut off and emotionally damaged of all.

With school parents are stuck in the middle. Apart from their own baggage, they now have to contend with the social, political and bureaucratic expectations and demands that the teachers themselves have to meet. For schools generally operate within what are perceived as normal and desirable goals, structures and behaviours for children. *However, if we put preserving aliveness at the top of the agenda then things look very different.* For how can it be in any way valuable to force a small growing human to contain him or herself for hours at a time within one room, sitting on a hard chair facing a desk, often in front of a computer; not allowed to talk except when asked or to move the body around beyond minor adjustments? What is really going on here?

All the while being required to listen to something they may not be the least bit interested in, that feels it has no relevance to their lives; required to store this unwanted information and regurgitate it at exam time or suffer the consequences – low results, culminating in teachers' and parental disappointment and disapproval, even anger and scorn. What is this teaching children? Then to be released for short breaks to express their pent-up energy in loud noise, and maybe taking out their feelings of frustration on their fellows. Undoubtedly schools serve a function; apart from teaching children to conform and limit their aspirations, they serve to contain them, to keep them out of trouble so parents can go to work. Do I sound cynical? If you were to design the perfect program to stifle aliveness, would it look that different?

Make no mistake, full aliveness is dangerous! It does not conform to others' requirements; it does not lend itself to social control. Like a forest fire it is unpredictable: it may cross boundaries and leap in any direction at any moment, according to where the wind is blowing. It has a natural, anarchic energy. And this is felt as a terrible threat to any external form of order and authority. It must be doused and brought under control, and any remaining flickers rapidly stamped out before it sets light to its surroundings. Plays have been written about this, of which *One Flew Over the Cuckoo's Nest* – where a sane but rebellious inmate in a psychiatric hospital ends up getting lobotomised for challenging the head nurse – is perhaps the best illustration. And of course there was Jesus, who paid for his preaching dissension to his followers by being strung up on a cross. Is this really the lesson we want to teach our children? 'See! Look what happens when you disobey and speak your truth!'

So what to do? How best to preserve and foster aliveness in children? In looking for better solutions, whatever these may turn out to be, it is important this comes from a place of *intuitive connection with our deeper nature.* Don't rely on the mind to know what is needed; you can feel and sense and intuit a great deal of accurate information about priorities, these give weight to any fresh, creative options you may uncover. Take your courage to keep on looking beneath the surface; keep turning over stones and remember (and this holds true for any honest attempt to see what is true) even if you find things underneath that are hard to look at – ugly, smelly or seemingly beyond hope – you are letting in fresh air and sunshine, bringing in the light of awareness to see what is needed. There are so many possibilities for doing things differently. And with conscious awareness we can be lifted up into this place of love and freedom where we belong – where we *all* belong.

Staying alive

Intuitively, I felt the importance of retaining my aliveness despite the complete lack of awareness of this amongst the society I grew up in, out in the world. In many ways my rather unusual upbringing insulated me from the attitudes of society around me, especially the fears and insecurities expressed as 'You can't do that' or 'You had better do this if you want to succeed'. I remember being motivated by a sense of wanting to explore life away from the constraints of any school curriculum, so I left school at the earliest opportunity (at fifteen, which you could do then).

In many ways I was much clearer about what I didn't want to do than what I did. I didn't want to be a nurse, a secretary or a teacher (the regular job options for middle-class girls then). Nor did I want to keep on studying and stuff my head full of what I perceived to be dry information at some university. More than anything I was absolutely, totally clear that I didn't want to spend my life in a nine-to-five job, stuck in some stuffy building miles from the natural elements, with people I imagined to be boring, bitchy and bossy, climbing a ladder to nowhere. I wasn't looking to 'settle down' and have a family either.

So what to do? When I told the headmaster of the State school I briefly attended that I was interested in farming, his response was a sarcastic 'They farm monkeys in Africa, you know.' He was no doubt pissed-off that I had declined his offer of higher education. I liked being out in the open air amongst the elements and I liked animals, so I tried it anyway. That soon got rid of my romantic notions, stuck amongst the concrete and cow-shit of modern farming methods, with frightened wild-eyed animals called by their numbers and stripped of their bovine dignity (yes dignity! If you get to know cows individually you realise they each have their own character). Slicing day-old piglet's balls off, ringing lamb's tails and clipping chicken's beaks – no thanks! I knew what felt good and it surely wasn't that.

So I tried Art School, but that represented the too familiar world of my parents, who were anyway better than me at both drawing and painting, and I wasn't really motivated. If I had been a boy maybe I would have got hold of a Harley Davidson and headed off into the sunset, but I wasn't too confident around machines. I just loved the feeling of freedom I got from picking up some newspaper or magazine, looking down the job columns and knowing I could be living anywhere, doing anything – anything in the casual line anyway. I wanted to find out about other people and how they live; to explore different kinds of work and different landscapes, different cultures, different countries. I was thirsty to expand my experience of the world.

In my late teens and early twenties I managed about sixty different jobs, with an average of about three weeks each, interspersed with bouts of travelling. I don't know where I got the clarity and confidence (some would say the self-indulgence and irresponsibility!). I suppose this was a mixture of being sent to a free school, where kids were encouraged to use their initiative, to question and think for themselves, and a parent who was great at supporting me in going for what I wanted, as she herself had done in her own way. I think I just saw the world as a place to play in, which outraged not a few people around me. However, I was just sublimely unaware of what other people thought, of what they saw as risky – like the lack of a secure future and opportunities that come through persevering at one thing.

Looking back, I think I instinctively knew I couldn't afford to pay too much attention to the future, that it represented a ransom, a sacrifice, a price I wasn't prepared to pay. During this time I was also busy exploring relationships and the roller-coaster of my feelings and emotions. Later, I became enthused about expressing my creativity through interior design before becoming pregnant, which re-oriented my life around what I imagined to be the ideal scenario for raising children: first a cottage, then a farm full of animals in the countryside. The world seemed full of endless possibilities (This was the late Sixties/early Seventies, don't forget). How very different everything looks for young people leaving school today!

The unintended consequences of unconscious parenting

Looking back, amongst whatever we may feel we did well as a parent, it's hard not to see things to regret too, things that were not recognised or attended to at the time. There is no organised preparation or support for parenting, so we have to practice on the job. And this leaves all kinds of unconscious material hidden and likely to get ignited along the way. In my own case, in my ignorance and arrogance and tendency to go my own way, I didn't want to listen to others. And not all advice is helpful or appropriate anyway, especially if this undermines our confidence. However, there are some basic questions that can help unearth unconscious agendas.

For instance, it's curious, isn't it, how nobody asks the basic question 'Why *do* parents have children?' Why do they *really*? Beyond the obvious reasons that is, like the instinct to procreate, to bond and fulfil a relationship, to please the grandparents, carry on the firm, whatever. Or the less talked about but nevertheless common idea that being a parent will bring us a certain status in society, especially women, where it may be used to avoid or put off going out into the world of work.

Then there are the motivations we don't talk about because we prefer not to ask these questions; it feels too uncomfortable. Without doubt, having a child bestows *an enormous power to influence and control the development of another human being*: an opportunity to mould them in our image. It brings all kinds of possibilities such as identifying with our offspring, finding success *through* them, attempting to replicate our own values, dressing them up and presenting them as trophies, etc. – quite a potent mix of possible ego-based agendas! And this is apart from such a simple motivation as providing company so that, until they leave, we need never feel alone (in the Western world at least, people have largely given up on the idea that children will look after us in our old age).

Does this sound cynical? Well, but if you have followed the earlier chapters about the egoic mind, why would having children be any different? Why *would* the conditioned mind *not* interfere in this most delicate and important role of parenting? For most people this paints too stark a picture; they prefer to erect a sentimental screen and believe everyone had a happy childhood, including themselves; that only an unfortunate few are treated badly by cruel or indifferent parents. And in my experience, this is simply not true. By avoiding looking into all this we simply continue the harm, albeit unconsciously. Then, talking about why children drink and take drugs, self-harm and even commit suicide, or why so many adults live unfulfilling lives and suffer from depression or anxiety and various forms of mental illness, is like seeking to cut off the head of a weed without ever examining its root.

Don't misunderstand what I am saying here; most parents have the best of intentions. We care deeply about our children and go to great lengths to try to give them what we believe they need and should have. It is not easy being a parent; in fact nothing is more challenging. Whatever we do there are always things we can regret and – apart from those parents who are themselves too damaged to feel this – this is true for most parents, and it is painful. However, bringing up children is also a profound learning opportunity. They can teach us about the real, unconditional love of our hearts: how to keep accessing this even when we feel most exasperated or out-of-sorts.

They get us up in the night to feed them, change a nappy, soothe them, over and over again when we are completely exhausted. Or to help them with their homework or take them somewhere, fix a puncture on their bike, cook their favourite meal; we listen to them, comfort them, encourage them, pick up after them; we pull on all our resources, the last of our patience, all of our ingenuity. *Nothing* takes you to the wire like your child in trouble or hurting in some way, and you happily give up your own needs when things get hard. This is the heart in action. This is love expressing itself in human form *despite the egoic mind*: this is you being who you *really* are, beneath any conditioning.

Nature connection and presence

A simple and powerful way to open up to full aliveness is through connecting with nature, especially if this was lacking when you grew up. By 'nature' *I mean everything that is alive that is non-human* (even though in reality we are also part of nature). You can do this from a window sill, a balcony, a front porch; it doesn't have to be out in a garden or the countryside. A spider spinning a web on the ceiling is part of nature, or you can connect with a pigeon on your windowsill or perhaps a squirrel in the branch of a tree. If you have a garden you may see a hedgehog or even, if you are lucky, a fox. Developing *an ongoing relationship* with a creature you can see and relate to everyday has a particular benefit: then you can really get to know this being and how it behaves.

It can be surprising how many creatures you can spot in urban environments. The more open you are, the deeper the connection, so just your intention and a little time and patience can bring miracles. In terms of the quality of communication, this is essentially no different in an urban environment to more dramatic experiences 'out in the wilds of nature', like those I had with a whale and a lion. True, some of the energetic experiences I had whilst camping alone in the

Australian wilderness were certainly helped by taking time out from 'civilised' human society and its manifestations; this allowed for some unusual and intense connections that held a particular power – and for this very reason they were not always easy to stay with.

For instance, one time I was with a group of people that included an Aboriginal elder and his friends, visiting a certain rock (no, not Ayers Rock, or Uluru, to give it its Aboriginal name). I had a large canvass bag with me that was both bulky and heavy and – for some reason I can't now remember – bare feet, and yet I found myself climbing easily up this in places almost vertical rock, in the dark, with a clear sense of presence calling me. I got separated from the others and was sitting amongst a pile of smaller rocks at the top when I felt and heard an enormous rumbling underneath me and I 'knew' the spirit within the rock was rising up. Sadly, I have to confess, I was not brave enough to stay put and moved to rejoin the others.

Another time, out with a group of friends in the Blue Mountains (which are densely forested) we stayed out too long exploring a hidden valley and it became dark. Even though there was a full moon, we still had no idea how to find the path back to our camp. So we just climbed up a ravine and, after walking a short distance, found ourselves *at the precise spot where the path to our camp ended*, beside a cluster of bee hives! And something in me 'knew' this was no coincidence.

Yet another time, my children and I were exploring that group of rocks known as Hanging Rock when we came to a big hollow boulder sitting on top of another one. We climbed up inside and discovered that when we made sounds these were magnified to create the most extraordinary resonance – a bit like the effect of 'overtone singing' (which the Tibetan's use in their religious chanting), and this powerful sensation, of sound distorted and mixed with vibration, went far beyond words.

For me Australia, with its vast red deserts, its endless coastlines and unique flora and fauna is a land that allowed me an intimate glimpse of itself; a communion that was made easier by the absence of human activity in so many places. In some ways, in its untouched qualities, *it felt like aliveness personified.* You can still find places where there is a sense that no 'white fella' has been, and much of it – for me at that time – felt like a kind of initiation into the spirituality of non-human reality. As the famous Sufi poet, Rumi, puts it 'When God gives (you) this knowing, inanimate stones, plants, animals, everything, fills with unfolding significance.' In this living reality, connection can happen anywhere.

Many years ago, at the Findhorn Foundation in Scotland, I had two simple but striking and completely unexpected instances of this connection with nature. In the first I was sitting beside a lawn – looking at nothing in particular – when I noticed a patch of grass that appeared to be waving at me. I realised the wind was blowing in the opposite direction so I was startled and didn't know what to make of it. On a different occasion, while working in the Findhorn gardens I had another experience, this time with a tree. I was upset about something and felt moved to stand in the centre of this tree (there are firs growing there with many trunks rising out of one base, so you can stand in amongst them). As I stood there I had the strangest sensation that these trunks were gathering in around me, emanating a loving energy which was intensely soothing. 'Nonsense! That's just wishful thinking or an over-active imagination' says a sceptical mind. In which case a more recent experience will sound even more bizarre.

I was with Jon Young (the man who teaches Intuitive tracking) and Anna Breytenbach (the animal communicator) and a group of people, once again at Findhorn. Jon shared how two musician-songwriters he knew but who didn't know each other, had each, on separate occasions, approached him with a wordless song they said was given to them by the Elderflower tree. It turned out each was a perfect harmony for the other! He taught us the song and we went to where a group of three Elderflower trees grew in the forest, where we stood in a circle and sang this song.

Now, if I tell you that whilst we did this I saw a series of little faces, made out of what looked like carved wood, with pointy noses and bright eyes, some with beards and some made of stone with moss and lichen caps, you would surely think I was 'off with the fairies' – and you would be right! At first they looked quite solemn, even a bit sad and then, as we sang, they burst out into the most gleeful laughter, bringing such a feeling of joy and delight. What or who were they? I don't know, but Dorothy McLain (now 95, one of the founders of the Findhorn Foundation, whose interest was working with nature) calls them 'Devas' or 'Nature Spirits', and many people, especially those visiting Findhorn, claim to have seen them. I remembered I had actually glimpsed them before, but – as happens – *I had not really registered this at the time*: they simply appeared in my 'sight', I wasn't looking for them, I didn't expect them. But they do seem to be representative of the many beings and forms of life we usually don't see, or pay attention to.

Normally, if one talks about such things people either look at you askance – perhaps writing you off as some dippy woman with her fantasies – or, they get tremendously excited about it and tell all their friends. In other words, people tend to be either credulous or dismissive. Wouldn't it be great if we just opened to the many full-of-wonder experiences life offers without needing to emotionalise these? Just because something doesn't fit with what we have been told is real – because we ourselves have not had such experiences up to now – is no excuse for denying it may be true, either. Imagine if trees could speak, what might they have to tell us? Well, they can! Just not in the way we are used to hearing things. What they have to communicate enters directly into our awareness; it doesn't need words: *this is the universal language I spoke about earlier*.

So, sitting in a spot I had been frequenting under a small birch tree, one day I found myself feeling overwhelmed with sadness for the harm humans are causing to the natural world out of our ignorance and greed. I had anticipated trees might feel angry and aggrieved about this, but when I asked this tree if it would help in reversing this tragedy, it simply responded with a wordless 'of course!' No drama at all. One of the things I like about Jon's work is how he grounds the spiritual, intuitive and psychic in practical ways that can be used not simply to communicate, *but to validate the wholeness of this world: the Being-ness that exists within everything.* The Being-ness that manifests as a hedgehog, a pebble, a human, a tree; the wind, the ocean, the stars – even the smallest grain of sand. Then, as we humans recover our aliveness, so we recover our sense of connection as part of this whole.

In his book *The Man who made things out of Trees,* Robert Penn talks about how the Japanese do something they call 'Shinrin-yoku', which means 'forest bathing'; how nearly a quarter of the population regularly go for a stroll in ancient woodland, and how this has been widely known as *a standard form of preventative medicine* since it was inspired by Shinto and Buddhist practices in ancient times. Isn't that beautiful? A true example of intuitive intelligence.

However, more recently – and notably this time in the West, which is far more reliant on the mind – an American biologist E.O. Wilson came up with a theory he called 'Biophilia', stating that we have a deep affiliation with other forms of life, like trees, which is instinctive and rooted in our biology, and a professor Roger Ulrich made studies in what is now called 'Environmental psychology', where he found hospitalised patients in rooms with a window facing natural surroundings needed less pain-relief than those facing a brick wall. (What a surprise!) Yet more research shows that humans respond positively to wood in interiors, both psychologically and physiologically, and that spending time in nature improves cognition, helps with anxiety and depression and even enhances empathy. Studies show how trees affect us on a molecular level, in our cells and neurones, and try to work out how they do this; how leisurely walks in old-growth forest can reduce heart rate and lower blood pressure, decrease sympathetic nerve activity and lower levels of the stress hormone, cortisol.

Now this is all very impressive, Isn't it? Notice how you respond to all this carefully researched information, because this has a very different origin to the practice of Shinrin-yoku, which comes from tuning in and *having a direct relationship with what is here*. The second ponderous approach relies on developing theories and testing these against what we call the 'evidence'; and if this can't be found, or changes, certainty is lost and the whole theory may collapse. Personally, I find these examples of how the mind tries to grasp and analyse life and aliveness somewhat hilarious. But they are instructive because they let us see how *only when something has been named and classified and to some extent explained, are we safe to believe in its existence*. Thus we create our own 'reality': with the mind. Remember Jean Liedloff? And how people needed to read about it in a book before recognising the value of touch? Unlike children before they have learnt this, most of us do as we have been taught to do and allow ourselves to be convinced only when there is 'evidence'; and when this has been authenticated by those claiming authority.

From this we construct common agreements about reality. So the wonderful thing about re-orienting ourselves from an intuitive perspective, is that all of the effects mentioned in the paragraph before last can be *felt, sensed* and *known* without any need for the mind to intervene. *No intermediary is needed.* We become sensitive to them as we connect with the whole of life. What the conventional scientific approach, based on a compartmentalising, dualistic mind fails to understand is that this knowing *requires direct connection*, not the calculation of mind. And going deeper still, what we are essentially connecting with *is part of ourselves:* because in intuitive reality we are not actually separate – not in the way we have learned to believe.

I am not saying here that there is no value in a scientific approach. Clearly there have been great benefits (as well as discoveries that have led to unfortunate consequences, such as the discovery of the atom). There is even an apparently new discipline called 'Bio-inspiration', where scientists study nature for inspiration. As one of these, Leif Rostrum, comments about researching storage of solar energy *'The leaf as nature's solar panel is a great example: scientists have been trying to better understand photosynthesis for a long time, even well before we wanted to collect and store solar energy for ourselves'.* What I am intending to highlight is the limiting effect on humans and our view of reality when we conclude nothing has value until it can be explained and validated in these ways; when this approach is used to dismiss our *actual* experience.

In his book *Feral*, George Monbiot talks about re-wilding and the need for humans to re-connect with and value wildness, both in nature and in themselves. Despite his faith in science and the intellect, I would call his trust in life to find its own way the wisdom of the intuitive heart, his distrust of spirituality and religion an instinctive resistance to the misuse of these and his passionate concern for protecting but not dominating all life a great role model for men. It is clear from his writing that he has had deeply spiritual experiences and his anguish at the destruction of the natural world is held within an undeniable love.

I want to include a passage Anna Breytenbach wrote about her experience of connecting with dragonflies here, because this illustrates something of the subtle nature of our relationship with other forms. On seeing and moving close to a couple of dragonflies she says *'Bringing myself present, I was in genuine wonder at his or her physical characteristics – but without sending my energy outwards in a sharp spike of cognitive curiosity that would have been an arrow of disturbance. Instead I stayed in my heart, simply opening to the experience of shared space. After a while of peaceful no-thought, my hand spontaneously stretched out towards the dragonfly and hovered close to the gossamer-thin wings. At which point I became aware that the insect was wondering what my* skin felt like to touch. Again, aware that my human clumsiness might inadvertently harm this delicate body, I reached towards his or her back and softly made physical contact. What followed was a timeless space of a few minutes of mutual sharing, the dragonfly leaning in to feel me more solidly as I softly tickled their back. In those sacred moments we exchanged so much! We learned what it's like to be the other species. We met at the frequency of unconditional love. We felt mutual understanding, awe and enjoyment. We knew each other.'

The creative impulse as an expression of aliveness

One vibrant and visible aspect of aliveness is creativity. But what actually is this? We associate this word with people who create art, music, writing, poetry – all kinds of activities that we believe you need to be an artist to do. Yet in reality, creativity is just an aspect of aliveness: a natural expression and response to external stimuli. It invites curiosity and even wonder, because in order to be truly creative we have to release rigid ideas of how everything *should be*; we have to be open to both receiving and perceiving something new, something that is neither known nor expected and may well seem – at least at first – beyond our grasp. There can be a certain tension, an eagerness in the anticipation of what this may be, but whether it is a slight glimpse or a fully completed image, what arrives can neither be anticipated nor controlled in any way, shape or form by the intellect – *not if it is true.*

This is why artists are often seen as rebels: wild, nonconformist, out on the edge. They tend to have a far less fixed view of the world, a wider view of reality because when they look, instead of seeking to control what they see through recognition – by identifying it with something known – they are open to looking at what is *actually there*. Looking, for an artist, is a form of embracing. He or she touches and explores what they are looking at with their intuitive senses, as if they were extending some fine and delicate instrument to wander over and explore whatever they hold in their view. They *feel* into it and don't stay on the surface; they are willing to know it, intimately, in a way that most people are not. They are not interested in mere surfaces but in what lies beneath them; what is seen, felt and intuited that can be met, reflected and interpreted through the medium and materials they choose, using colour, shape, texture, light and shade. And in true artists – the so-called 'great' ones – their individual *interpretation* of what they see, combined with their skill in using their chosen medium, allows for something of their very essence to be brought forth and expressed.

This is the gift artists bring, which has no real relationship to the money they may receive (even though they need to eat!). Even if they don't understand this themselves, even if they are caught up in a variety of ego games – such as wanting attention, wanting to be special, to impress, whatever – what they produce is really an offering. It truly belongs to no-one, irrespective of who signs the cheque and takes possession of the physical item. Whatever the artist's chosen subject, no matter how they wish to interpret this, *if it is authentic art it carries a voice of its own*. Hence the true artist is both receiver and interpreter of a living expression of Being.

He or she is a conduit, and regardless of their personality or temperament, they transcend this while in action. It can feel literally like seeding, gestating and giving birth: nothing can be forced, things arrive in their own time, unfold as they will and complete *themselves*. The artist participates in this process, of course, but is not in control of it (in the way the mind uses control). So, she or he gets a feeling when to leave it alone, when to work on it; and, if they are alert and not pressured by other agendas, they *recognise* when it is finished. They *see* this, they don't decide. *So this whole unfolding of the creative process can be seen as a metaphor for living with intuitive reality.*

The art world is full of examples of so-called art that has no real sense of aliveness. Money, fashion and a requirement that it explain itself in *concepts*: all these tend to deprive art of its immediacy and power. They interfere in the production and exhibiting of authentic art: that is, art that is vibrant and alive. Here and there something gets through, something bursting with energy and originality, art that takes us beyond the mundane world and refreshes us with glimpses of what lies behind this. We instinctively recognise this, but again, people have been so conditioned to accept others' opinions as to what has value that many ordinary souls have simply given up on art altogether: much of it no longer touches us, it fails to satisfy.

One could ask here 'Is a statement by itself art?' Or is it something else, a commentary perhaps? Tracy Emin's used bed sheet comes to mind. And this idea of demanding that art explain itself in words: so-called 'conceptual art'. But how can art be defined in concepts – which are essentially mind-based – when the whole power of drawing and painting and sculpture transcends a need for either thought or words? In fact allows the viewer to perceive *that which cannot be put into words?* That which is beyond all words and concepts? Beyond mind? Inspiration comes through intuition, it is not a function of the mind. As with great music we are moved by great art; this enters the domain of the heart, with its potential for aliveness: we are touched.

This absence of aliveness is not just true about art, of course. If you look around in many circles of life you can see aliveness suppressed and not valued. It is inconvenient, subversive, potentially disruptive; it won't be controlled nor fit into the tidy formulas and filing systems of mind. There is evidence all around us of how aliveness has been subjugated and too often ignored. Perhaps you have observed this suppression of the creative in children? How, in nursery or primary school creativity may be allowed, even encouraged but soon enough, through a schooling system that obsesses over gathering information – to be filed, stored and displayed on demand – creativity gets suppressed, *along with our vital life-force.* Inventiveness and ingenuity are part of this aliveness, along with various internalised ways of perceiving, receiving and responding to life. The opposite of create is destroy, so when we inhibit creativity we not only stifle aliveness, we encourage all kinds of self-destructive behaviours.

I was only fifteen when I first went to art school (between forays into farming). In those days your entry depended entirely on the quality of your portfolio: no need for maths and arithmetic (which many of us would have failed anyway). The head was a respected landscape artist, who wore a silk bow tie and kept a whisky bottle on top of his desk. Art schools were hives of innovation in those days, one of the few places where aliveness flourished and, unlike many schools at that time, they were mixed. Some of the boys played in 'trad' (traditional jazz) bands and the top room was often filled with the wonderful sounds of sax and trumpet, clarinet and trombone (with a couple snogging behind the long green curtains in the window alcoves). Girls turned up in hessian sacks (a style the fashion industry immediately adopted), pyjamas, men's shirts worn over tight black jeans which looked like they had been painted on (nothing new now, but this was the Fifties).

We drank builder's tea or disgusting powdered coffee and cheap wine, and occasionally went to a movie. We talked and danced and read poetry and sex was no big deal: you did if you wanted to, usually because you were connecting with someone you liked, or you didn't. There was no pressure from boys, none of the sleazy groping behind the bicycle shed of State schools. And we painted and drew and sculpted, sometimes late into the evening, *because we wanted to*, because this was what most of us loved to do. Looking back now it seemed about the only real, alive place to be. Then the head shot himself and a new man arrived wearing a suit and handwoven tweed tie, intent on regulating the hours we attended and controlling what we did during them. I remember painting an oak tree in scarlet oils and he pronouncing 'Trees are not red!' Bureaucracy had arrived.

I am not intending to suggest here that art is the sole province of 'artists' – far from it. Anyone can express themselves in a simple act of creation, which is an important part of what we *are*. For sure, some people have a greater gift for seeing and greater skills in translating that seeing (which might take the form of writing or playing music, writing poetry, dancing, whatever), which others may then appreciate. But despite this, I would be rich if I had a fiver for every time someone told me they can't do any of these things! But not all forms of expression are intended to be seen or heard by others. What art does is it gives us *a way to explore life*: including ourselves and the world around us.

At least in the early days, most children are encouraged to use this as a form of discovery and play; it's only as we grow older that critical judgement – others' and our own – starts to inhibit what we feel we can do. Then we learn to deny ourselves this vital field of aliveness. With small children, before they encounter these inhibitions, there can be a wonderful expression of free energy and curiosity. For instance, have you noticed with children looking at illustrations, how they love detail? They love to see expressions on faces and be shown intricate descriptions of places and objects: this extends their imagination. Which is why I would love to bring back the stocks and encourage children to hurl rotten eggs and tomatoes at all those ignorant adults who insist on buying children's books filled with illustrations by adults, imitating children's attempts to draw like adults. How insulting is that for a child!

What is born? And born into what?

While we are talking about children – little growing humans – and aliveness, it is interesting to pause and ask: just what *are* children, really? *What is it that is born?* What is it that appears to come alive? We are so accustomed to seeing conception, birth and babies in terms of biology: sperm and egg get together, import some genes from parents, who imported them from their parents, and so on back to Adam and Eve (or the primordial swamp, depending on your beliefs). It's all a matter of biology and physics and chemistry and, ultimately, a matter for science. But these 'answers' don't address the question; rather, they limit the scope of the question to fit the available answers (just as we see politicians attempting to do as they manoeuvre and dissemble on television). However, if you come from a fresh perspective and imagine Being existing in timeless reality: a reality that has no physical structures and no such thing as the progression of time as we know it, that has no sense of individuality – or even the *possibility* of separation from the whole – we glimpse a very different picture.

As we noted in the first chapter of this book, through our limited scientific perspective we humans have assumed we are the superior species of this, *our* world. That anything approaching our intelligence must be some kind of manlike form (even if it has only one eye, three legs or green skin). The idea that we may be simply *a particular manifestation of one whole, one consciousness*, is still barely knocking at the doors of the mind, at the portal we call quantum physics. As mind exists in duality, there is really no way it can grasp this. It can *talk* about it, *theorise about* it, philosophise about it; but it cannot be *known* by mind, which lacks the capacity to realise what we are. Any more than mind can relate to nothing: the void where no 'thing' exists and out of which every 'thing' is born. These remain as spiritual *concepts* for the mind.

However, *when it is filled with light* – enlightened – the mind has no need to claim anything. It can relax and give up the role it has assumed as director of the show. And of those teachers who speak about spiritual matters (Adyashanti being one whom I find exceptionally clear), the wise ones know the truth of what we are cannot be described, and so support you finding out for yourself. Here, I simply want to suggest that children are not what we believe them to be. That, in reality, they are little body-Beings – that is, *Being appearing as bodies* – the one appearing as many. This Being that has no identity, no name and no form; by some miracle 'this' *takes on form* and then, gradually, a sense of identity helped by being given a name. This body-Being *assumes* a genetic history along with the 'apparent' human beings it is born to, whom, later, it will learn to regard as its 'parents': people it *belongs to*.

Can you begin to imagine the immense confusion and shock of being evicted from a warm, dark, safe home in the womb, out into the glare of a hospital 'birthing factory'? The potential for absolute terror at being cast out from the security of oneness into this world of apparent separation and duality? With a whole host of unfamiliar sensations and input? Especially – as happens too often – if it is denied the immediate sensual reconnection with the body it has inhabited for nine months, with a loving mother to nurture and protect it? People are naturally concerned that a fully functioning physical entity is born. However, we forget that (or are ignorant of), *in terms of a child's ability to be fully alive,* this is also dependent on its capacities to receive and express; on many subtle and highly sensitive, intuitive, sensory and feeling levels, prior to any mental development.

It is here that the infant meets the limitations of our expectations and beliefs. It is immediately subject to things that affect it, that are frightening, confusing and utterly outside its field of reference. Perhaps, one day, children will be seen for what they truly are and given what they need to flourish in this strange place we call 'the World.' Perhaps we will come to remember just how precious they are – and not just to their immediate family; to give primacy to this, valuing and supporting those who care for them *above all else*. In the meantime, this unique entity that we call a child – *with its innate capacity for aliveness* – will struggle and strain and, hopefully, retain enough aliveness to remember what it has lost and set out to reclaim it. And the wonderfully affirming thing about this process of reclamation is that it often seems to lead to helping others to reclaim their aliveness too: meaning the unfolding into our true nature can gain momentum.

Here and there I have come across places and people with a 'spiritual' intent where children are not welcome. For instance, I once asked one of the older members of the Findhorn Foundation – which is, after all, a community dedicated to New Age values – why there was no children's playground (this was before they replaced the caravans with houses; now it has become more of an eco-village and there is one). This woman amazed me by replying 'Children get in the way of spiritual development'. Can this be true? I can see that during periods of silent meditation, on long retreats or immersion in certain emotional and especially cathartic processes, a child-free space may be needed. But outside of this? It's strange, isn't it, to see how *the expression of aliveness* and the celebration of life this brings – children being exemplars of this – seem to be lacking in many forms of spirituality and mainstream religion? Here, it would seem that quietness, patience, self-discipline, earnestness, humility and the willingness to be good and kind are the qualities one needs to inculcate. And the reward for this will be either heaven or enlightenment (or some wonderfully elevated spiritual status) and this will free us from all difficulty and pain: life will flow in continuous bliss with the ability to meet all that comes with ease.

Nice idea! Because idea is all that this is: an idea that becomes a belief. A shame really, as the prevalence of this attitude puts many people, especially the young, off the whole notion of looking for meaning in spirituality. Or it attracts the same old egoic need to *do* or *present* in order to *get* (what ego thinks it wants) – and all the while something precious and obvious gets overlooked. For how can you reach deeply into your being-ness *without fully engaging with life?* Without responding on all levels? Without ringing all the many notes your internal bells are capable of? We are here to make divine music! How is this possible without accessing the *totality* of our feeling, sensing, intuiting nature? How can you thank life for its gift without celebrating?

Celebration – falling in love with life

In days gone by there was much opportunity for dancing, singing and celebrating, in all its forms. While this may still happen in places like Africa, India and South America, such displays of joyful celebration of life are often lacking in Western societies, outside of religious-based ceremonies. We watch other people's celebrations on television: we cheer a football team, our country's athletes at the Olympics; we applaud awards given to people in the film and music business; we cheer celebrities of all kinds and that's about it. Oh, and we try to revive a few stilted forms like Morris dancing at country fairs. True, certain Christian-based churches encourage their own form of joyful celebration but these are very much in a minority. For everyone else there is nowhere to come together to celebrate life itself.

Osho used to say we need to bring Zorba and the Buddha together (Zorba being the Greek character played by Anthony Quinn in the film *Zorba the Greek*, based on the book by Nikos Karantzakis), whose life was filled with celebration; just not in a nice, 'spiritual' form for he enjoyed dancing, drinking, friendship and loving women. 'Nothing new here' you might say, but actually there is a difference, a difference in his attitude, a willingness to fully engage with life. Most Westerners only dance wildly, if at all, when they are young, in clubs or at parties, high on alcohol or drugs (or in someone else's country). Feeling a buzz is not the same as real joyfulness, the expression of aliveness in the full sense of the word. Alcohol is not so much enjoyed as used as a means to an end – to overcome inhibitions. Unfortunately, excessive drinking just deadens the senses, limiting full aliveness as it does so.

Expressions like 'depth of engagement' and 'being with your energy' speak to this sense of aliveness. What being fully alive *does not mean* is blindly running around making a lot of noise, catharting and having tantrums all over the place; it doesn't mean teenage-style rebellion (though this may be an attempt to reclaim it) or forcing your energy onto other people, regardless of where they are at, under the misapprehension that you are being 'real' and 'authentic'. They run a workshop called 'OSHO Born Again' in Osho's commune, (now known as OSHO International Meditation Resort) in Pune, India. This gives people permission to feel into and act out their childhood wounds. You can always tell when this group is happening: you see tearful people walking around clutching worn, soggy, one-eyed teddy bears. However, what is always made very clear (and this applies to all the workshops) is that you don't act out outside of these groups. If you keep doing so you are likely to be asked to leave the commune and this is quite a useful learning in itself.

Aliveness is juicy, full of energy – *even* (and this may sound surprising) *when that energy is still*. We are open and accessible to life: to joy, to pain, to laughter; to both receiving and expressing. We are open to a kind of energetic, spontaneous combustion that is contagious, and any expression – *when we are connected in this way* – is itself a celebration! It is an expression of thankfulness. I remember dancing with thousands of others in the meditation hall in the commune, each person totally with themselves and their blissfulness, yet all of us together *and aware of being together,* in one space. All in white, on a white marble floor, under a white canvas roof; the tall bamboos strung with fairy lights creaking in the darkness outside. This was a totally unique experience for me, as it would be for most of us; and it's not something I have found anywhere else. Carnivals come closest, but they tend to express the Zorba energy without the Buddha. This was an expression of totality, the union of both: of the one in its many forms and faces dancing with itself.

Surely many of us have experienced moments where we feel a deep stirring at our core, a sense of being moved by something that is powerful, but difficult to put a name to? Certain things can provoke this, like falling in love or standing on top of a mountain looking out across some grand vista, but it may arise when we are just sitting quietly somewhere doing nothing in particular. We get a taste of something, a twinge of exhilaration, an energy wanting to expand and move that is not, in itself, physical. There is an awareness of a sense of passionate aliveness that is to be found through the body – as if we are lit up by spirit and may become, like the sun, one ball of blazing energy and light. Life itself may not need a body, *but to live as a human expression of itself it absolutely does!* So when we wake up and stop being intimidated by our fears and fantasies it can be shocking to discover how much we have limited ourselves, limited this expression of life. And all the while life is just waiting to know you! All around us everything, everywhere, is presenting the invitation: here it is, come out and play! One could even say the planet herself is holding her breath for humanity to wake up and *let life in*!

Home-Play

1. Take a pause to *let in*
- Stop. Breathe. Consciously let *in* on the out breath.

  Repeat frequently throughout the day. You may notice a slight tremble, a little fear as you do this, so remember to treat yourself with tenderness. All is well.

2. The unwanted child: including what is being left out
- Using whichever one of your arms feels right, extend this arm out beside the body, palm facing outwards, as though pushing something away. Feel the urge to reject, to suppress, to get rid of. Feel this in the body: the not wanting to own this part, the unspoken message of 'Go away!' towards this energetic presence (and whatever it represents to you)
- Next feel your heart, take a breath and (this is extremely subtle) allow this feeling of wanting to push away relax as you let in the possibility of dropping this reaction; and, instead, letting something in. The sense that it might, after all, be accepted, even wanted, even welcomed! (It is essential that you stay in contact with your feelings here and don't try to change or force anything. It has to be a true response and this can only happen in its own time.) Allow the hand to sense this energetic possibility. Moving the fingertips, feel into this and notice how the hand may start to turn a little towards you (it may waver in this process as your feelings waver) until the palm is now loose and facing towards you.
- Now, very slowly, very consciously, bring this arm in towards you: Inviting, welcoming and encouraging this that has felt unwanted and excluded. You might call this your 'inner child' (labels don't really matter) - any small vulnerable part that has been shut away, abandoned, avoided or denied.
- Stop moving the arm at about the distance this arm would be if it were holding someone close; don't try and pull anything towards you. It is enough to hold to the feeling of being available, expressed in the movement and positioning of the body. Once again, slowness makes this more powerful.

3. Saying Yes! to life
- Sitting comfortably, feet on the floor, buttocks on a seat and spine reasonably erect, breathe into the cradle, and then focus attention on the heart.
- Bring the hands in front of the heart, with the fingers facing it and elbows lifted. As you breathe out, open the arms into a wide open gesture, feeling the chest expand as you do so, with a sense of defences melting, letting everything both in and out. Say the word '*Yeeeessss!*' as you do so.

  With this exercise, it is important to wait until you feel the body is ready to respond spontaneously: never force it.

Sacred sensuality

'I believe in the flesh and the appetites; seeing, hearing, feeling, are miracles, and each part and tag of me is a miracle. Divine am I inside and out, and I make holy whatever I touch or am touch'd from; the scent of these armpits, aroma finer than prayer; this head more than churches, bibles, and all the creeds.' ~ Walt Whitman, Leaves of Grass

'What was invented with civilisation was the ability of some to deny sensuality to others.' ~ Richard Manning, Against the grain: How agriculture has hijacked civilisation

'I don't have a philosophy: I have senses...If I talk about Nature, it's not because I know what it is but because I love it, and that's why I love it. Because when you love you never know what you love, or why you love, or what love is. Loving is eternal innocence, and the only innocence is not thinking.' ~ Alberto Caeiro, The Keeper of Sheep

Sensuality is very much part of aliveness. Do you remember when you were a child splashing in puddles, what fun that was? Or holding a kitten and stroking its soft fur, how warm and alive it felt? Running a stick along a railing to make a musical sound, or holding a pebble and feeling the smooth surface in your hand? I had a whole collection of assorted treasures, including a soft owl's feather that I loved stroking across my cheek, a broken green glass statue that, when I looked through it, coloured the world green, a delicate white crab's shell, a shiny blue bead flecked with purple and gold like some exotic bird's egg and so on. Children are natural magpies and have no interest in objects needing to have a monetary value. I collected the down from dandelion clocks and made it into soft balls and pulled the stems of long grass to suck the sweetness from the stalk.

These were simple sensual pleasures that had nothing to do with what adults saw as important. We could say that these times were full of an innocent aliveness – filled with connection and response to what we found around us – without the mind coming in with all its assessments and judgements and condemnations. There seemed to be time to just explore and delight in such simple pleasures, and even now – a long way from my childhood – I can't walk down a street in summer without stopping to smell the roses I pass and run my fingers over lavender heads to gather their scent.

One of the wonderfully relaxing things about being an older woman is not drawing the attention of men; not being checked out by some predatory, lustful, or even just hopeful member of the opposite sex. I know that sounds strange, so let me explain: this absence of attention allows one the absolute freedom to just be; to watch others if you feel so inclined without a sense of being part of a game – and I enjoy this enormously. It doesn't mean if an admiring glance comes my way I can't appreciate this. It has nothing to do with being cut off from forming friendships or meaningful relationships; these can still happen, but they tend to be more genuine and formed out of shared mutual interests, although there can still be an energetic attraction too. Yes really! Age is not a barrier to energy; there may be less of the physical kind but the energy of attraction is not physical in that sense. It's more about subtle energy, and this is influenced by the senses: especially the sense of smell, but also touch and voice and all the feeling responses of the heart.

So not being watched in this way by men in general removes one from the game of pursuit. Nothing wrong with playing if that is what you feel to do, but so many women put themselves under constant pressure because of this: pressure to look their 'best', to focus on image and presentation of the packaging. And this is essentially goal-orientated, to get: to get attention, to get a man (for a lover, boyfriend, husband, companion) or to keep the one you have. Underlying this is a sense of insecurity, and this doesn't allow for a relaxed spontaneous being-in-the-moment, where natural affinities can ripen and grow by themselves. This is why it can feel such an enormous relief to no longer need to fuss about all that.

None of this means I don't enjoy clothes: styles, fabrics, colours and textures and varying combinations, nor enjoy having these appreciated; that I don't bother how my hair is cut and never paint my toenails. However, I now do these things to please myself. And sometimes I do choose to dress for others. For instance, if I have occasion to travel on the commuter trains to London where everyone wears black and dark colours, or when the weather feels overcast and oppressive, I sometimes feel to wear bright colours to cheer everyone up. Not wanting to play the hunting game doesn't mean I can't enjoy relationships either. What I have seen is that women who are no longer caught up in these games don't approach others *from a feeling of lack or desperation,* and in consequence relationships remain cleaner and can go deeper. We have learnt to enjoy being alone and discovered that the truth is, *in or out of relationship,* life brings challenges and joys – including loneliness and including pleasure. So what I am saying is that while we are still playing out this need to get someone else to fill a role in our life, we are not able to simple be; not able to pay attention to what we feel and know, and what does actually bring contentment. Released from this need, we are still free to play – as we did as children – for the sheer fun of dressing up.

Although sensuality and sexuality are intimately related, sensuality doesn't have to invoke a desire for sex. Sensuality simply means appreciation of the senses. It happens in our bodies not our thinking mind, and is a direct response to both our inner feelings and outer stimulus; it is both an intimate connection *with* and an expression *of* this connection. *So it binds us to life in a way thinking cannot.* And, although sensuality is an absolutely natural function of the body (as of course is sexuality), it is rather sad that in our Westernised culture, sensuality has become so associated with sex that most people don't seem aware of the difference. This means that a load of inherited moralistic and cultural attitudes towards sexuality overlap into – and interfere with – the normal, naturally sensual expression of our bodies.

In fact, to speak about bodies and not include sensuality is like talking about food but ignoring taste! Wouldn't it be wonderful if we could re-value sensuality and see it for what it really is? The most marvellous of our capacities for connecting with life, for responding and relating with everything that is? This sensual expression also includes the giving and receiving of pleasure, and when they are allowed to be spontaneous bodies are naturally sensual. Free from stress and inhibition, they move in an easy, relaxed way, with a grace and swing we often associate with certain animals. We say graceful as a bird or lithe as a tiger. What is forgotten in present-day culture is that *this sensual expression is actually a veneration of life.*

The cost of repression

Children are born into a body built for pleasure, and they will explore and play with this until, sooner or later, the adult world interferes. Can you remember this happening to you? Those subtle or not so subtle signals from parents, teachers and others: that enjoying and expressing pleasure with one's body in public – or where others can see you – is not acceptable? I am not just talking about exploring the genitals. It is actually tragic that, as we grow older, a combination of adult disapproval and inner insecurities lead most children to begin to unconsciously stunt their natural bodily expression and pleasurable response; how quickly we lose the flexibility of a body free to express its delight in itself and the world around us.

I remember an old boyfriend telling me about a time when he was a boy, when the family were gathered around the dining table and he found himself running a drinking glass across his mouth, savouring the feel of the cool, smooth glass against his lips. After a while he became aware of his mother's discomfort and disapproval so that, even though she didn't reprimand him, he too started to feel uncomfortable and stopped. So these repressive forces, often passed down through families and the cultural norms they themselves have absorbed, get passed on, often without even mentioning them. Children feel these powerful forces and rarely question them. At least until they reach a more rebellious age, by which time the harm is done; the feelings have been repressed and stored underground, in the body, where we have no conscious awareness of them. And so begins the whole terrible, damaging business of repression: because when natural responses are repressed they seek an outlet, and this is so often a destructive one.

Maybe you remember, or have heard about, how D.H. Lawrence scandalised his contemporaries by daring to write about not just sex, but sensuality, in *Lady Chatterley's Lover?* How the unexpurgated version, which venerated the sensual joys of the body, was banned? Currently, the repression of our raw animal nature is most visible in men, especially older men in Anglo-North American cultures. Here, the natural ability to combine *sensuality with dignity* – that can still be found amongst men from Mediterranean countries, for instance – has been largely lost (watch an older Spaniard dancing the Tango or the Pasodoble and you will see it).

Whereas there is this sense amongst so many Westernised men now that it's sex or nothing – as if they don't know how to just be sensual. And this brings with it a huge loss, both to themselves and to women. The way so many men live now, with deodorised, be-suited, sedentary lifestyles contributes to this sense of fear of their sensual, 'animal' nature. In the past, men were far more engaged in physical work like farming or mining; naked, sweaty torsos and the grunts and groans of physical labour were normal. Now, this is largely relegated to the boxing ring or a rugby scrum, which only represent one aspect of our physicality. These lack the sensuous combination of grace and rhythm of other activities that people can enjoy watching or participating in, like dance or athletics, without needing to end up in bed! The bald, erotic titillation of the strip club, that has come to be portrayed as 'fun', and sensuality used in advertising to arouse and entice people to buy, all of this speaks to this loss of the innocent pleasure in our body. A disconnect has been created – leaving a gap, filled with promises that don't deliver, that fail to nourish us and leave us feeling less than we are.

As I have come to see it, this loss is central to the mess we have got ourselves into, disconnected – as so many people are – from the wisdom of our bodies. Perhaps you have noticed how people from non-Westernised cultures, like Africans, South Americans and especially Islanders from warm climates, tend to be more uninhibited? How relaxed they appear? How natural it is for them to use their bodies to express their feelings? Where many of them come from the villages and city streets are full of colour and exotic smells and tastes. I remember attending the Notting Hill carnival many years ago. How wonderful it was to see all those black people, mainly of West Indian origin, dressed in such exotic, sexy and colourful costumes, dancing in the streets to the rhythm of steel drums. It was hilarious to see a few white people trying to join in, twitching a hip here, a shoulder there, but generally looking self-conscious and awkward; and it was all pretty new and wild for sedate Londoners at that time.

Memories of this include an old grandmother, in a skimpy turquoise skirt and top with gold fringes, and a virile young man covered in beads and paint, gyrating in the street in front of us; a strong smell of jerk chicken and curried fish, wrapped in silver foil by local people, cooked and sold from tables in their doorways (wherever were the health and safety inspectors?) wafting over us – along with the scent of roasted sweetcorn sprinkled with coconut and brown sugar from stalls beside the road, and lots of Rastas and bongs and heavy incense (this was the Portobello Road before most of the area got gentrified and packed with tourists). I remember thinking thank God for these wonderful island people who knew how to celebrate, how to fully occupy and enjoy their bodies: how needed they were to shake up our stiff old English way of life!

In a way sensuality seems to have been even more firmly suppressed than sexuality; it has attracted more subtle condemnation. Now why would that be? If you look back on European history you see that the clergy – with their hunger for power, and hence need to control the masses and subjugate them to their own version of how to get to God – were responsible for much that has disconnected us from our bodies. Also, an emerging desire amongst people to be seen as respectable (an important part of moving up the social scale), this had its influence too.

But isn't it ironic that those who preach religion, intended to be a means for worshiping God, are so afraid of the spontaneous expression of our God-given form? (The Afro-Caribbean Gospel churches being a clear exception). And this applies not just to Christianity but other religions like Islam, too. Yet if you look closely, you see that it is this very repression of our instinctual bodily responses – taught, inculcated and lived by so many for so long – it is this that is the actual source of so much misery; along with violence and hatred and misogyny and sexual perversions of all kinds. We see how the very act of *conscious control* then puts pressure on the *unconscious* to act out what has been repressed.

The body is a vehicle for expressing a whole repertoire of feelings, so when it is not allowed to do this naturally, trouble is bound to ensue. As we mentioned earlier, bottled up feelings and emotions start to fester; they become toxic and seek an alternative outlet. Hence the terrible and tragic behaviours people exhibit, like the abuse of heavy drugs; or rape, paedophilia and so on. People with a lot of repressed feelings and emotions are potentially dangerous, to others and to themselves. These feelings, when provoked, can erupt beyond our control and cause real harm (as with the man who killed his wife), and of course master manipulators like Hitler exploited this for their own ends. In its extreme, emotional suppression leads to sickness of mind and body and even death, yet you don't hear any of this talked about. Strange, isn't it? Words like *suppression* and *repression,* which hold such power, are not part of our common dialogue. These words – *and their crucial relationship to our behaviour* – are never referred to in the media, and are certainly not taught in schools.

One man who tried to address this as far back as the 1920s was Wilhelm Reich. He saw repression as the root cause of all neurosis. However, both his radical approach to his patients (he actually *massaged* them!), and his active encouragement of young people to explore their sexuality (providing them with the means for birth control), along with his pro-Marxist and antifascist sympathies upset his psychology compatriots no end. (This was in Austria, a Catholic country don't forget.) And even when he moved to America to escape Hitler he was vilified, his books burnt and he himself thrown into prison (for violating an injunction) where he died two years later.

Amazing, isn't it? How threatening recommending exploring and reclaiming our true nature – especially our sexuality – can be! (And still is to those who wield power, if Osho's rumoured Thallium poisoning by the CIA is true.) Whatever Reich's personality (which seems to have been quite dominating), he nonetheless had a big influence on the development of alternative therapies, in particular body-therapies that include emotional release like Bioenergetics and Primal Scream Therapy. Here, it is sobering to note that despite the whole cultural revolution of the late Sixties and early Seventies, during which there was a flowering of what was hastily dubbed 'sexual permissiveness' by straight commentators, so many people are *still* unable to connect deeply with either their sensual bodies or their sexuality. And at the same time, we have ever-more-explicit depictions of sex in films and a big rise in the watching of pornographic material. Could there be a connection?

Why are religious and other authorities so afraid of sensuality and sexuality? Could it be because they are both essentially anarchic? Heaven forbid! Because if we listen to, trust in and start to follow our bodily experience and intuitive knowing, we are no longer subject to control by the arguments and opinions of others, including their concept of morality. We are no longer convinced. We may stop listening, stop paying attention and stop seeking an outside authority to tell us how to behave. Instead, we may start listening to something deeper: listening to life and obeying its call. Then, we no longer need priests and Popes if we have direct access to a living God that includes us all. If we now have access to our own guidance – *anytime, anywhere* – this effectively undermines *all* outside authority including the church, but also any political interests: *in fact any external source that seeks to control us for whatever reason.* No wonder intuition and sensuality are seen as a threat! As too are Pagan religions, with their encouragement of sensual pleasures. (That Christian churches, including the Vatican, are erected on Pagan sites bears out the theme of Christians seeking domination and eradication of all competition.)

But however appreciative of the senses, Paganism too is bound by its own rituals and roles and beliefs, such as the Norse Pagans with their *Nine Noble Virtues* and the Wiccan Redes *'do as you like, but do no harm'*. Even The Charge of the Goddess *'For my Law is to love all Beings'* (according to Doreen Valiente's version), for all its undeniable beauty, is given as a command rather than simply offered as guidance. Ultimately, despite the acknowledgement of all that is non-man-made – including the nature-spirits – being part of the Divine and, as such, inviting of worship, something deeper seems to be lacking.

The sense of celebration and expression of delight in life and its cycles are wonderful. Perhaps less wonderful are some of the hierarchical forms and rituals that are entangled in beliefs of the mind like ivy around a tree. As always, without conscious awareness the egoic mind, unseen, can creep in and strangle the very life such forms are intended to celebrate. The underlying message is the same: control – celebrate my way. And of course you can't do that if you are going to be true. That is what I mean by saying sensuality itself is essentially anarchic: *it is a direct path of communion* needing no form, no rituals, no-one to intercede for us. There is no place for the beliefs of mind, as sensuality offers – potentially – union with what we essentially are. Which is where a focus on what is true is needed to allow this to blossom: then sensuality becomes sacred.

But if we were to simply live 'as the animals', free to respond to our senses and enjoy expressing ourselves through our bodies, surely we would all become savages? And it is true, *in the service of ego* the senses can be abused. As with the Romans, who (or so the story goes) reclined on couches and gorged themselves, only to dangle bacon rind down their throats to make themselves sick so they could continue to feast. But even then, this is just an absurd and rather ridiculous way of gratifying the senses, that reflects a deep and unconscious level of disconnection: a disconnect with Being, with our true nature.

So we come again to the (by now, hopefully obvious) recognition: that it is this disconnect – held in place by a belief in, and identification with, the egoic mind, and the version of reality it presents us with; it is this that prevents us living in harmony with life. Words like 'greed' and 'excess' are used by the mind to condemn, and thereby attempt to control behaviour through learned codes of morality. However, it's not bad or wrong to want to eat a lot, and who is to judge what is 'excess'? It's not wrong to be disconnected either, but all of these things do have an effect. We can see that this extreme emphasis on seeking pleasure for its own sake is just another symptom of our inability to find *real* satisfaction in our lives. We seek more, and then more again, rather than stopping for a moment and allowing ourselves to feel the underlying pain and loneliness and insecurity of living out of alignment with our true nature.

Exploring the senses: Sound

We have already talked a lot about touch, so what about the other senses? Like sound? This too brings a fine level of responsiveness. A man called David Hendy has made radio programmes and written a book about this. In *Noise: A Human History of Sound and Listening*, he talks about the often unrecognised effect of sound on our lives, and indeed our evolution. He speaks about how sound can be subversive, encouraging people to rebel and resist being dominated by the powerful. This was why, he says, in the Middle Ages until only a couple of hundred years ago, carnivals and public celebrations were prohibited, inciting – as they did – the church's outrage at what they saw as encouraging 'riotous and lewd' behaviour. So although sound has been used by humans for millions of years to express feelings and communicate and celebrate, it too has more recently been seen as a threat to order and, where possible, banned or discouraged.

Hendy also talks about the use of sound as a sophisticated means of defence, through long-distance communication. How, for example, native tribes living in the dense forests of West Africa had developed sound to a fine art. They could pass on surprisingly detailed information almost instantly through the rhythm and timbre of their drum beats; so when both British and Dutch armies tried to invade them, they were greatly hampered by needing days or even weeks to get their messages through.

Sound is such a subtle form of communication and can invoke such a powerful feeling response, a response that often carries associations with the past: like church bells for instance, rarely heard in many urban and suburban environments today. (Birdsong, on the other hand, is flourishing in the suburbs, where it is dying out in the countryside. What a strange topsy-turvy world we have created!) In fact, sound *as noise* has become difficult to avoid, along with vibration and the low levels of stress these can induce. One of the things I love about being in the mountains is the silence, broken only by the occasional dog, donkey or cockerel; though places like this, where humans can live in relative peace, are fast disappearing.

But it is as a means of evocation, of moving us on a profound *feeling* level that sound – in the form of music – is most powerful. Perhaps more than any other sense, sound can change our mood and raise or lower our energy; we can be transported to realms that lie beyond the bland material. For music is not only a great leveller, it also gives permission. So people who would otherwise be too inhibited to show their feelings can privately indulge their emotional repertoire whilst listening to music; and this includes of course, singing, where the body itself is the instrument. If you watch a singer, especially one of the great singers – whether of opera, jazz, flamenco or another form – it is extraordinary to listen to what can not only be heard, but *felt*. This can stir feelings that connect us with something so much more vast than our little everyday lives, and so reconnect us, momentarily at least, with something divine. To quote the musician Carlos Santana: *'Music cuts right into your subconscious, it speaks right past your head and into your soul.'*

Colour

What about colour? This is one of the most misunderstood and undervalued influences on our perception, our experience of reality. Most of us have little awareness of how this is affecting us, all day long, whether we pay attention to it or not. And this is not just on our feeling state but also our aura, or subtle energy body; the colours we use impact on the world around us, influencing the way we are perceived, hence the energy we attract: and all of this *affects our sense of wellbeing and vitality* (hence the use of use coloured lamps to treat people). We are even affected by the colour of the food we eat!

So it just makes sense to tune-in when choosing colours for your home (especially a child's bedroom), the sheets you spend up to a third of your life sleeping in, the car you drive, and so on. Bob Moore (Anne Parks' teacher, who understood more about subtle energy than anyone I have met) used to bring builder's colour charts into a class. He talked about how not just the main colours, but each hue and shade has a distinct resonance. So this is another of those places to listen in and trust what you find; to experiment so you can discover for yourself your capacity to sense colour and its impact.

As more evidence emerges of the previously unknown effects of colour, so health professionals and others are beginning to realise its significance. For example, new research by students at the Netherlands Institute of Ecology shows how colours affect free-living songbirds nesting under red, white, green lighting. White light was shown to increases levels of stress hormones (corticosterone concentrations). Nesting close to red light produced even higher levels, whereas under green this was negligible. As this relates to wavelength it is likely blue, being shorter still, would create even less, if any, stress. A difficulty here is that whilst such experiments are no doubt useful to prove the influence of colour to the sceptical, they tend to be translated into immutable 'facts', and these can miss the very fine impact of colour on different people at different times. So remember: you need to tune in in the moment rather than adopting rules.

When I was in my mid-twenties I went back to art college, this time for a course in interior design, and they took us to a lighting factory. Here I was utterly amazed to see how colours of light and the way they mix is totally different to solid pigments. A child of artists, I grew up with the smell of oil paint, turpentine and linseed oil and from a very early age, I was *sure* the primary colours were yellow, red and blue; I was *absolutely certain* red and yellow make orange, yellow and blue, green, red and blue, purple. Well, with light they don't! Blue, red and *green* are the primaries and red and *green* make yellow, blue and red, magenta, blue and green, cyan. I felt like one of those people who was convinced the Earth was flat and then was told no, it had been proved to be spherical. I later realised it is these colours of *light* that I 'see' psychically'. I was made acutely aware of this intimate connection with colour in my mid-thirties, when I began to notice my whole vision would fill up with this very light blue. It was on the Indigo spectrum but very pale, and it somehow made me feel safe and treasured: *I knew it was important because I intuitively sensed and felt its impact.* Shortly after this I was diagnosed as having an overactive thyroid, and I sensed a connection. As I attended to this so the colour faded.

When a client comes for a session we explore colour and it's interesting to notice how inhibited many people are around this, especially men and depending on culture. So most Western men will happily hide out in dark colours, with maybe a bright T shirt at weekends; oh, and those fluorescent yellow and green slippers with dragons heads on they were given for Christmas – at least around the house! Contrast this with men from Asian, African or South American countries or Pacific islanders, and you get a sense this has to do with a fear of expressing both aliveness and also, interestingly, vulnerability.

We Westernised women too have our restrictions, usually dictated by fashion, age or size; hence the tendency amongst larger women to gravitate towards black, hoping it makes them look smaller, and older women to avoiding bright colours. But go down Brixton market – or anywhere with a strong mixed-race element – and you will find grannies dressed in the wildest of colours. I mention all this self-imposed restriction because it's yet another area where we limit our capacity for self-expression and intuitive discernment. It stops us playing with colour, which would allow us to express our vibrancy along with a changing, subtle, energetic response to life – not the old 'autumn', 'winter', 'spring' diagnosis, but tuning-in to our *body*, connecting with our mood-of-the-moment. Keeping a wide range of colours in your wardrobe in rainbow formation, allows you to just pick something out without too much hassle. Try stopping to *feel* and *sense* colours before you get dressed in the morning. Notice how wearing these makes you feel. Experiment. Best not to make any hard and fast rules – there really are none, and things can change.

One of the best things about England is its gardens; here you can walk around and pause in front of different coloured flowers, letting these into your awareness – *receiving* them. As you become more sensitised, you will notice how certain colours draw you, how each has a distinctly separate energy.

Lastly, don't get too serious about all this. It's fun to play, and yet another way of enriching one's life by focussing the senses and enjoying them. See if you can let go of restrictive associations – pink is for girls, black is negative – but would you really want to sleep in broad daylight? Or deny the beauty of an ebony carving? The truth is we live in a paradise of colours, so why miss out on the feast?

Movement and dance, smell and taste

Another form of sensual connection and pleasure is movement and dance. Have you ever wondered why programmes like *Strictly come Dancing* are so incredibly popular? And sometimes with the most surprising people? It's not just the celebrities and sexy partners that attract: watching all forms of dance you can *feel* the energy – from a slow, graceful, lilting Waltz to an intensely erotic Argentine Tango – there is a strong *feeling* content. And I don't imagine I am alone in being able to feel the movement others make in my own body – we just don't talk about this. The Pasodoble, with its Spanish bullfighting theme, carries echoes of Flamenco, where the mesmerising movements reflect such passion, and the Rumba is very sensual to watch. There can be a sense of *duende* in these dances (this word referring to the magical quality, the spirit encountered when the dancers lose themselves in the dance and something deep and impersonal takes over). Remember, Being celebrates life through the body, and in watching we are able to melt and merge to become a part of this. As Abdiel Cedric Jacobsen, of the Martha Graham Dance Company puts it *'Dance is a reflection of life: there will be many moments of excitement, fear, great joy, and great pain, but, as in life, each moment brings its own blessings.'*

A master of Tantra, Daniel Odier, who was born in Geneva, teaches something he calls Tandava from a space of great depth and knowledge but also simplicity. When you listen to and watch him it feels as if he is just so naturally extracting the very essence of what movement is in his talks. Like a snake charmer, as he demonstrates and within the flow, something subtle and exquisitely beautiful reveals itself, something that can easily be overlooked: the sacred expressing itself in form.

Let's not leave out smell and taste here, which are closely related. In another extraordinary feat, Octopi are able to smell and taste through their limbs! *'The majority of their 500m neurones are in their arms, which can not only touch but smell and taste – they quite literally have minds of their own.'* according to Peter Godfrey-Smith, author of *Other Minds: The Octopus, The Sea and the Deep Origins of Consciousness*. I can't resist including his recounting of an octopus taking his collaborator by the hand on a 10-minute tour to its den, "as if he were being led across the sea floor by a very small eight-legged child". What a truly magical world we are living in!

Any garden-lover knows how important smell is (people who create roses without scent are another candidate for the stocks!). And those who love cooking (and eating) love the smells of a kitchen. Fresh sawdust, new-mown hay, parched ground after a sudden downpour: smell is powerfully evocative; it is a primary factor in sexual attraction too (which is why perfume-makers study pheromones in order to produce smells that attract). I once participated in a workshop where everyone was blindfold and then told to move towards someone they felt drawn to. Imagine how disconcerting to find, when the blindfolds were removed, that this person was not at all someone you thought you might be attracted to! And, of course, as is well known about the skunk, smell can be used to repel. In fact smell is the most subtle of communicators.

In his extraordinary book *The Hidden Life of Trees*, Peter Wohlleben, who has lived for many years tending the same forest, talks about how trees feel and communicate; how they use scent to communicate with each other to defend against attack, for instance. Acacia trees in the African Savannah are able not only to fill their leaves with toxic substances (as can many other species) – in this case to ward off attack by giraffes – but to emit a gas, ethylene, to warn neighbouring trees about the approaching threat.

With taste, we tend to associate this with eating and perhaps sex, but there are so many other subtle levels of taste: one can taste the earth, the wind, the air itself. As with smell, we are constantly receiving input that goes unrecognised. Maybe you have a dog or a cat at home? If you do you will have seen how very important these senses are to them, and not just in obvious ways – like telling them when food is coming or who is sexually available. Smell especially, along with taste and sound, is not only a primary means of navigation, but how animals communicate with one another.

It is *we humans,* through our learned inhibitions – and over-reliance on our eyes and ears as a consequence – who largely live in a world of sensory deprivation. Encouraged by things like television and film, we have become overly dependent on these two forms of input; we don't notice that in watching a screen we only receive *partial* sensory information, information that is entirely devoid of taste, smell and, of course, touch. With reading or listening to the spoken voice, this involves a more-wide-ranging sensory response; we translate words into images that may *invoke* sounds, smells and even taste: but again, not touch. And this is important because touch – amongst all the senses – *can ground us in the here and now of reality,* and touching another living being is an act of connection and also, inclusion. In the West, sadly, we have become so adjusted to receiving only partial sensory input that, along with more general inhibitions, we have shut ourselves out from much of the grand theatre of life into which we were born. The senses connect us; and one could question whether the amount of time and attention so many people, especially the younger generation, spend with some form of mobile transmitter glued to their ears, is not actually a rather desperate cry for connection from those who have lost a sense of where to find or how to access the real thing.

Norman Doidge (whom we quoted earlier) wrote two books: *The Brain That Changes Itself* and *The Brain's Way of Healing*). In these he talks about how spending long periods of time watching screens changes the very structures of our brain. He says of his experience *'truth be told, the real scientist begins not with a particular task but a sense of wonder at how the world works. I became comfortable with wonder, writing both of these books – it triggers curiosity and pulls you towards it, but it triggers anxiety at the same time because you don't know what is behind it. I have tried to explain over and over again how mind changes brain structure and function but nobody alive has yet properly defined mind and no one has explained properly how so-called ethereal thought can change so-called material structure. The whole subject is filled with wonder.'* One is left 'wondering' just what effect a lack of touch is having on people; whether it is, actually, slowly dehumanising us?

Sensuality as reverence for life

If you allow your body to move in sensual ways, what do you notice? Bodily movements that are sensual are essentially *slow*. They involve curving, flowing, swaying, undulating, rhythmic movements and things like subtle shaking or shimmying (as with belly dance) and rippling of the body. Indian religious music, Kirtan, is profoundly sensual. The Hindu religion doesn't separate sexuality from religion in the way Christianity does, and the movement of the women's hands in classical Indian dance also show this sensual quality. The Sufis too express this sensuality in their poetry.

Sensual movements can be likened to water flowing, a tree swaying in the wind, flames curling and flickering, a snake wriggling across the earth – they share such clear common ground with the elements and natural forms. And something I have noticed is that I experience a pleasurable sensation in my body on seeing and moving through countryside with rolling hills or sand dunes and various sensual landscapes. I suspect we are all affected by these natural organic shapes but this seems to be largely unconscious and, therefore, unaddressed.

It is no less than tragic to see how this disconnection from a natural sensuality leaves so many of the more recent of our species stranded; prompting knee-jerk titters and awkwardness or sly smirks when something overtly sensual presents itself. We have forgotten how to respond naturally, spontaneously, without heading this response off into a sexual direction. *With conscious intention*, participating in a sensual feast can offer profound healing for a body and psyche infested with self-censoring inhibitions. This can re-connect us with our body as a source of pleasure and delight in an *innocent* way, as when we were children. And I have witnessed how this recovery can be supported, delicately, appropriately; to allow for both dignity and a genuine delight in this gift of a body – in union with Being.

A deep truth is that when we express ourselves in sensual ways, the body can become a conduit. Not only does it allow us to express our delight in moving like this, we become one with what we are moving *within*, with the elements and nature – one with the whole. In order to fully allow this we have to let go of all thinking, let go of the mind altogether and allow ourselves to become vessels: vessels for the expression of something that is deeply felt and intuitively known but cannot be categorised; indeed, cannot be described or explained at all. There is no English word for this although, as we mentioned earlier, the Spanish use this word 'duende', which is rumoured to have its origin amongst a spiritual group of women in Morocco long ago. The Sufi Order International with Per Vilayat Inayat Khan – the so-called 'whirling dervishes' – illustrate this quite beautifully. In this movement the intention is just that: to become a conduit for divine light, for consciousness, for God: to receive this and channel it down into the world of form. Movement is used in many kinds of celebration and ritual, the power of this being entirely dependent on the intention of the participants and their ability to surrender to this. Then, even when the movements become frenzied, a certain *connection* is retained, with the mind totally absent.

When we are in deep communion with our bodies, we are not really so different to the animals and other non-human beings – except that most of us have come to see ourselves as vastly superior: a superiority we measure with the intellect, believing that our clever mental gymnastics somehow mean we are more intelligent. But when you look around you, at what we do to ourselves, each other, and the world we depend on then it looks rather different. If intelligence were to be measured by what we have achieved with our minds, we don't look too clever after all. Not much use getting to the moon and harnessing electricity and all our technological wizardry if we can't live together in peace and harmony. Curious isn't it? How learning to read and write and all our vast accumulation of knowledge doesn't seem to have given us more wisdom, or made us more able to love and care for one another – quite possibly the reverse. It can be hard to accept this is so; to recognise what could be judged as a failure; to see how, in our obsession with the intellect and its goals of dominance and wealth creation, we have entirely forgotten the body-Being – facing this can seem just too depressing. Here is where regaining connection with the eyes of the heart – so we can see what bodies really *are* and what they can do when they function through Being – can open another perspective entirely.

In fact, *bodies are a wonderful connector with intuitive reality, with truth*. Our senses allow us to have immediate relationship with our environment and to appreciate this. So, the feel of cool rain on your skin after a hot dry spell; the taste of a juicy plum straight from the tree; the sound of a dove cooing from a branch overhead; or the sensation of walking barefoot over grass, over sand, across mud, smooth rock, carpets of pine needles. Not just *watching* bodies – whether a graceful dancer or just someone walking down the street who is relaxed and at ease – *but being that yourself;* free to enjoy your body's desire to move in a whole variety of ways. I am not talking the kind of running or speed-walking that requires *will* to produce, with an adrenal rush as the reward. I mean your body responding to *feeling impulses*: so when happy we tend to move in a more flowing, loose and graceful way, and the opposite when we are stressed. A tense body can't really enjoy itself, it is restricted whether by the social and moral inhibitions it has imbibed or just filled with anxious, frustrated emotions and thoughts. So sensual movements are synonymous with relaxation.

It is truly life-affirming to notice how pleasure becomes something different when you are connected with Being. Then, instead of simple gratification, which is something the egoic mind uses to try to fill its lack, pleasure translates into direct *appreciation:* appreciation of everything that comes. This includes a sense of gratitude that is linked in with the heart: a place where giving and receiving are united, the same thing. And again this emphasis on slowness, on slowing down. So, fully tasting an apple, letting yourself be entranced by a blackbird serenading or the smell a rose: all these are things that cannot be enjoyed if we are in a hurry.

The word to *savour* implies this: we can savour life as David Thoreau did and later recorded, in his classic book *Walden,* where he eulogises the pleasures of a slow life in nature, spending hours simply being present with his senses to what presented, what was there. It's important to recognise the *totality* that is expressed through sensuality, that doesn't have to depend on escaping the world but can accept whatever arises, wherever we are. To flow freely, we have to meet anything that gets in the way of this flow, including any social inhibitions. In the totality of experience I am speaking about, *both sensuality and sexuality are given a place in spirituality,* including the spirituality found in nature. We forget that spirit expresses itself through sensuality too! In one sense, this is the essence of what I am writing about because without sensuality the body is denied, our full expression is denied; absurdly, life itself is denied! Along with the power of the body to celebrate this.

So then in *true* sensuality – that is, sensuality empty of egoic drives – we are not only relaxed, we are open to receiving: a smell, a touch, a taste; open to responding too and, essentially, this means we are open to connecting, in the moment. We are undefended. There is no barrier between us and Being, between us and reality. *We are alive!* Then, to the question 'What is my function?' comes the response 'To taste life.' Why? Because I can; because this is a way to worship this that I am, that we all are a reflection *of*.

Home-play

1. Sensual movements

- Practise letting your body undulate. Imagine you are in a river and the waves of a passing boat are going through you, causing the body to ripple. Or you are floating amongst the waves in the ocean, being lifted up and then sliding down into the troughs, letting the pleasurable feel of this movement enter your whole body. Shimmy with your hips (this is very freeing). As with classical Indian dance, move your hands, weaving and flowing together. Imitate a snake being charmed out of a basket or the tendrils waving on some under-water plant. Lie on the floor and wriggle, or you might want to imitate a caterpillar walking or a cat stretching after a nap. Make this both a game and a habit.

Notice any feelings of foolishness or embarrassment and remind yourself you are loosening up from all the conditioned inhibitions and control patterns you have absorbed during your lifetime, letting your natural bodily responses free to just enjoy themselves.

2. Exaggerate bodily constraints

- Imagine you are wrapped up tightly like a mummy or bound in a straight jacket; or practise moving like a robot with sharp, jerky movements.
- Then stop, shake and move with sensual movements and *feel* the difference, the contrast, *feel* what happens to your body on all levels, including the breath.

Again, recognise how you have been constraining your energy and limiting your natural, joyful, sensual response to life. Be present to any feelings that may come up, of sadness perhaps, as a result of this.

3. Allow yourself to enjoy being touched by yourself

- Touch any part of your body. Don't intentionally exclude the sexually erotic zones but you don't need to include them, either. As you stroke yourself notice all sensations; different textures; warm and cool places; how this makes you feel. Let your fingers express love and tenderness. Treasure this body. Pleasure too is God-given! Remember; enjoying your body is Being enjoying itself.

Sexual union & the search for the inner lover

'He who penetrates the body's nature is liberated' ~ Abhinavagupta, 10th century Kashmiri philosopher (from a quote by Tantric master Daniel Odier)

'When I touched her body, I believed she was God. In the curves of her form I found the birth of Man, the creation of the world, and the origin of all life.' ~ Roman Payne

'Orgasm is the involvement of the total body: mind, body, soul, all together. You vibrate, your whole being vibrates, from the toes to the head. You are no longer in control; existence has taken possession of you and you don't know who you are. It is like a madness, it is like sleep, it is like meditation, it is like death' ~ Osho

Sexuality can be one of the most deep, powerful, beautiful and fulfilling of human experiences. It has enormous potential to enrich out lives. And yet, this word is one of the most loaded in the dictionary, it carries so much baggage. It carries such association with things which are anything but beautiful – with pain and shame, disappointment and betrayal, with jealousy, frustration and the struggle to achieve.

Much of what I have already said about sensuality applies to sexuality, especially around repression. But before moving on, I want to take a look at what too often gets left out and remains unseen in attempts to explore this illusive potential; at what lies buried amidst the rubble of confusion and failed attempts to find the promised 'holy grail'. We think we know what sexuality is, but do we really? What if it is so much more than our *idea* about it? Even when this is based on some experience? In fact most people, as they grow up and begin to explore this, acquire a very limited and often quite distorted notion of what sexuality is. So just for a moment, can we let go of what we think we know and allow ourselves to play in the land of possibility?

For instance, supposing that instead of sex being simply a means to have an enjoyable experience, relieve tension, bond with a lover or create children, what if it is also a natural way of replenishing ourselves through connecting with the whole? What do I mean by this? Well, take sleep. Nobody knows what we are doing when we sleep (I don't mean dreaming, but during what is called 'deep sleep'). I once had to research something for a design project that involved sleep and I was amazed to discover how very little is known about this subject. Yes, we know that parts of the body get busy regenerating themselves, but what about the mind? It seems that during sleep the mind takes a break; that were it not to do so, and for regular periods, the body would be unable to continue. It appears that a tremendous amount of energy is needed to maintain this mind with its sense of personal identity, so sleep is a way of re-charging our batteries.

Then, during sleep, we no longer need to keep up the idea of a mind and a self and being a separate 'someone'; during sleep mind as we know it fails to exist. The blueprint remains, the basic archetypal, physical structures, including limited brain activity, *but the psychological aspect that is contained in identity is absent during sleep.* The question children often ask: 'Where do we go to when we sleep?' is answered by 'nowhere'; because during sleep *'we'* do not exist (though a body that others might identify as 'us' may do). Now what if this dissolution of the mind, with its sense of self, allows us to reconnect with the whole? Even that it is this disappearing back into the One that is *essential* to our continuing to remain alive? Continuing to make an imprint on life as an apparent individual? Mind itself cannot know if this is true, but the intuitive connection with Being can sense or intuit this.

Coming back to sex, what if this is *also* a way of recharging our batteries? Because in the moment of orgasm – as in sleep – we merge into the whole and, however briefly, let go of our separate selfhood (what is known as 'the little death'). If we take this even further, we might say sex is a way of penetrating the veil between the inchoate nothingness and the manifest in the form of a human life. So that when we orgasm together, male and female, we create a portal through which spirit can enter in the form of a child, the sperm and egg containing the blueprint and physical building materials. And that when humans enter this sacred portal *consciously*, they allow something of the divine to flow into the mundane world. Whether this is consciousness itself or some unknown elixir of the sacred Being, who knows?

Could it be that in this act of conscious sexual union humans create an exquisitely alive and potent 'force' that has enormous potential? Including for healing and the enlivening of Being-ness everywhere? You can accuse me here of wild and absurd fantasies but the truth is no-one knows: that is no scientist, philosopher, theologian or academic – none of the accepted guardians of 'knowledge'. But then wisdom, *the knowing of truth,* cannot be learned from a book, hoarded or claimed: it can only be recognised and lived.

Whatever the truth of all this, which you need to discover for yourself, it is clear sexuality holds an extraordinarily potent and beautiful opportunity for surrender; an opportunity to allow the experience of individuality to dissolve into the whole, into the Oneness of Being. And yet, tragically, this so rarely happens – in its full flowering anyway. Instead, sex has come to represent the most confused, contentious and misunderstood aspect of human life. Condemned and constrained by so many religious organisations, clumsily disbursed as biological 'facts' in school curriculums, frequently a source of anxiety and dismay amongst parents; with its power ruthlessly exploited by both media and corporate sales interests, sexuality remains to many a mystery.

In spite of its potential for bringing joy and deep satisfaction, widespread frustration and disappointment is common. *'We have never been freer to define our own relationships, and follow our own pleasure, but despite this we are far from satisfied'* says Philippe Brenot, a French psychiatrist, in his book *The Story of Sex: From Apes to Robots,* where he attempts to understand sexuality by examining our social history. *'People think sexuality is just an instinct, that it is natural like eating and drinking. No. There is no gene that drives sexuality. All sexuality is learned.'* (Here we have a perfect example of what the mind does when it tries to study something beyond its grasp: the utterly absurd conclusions it reaches.)

So what is really happening here? When we look closely, using conscious awareness combined with our intuitive insight to feel our way into this, we can recognise how, in the attempt to exploit sexuality *for emotional and sensory gratification,* we unknowingly limit its potential and something extraordinarily precious gets lost. If you look with fresh eyes at how sex is often pursued, doesn't it seem odd the way we go about doing this in our culture? For example, someone feels horny so they look up an internet dating site, arrange to meet a perfect stranger and after a brief drink, chat, whatever, go to one of their homes. There, they peel off their clothes and proceed to attempt to arouse each other as they enter, or are entered by, the other's most intimate body part. Doesn't this strike you as a little strange? Yet this is what many people do in the quest to find sex and/or intimacy – whether that's a one-night stand or looking for someone to share the rest of their life with.

What I am pointing to here has nothing to do with concepts of morality, by the way. It has a great deal to do with a failure to trust the body and listen *in;* to listen to the discerning heart; to the intuitive, feeling, sensing body that knows about timing and appropriateness, instead of overriding this with lust or desperate hopes and fantasies around finding a partner. When we listen to this that doesn't get swayed by old fears around wanting and not being wanted, getting and not getting and so on, we *know!* We are in tune with ourselves. I am talking about bringing conscious awareness in and listening to this that sees when, as so often happens, we get distracted and listen instead to the longings of our insecure child.

What we are talking about involves a failure to really connect, with ourselves and with the other, so ignoring true relationship and separating sex from our essence, from Being. We turn sex into a commodity. Then all the potential for depth and richness and profound moments of meeting and surrender to Being become buried – buried under an avalanche of grasping or avoiding, failing or succeeding, bargaining and pretending; or, if that is what is wanted, dominating and being dominated: along with either brief excitement and temporary relief, moments of feeling wanted and desired, or feelings of frustration, inadequacy, even despair.

As the subtle world of intuition, of deep feeling, delicate sensing and all the body's wonderful capacities for response get overlooked or overridden, the innate beauty of sex *as reverence for all that is* gets lost; lost in the struggle to obtain 'great sex', and our programmed ideas of what this should look like, so often with the emphasis on appearance and technique. We have been given such a great gift and we don't know how to receive it.

Sex as a path to surrender

There are numerous tensions between men and women, or partners of any gender, and these play out in our sexual lives, causing upset and feelings of separation. When we take gender roles to be the ultimate definition of who we are – when we believe we *are* the body-mind – then sexuality gets taken out of context; then sex comes to be seen, almost inevitably, as a commodity. We use it to gain something, to seek pleasure and procreate without acknowledging its deeper significance. Yet intuitively we feel this, especially women. Because whatever our mental attitudes, instinct naturally inclines us to move towards sexual fulfilment, especially when we are young, even if we try to deny its potency in our lives. Even the most thought-addicted individual comes to let go, temporarily, if s/he surrenders to the pull.

It may even be that a variety of bizarre sexual acts and extreme behaviours are an attempt to reach into a raw potential, into something we sense we have lost – lost in the habit of controlling through our conditioned mind. Hence the attraction of films like *Fifty Shades of Grey*, as people seek stimulation in ever wilder ways to break through the ice; and greater desolation and despair is often the result, because our true nature doesn't respond to this approach and cannot deliver the deep *satisfaction through connection* that we crave in these ways. All it can do is focus us momentarily on the body instead of the mind, but even here, a body unoccupied cannot suddenly deliver. And so we miss out on one of the greatest joys in life.

What was your initial sexual experience like? Many people I know were unable to gently explore their sexuality with another when growing up, with mutual respect and kindness, in a friendly atmosphere free from pressure and judgement: not just of parents and society but also our peer group. As a girl growing up in England in the Fifties there were three choices: you either didn't and were a 'good girl' – meaning you were worthy of respect and even marriage by 'nice boys' (and being called frigid by others, including some of the 'nice boys' behind your back), or you went 'all the way' – which put you firmly in the 'fast' bracket (in which case you could be called a tart and looked down on by 'nice boys' and their friends) or you took part in a sleazy ritual, often carried out in the backseat of cars, where the two combatants played out their respective roles: the boy to go as far as he could, and the girl to keep resisting as long as she could, and basically stay in control. The terms A, B and C were used to denote stages of progress, and lively discussion with your own gender went on afterwards as to how far you had got (boys) or how far the boy had been allowed to go (girls). Either way, it was all pretty sordid and frustrating.

It seems sexual experience for young people hasn't really changed that much, although there are fewer half-way games. There is still external pressure (especially from social media) and, it would seem, a cult of disrespecting young girls regardless of whether they perform. Although it is generally acceptable now, in the West at least, to have sex outside marriage *there is still an almost total lack of insight into what sex can be*. The Sufi poet Rumi said something like 'Be careful about shaming sexual behaviour in an adolescent or anyone who hasn't yet had his or her fill of erotic trancing. Often, the closest we come to surrender is orgasm.' This points to a need to allow sexuality to flower without interference, learning to honour this as a way to experience surrender to our essential Being-ness.

For women especially, sex is often deeply disappointing. We long to be met and to merge and so often end up frustrated, blaming either ourselves or our partner. I remember a time when this was happening for me: the misery of lying awake for hours with this deep feeling of sorrow and loss, feeling let down by something I could neither articulate nor control. There was such a sense of desolation, of moving towards something only to find oneself somehow left behind, and what felt like abandonment despite the best efforts of my partner – as if the tide had come surging in and withdrawn again, leaving me like an empty shell, feeling flat and exposed on the sand. We read books, tried a variety of techniques and all that seemed to lead to was the label 'frigid'.

What I didn't understand at the time was that beneath my apparent inability to let go, beneath what seemed to be a fear of loss of control, lay the fear of not being truly met, 100%, and fear of consequent feelings of abandonment that I ended up feeling anyway! It took me some years to begin to get a sense of something: partly because it was subtle, but also because I had never heard anyone talk about it. What I eventually realised is that the female body has an inbuilt spontaneous defence mechanism and knows when to protect itself, and that this can *and needs to be* trusted: it can't be cajoled or forced.

In this way, women are very different to men. We can liken a women's internal sexual landscape to a cave: a cave that holds her most treasured jewels – her essence. Whatever you call it or see it as, it's precious and there is an integrity, an inner knowing in women about the right partner, the right time and the right approach that needs to be honoured. Women in the past (perhaps those who worked as temple priestesses?) doubtless had their own ways of dealing with this, but in today's world very little is known about women's true sexuality. Although, as we mentioned in the previous chapter, there is a growing interest in anything that calls itself Tantra, this often has more to do with coming free from sexual guilt – and in the process, something far more precious and delicate gets overlooked. What this is doesn't generally sell workshops: it can be known *by you* and is entirely personal *to you*; then the sharing of this can be sacred.

When it is in service to the egoic mind, sex becomes about pleasure and power rather than intimacy. Sexual intimacy infers feelings of longing for closeness, union with a *particular* individual, as contrasted with desiring someone simply because they arouse your sexual appetite, which (usually more with men) can take the form of a sexual conquest, and include feelings of power and domination that have nothing to do with love. We could describe this difference in terms of energy centres or chakras, the base chakra being concerned with an *impersonal* sexual arousal and the second chakra with the personal: that is, arousal and desire dependent on a specific other. The solar plexus is (in part) concerned with power and the heart with love. (Once again, these are *tentative* descriptions designed to give you a *feel* for something related to your subtle energy body.) So then we can see how the solar plexus can interfere with intimacy, especially when the heart is closed off (defended), by pulling attention into fears of inadequacy – and into a consequent unconscious desire for power and domination, most often in men. (This cycle of fear of inadequacy leading to a desire to overpower is a thread that runs throughout men's relationship with women.) In this place of sexual conflict and energy blockages, there are certain exercises you can do to help free energy, but my experience is that whatever you do, *you have to meet the issues that are causing blockages and imbalances* or these simply return, or shift into another area. However, there is one thing that *can* bring relief and support to women and this is to connect with her own inner male.

Finding the lover within

The longing for union with another, which I am saying is part of a deeper longing for union with the whole, finds expression through sexuality. Yet it is perfectly possible, *though not widely known,* that we can achieve this sense of completeness that comes from union with our opposite gender, within ourselves, without the physical presence of another. Here, it is important to recognise that this does not have to take the form of *physical orgasm*. I am talking about an *energetic, felt sense of connection*, that satisfies on a profound level. I sense this connection around the back of the sacral area in the lower body. When this happens it can be quite amazing, even earth-shattering to realise you can feel the same feeling of desire and attraction you feel for another, within yourself! That what you thought of as something that only gets aroused by another – their presence or your thinking about them – can actually be activated within your own energy-field by your focussing your awareness on this. Then, when a partner appears, they catalyse this energy for you; they add the dimension brought by another body and another personality, with its own particular qualities, desires, preferences and so on.

Then our experience expands beyond the simple essence of male and female, gaining in all kinds of interesting dimensions. Does this sound strange? Can you feel a sense of what I am saying here? It is extremely subtle and requires all of your sensitivity. I am not referring to pleasuring yourself, bringing yourself to orgasm. What I am talking about is you being able to feel this sense of union *within yourself*, hence coming free from a need for an *actual other* in order to experience desire and *energetic union*. Then if you are alone, you can still access this sense of a deep bond with this energy and be satisfied *by the felt presence of the other gender* creating a sense of wholeness. No need for dependency on a separate other to experience this. No need to feel split and alone in your limited gender role. Extraordinary to realise we can experience communion with both genders *within ourselves* without needing to be some sort of boring hermaphrodite!

There is much talk of finding your inner lover in tantric circles and, as we have noted, this tends to be focussed around pleasure. Nothing wrong with that but what I am talking about here is something else: an inner relationship that is not focussed on orgasm. Because for a woman to see that *as a woman,* she can experience her counterpart, the male, as always being there for her, waiting to meet her – ever present, never absent – can be life-changing. With this comes the experience of her wholeness *beyond* gender: meeting who she really is.

It is a bit like the way you can experience both hands separately and yet they are joined to the one body, but this difference goes so much deeper than that: it has a profound intuitive *feeling* quality that is both fulfilling and nurturing. It brings the sense not just of being met, but *completed;* at peace and resting in the knowing that this is so, always has been so, always will be so. Woman is usually far more aware of this potential than man: she senses it, longs for it in the deepest recesses of her feminine human Being-ness. And because hardly any women know this inner male – that can also be represented by the outer – she is always trying to find this in a partner. And if she fails to be deeply met, as many women do even *with* a partner, she can start to shrivel inside and blame and reject men as a gender.

Because I am speaking from my own experience as a woman here, in terms of men finding and meeting their inner woman – and being able to find completion as a result – I can't speak directly. But it would seem likely that man too can experience his internal woman being there for him: ever present, ever waiting, eternally his to penetrate and offer himself to – and thus unify with, energetically, *internally*. I see man's true nature as protecting and giving: he has the instrument of giving to prove this, whether this involves giving his sperm to form a child or giving pleasure or comfort, demonstrating his love or surrendering himself through the woman to unite with Being (in the deepest sense, this could be seen as the ultimate form of giving, or offering).

A spiritual teacher called Barry Long used to talk about the woman containing a special essence and about man's role in gathering this through the sexual act of penetration. But regardless of this possibility, the man essentially penetrates the woman, and this act of penetration can also be withdrawn. Hence it is easier for men to offer themselves around because they don't have to open and allow someone to enter deep into their most intimate province – they are not *receivers*. If a child is created they don't carry it in their bodies and feed it from their bodies. *They can leave*. And of course women know this and it can affect their feelings and behaviour towards men. A line from that old English ballad *Early One Morning* comes to mind: *'Oh don't deceive me, oh never leave me, how could you use a poor maiden so'*.

Woman's bodies are *essentially* different. We are not just naturally more receptive by nature, our bodies are designed to *be* receptive; as I have just said, we receive the male organ deep into our bodies. And permission is needed here which is why rape is such a violation. It not only violates the sanctity of a woman's body but in so doing, in over-powering her by force, it takes away the ability of the woman *to choose* who enters her body and when, forcing her to receive what she is designed to *select*. Overriding her nature and destroying her dignity and integrity in this way profoundly wounds a woman. And what is not seen or talked about is that for a man, who is usually more powerful physically, to force entry into a woman he must also betray *his true nature*: forsaking his power to give, *to bestow*, and his dignity as someone who is *chosen and welcomed* and *received by woman* – along with the integrity of his role of honouring and protecting her and, potentially, her child.

What I am saying here is that this act is actually damaging for the man too, on emotional, psychic and spiritual levels. Contrary to the infantile message believed by some men with issues around power and inadequacy, he has abased himself and admitted his inability to *be* a true man, true to his gender; along with his deep-seated sense of powerlessness and fear of women. Macho bravado is designed to hide an underlying shame (visible to those who care to look beneath the surface of characters like Donald Trump), hence the unconscious collusion amongst male authorities like the police in resisting pursuing and prosecuting rape. So we try to control and deny what we are afraid to meet.

Sexual healing

As with sensuality, there is much to reclaim via the body; much distortion and pain to heal and, as we find our way back into the heart and begin opening to love, much to be discovered, enjoyed and deeply met. Indeed, we could say that sexual healing is one of the most urgent needs in society. The pain, which is stored in the body in the sexual areas, can lead to all kinds of self-and-other destructive thoughts and behaviours. When sex gets mixed up with power, and unresolved issues around this, it becomes dangerous. We could even say it underlies the drive to make war, to conquer other countries. So being willing to look and to meet what we find, and seek help when needed, is invaluable.

There are many books, courses and teachers available; exploring by following your intuitive heart will enable you to find what works best for you. Connecting with your inner opposite-gender can be greatly healing; as can just spending time feeling into this area of the body, sensing old wounds, creating rituals with candles and incense: whatever allows this to come free. You will know this through the levels of tension felt in the body and a sense of release or lightening of this tension. Persistent cystitis and other diseases in the sexual region are affected by our beliefs; so if you can identify these, such as: 'I am unattractive therefore nobody will desire me. I can't expect to be really loved, therefore I must be grateful for anything I can get.' this really helps. Those who suffer most from such beliefs may attempt to compensate for the feelings and emotions these engender through fantasising, and this leaves an inner emptiness. We detach from the here and now and, therefore, the sense of aliveness that comes from fully engaging with life. In retreat, we cut ourselves off not just from the possibility of hurt and rejection and disappointment, but from the joy and delight and wonderment of participation in the flow. How very sad.

So where to go to find help? A plethora of books and courses and workshops that tend to use the word 'Tantra' has grown to meet a growing interest in sexuality. (Julie Henderson's *The Lover Within* is a classic.) The majority of these will attempt to teach you how to get more and better – more pleasure, more uninhibitedness, more excitement, more and better partners, better orgasms. In other words, more of what the egoic mind thinks it wants. Real Tantra has nothing to do with this. It is a way to awaken through the body and its energy systems that involves the exact opposite: *letting go of wanting*. How do you have sex without wanting? Who is asking the question? What is it that wants? Aha! There is that pesky ego again – we come back to the same place. Here, a useful to question to ask is 'What is it that you *really* want?' And if, when you dig deep enough you find this to be union, even if that is a vague yearning and you don't really know what with, then wonderful! Let yourself be taken, devoured; dissolve into the one Being that you never truly left. Rest and refresh.

Sexual healing groups and sessions can actually be of great value *as long as the space is held with safety and respect*, and the best of these will allow your experience to go deeper. A woman called Marlies Cocheret does some wonderful, very delicate work in this area that is grounded in stillness. Her video *'Awakened Lovemaking'* (on her website) contains the most beautiful, simple and relevant comments that cut to the heart of what this is really about: trusting the body, *because it is bodies that know how to make love*. Here is where mind has absolutely no place.

So ultimately, the core of resolving our dilemmas remains the same. If we can recognise and meet whatever is there, especially if we can do this with compassion; if we can open through the body-Being to what we really *are* then all misunderstanding and confusion falls away, in its own time. And – once again – this is greatly helped by a willingness to see the limitations of mind and stop believing it's stories; instead, trusting the intuitive wisdom of the body, trusting our love so we can let go of all that gets in the way of resting in Being. Then any connection through touch becomes a sacrament.

Funny how we always seem to come back to touch, Isn't It? One of the most effective ways to bring the energy down out of your mind is through touch – stroking and caressing your body, getting physical and enjoying this. Getting to know your body. Noticing the warmth or coolness of your skin; parts where it is rougher, others silky smooth, some areas that are more sensitive than others. Just by bringing your attention to your body in this way it is easier to forget about thoughts. If this touching wants to go in a sexual direction, into pleasuring yourself, that's totally fine, although this isn't necessarily the intention. Whoever invented the gross and hideously cumbersome word 'masturbation' is another candidate for rotten eggs.

As for that awful label 'frigid' – my God! Why do I sense these words were invented by some joy-less, out-of-their body, intellectually-constipated prat? Certainly they came from a mind, with its love of labelling and categorising and blind indifference to the harm this can cause. Have you ever heard a man being called frigid? Impotent yes, but problems getting an erection are not the same: this doesn't imply an inability to orgasm, to climax; *to feel, to let go*. Rather, it refers to a failure of the scaffolding, a functional disability, even if this does have psychological causes and ultimately prevents orgasm. The simple truth is that this label 'frigid', that has been the cause of so much stigmatising and pain and hopeless self-criticism amongst women over the years, *is actually a lie*. There is no such thing as a frigid woman, a woman unable to have orgasms; there are only defences – defences erected to avoid pain and inappropriate liaisons.

Sex, love and intimacy

Can we bring in the word love here? How about that sex without love is tantamount to saying 'connect organs without connecting with who you are with'? That this sits in denial. Is this a fear of the other? A fear of intimacy? I hesitate in using the word 'love' because, as we saw in the chapter on feelings, it is used to mean different things. What about if we include respect and affection? Out of all the spiritual teachers, Osho stands out as a shining exception in his willingness to confront sexuality. Here are a couple of interesting comments he made: *'In love the other is important; in lust you are important'* and *'People who are afraid of love are not afraid of sex. Love is dangerous; sex is not dangerous, it can be manipulated.'* Here we are faced with one simple truth that awaits our willingness to recognise it: as an expression of our wholeness, our true Being-ness, *sexuality has to involve intimacy*. This may seem obvious but what real intimacy involves is dropping all our defences.

So many people remain unaware of their defences or, if they are aware, have strong resistance to letting these go. It's scary stuff to meet another *truly* naked – hence all the games, such as advocates of so-called 'free love', where someone demands their 'right' to have lots of lovers, which handily protects them from ever having to go to this deep and scary place with another: to risk. What would they be risking? Being hurt; feeling rejected, abandoned, engulfed, guilty, betrayed; dominated, dependent or depended on – all the patterns and behaviours that replicate whatever circumstances we were raised with. Instead, we can just move on to another object of desire.

Sex, if allowed to be real and go deep, will bring *everything* up. So when you recognise this, it comes as no surprise that humans get into such messes around sexuality, does it? It takes courage to step up to the plate: *emotional courage:* a quality greater than any act of physical bravado. And there are no guarantees. You don't know when you go into it how things will turn out. Which is why if you can see it as a way to open your heart and let go into life, you can't lose. No matter how painful the experience, only love will bring you through. Here a deep connection with Being offers strength and refuge. We each have our own lives to unpack so if sexual relating is there in yours can you open to receiving the gift?

For sure there are times in our lives when sexuality isn't happening, isn't a focus. But when it is, it opens up Pandora's box. So when we can see to untangle the undergrowth blocking the doorway, and take our courage to step inside, there is a world of enchantment that awaits us. This can extend from the slowest, gentlest whisper to the wildest dance as the two bodies each follow the energy and interpret and respond to the intuitive signals between them. In this process of moving towards the intensification of desire, a myriad subtle sensing, feeling, intuiting sparks ignite: a delicate drawing together, moving apart in which dissolving happens. We are surrendered beyond all ability to control as we offer ourselves to the divine in all of us. What bliss!

Home-play
1) Tuning-in through caressing
- Set aside a special time to be together with your partner and remove all obstacles to remaining undisturbed. Remove your clothes and lie together on a comfortable surface, Give yourselves lots of time. Choose who will go first and then do nothing.
- Feel the energy in your cradle and when this connection is made, bring your energy up into the heart. You can create a breathing cycle together between cradle and heart, the woman breathing in through the cradle and out through the heart, the man reversing this.
- Now, allow one of your hands to move towards the body of the other, slowly, tentatively, fully aware; present in your body and savouring every moment. Know that you are already In each other's energy-field and see if you can sense permission from the other to touch.
- Then, as with the introduction to giving a massage, let your fingers come to rest as lightly as a butterfly landing on a flower and wait. Only when you feel a genuine sense of connection begin to move, caressing the body of the other very slowly, taking time to pause and do nothing. Continue moving and exploring and keeping the focus on a sense of wonderment as you do this. (You may have had a sexual relationship with your partner for years, but this time, see if you can approach them as if it were the first time.). *See if you can let go into allowing your body to guide you.* Remember, the mind has no place here, so send it off for a walk.

For men especially, this process can be difficult if anticipation causes an erection and desire to ejaculate. What can help here is stopping all movement and shifting attention away from sex. Reading can help and you might want to bring a book of poetry, for instance, to share together, to keep the energy focussed on something uplifting.

2. Healing guilt and shame around sexuality
This is an exercise to do alone. Light a candle and maybe burn some incense if this helps give this a sense of ritual and once again, take uninterrupted time for this.
- Imagine all the various sensual experiences embodied in the form of a God or Goddess-like lover, whose sole existence is to be there for you; whose sole tender intention is to bring healing into your body with their Being-ness.

- As this lover penetrates/receives you, visualise yourself dissolving into this field of love and wholeness, letting go of any old feelings of shame, guilt, sorrow and regret. Know that who you truly are cannot be tarnished by any human act.

NOTE: you may wish to include orgasmic release and/or any visualisations and rituals of your own. There are people (like Marlies Cocheret) who offer sexual healing practices that can support this process which are beyond the scope of this book.

A living spirituality

'Flow down and down in always widening rings of being' ~ Rumi

'I just want to move within God' ~ Anne Kennedy (who was) an 'ordinary' wise woman and very dear friend.

'There is a historical and paradoxical dividing line in spirituality that is breaking down. It is the division between the inner life of revelation and the outer expression of that revelation. We should not assume that just because we have deep spiritual realisation that this will automatically inform other areas of our lives' ~ Adyashanti

Do you remember the song of the body-Being from the first chapter? 'Return, return, return...'? Within everything that we are looking at in this book lies this sense of returning to some indescribable place of belonging: of knowing this and resting in this. So that all our responses come *from* this and we can let go of all striving. What a relief! The word 'spirituality' comes from spirit and refers to this true, core essence of life. And we come to see that this spirit – what I am calling Being – cannot be achieved, obtained or purchased. We cannot be spiritual consumers (what a Tibetan teacher called Trungpa once described as *Spiritual Materialism* in his book of that name): this does not work. Rather *we are consumed by* this that cannot be controlled or co-opted in any way.

So what to do or not do to invite this? Whom to follow? What to trust? It's easy to say just follow your intuitive heart, your inner knowing; be obedient to that which looks like a kind of spiritual anarchy. But this just brings more questions such as: 'Obedient to whom or what?' and 'What is true obedience anyway?' Then we may glimpse a deep truth: that we can only listen to and follow and be obedient to *what we are*. (Don't worry if the mind feels confused here.) And finding out what this is involves us in recognising what we are *not*.

We could say about the term 'spiritual anarchy' that this refers to 'following the little bit that we know to be true' that the teacher John de Ruiter talks about: what Osho speaks of as rebelling *for* (one's truth – as did Jesus) rather than rebelling *against* (some form of external authority, like the typical teenager); and Adyashanti distinguishes as being free *to*, instead of free *from* (referring to true freedom): these being subtle but very powerful distinctions. Spiritual anarchy refers to finding our own way, making our own mistakes – and all the while listening out for the quiet voice of knowing that calls to us through the body's sensing, feeling, intuitive abilities. Sometimes there is a heavy mist and it's hard to see, and then – in an instant – things clear and there it is, shining in broad daylight! Sometimes we just have to let go and relax, trusting, with no sense of what comes next. Seeking support and a clear reflection from someone else, whether in the role of spiritual teacher or any other form, is part of this willingness to be open and take risks. *We come to see that living in intuitive reality can only truly happen if we remain willing to make ourselves available.*

Meditation: the mainstay of spiritual practice

Most spiritual teachers talk about the importance of meditation. But what does this word actually mean? Osho, for instance, has a lot to say about it that suggest he saw this as a way of life. For example *'My effort is to leave you alone with meditation, with no mediator between you and existence. When you are not in meditation you are separated from existence and that is your suffering. It's the same as when you take a fish out of the ocean and throw it on the bank – the misery and the suffering and the tortures he goes through, the hankering and the effort to reach back to the ocean because it is where he belongs, He is part of the ocean and he cannot remain apart.'*

He also comments: *'Millions of people miss meditation because it has taken on a wrong connotation. It looks very serious, looks gloomy, has something of the church in it, looks as if it is only for people who are dead, or almost dead. A really meditative person is playful: Life is fun for him, life is a play. He enjoys it tremendously. He is not serious. He is relaxed'* (or she, obviously), and this *'Meditation is a surrender, it is not a demand. It is not forcing existence your way, it is relaxing into the way existence wants you to be. It is a let-go.'*

Have you been to one of those meditation classes where you are told 'how to'? Where you sit there striving to follow the instruction to 'Watch your thoughts' or 'Just follow the breath?' Holding your back rigid and struggling to force your legs to adopt the lotus position? All in stiff silence where unnecessary sounds or movements are discouraged? The idea that this is a practice that represents the pinnacle of spiritual achievement? There may be variations of effort and intent, but basically it's about getting it right, doing it. Or is it? Who told you that? How is it that meditation – the simple act of being fully present – can become such a chore?

To stop ourselves in the middle of a life struggling to achieve and get things done can feel like jamming the brakes on in a runaway train. Not surprising then that we bring the same attitudes we have been taught into the 'practice' of meditation. So we strive and struggle to achieve results. We get busy suppressing and forcing ourselves to conform to what we believe is required. And all the while what we don't do is look at our *motivation*, where this effort is coming *from*. 'But I must find a way to stop my thoughts.' Really? 'Yes! They are driving me crazy!'

Or 'I am stressed out and meditation will take care of that' (without me having to look at why, or change my lifestyle). Or 'I am not enjoying my life and I've heard meditation can make me feel blissful' (*and I want that* goes unsaid, unregarded). So the egoic drive remains unchallenged, firmly holding the reins.

What would happen if we simply relaxed and, as Adyashanti recommends, just let everything be as it is? If we rested in Being? True, it can be useful watching our thoughts; interesting to note how they appear and disappear, often directed by some juicy feeling, taking us away from the present moment with seductive content like intended holidays or old disputes, borne away on the current of our emotional repertoire – we may even notice their repetitiveness. But this is not meditation. Watching the breath may help prevent our attention from wandering. But this is not meditation either.

Taking a quiet space of non-doing, with no pressure, we may become aware of something, something that is here all the time. A spaciousness, an empty-of-happening space. Something that doesn't fit into a tidy definition but is nonetheless present. Something we sense that lies beneath all apparent change, that remains constant: *even when we pay it no attention*. It makes sense to focus this in our lives, even to develop a thirst for it. Once we have seen how thoughts act as a filter on the vibrant, alive quality of being fully present, this becomes a natural desire. So forget all your ideas about what meditation can give you, how it is good for you, will make you a more peaceful, contented person, how you will gain spiritual kudos amongst your friends. Forget the 'should-ing' and the trying – just feel how your heart loves to rest in this quiet place of Being, immersed in the fragrance of life in all it's silent fullness.

None of what I am saying here is intended to rubbish people's attempts to find how to step out of the chains of the egoic mind and its conditioned beliefs through meditation. And structures have their uses. There are spiritual traditions, like Zen Buddhism, where formal meditation is the core of the teaching. I am not intending to say techniques and teachers can't help in overcoming stuck spaces. These teachings have existed for thousands of years. But it is interesting to wonder how many of those who follow these traditions move beyond the control of the egoic mind and how relevant these rigorous processes are for us today; and to observe how this word 'meditation' – like so many words – has become loaded with *ideas* about what this means. Bringing our attention to what is here, now, does not require any particular form.

True meditation feels more like a way of *being*, a way of resting in life. It's like stillness has within it a flow that can be connected with. What feels essential here is that we come into trusting the body-Being, regaining our natural place as conscious beings flowing through human form. And it seems to me this is best done slowly, softly, gently; through learning to listen to and follow the many subtle forms of information, invitation and movement that emanate from this body-Being. It is true that to hear these it may help to be quiet; to take gaps in our busy doing and thinking-about-what-we-have-been-doing and what-we-need-to-do-next lives. But *if you allow it,* life will touch every part of you and bring it back into full aliveness. Then, all that is required is trusting this process and noticing when mind interferes.

Very much connected with meditation is the word 'stillness', this has a beautiful ring to it, doesn't it? So it's a shame when it too gets misunderstood. We can take stillness to mean being literally still, as in not moving. But of course stillness is speaking about a *quality* – a sense of something still within us that is present no matter where we are or what we are doing, *no matter whether we notice it or not.* Again, it's one of those words that is hard to describe, depending as it does on our experiencing it and noticing it. Classes in meditation are now relatively popular, where people are often taught that sitting is necessary; keeping the body still and resisting its urges to move and fidget. But why? If we spend the vast majority of our time occupied in thinking, or plugged into some information or entertainment source, then it makes sense to unplug and not think for a while. However, although sitting still doing nothing can be precious, we don't need to be either still or do any of these things to connect with stillness here, now, present to ourselves and what this stillness actually *is*.

And what about love? How does stillness relate to love? To falling in love? 'What a strange question' you may think. But let yourself fall in love with *everything* and see what happens! Then, instead of moving up and away from the human experience into a vast emptiness where nothing is required of you (as the sense of 'you' no longer exists), 'you' dissolve into this human experience that, paradoxically, still requires to be met. Then the heart can be seen to be a moving stream *that moves from stillness:* a stillness that radiates.

Then, this idea of 'being spiritual' that many people have, where you sit there chanting 'Om' with your legs wrapped round your neck trying to get to somewhere – somewhere where there are no thoughts, no emotions: a kind of 'dead zone' – looks rather absurd. Here we are! Where do you want to go? Why avoid fully engaging with life as it is? Because *stillness is buried within life*, it is the very heart of life itself! Then what we call 'love' is how stillness engages with life: with ourselves, with everyone and everything. For me, the word 'Being' encompasses this union of stillness and movement. It is the mystery that awaits us when we are – finally – willing to let go of hiding out in the mind and just dissolve into 'this'. As the Sufis put it so beautifully 'God is a hidden treasure waiting to be found.'

The meanings within spiritual terms

Once you are bitten and get a taste for following this intuitive flow into the unknown but also somehow *known* true reality, you may find yourself getting involved with some kind of spiritual approach, and here certain words and phrases keep cropping up, like the phrase 'Here and now'. Lots of people have read Eckhart Tolle's *The Power of Now* and have some sense of this, but I have also noticed a certain confusion around phrases like 'Being here now' and 'Being in the present moment'. Because, in one sense, we are always here as there is nowhere else for us to be *but* here, now.

So what most people are referring to by these phrases is *attention*: having our attention free to experience what is going on within and around us, versus our attention being engaged by the mind, meaning thought. That is, thought either *commenting on* what is going on around us, or *thinking about* how to manipulate what is going on around us, or else engaged in *thinking about* the past or the future (and often how to manipulate that too) all of this threaded through with self referencing, together with any *reactive emotions* that are triggered by these thoughts. So being fully present assumes our attention is free from thinking and emotional reaction, free to simply be aware of what is here, already present, with all our senses fully operational.

As George Monbiot (this time writing for the Guardian) points out in an article titled Our Greatest Peril: Screening ourselves from reality: '*For those who still see the rainbow arcing over the town while everyone else is buried in their phones, life in the real world can feel lonely*'. For tribal people this being fully present in the here and now has, apparently, been their *normal* state of being for thousands of years: being attentive to what is here, including other humans and indeed everything around them. For most people living now – and this is especially true for Westerners – being 'lost in the mind' is *our* normal state, where we have cut off awareness of much of what is actually here to concentrate on what our mind is doing: i.e. the place 99.9% of us spend most of our waking time. Unless, that is, we are engaged in some form of activity that necessitates our attention being focussed on the here and now. Things that can be dangerous, like crossing a road, usually bring our attention here. Accidents often happen when people go on automatic, their attention absent, and repetitive work invites this state of absence.

You might think something like farming, being directly engaged with nature and the elements, needing focussed attention to decide if a field of wheat is ready for harvesting or a calf struggling to be born needs help, would keep us present, wouldn't you? In fact however, much of farming today is on an industrial scale that involves things like sitting on a tractor going in endless circles, wearing headphones to keep out the noise, and generally using a lot of big machinery and mechanised repetitive processes. Much of the office, shop or factory work most people are engaged in doesn't require our full attention, beyond a certain mechanical response.

As these environments are often not particularly inspiring or nurturing places to be, where natural daylight is often replaced by fluorescent lighting and we are surrounded by synthetic materials, machines and technology, this all contributes to a desire to escape into our thoughts. Travelling home, people talk on their mobile, use a laptop and are variously engaged in more of this thinking process, so when we finally arrive we just want to relax and likely watch television, read the paper, go on Facebook or do something that again engages the mind. Days, weeks, months, years are spent in a sort of no-man's land of attention continually focussed in the mind, far away from the alert, alive, warm human intelligence that is connected with the body and heart. It is in this context that the invitation to 'be here now' is the equivalent of 'wake up and live!'

What exactly is presence?

How about this word *'presence'*? How many people really know what it means? This term gets used to refer to someone with a big personality, big energy, charisma (and just what is *that* exactly?) or of whom we are acutely aware. We say so-and-so has a 'big presence' and imagine this to be a quality that some people *possess* and others don't: in other words, *we think it belongs to us*. And all the while we don't really know what presence actually *is*. Not surprising really, as mind can't grasp it; can't analyse, categorise, understand or say much about it at all. Presence is something we *recognise,* that we may feel and sense and intuitively *know*. Try it for yourself: watch how you are perceiving this. What I have found is that this is very different to our accustomed experience of the senses.

So, for instance, if someone were to ask you to listen to something, you have some idea of what this is like and you will focus your attention on your hearing, on perceiving something through your ears. You already have an expectation about this and to make it easier you will likely go quiet, maybe angle your head and screen out background noise. Or if someone asks you to feel something, you may anticipate a touch and bring your attention to your physical body – same with the other familiar senses. However, presence is none of these things. And although this word is used to refer to a sense of *individual* presence (and for some this appears bigger than others), what we are referring to here is more of an energy-field with a quality of stillness, of being *fully present,* attentive to the here and now.

Then there is presence independent of any form, presence that is everywhere. And what I discovered for myself is that if I choose to focus on presence itself, I find it by letting go: letting go, that is, *of what is in the way of perceiving this*. Then it is simply here, known. It hasn't arrived from somewhere and it doesn't leave. It is always here and when I bring my attention to it everything seems to lose a little of its apparent individuality. There is a sense of alive, alert intelligence in everything, everywhere. Or, another way of saying that – everything exists *within* presence; so it's like a shift of attention. We could say it includes a heightened state of awareness that may be felt by those around us, but it is more than this. I can say about it that presence has no limits, no boundaries; that there is no 'me' and presence or 'you' and presence: it is both empty and full, and there is no discord between this apparent paradox. I can say presence has no smell, no sound, no colour; that it has nothing that my familiar senses can probe or my mind apprehend. And yet we know it, we recognise it – *intimately*.

I mentioned earlier my fear of flying. Here I discovered something profound about presence (which anyone can try). When the plane I was flying in hit a patch of turbulence, my awareness seemed to divide. 'I' was watching these sensations of fear rippling through my body; I was even able, at moments, to detach enough from the body-mind's programming to survive to find these sensations interesting, even exciting. And then awareness moved to focus on this sense of being part of the vastness: 'I' became limitless. From this locus of awareness which I associate with 'myself', presence – *or the vastness itself* – was looking. This reaction of fear within the body-mind was seen from *within* this vastness, this sense of presence. And this had no fear of dying because there was nothing to die. Does that make sense? Like presence itself can see. There are spiritual books and teachers who speak eloquently about this, but you have to know it for yourself to truly know what presence is.

Many years ago I discovered I could trigger this awareness of presence. I used to make circles on the wall of a room with old cards people had sent me. I would create a spherical centre and then make a circle around this and then another circle around that, so I had two circles and a centre – no particular reason, I just liked it. Then one day I found myself focussed on imagining moving one circle to the left and the other to the right *at the same time,* and something in me opened and shifted. I had already had this experience outdoors gazing at clouds, movements in water, trees moving in the wind, leaves dancing, and so on. I noticed it again in the introduction to Adyashanti's DVDs (whether this is deliberate I have no idea). There is a full moon reflecting on water and the water itself appears to move both up and down and in opposite directions, creating this same sense of a shift which I feel in the belly. It is interesting to experiment and just notice what is there.

Another very approximate description of presence (these are more like hints really) would be to say it's like living with bad eyesight: when you finally get glasses and suddenly the world comes into focus and is crystal clear. There is a certain vibrancy to everything when you are fully present that is lacking when you are caught up in the mind. Another analogy could be watching a movie: you have been entranced, under a spell. You come out of the cinema blinking into the light and everything around you now reverts to something that is *real*.

Visually, presence reminds me of an endless circle disappearing into itself, appearing and disappearing simultaneously: there is no difference between this and eternity. We think of eternity as somewhere *out there*, in the future, and I remember as a young child trying to visualise it. The garden of the house we lived in at that time had a brown wooden fence around it and no matter how far I looked out into space, my imagination always ended up at this fence. There is no way the mind can grasp the truth of timelessness! That eternity sort of truncates into being the same as being *fully here now*. Presence is neither rational nor logical; it's more poetic, and one can feel how the Japanese use of koans (riddles that can't be solved by the mind) operate to provoke this recognition.

My own awareness of presence seems to vary. When I am working, I somehow know how to let go and be present with no effort or idea about how or what I am doing. At certain moments it appears to become intensely focussed, and it seems to be its nature to be intuitive. An example of this intuitive quality of presence was a time when I was standing gazing up into a mass of brilliant orange clouds in a sunset and I received the knowing that it was time to leave both my lover and the community I was then living in, in the Australian countryside. This insight happened in a moment of clear presence, outside of time: known beyond doubt. If something like this happens to you don't pay attention to the doubts of mind; just let the mind do its thing but don't listen. Rather, stay relaxed and at ease with a sense of no need to try to make anything happen, no need to force or coerce. Just let yourself be totally fine resting in this place of receptivity, where nothing needs to happen. And this in itself can bring such a wonderful sense of relief!

From this place of presence, intuitive knowings are free to come and go. And sometimes there would seem to be much wisdom in what appears. Do I always follow this? No. I, perhaps like you, move in and out of clarity and can still get caught up in doubt and resistance and the fantasies of mind. Like the glaciers melting, this is becoming less and less and thankfully I can remember: remember to pay attention to what I love and from here, sooner or later, return to connecting with what I know, what I am.

It gets easier when you start to realise it really doesn't matter! You drop this pressure on yourself to perform and achieve and get to some place of spiritual seeking that you have envisioned: you stop giving a fuck. What? Yes! You just open to this sense of loving presence, or Being, and let that do what it does to you. In that sense love is like water when poured onto a stone: eventually it leaves nothing, your idea of 'you' is dissolved. As you get to taste this reality, you recognise that love is a power like no other: it can dissolve even your very core sense of who you think you are, *and that's just fine* – even when your egoic mind is fighting this with everything it has. Maybe this happens more easily when you get older, you get tired of resisting? I guess we shall all, eventually, find out.

And consciousness and awareness?

'Consciousness' and 'awareness' are both terms used a lot in spiritual circles, but what is really meant by these words? If we leave aside the physical state of being conscious versus unconscious, referring to our brain function, we are talking about the *knowing* of something, being aware without the thinking mind. When we are awake we are conscious but we are not always *consciously* aware. For this we have to be *self*-conscious: conscious of a sense of self: we *know* that we know. For example, with awareness, we might *become aware* that someone just walked into the room, we noticed this. But what if we are aware that we are feeling shy? In the first we are aware of an outer physical occurrence but in the second we are focussing attention on our *inner* world, in this case our feelings; we are conscious of these, we could say we are *consciously aware*. Someone not in touch with their feelings would not have been aware that they were feeling shy.

It's almost like awareness sees and *consciousness notices or pays attention to* what is seen. For instance, you may have been aware of a noise on some level for some time, but then you become conscious of it, *you notice it:* it comes to your attention. In this sense, to be conscious of something feels closer and more personal than just to be aware. So subtle, and given the way these words are often used interchangeably, maybe better not to try too hard to distinguish but rather just get a feel for what is meant.

This urge to explore and become conscious, to have an inner knowing of what is going on with us, seems to grow by itself. Along with awareness, it is given great importance in spiritual teachings because it is *this* that makes such a difference, *this* that clears our view. Hopefully by now, if not before, you are able to recognise your egoic mind and the many games it plays, the many guises it comes in? A common question in spiritual circles is 'Who is aware?' (rather than 'Who is conscious?'). Perhaps this gives a hint of this subtle distinction in the way these words are used; there is a sense that awareness is aware, but in saying 'conscious of' something personal is implied, a some*one* that is conscious. Here we might ask 'what is this sense of self that is conscious, that knows?'. When I heard Adyashanti say that we all need a rudimentary sense of self in order to function in a human body, this made sense to me. It is when we become attached to this sense of a separate self and start to *identify* with it, to the extent that we lose our connection with Being and our knowing of who we truly are that trouble ensues, as the illusion of the egoic mind takes up occupancy – is believed and seen as real.

Here more than anywhere, when we are talking about what is seen as spiritual, it is important to remember you have your own bell that rings out in warning when something feels untrue so *listen* to it. Don't take anything on trust (including what I am writing here). Who cares if they are famous and all your friends hang on their every word? And don't invite the mind in here. This looking at what these words and phrases mean is not about analysing and trying to order reality, it's about inviting clarity in; an attempt to brush away the cobwebs that have hung over many of the terms and concepts we have about spirituality, so we can take a fresh look at what, at its core, remains a mystery. But a mystery nonetheless that draws us in from this sense of wanting to know what is real and true, wanting to live our love and joyfulness and come home to rest here. An image comes, showing each of us as bubbles rising up in the swamp of unconsciousness, popping and bursting open and releasing our fragrance. In that sense there really is nothing to do.

The Absolute and terms for awakening

In the nothing-to-do and no-one-to-do-it land of non-duality, terms like the Absolute are used to refer to the ground from which everything arises. The vast nothingness, an emptiness potent with possibility and a fullness alive with everything that is constantly manifesting and unmanifesting: two sides of the same coin. Other words used for this are Infinity, Eternity, the All-that-is. Terms like *awakening* (from the dream state of mind we call 'the world'), *enlightenment* (signifying moving into the light of consciousness from the dark of unconsciousness), *self-realisation* (realising our true nature, which cannot be spoken) and *liberation* (coming free from all illusion) are used by different teachers to speak about an instantaneous, spiritual occurrence – a revelation if you like, even though this may not be permanent, often recurs and is anyway, some teachers say, only the first step; a step towards what could be described as the ultimate dissolution of the self and that which lies beyond description.

There are and have been some wonderful, true teachers who have spoken about all this; those from whom one senses the outer egoic forms have largely melted away like candle wax from a wick, leaving just a pure, alive and sometimes delightfully humorous flame. Here, as a silly and playful way of speaking in these lofty halls of spiritual matters that can become overly serious and solemn, we could ask: 'If we all contain a wick, who or what carries the lighter?'

Something that soon becomes obvious is that awakening stands beyond all possible explanation and control: of the mind, of religion, of any given version or idea about reality. Do you remember in the chapter on mInd, speaking about the absence of a someone? This insight, *as realisation rather than simply a concept,* that there is no separate self, is what occurs in awakening. In fact, it is the focus on this that distinguishes true spirituality from *ideas about* spirituality, that may involve concepts such as guardians, angels, soul-mates and so on. Or God and the Devil as the good or bad parents and overlords. (As distinct from using a variety of Gods and Goddesses as *archetypes,* as do Buddhists and Hindus and other religions.) So with awakening we bring something 'extra'-ordinary into view, something the vast majority of Christian-based and mind-orientated Western societies are not informed about: the reality that there is no actual *person* in residence, no person running the show! And this is hugely challenging in many ways but especially to religions that deny this.

And yet, in talking about spirituality in this way, about the Absolute, awakening and all these words and phrases that help bring a focus to this – a sense of something to pay attention to and explore – there is perhaps something else that gets less attention. Meditation, 'Being here now', 'Being fully present', 'Consciousness', 'Awareness', 'Stillness' and 'Presence': all these terms are very powerful in allowing something to open and be recognised, and can help in letting go of the domination of the egoic mind. But what about intuition and the amazing capacities for connection inherent in the body-Being? For many men, the former are more appealing. They offer a way to transcend daily strife and not have to deal with the rawness of humans living together with unconscious egoic drives controlling the vast majority. There is no requirement to *meet* the world as dream, not head on but with the heart.

My sense is that something important is missing here; something left out, not included. Can that be true? Well, at the very least not emphasised. And this has everything to do with the feminine, and with the body-Being; with our *relationship* to reality and the capacity to connect *directly* through the intuitive, sensing, feeling body. Here, I found Osho to be unique in both recognising the body's value and encouraging exploration of this and, although teachers like Adyashanti also refer to the body and emphasise the importance of things like *listening in,* there seems to be a general lack of focus amongst many spiritual teachers on this more feminine approach; on the body and its capacities to inform us: to help apprehend and bring us back to true reality *while living our lives.* An interesting question to ask ourselves here might be – If we are willing to become intimate with the Absolute, why is there resistance to being intimate with each other?

In what appears to have been be a dearth of teachers able to embrace this wider approach, it's wonderful to find exceptions, like Marlies Cocheret whom I mentioned earlier, who works so beautifully with the body, and certainly there will be others and these often tend to be women. Perhaps there is, or has been, a tendency amongst women to ignore or dismiss what Adyashanti calls the 'ground of Being', to focus on the practicalities of caring for the family; but the way we live our lives is changing, women have more opportunity beyond this. It is as though a different focus is now needed to complete something: something to do with life in a human body as an opportunity for *living* spirituality, as spirit expressing itself through a body, in the here and now.

Not in a cave, not in some monastery separated from people's ordinary lives, but here in the marketplace; where people have relationships: with their children, families and friends and in the workplace. Opening this up seems to be manifesting through women, who are – as we have noted – generally more in touch with their feeling, sensing, intuitive qualities and more interested in living 'this' in a body. So altogether a more feminine-aspected spirituality that has its roots in the earth and flesh of the multiple Being that inhabits everything, on all levels and none. For surely, as we keep seeing, in true spirituality *nothing can be left out?*

What is the relationship between psychology and the body and spirituality?

One thing that is evident amongst some who either seek or teach 'spirituality' is a division between this and psychology, which is seen as belonging to the mundane world and, as such, neither useful nor relevant, even a potential distraction. And I find this both unfortunate and misleading. Just because psychology itself operates from *within* the mind – with its complex terminology and theories and programmes of analysis, its attempts to understand and compartmentalise using the mind – doesn't mean that *attending to the mind itself* is not a useful, even an essential part of freeing ourselves to live our spirituality. And this is true both for the mind with its conditioned beliefs, and the emotions mind creates out of these. It is this interplay between mind and feeling and emotion that is generally known as psychology. The difference here, *which is a crucial one*, is in how we approach this. When we bring consciousness in to shine its light onto what is *actually here* – no matter what that is – this changes everything. Then, *anything* that supports us in meeting what is seen impacts on the spiritual by enabling us to live what we actually *are*.

When you look at spirituality from this perspective it seems obvious, doesn't it? For, as we have just said, how can true spirituality leave *anything* out? As we have seen, spirit inhabits even the most dense material levels, so where is this territory in which it is absent? Is there some unspoken agreement to try to exclude this? And if so, why? 'But surely that is what awakening is: it frees us from all the messy stuff in one glorious burst of realisation!'. Does it? Just because it gets so little attention I want to re-emphasise this split between the body and spirituality, that mainstream psychology tends to perpetuate. There is a sense here of something resisted – particularly in spiritual traditions that have been run by men (and that is most of them) – a fear of including the body, with its feelings and desires – *especially in terms of human relationships and sexuality* – along with the testing realities of ordinary life, such as the raising of children.

True, there do appear to be some 'spiritual innocents', who haven't needed to go through a process of inner 'looking' to become conscious, but maybe these people somehow lived without ever getting caught up in the egoic web the rest of us struggle with? Maybe they somehow never lost touch with knowing who they are? My own definition of 'spiritual work' includes *anything* we do with the conscious intention to become fully alive and free ourselves from what is in the way of living what we truly are. And if there is a constant, it is that this has to include both meeting dark and difficult feelings and emotions, and seeing through conditioning and the construct of the egoic mind.

There is something else here that too often gets ignored, that conventional approaches to psychology and spirituality seem reluctant to include. Yet this is extremely important. What I am speaking about is using simple, direct and powerful *physical* and *sensory* processes, of the kind I have been describing in this book (including those in the last chapter on unravelling) to free us from the dominance of the mind. For instance, one might think that ways of externalising and making concrete what is often nebulous and seen as 'internal' would be part of a psychological approach. And yet, even when there is an attempt to include the physical and sensory – as in Jung's use of sand-play and later Assagioli's use of painting in what he called *Psycho-synthesis* – these fail to see the mind as a construct in itself, a filter through which we attempt to perceive reality. As long as the focus is on *integrating the so-called 'psyche'* what is beyond the psyche is not seen.

To add to the confusion, this word 'psyche', used by psychologists to represent the mind and emotions, is actually derived from the Greek word meaning *soul*. So without a clear understanding that what we really are is *not* the mind, any approach to freeing ourselves will be limited to improving our ability to function in the world and making us feel a bit better about ourselves as we do so. And in an ironic parallel, it would seem that as long as those seeking spirituality focus solely on awakening, and ignore the psychological, including our feelings and the body, the capacity for *embodying* spirit remains limited. In other words, neither psychological nor spiritual approaches are complete without including each other and the body. Being-ness means wholeness: holy-ness. How can there can be any true segregation?

Once this openness to include all levels is there, a flow can start to happen by itself: Being moves more easily. Remember what I said: 'there are no rules'? Well, once difficult, dark and painful feelings have been allowed to surface and be met, something starts to happen. I didn't know about this until one day, sitting with various uncomfortable feelings, I heard this voiceless voice saying 'come into your bigger-ness', and I instantly understood. Something in me let go and it felt like the energy just expanded, and as it did so the concern for what I had been feeling fell away. I was left just being present *(being presence* is actually more accurate) with a sense of calm serenity. What I saw from this is that *once you are no longer resisting a feeling, you don't need to keep sitting with it* (nor endlessly ferret around in the refuse bin of past feelings and sensations, like a fanatical housewife intent on removing every last particle of grime!).

In my understanding, this is where both psychological approaches that continuously recycle feelings and emotions, and spiritual teachings that seek to avoid them, miss the point. In the latter case, you can't simply step away from deep feelings. You can practise detachment certainly, and this may work to close you off from feeling them, which may have a certain usefulness. However, teaching this as a way to 'deal with' uncomfortable feelings and emotions doesn't really work – any more than hoping if you just meditate long enough, you will achieve a state of such profound peace and harmony that you won't need to be bothered by uncomfortable feelings at all! So to be clear, I am saying be willing to feel what is there, but beyond that don't hang around unnecessarily, don't get caught in a belief that concentrating on feelings and emotions is what you are *supposed to do*. There are no 'supposed to's', there is just you in your beautiful nakedness experiencing what is – *however that appears*.

The significance of prayer

Ah, prayer. This is such a central part of our Christian conditioning and invites all our egoic fears and desires. We so often attempt to lift ourselves out of despondency with hope rather than true connection. Usually, prayer involves asking for something to happen or not happen – asking that whatever happens it will fit what we want, *with what we hope for*. Whether we pray for the health of a child, water for our crops, success in getting a job, a partner: whatever we are praying for, we are asking that life be arranged to accommodate our request. So we pray to what we believe may fulfil our hope, whether we see this as God, the Virgin Mary, a Higher Power, another deity, the spirit of an ancestor, the Universe, whatever. And we often try and deal; to please or appease whoever or whatever we are praying to – to attend church more often, to be good, to offer a gift, a sacrifice. Here is where we can spot the fearful, manipulating egoic mind.

And yet true prayer offers the possibility for something else, for surrendering to something unknowable. In exposing our vulnerable heart *we relinquish all hope*, and acknowledge instead that we cannot know what needs to happen. We may experience fear and hurt but, ultimately, as we stand naked in our trust in life – in the knowing that whatever occurs we will honour and accept this – this burden falls away. Then our prayer may be that we find the courage and openness to meet this, and to see how we may align ourselves with what is true. Because what is rarely seen in the way prayer is regularly used is that *living life itself can be our prayer*, living true to what we know. How can this be anything else?

There is something practical we *can* do around prayer, and that is to join together to offer our hearts in love for the wellbeing of all life, without needing to be part of any religion or particular spiritual path. On a Sufi retreat I once attended, we did a practice that was originally taught by the spiritual teacher Gurdjieff. There was a lovely old walled garden beside the big country house where the gathering was held and in the morning we were asked to weed this together; then, every half hour, we stopped and stood for one minute in silence before starting work again. This all stopping together, standing still in silence together, was powerful. In this case, there was no stated intention beyond being present, but there could be.

Something like that can and does happen on a regular basis in all kinds of places and it could be extended to happen internationally, all over the world. Wouldn't that be something? For example: a time could be set aside – say Sunday at 4pm (in your country) – and then, if everyone stops at that time *wherever they are, whatever they are doing,* and tunes in to their hearts together for, say, one minute, with the shared intention to direct this to holding the world and its occupants in love and healing, this has vast power. The time difference would create a wave of continuous loving energy over 24 hours every week (and nobody has to get up in the middle of the night to join in!). We could call this the 'One Minute Moment'. Imagine if this were to be extended to every day, it would create a continuous cycle of healing energy around the earth!

Religions like Buddhism and others regularly use prayer with these intentions, as do many small healing groups, but we are talking about something secular here, something anyone could join in with without needing to belong to anything like that. Why do we associate joining together in prayer as something only certain kinds of people do? On certain occasions? Why do we separate and thereby limit our lives in this way? Why could prayer for the world not be something children are encouraged to do at school, for instance? After all, it's they who will inherit the mess we are making. Or the audience at a theatre? As part of a sing-along program for the elderly? At a football match? Let's go one crazy step further. How about that this kind of group prayer even has potential *political* ramifications as it could be linked to a new and very powerful way of doing politics, that *includes love and embracing the world and each other*. Conflict resolution on a truly vast scale! A healing not just for the recipients but for those who participate too?

Is there a soul?

Many people into spirituality use the word 'soul', a word that suggests something beautiful and significant and clearly holds great meaning for some people. It has a poetical element, as in when the Sufi poet Rumi says *'When you do things from your soul, you feel a river moving in you, a joy.'* We sense what he means. And we use the term '*soulless'* to indicate something that lacks a sense of this. Yet it remains nebulous, indefinable. It is something science remains ignorant about, it cannot relate to the term, it goes beyond its prescribed terrain which lacks a connection to the deeper mystery of life contained within Being.

Only those few exceptional scientists who operate with great humility are enabled to see beyond the apparently functional to glimpse what is *actually* here: what is really going on. I say this because to fully open to existence you have to take all your clothes off and stand naked: naked before life and allow yourself to be showered with truth and washed clean of the arrogant hubris of the mind. Then you know: there is nowhere else *but* here, with what is in front of you, surrounding you and also within you. There is nowhere else to go! Perhaps it is significant that we are able to grasp the meaning of 'soulless', despite failing to find meaning in the word 'soul' itself. Hence, it is recognised by its absence.

For many, the soul is seen as part of our spiritual makeup, a kind of guide that has an overview, and may even somehow orchestrate our lives (past and present). I confess (and this is entirely personal) I don't use this word now, although at one time I did. It doesn't seem to have a place and I find it too easily invites mind in to formulate all kinds of conceptual frameworks, esoteric explanations and hierarchal beliefs. Although, unlike the words 'Higher self' and 'Inner Self', the word 'soul' is given no *location*, all three seem to belong to the personal; all of these terms invite a sense of ownership – even though we may also talk about 'group souls' and 'over-souls'. Even the term 'World soul' has this sense of our world versus other worlds.

So then we can see how, if we are interested in what lies *beyond* the personal, the concept of soul might get in the way? I can imagine there are teachers who know about many deep mysteries – of which the soul may be one – but are wise enough not to talk about them, knowing our tendency for trying to grasp the unknown and turn it into manageable concepts. Here is where the word 'Being' is like the impersonal meeting the imaginary personal, which could be described as unfolding from nothing into something and back into nothing again, in an unending movement that comes from, and is not separate to, stillness itself. All of which speaks to how impossible it is to catch this illusive 'this' in words!

Being, interestingly, is both a noun *and* a verb, implying no action as in no-doing but yet something continuous. So you can 'be' but you can't 'soul'. And words like 'enlightenment', 'awakening', 'realisation' and 'liberation' all suggest an event, an instantaneous occurrence: a rending of the illusive clouds of egoic mind so we glimpse what is real and what – as with the sun behind the clouds – has been there all the time. Then what is not real appears to fall away – *at least in that moment*. But clouds can return. Teachers speak of abiding awakening but this seems exceedingly rare.

Or so it would appear, because who really knows who, and how many of us, are awake? Are living awake-ness? How many Buddhas and Jesuses and Krishnas and Mohammed's are walking around amongst us, unrecognised, today? So in the way that I am using it, the word 'Being' unites with a sense of movement, a sense of flow: like waves on the seashore it flows to and fro yet remains – always – part of the sea itself and, also like the waves, *it always returns to itself*. It appears to flow into human beings and yet remains always itself: Being. So we are continuously coming into Being, yet we never leave it: a wonderful mind-scrambler, that! But with our knowing that is beyond words and concepts, we can *feel* this, *sense* something; recognise the truth this is pointing to.

While we are looking at words and their meanings, how do you relate to the word 'spirituality' itself? What does that word trigger in you? It seems to mean so many different things to different people and some of us have a strong allergic reaction to what can seem to suggest membership to an exclusive club, with its badges and rituals and expected behaviours; whose members are – or believe themselves to be – somehow elevated and superior to everyone else. It has an association with educated, middle-class, older people all behaving rather tidily.

Growing up, I remember I had no interest in the concept of spirituality and yet I have always had a sense of the 'more to' of life, a sense of connection with *something* – even if that something felt rather vague. I remember in dreams a sense of *presences*, of meeting with special 'beings', and my childhood, during which I spent long hours alone in nature, no doubt nurtured these experiences. As mentioned earlier, I grew up intent on exploring life around me: who needed spirituality? The whole concept felt alien, somehow dry and unappealing. I had heard my mother and her friends speak of people like Gurdjieff and J. G. Bennett and something called 'Latihan', and later I watched the Hare Krishnas dancing in the street. But life seemed brimful and by the time I might have taken a second look, I was busy with children, 'the bomb' threatened and we were immersed in creating an alternative lifestyle in the countryside based more on the tales of Beatrice Potter than spirituality (or reality!).

This lack of wanting to explore spirituality in the usual ways seems to be common in young people. They want something fresh and immediate, and tend to look more to music for sharing a common sense of angst or enthusiasm. So I was tickled to note when, a while ago now, the same popular and outrageous comedian who speaks out about political disengagement, Russell Brand, also talked (albeit more quietly) about his involvement with God and spirituality and recommended people practise meditation. We live in interesting times!

Are 'past lives' real?

Do we really have past lives? And if so, what do they mean? As a belief in people having many lives is part of major spiritual traditions, let's take a look. Both Hindu and Buddhist teachings say that past lives are real and contain information about how we evolve through these lifetimes (hence *The Tibetan Book of the Dead* where, it's interesting to note, none of the potential horrors portray anything more terrifying than what is already being experienced by people here now, in this lifetime!). Unlike the teachings of Christianity, with Heaven or Hell and the waiting room of purgatory being the end of the story, this presents an opportunity for a soul – or some kind of 'core identity' – to evolve. Indeed for the Indians, their whole structure of society relies upon past lives and beliefs about

Karma to justify the caste system (the Dalits or 'untouchables' being an integral part of this).

Here in the West, past life 'readings' have become part of the menu at holistic fairs, and an accepted belief amongst many who reject Christianity and seek alternative forms of spirituality. So how does this belief impact those who follow it? Because, embedded in this teaching lies the invitation to believe in a linear sequence of events, where we gain kudos to 'get there', so to speak – to reach enlightenment, the finishing-line, at last – whew! Except that doesn't seem to happen. In fact, this seeing of enlightenment as a goal just seems to get in the way. Here we see once again cunning old egoic mind hiding behind the pressure to achieve, with false promises of the 'if I do this (meditate three hours a day, live a good, worthy life full of charitable actions, avoid too much sex: whatever constitutes your idea of correct spiritual behaviour) I will be rewarded in the next life and, ultimately, with a 'permanent bliss' kind of deal.

For myself, despite having read about, had 'readings' on and directly experienced apparent past lives, I am not sure what these really are or, more importantly, *what is their relevance*. True, I participated in past lives workshops and had experiences in these that seemed to be real, that sometimes seemed to connect with something in my present life. But what I noticed was how this whole area, as with the psychic, carries a certain fascination, a magnetic draw. It pulls on our curiosity and easily becomes a playground for egoic interests. In the early days of working with people apparent past life incidents would occur every now and then. For example, during a session with a female client I 'saw' an image of a woman in a long dress whose foot was caught under a plank in a burning house. Although my client had no memory of anything like this, it nonetheless triggered a cathartic response, an opening into a deeply buried fear which proved helpful at the time.

These days such images – of people and places that seem to be in the past – are less frequent, less dramatic and, significantly, tend to restrict themselves to the silent time on the bench. Perhaps they are carried in that person's energy-field? Or are 'borrowed' from others? From a collective store? Who knows? Sometimes these images (that may include words or sounds) can trigger a movement of energy *now*, in this moment – this is useful. Beyond that I have no interest in looking for meanings. Who would be looking for these, anyway? Like a butterfly that meanders briefly into one's path, I feel to acknowledge its presence but with no attempt to capture it. Maybe these images are just memories we draw to us from the collective pile (a collective mind?) that hold a resonance for us? Perhaps they exist on a level other than mind, which has its own mysteries? There are certainly people who claim to know so you can take your pic, or listen to your own intuitive sense about this. In terms of our being a unique entity, that keeps evolving through many lifetimes if, as I once heard Osho poetically describe death, we are like dewdrops dissolving back into the ocean, what is there of uniqueness to be reborn?

Spiritual conditioning and the 'spiritual ego'

This seems to be a good place to talk about *spiritual* conditioning. For those who are on a spiritual path there is much to be seen here, much to recognise and come free from and, in amongst this, the recognising of the spiritualised ego. It's amazing how well the ego thrives in these domains; hiding under the guise of the 'subtle ego' it is, by its nature, *always* seeking to get something for itself. How can it do anything else? After all, that is what it *is*, nothing more than *the belief in a separate self*. As we have seen, it is this belief that we are separate – which is developed as we lose our sense of being part of everything and learn to function in the world – that creates the drive to get and to avoid. Most of us associate egotism with blatant demands by someone to get what they want. We think of pop stars and film stars and actors on stage gulping down approval and adulation.

I first became aware of this subtle ego while working as a volunteer in the Findhorn Foundation. The community used this phrase 'being of service' and I began to notice how some people avoided the blatant and, instead, acted out a sort of undercover version of ego by presenting its opposite (all of this being unconscious, of course): a helpful, humble, self-sacrificing exterior. I don't mean to imply that this tendency was invented there; clearly this gets acted out in other scenarios, but perhaps most often in religious and spiritually-focussed organisations. How uncomfortable it can be to recognise things like this in ourselves, even when we see it as inevitable – because ego doesn't pick its victims! So it's good to remember we *all* are influenced by this that we call ego, every last one of us; and, mercifully, some get to see through it!

In the same vein, it is interesting to examine this word 'helpful'. When you look closely at the urge to help others, what often seems to be hiding under the surface is something that wants something for itself. We want to be *seen* as helpful, we want to be valued; we want others to look up to us, to need us and perhaps even to rely on us, and then we get to feel good about ourselves: worthy, important, acceptable. – or just plain needed. You can see how this desire to help – *when driven by egoic mind* – comes from a deep feeling of unworthiness which is often hidden from view. So when someone tries to be of service they are often caught in this unconsciously-motivated desire; we put on an appearance and deceive ourselves in doing so.

And so the subtle ego attempts to get what it wants, while avoiding being seen as egotistical with the disapproval this incurs – *especially in spiritual circles*. Don't be discouraged by this; once you take a good look at how ego operates, once you have seen how we are *all* acting out of ego some, or even much of the time, you realise it is simply a matter of visibility. It plays rampant or stays hidden, but whatever the game it plays, it is still ego. The important thing is that we spot it: *that it is exposed*. 'Of course! I see now, conditioning operates in spiritual circles too!'. When we are disconnected from our innate Being-ness, it is natural to want to be loved, accepted and appreciated; even for those who appear to be indifferent – unless they are one of those rare people who are totally free from egoic drives. Have you met someone who is?

A note here about giving and receiving that relates to helping. There is a strong influence from Christian, and especially puritanical teachings, that influences all this. We have been taught that it is better to give than to receive. But is this really true? *Because when the heart is fully open there is no distinction.* Take a look: next time you give or receive something, notice your responses to this. Notice how you may get to feel good about giving but not always comfortable about receiving. Perhaps you don't really let this *in?* Have you met one of those people, usually women (my maternal grandmother was one), who make it almost impossible for you to either give them anything or do anything for them? Who look really put out, even offended, if you insist? What these people have not been able to discover, because of the tight hold of their conditioning, is that it is actually an act of love to receive: to *fully* receive, that is. Gratitude is part of love, so then allowing others to give to you can be a part of this.

This word 'spiritual' is so often used as a value judgement about something, instead of value being seen as the qualities we *bring* to something, as in a genuine concern of the heart that is willing to engage without wanting something in return. How do you see spirituality? How would you define it? And what part does it play in your life? These are not questions most of us are brought up to ask, unless we have a religious background, that is. So it can be illuminating to recognise how spirituality – *or our idea of this* – can become a kind of trap: a place of aspiration that is separate to the rest of our lives. We make it our Holy Grail, when in fact this can be just as much an illusion as ego itself. It can have a lot of the same qualities, bringing in all the old unconscious motivations and pressures to perform that we have been taught, and which have become unconscious habitual behaviours.

So we find ourselves getting anxious and stressed: we haven't been meditating enough, we forgot to do our mantras, we've been eating junk food (again!), we've been watching telly instead of watching ourselves; on and on. Or secretly competing with others for the attention of a teacher, or comparing ourselves and feeling superior or inferior to those around us, and – ridiculous as this may sound – judging who is more awake, and so on. We so easily bring the same conditioned approaches, the same 'oughts' and 'shoulds' and ways of competing and pushing ourselves that we adopt in the rest of our lives, into this that we call spirituality. The ego is such a trickster! When the truth is, it is really, really simple;

and letting go into relaxing is the most basic necessity for letting ourselves be: be connected, be still, be present, be here now. Just *be*.

Having said all that about the ego, it's handy to become aware of a common occurrence in looking to come free from its influence: starting to see the ego itself as the enemy, the big, bad wolf stalking us throughout our lives. The word 'possession' is used in religious and psychic circles (and now in horror stories and films) to refer to someone possessed by evil, possessed by the Devil. And in a strange way we can be possessed, in fact, most of us *are possessed,* at least some of the time. But what possesses us is really a construct, a belief; we may call this ego, but actually it is an identity *that has no true form*. And yet, without this construct and our believing it – without ego – there would *be* no dance!

Imagine if we were all self-realised, how dull and predictable we might be, all sitting around in bliss or chanting 'Om' as we carried water and chopped wood; never an unkind thought, word or deed; always loving, harmonious, at peace. At first it sounds unbelievably wonderful, heaven on Earth! And then...hmm. Seen in that way the possibility dawns that, however apparently terrible and full of suffering life may appear, it always carries this spark of potential for awakening, for full aliveness just waiting to ignite. Then the becoming conscious, the recognising and remembering and intuiting provide a basis for a theatre of unknown and always changing dimensions. It may sound contrary to say this, but maybe even the ego can be honoured for its part in this play – however non-existent it may ultimately prove to be!

New Age, counter-culture and alternatives to Christian beliefs

Who is old enough to remember what happened at the end of the Sixties into the Seventies? That vast explosion of energy, mainly amongst young people seeking to come free from what were perceived as unnecessary constraints? In the US, the Vietnam war spawned its opposite: with John Lennon's famous call to *'make love, not war'* and George Harrison's embrace of the Maharishi Mahesh Yogi, the world opened up and permission to explore – drugs, free love, music and spirituality, suddenly arrived. Communes, music festivals, student protests mushroomed and, interestingly, the long-held macho image of the John Wayne variety was overtaken by a wave of long-haired gentleness. Men were allowed to to be sensitive and women to stop playing housewife. Opportunity seemed to be everywhere, anything possible. And before it was carefully harnessed and re-directed back towards material gain, there was an enormous expansion of human creativity and connectivity.

In the UK in Scotland the Findhorn Foundation – of the giant cabbages fame – was founded on New Age philosophy and has gone through many changes since I worked there as a volunteer many years ago, especially with people like Eckart Tolle visiting. Unlike the younger, drugs, free love and music-oriented counter-culture, with its determination to break down social barriers and share and experiment, Findhorn tended to attract an older, more respectable, middle-class and largely white group of people, so activities were more restricted. The focus was on building a spiritually-oriented community and ways of living together with nature channelled by two women, Eileen Caddy and Dorothy McLean, and following the ideas of people such as David Spangler.

As New Age philosophy evolved it expanded to include things like Shamanism, Wicca, Neo-Paganism, the Occult and a deluge of spiritual practices from the East, with lots of emphasis on alternative medicine and healing. Terms like 'the universe' and 'holistic' were used to refer to a non-religious sense of connection with, and practice of, all natural forms. And this was all pretty new at that time.

Looking back, it would seem that both the so-called 'counter culture' and New Age spiritual beliefs evolved out of an attempt to come free; free from the limitations and distortions of a rational, mechanistic and materialistic approach to life and also the oppressive, guilt-ridden beliefs taught by Christianity, contaminated as its teachings are with the anti-life attitudes of Puritanism (though I still found the Protestant work ethic alive and well at Findhorn). This surely drove the growing interest in other religions in the West, especially Buddhism, which contains no concept of original sin nor wrathful God, but rather emphasises peace, awareness and meditation.

At one time, I regularly visited someone living at Samye Ling Tibetan Centre, situated in the wilds of Scotland. This was the first place created in the West for Tibetan Buddhists living as refugees after the Chinese invasion. And something I noticed there was how the monks had very little understanding of our Christian conditioning. So, at first, they taught practices like 'loving kindness to all beings' to people who not only couldn't feel this towards themselves, but who were filled with unconscious shame and guilt and hang-ups around sexuality. And this was all new to the Tibetans at that time. Something I found curious was what happened with some of the people who entered a three-year retreat. After completing a rigorous program of meditation, prostrations and so on, in solitude, they would eventually come out, get involved with a partner, who maybe had children, and things would start to get messy.

From all this, I learned just how important are the processes that can help people come free from conditioned beliefs, especially moral beliefs, and meet the tangled feelings and emotions these inspire. And it was not only the Tibetans who were puzzled: most of the Indian gurus and teachers that people from the West were beginning to visit were ignorant about this too. I heard that when all these Westerners started turning up to hear him (this was in the early Seventies), Osho taught himself speed reading and read everything he could find about us: our history, our religion, our philosophy, psychology, politics – *everything he could to understand our different conditioning*. Which is why he was able to see that meditation and other 'normal' Indian spiritual practices alone couldn't work for most of us. Recognising this, he provided the space, devised body-inclusive 'meditations' and imported the best therapists to help us undo the knots, so practices like meditation could be of genuine use to us.

Meantime, back in the world of New Age ideas, certain beliefs took hold: for instance, that we choose our parents and are born into a situation in life to learn lessons; that we all have a life-purpose and that things are 'meant to be' (in other words everything being synchronicity – there being no such thing as coincidence). People sought guidance from a variety of sources, including a 'Higher' or 'Inner' self, channelling, astrology, the Tarot, etc. And one of the New Age's main credos became 'you create your own reality'. For people caught up in victimhood and blaming others, this idea can be life-changing. It helps in recognising just how negative and limiting many of our attitudes and beliefs are.

Ultimately though, I found something crucial was missing within this movement. Despite all the beautiful concepts and aspirations, I found it lacked a deeper insight, a questioning around what this reality that we are supposed to be creating actually *is,* and *who* it is that is creating it: in other words who, or what, we *really are*. After returning to the UK from being around Osho, I experienced this 'something missing' at Findhorn, where – at least at the time I was there – I found a general lack of focus on stillness and permission for people to just quietly sit. I saw a lot of activity, a lot of *doing* and discussion about manifesting visions and – crucially – *no recognition of the conditioned mind and its impact on all this*.

But despite its shortcomings, the advent of the New Age none-the-less had a valuable impact. No matter how at times fuzzy, misguided or lacking in depth it may have been, it provided a much-needed attempt to widen our view of reality to include the intuitive realms, with a strong focus on nature and healing. Within this resurgence many diverse and important aspects of reality were brought back into visibility and included. Every summer Britain hosts a range of outdoor, often child-friendly, sometimes drug-free festivals, where town, suburban and city-dwellers can escape the pressures of a life dominated by the mind and material concerns. Places where people can get out under the stars and taste a whole 'alternative' lifestyle, with its many forms and opportunities to express our aliveness and regain a sense of balance and community. There are not many places you can go and feel at ease sitting around a bonfire all night with comparative strangers. It's easy to make fun of all this, but there is actually something of real value happening here – the smoky edges around dope and ungrounded forays into the psychic and quasi-spiritual notwithstanding; an opportunity to touch base with what lives within us but is so often repressed: our aliveness, our connectedness, our heart and Being-ness.

The 'Growth Movement' that was born at the same time not only encouraged but, significantly, *gave people permission* to take a look at their lives and face their issues with a whole repertoire of means to do this. And it did it in far more varied, powerful and body-inclusive ways than concept, theory and word-dominated psychology and psychotherapy. Okay, some phrases like '*self*-development' (not sure how you develop a self?) and 'achieving your potential' can invite egoic, goal-orientated drives and beliefs; there is no questioning of who and what needs to be developed or grow or discover its potential, as this approach often fails to recognise *what is already here*.

However, in the context of the narrow version of reality presented to us, with its highly circumscribed beliefs and ways of behaviour and tendency to focus on material goals, it's rather wonderful that such opportunities exist. There are people, including those with a spiritual orientation, who see this whole movement as self-indulgent and irrelevant, but in my experience this is simply not true. It has – and still does – offer much of value in exploring and re-connecting with our full intuitive, sensual, sensitive, authentic aliveness; celebrating this and opening to what lies beyond the mundane.

Death – the great leveller

In talking about such a wide range of 'spiritual experiences' and ways of looking at things, let's not leave out the end of life in a physical body: death. Death – a word that inspires such dread and every-which-way-to-avoid-it, including avoiding even thinking or talking about it, as long as we can. In spiritual circles it is common to refer to every moment as being a death, as we open to the new and let go of the old. However, in terms of living this life as a human animal, which involves being in a body, then the ceasing of this does seem like a big event; and not just to those who may mourn us. We grow accustomed to our lives: like a favourite old jacket or pair of shoes, it has been worn in. And of course conditioned mind is full of ideas and expectations about death and what happens after this. 'Where do we go when we die?' is a favourite question for children. So, if we can loosen up a bit around all the fear and superstition, we can see how death might be a very special time. Why not celebrate this and prepare for it – if we have time – and make it a revered happening? A wonderful *change* – we are exiting form. And that naturally means attending to the fear that this invokes: fear of not-being, so we can be fully present in the time when there *is* no more time; opening our arms to be received by Being, like a precious child or a lover we have been parted from: in our minds at least.

One time, walking alone in the ancient pristine forests of Tasmania, I came across a fallen tree that had obviously been there a while. A fragment of sunlight penetrated the canopy above and lit up its massive trunk with a myriad colours;

it was like a whole universe in itself. Covered in mosses and lichen, it sported an enormous variety of different fungi and tiny insects, all intent on their part in helping the earth receive it back into everything else, this journey including their digestive systems! I remember reading in the cult book of the Sixties *Stranger in a Strange Land* by Robert A. Heinlein (later made into the film *4 1/2* with David Bowie, and where the word to 'grock' came from), about a human child who is raised by Martians. The author describes their custom of ingesting the bodies of their dead compatriots and – I don't know about you – I rather like the idea of being eaten by my friends. To be feasted upon by people who love you (not those who hurriedly spit you out, of course): what could be a more gracious way to dissolve into whatever appears to come next?

Ultimately, death requires us to face the whole question of what reality truly *is*. We use this word so casually, not questioning what we mean by it. One could say there are billions if not trillions of realities: yours, mine, theirs – each with its own viewpoint. Then there is a more general, holistic way of referring to this. Here we could say, in a manner of speaking, that reality is something to be entered into; something to be touched, known – intimately. You appear to step into it, are embraced by it. It is depthless, boundless, it has no end. So where can you go? How can you step outside of this? You can pretend, and try to avoid it by narrowing your attention onto the thinking constructs of the mind. So it's interesting to ask here: what would happen if you stopped concerning yourself with the agreed reality of others? If you didn't worry about being seen as crazy?

The truth is that full, living, intuitive reality is already here! So why not claim it? Why not live it? Instead of denying it out of fear, love it; celebrate it, shelter within it – *above all, attend to it*. Like a garden full of roses, its perfume brings a sense of peace and delight and joyfulness. It is your sanctuary, your fountain of wellbeing: forever. Is it *really true* that we don't already know this? Of the ultimate mystery that is life, it can still be said that *something* is known, *something* is heard, *something* is seen, *something* is sensed, *something* is felt. We are touched by *something;* we are moved and melted and reformed endlessly. If there is no 'I', there can be no 'why?' either: there just *is*. So, dead or alive, here we are! Surely this is what spirituality means: being fully *here*. Where is 'here'? Haven't you noticed? Here is always where we are.

Home-play
1. Here I am!
- Movements to accompany these words are: raise the hands, elbows parallel to the waist, fingers pointing straight in front, palms facing down.
- Now bring both hands down hard, as though banging on a table, exhaling sharply through the mouth.
- Inhale while slowly raising the hands and repeat. Feel the sense of pressing down energetically, forcefully. Initially, you may find it helpful to bring your

hands down onto a physical surface, like your thighs, a sofa you are sitting on or a desk or table surface, but be careful not to hurt yourself. After a while you may notice a sense of pushing energy down and no longer need this physical contact. You can include rising on the soles of your feet and coming down hard on the heels, in tandem or separate from the arm movements.
- Experiment with only saying the first syllable 'Here!' while exhaling and making the downward movement. Then repeat saying just 'I!', then 'am!' (so, three times). Explore saying, 'Here I am' by putting the emphasis on the first syllable 'Here!' on both exhale and downward movement, pause and say, 'I am.' Repeat emphasising the 'I!', then the 'am!', with a pause in between each. Play with the emphasis, noticing how each affects you.

Remember, there is no correct way to do these exercises, and they are more effective if you let go of any intention to achieve something. What doing these exercises can do is give you a felt sense of something; a sense that has everything to do with being embodied without holding on to anything.

2. Just here!
- Wherever you are, whatever you are doing, there will come moments when you can remember to be present. Saying this phrase to yourself, either silently or with words, can help bring a sense of this just being present, and this being enough. Then, when busy mind is asking us to do something, saying the phrase 'Just here!' can help us stop, relax and be still.
- Allow yourself to *know,* as you do this, that you are home, where you belong. Being present with yourself, you are doing just what you need to be doing, in this moment, in synchronicity with what you are: resting in Being. There is nothing else and nowhere else that you need to be. This *is* the reality of Being, you being reality, living as Being: Being being you!

3. Sing in the shower 'I am awareness tra la la, la la!
Don't forget, playing with the absurd has great power to unseat the mind, as well as reminding you not to get too precious and serious about yourself. Experiment by changing the word.

5. A riddle
How do you touch the face of God?
Answer: with your finger tips! (literally)

6. A thought to keep the mind happy
How could God laugh without humans and hyenas?

Meetings with remarkable teachers

'There is a dream dreaming us' ~ The ancient San people of the Kalahari

'When you finally get here, without being anywhere else in your head, then you will see that everything here is the face of God' ~ Adyashanti

'In a spiritual sense, I was always on a search for something, I didn't quite know what. Now you might say I was on a search for God. There was a sense that something wasn't quite right' ~ Marlies Cocheret

As I write this, how many people are sitting somewhere, perhaps looking out of a window or just staring at something without seeing what it is they are looking at, and wondering 'Is this it?', 'Is this my life?', 'What happened to my dreams?' or 'Now I have achieved my dreams why aren't I happy?', 'Why don't I feel content?', 'Why can't I just relax and enjoy it all?'. Feelings of unease, perhaps boredom; a sense of not knowing where to turn, what to do next and this nagging sense of something wrong, something missing – even a feeling of being deeply alone in all of this: perhaps these feelings are more common than we realise. And this illusive state called happiness, what is it really? It seems to be a temporary sense of well-being that for most of us is highly mercurial, disappearing the minute we notice it. It's like the very movement of trying to hold on to it makes it dissipate; so apparently fragile, so tenuous: who on earth invented the impossible phrase 'lasting happiness'?

All this is painful, especially as underneath many of us blame ourselves, however much we may seem to take our disquiet out on others around us. In people in their forties and fifties we call this the mid-life crisis but it can happen at any age. The most common conditioned response is to ignore the feelings by distracting attention, and the world is brimful of opportunities for this. However, sooner or later the unease creeps back and this is where a sense of confusion, frustration, and hopelessness, even despair may start to turn into what we call depression, along with anxiety, panic attacks or inappropriate displays of anger. Suicidal thoughts and various forms of so-called 'mental illness'; an obsessive need to gamble, to watch pornography, abuse drink and drugs and so on: these can all be part of this. And women, with our focus on having a desirable body and the perennial failure to meet our ideals, are especially vulnerable to food issues like anorexia and bulimia. All of these symptoms may have other causes but nonetheless they are often indications of a level of deep disconnection, we sense this goes beneath everything.

Or we may catch a glimpse of something, perhaps a brilliant inner light or inexplicable radiance, we sense the presence of something we can't quite see, we feel a sudden, unexplainable outburst of joy or a profound, unquenchable longing; this is when we may seek something we call spiritual and perhaps be drawn to find a teacher.

So let's take a look at these spiritual teachers. To clarify, by 'spiritual' I mean a teacher who is focussed on our awakening to the true nature of who and what we are and what life really is. And in my book, *a true teacher will always seek to support you in finding your own knowing about this*. Over the years I have met quite a number of different ones so I'd like to share some of the insights I gained from these experiences. Without exception, with each of them I found something of value, even when this took unexpected, uncomfortable and even painful form. So before sharing about these, I'll just say something about my own introduction to the world of spiritual teachers.

When I was young I had no particular interest in spirituality – that is, in what I understood this word to mean. It seemed to me that life was already full of interesting experiences, why would I want to seek what seemed to me a rather dry and lifeless world of spirit? Although we were not religious in my family, my mother was interested in spirituality, and one day I found a book lying around by J.G. Bennett, about the life of a man known as the Shivapuri Baba. He had spent forty years living alone in the jungles of India, later refused to teach or be made into a guru and *walked* all the way to England to meet Queen Victoria! But what caught my attention were the photographs. At aged one hundred and twenty he looked about forty and I have never, ever – then or since – seen such extraordinarily innocent radiance. I saw *something* and although I didn't pursue it at the time, I suspect it had a powerful impact. Later, when various people I knew were reappearing from trips to India with strings of beads around their necks and talking about meditation and mantras and yoga, I was still too fully immersed in exploring life around me to take much notice.

Then, in 1977, there was an event that seemed to change my life. At the time I was living out a fantasy in a romantic tumbledown farm in Cornwall with my small children and their father. I had become ill with an overactive thyroid and was seeking alternative treatment in London. There I met a man who was to play a significant role as catalyst in my life. He invited me to a weekend Sufi retreat in the country where he introduced me to an Englishman called Reshad Feild, who was at that time a Sheik of the Sufi Order International with Per Vilayat Inayat Khan. I remember this tall man with piercing blue eyes pronouncing 'Your life will be different from today!', and staggering outside into the early morning mist amongst the yellow spring daffodils, accompanied by a sound like gunfire echoing in my ears as the beechnuts popped on the enormous trees all around me.

Only later, did I realise I had been like a ripe plum on a tree and this man had simply seen this and given me a push; given me permission to follow my intuitive knowing – and so I did. Was this really an instantaneous revelation? In a way, but I had been feeling out of touch with my feeling, sensing, intuitive self for a while, living an unreal life with a partner with whom a deeper connection was lacking. Like the mole I mentioned earlier, tunnelling away underground, I had finally popped my head up and seen the truth. So I moved back to London where, despite having no notion as to what or how, I felt drawn to explore my inner world and engage with whatever, along with my children, engaged my heart.

I have already talked about Anne Parks, whom I met shortly after this through this same friend. I also met her teacher, Bob Moore, and although he never made any claims to be enlightened I was touched by his utterly simple, humble way of relating with us, despite clearly being an extraordinarily gifted master of energy, and I felt so much love emanating from him. A year or so after this I went travelling with my children and French lover and ended up in Australia, where, as I mentioned earlier, I had some extremely powerful and deeply moving experiences camping alone in areas of wilderness. There is something so vast and ancient about that land; despite the invasion of white men, places exist that feel almost untouched and there is a powerful energy, magical if you like. And then the tectonic plates shifted (in my inner feeling realm anyway) and I was tipped back out of Australia and into the next phase of my life. And here I met Osho.

Osho – the most dangerous man since Jesus Christ!

About ten years before this, I had had a powerful dream. I was in a big, white-washed dining-hall in a Mexican-style farmhouse, maybe California? It felt very light everywhere and lots of people were sitting around at various long pine benches, and despite their wearing white not orange robes, I 'knew' they were sannyasins (disciples of Osho). Eventually, everyone left except for one old man with a grey beard who came over and sat next to me. As he was wearing purple overalls I assumed he must be the caretaker. This man then proceeded to tell me everything I wanted to know. Unfortunately, on waking up I couldn't remember a thing he had said!

A day or so later I shared this dream with Andrew Watson, a powerful healer (the same man who told me not to wait any longer but to just start working with people), and he looked at me and said 'Didn't you know? Osho has entered his moon phase and asked his sannyasins to change from wearing orange to purple or red?' So did I *really* meet this controversial but supposedly enlightened man in my dream? In spite of this strange event, I deliberately avoided going near him or his ashram – I didn't trust that wickedly playful, seductive smile, the sheer radiant beauty of the man; and why did his followers all wear his photo around their necks? And they were all so cliquey and always hugging each other and looking so disgustingly smug!

When I had to leave Australia and realised I needed somewhere to be with all the powerful feelings this event had stirred up, I simply knew this was the place to go, to Osho's commune in Pune, India. Arriving there was extraordinary. The commune felt like an utterly magical land, a place that somehow existed outside of time, outside the reality of the mundane world. Of course, to anyone who has been to India that in itself is quite a culture shock: getting used to the smells, the flies and the dirt, the noise and sheer number of people everywhere. Whereas within the commune itself all was quiet and clean, orderly and beautiful. It's still there, a place full of flowering trees and gardens, intersected by white marble paths and evidence of water everywhere (and in a dry dusty country like India, water is precious). There are waterfalls and fountains, ponds with swans drifting on them, streams and rocks and so many places to sit, often with a maroon-robed occupant already enjoying the space.

Being able to just sit quietly, undisturbed amid the beauty and tranquillity of nature, surrounded by people intent on becoming conscious – what a blessing! Increasing its otherworldly aspect are some of the buildings that are pyramid-shaped, painted matt black with blue glass windows, which gives them a Japanese Zen-like feel. Considering the huge numbers of people visiting at that time, people from all over the world in their thousands, the organisation was extraordinarily efficient. A place of peace certainly and yet full of so much vibrant energy: people meditating, people singing, people dancing and playing music; all kinds of therapies were available, along with the arts and martial arts. There were people embracing, sitting around in the cafés, restaurants or bars; taking showers, swimming or playing tennis. People cooking and counting, cleaning and typing, washing and generally occupied in the running of the place; and of course everything stops in the evening so everyone can attend Darshan: that is, sitting in the presence of the master – the most important event of the day,

Here I perhaps need to make a point. If you try to assess something like this, especially this sitting with other people in the presence of an awakened one, with your critical intellect, you will miss out completely: a lot of people make this mistake. In the case of Osho for instance, he was deliberately provocative: this was one of the powerful devices he used to help us in dropping the conditioned mind. So many people got stuck, and still do, on the ninety-nine Rolls Royce and the rumours of cults and sex gurus. They totally failed to see what was really going on: that a truly global movement involving tens of thousands of people, was providing a place for focussing awareness and self-discovery; a place to *take responsibility*.

What do I mean by that? I mean take responsibility for ourselves by seeking to drop, or see through, our conditioning and clear up the internal mess; to do this using a combination of therapy, meditation and celebrating life with laughter and love. And this focus on becoming conscious extended to a worldwide support network of communes and friendly people and places to stay to back all that up. It was both brilliant and extraordinary and *quite without equal,* before or since. And – what few outsiders understood – the focus on the 'master' actually allowed for a kind of spiritual anarchy; we were being asked to take the love that Osho inspired in us *and find out the truth for ourselves.*

And of course it was all pretty weird stuff to a world largely preoccupied with how to survive or get more goodies: a world of conventional priorities with a very different recipe as to how to live your life and what it means to succeed. So it's not really surprising that so many people reacted towards Osho and his sannyasins with such outrage. *Other* people were seen to be getting free from their conditioning and doing what they felt like doing. These people were joyful and laughing and expressing their emotions freely. They didn't care if they weren't seen as good or polite or fitting into the mould, and they weren't hiding it either. Not surprising that the media, our public control mechanism, excelled itself with such pure and consistently vitriolic wrath – all of this in complete ignorance of humanity's true nature, our real potential as humans *Being.* Looking back now it seems incredible that so much was invoked by the presence and vision of just one man.

Not long after I arrived in the Commune I attended the initiation ceremony where new sannyasins 'enrolled'. It was a special occasion and most people wanted to be there because it was so very beautiful – the music, the open heartedness, the feeling of joy in the air. Friends would stand around with flowers waiting for someone they knew to return from their initiation so they could embrace them; people laughing and smiling and dancing, so much love everywhere! It was a very blissful occasion and I just got this powerful feeling to go for it.

As it happened, the night before my own initiation they were playing a recording of one of Osho's most provocative Darshans, where he talks about how in the future women won't be needed for childbirth anymore; how we will all have test-tube babies and be able to order up an Einstein or a Picasso according to our whim. My mind was shouting 'How can you take sannyas with a man like that? He's crazy, evil; this is fascist thinking. What are you doing!', but my heart had no such problem. It recognised this man to be the embodiment of a rare and extraordinary love: *love without interference*, with no personal agenda. My heart simply said yes! I didn't question it; I followed it and have never felt any regret. For me it was another powerful lesson in trusting my heart before my head. And I am still in love with that which this man embodied, and in his case it was vast: it showed me something of what it means to be truly enlightened.

Of course there are people who didn't share my experience, which lays open the whole question about whether there can be such a thing as evidence of enlightenment, or what that term implies. There are lots of people for whom that particular man provoked an adverse, even outraged response. Does that mean he wasn't really enlightened? Or that enlightened people can act irresponsibly? Or does it simply indicate that things are often not what they seem, and that we can't use the mind as a tool to understand what is essentially beyond mind? To try and assess things which belong to the domain of the heart?

In Osho's case, there were many people who had been his followers who felt betrayed when things 'went wrong'; people who felt the therapies were too aggressive in the early days and others who had invested their life savings and did not get them back when the Ranch – Osho's vision of Utopia in America – collapsed. There are people who blamed Osho for the misuse of power by those he had allowed to take positions of authority in the running of things, like the infamous Sheila. Why didn't he act? Did he really not know what was going on? Surely the job of teacher is to take care of his followers? But is it? To what extent are we to be treated as children and protected from the consequences of our choices? Safeguarded from all risk (should this even be possible!)? Interesting questions. And, of course, there are the millions of others who never sat in front of Osho, never went near the commune or the Ranch or any of the other places he went to, yet felt themselves entitled to pronounce judgement anyway.

It is true it was a dangerous place. I have some reservations about a lack of adequate support for people who found the processes too strong, especially young people who were more vulnerable. For instance, some of the meditations prescribed – in particular OSHO Dynamic Meditation, that involves catharsis and a powerful breathing technique – could bring up too much too quickly; and for fragile psyches this could lead to real problems. There were counsellors to filter who took which groups, but that didn't always prevent a few messy outcomes. I didn't notice much emphasis on the need to get regular, ongoing, professional support after the experience of the commune, when people got back home (always supposing you could find someone whose approach was inclusive enough, that is). Sometimes, within the emphasis put on exploring, I felt a lack of recognition of and respect for the difference with women's sexuality; a lack of support for being more circumspect about sexual encounters, although we were always free to do as we chose.

However, that said, it is important to remember that it was all a gigantic experiment, so there were bound to be a few casualties with something happening on such a vast scale. And the overall benefit in bringing conscious awareness to so many people who were stuck in their conditioning has been enormous, with the impact of this continuing to have an influence on the lives of so many today.

By the time I first visited the commune, in 1988, Osho was already physically very frail. He had been silent for some time and although he had begun his talks again, he was not speaking to people individually, we just saw him for Darshan every evening when he was driven over (yes, in one of the Roll Royce), entered at the back of the hall and stood on the podium to namaste us. This is an Indian form of greeting (pronounced 'na-ma-stay') with the hands put together, as in Christian prayer, and bowing to the other. It can be translated to mean 'I acknowledge the beloved presence in you as being the same as mine.' This was tremendously significant – that an enlightened teacher was bowing to *us*, telling us that we were *all* the beloved; *we were all in this together!* (Not quite what the Pope preaches). He then sat in his chair and closed his eyes and we sat in silence for a lengthy period of meditation before he commenced speaking. Unfortunately, by this time he had to wear dark glasses to protect his eyes, so I can't say I saw much of him close-to; even the letter I wrote him was answered on his behalf by his secretary at the time, Hassia.

Many people outside the commune thought Osho wanted to be a Guru, but something he said shortly before his death contradicts this: '*I had always wanted not to be a master to anybody. But people want a master, they want to be disciples; hence, I played the role. It is time that I should say to you that now many of you are ready to accept me as the friend*' (which is a Japanese translation of the word 'Osho').

In fact his presence was tangible everywhere and I felt the power of his energy through the *transmission*, which refers to the transfer of energy to others; so sitting with someone who has realised themselves the energy around them can be both powerful and vast. Perhaps 'radiation' is a more accurate term as, contrary to what is often assumed, there is no deliberate transference, simply a radiance that can be felt: meaning everyone around them is bathed in this. Consciously or unconsciously, we respond: our Being-ness resonates. Which is where saying 'Yes!' to accepting the connection between you – whether you call it master and disciple or simply friends – *alters the experience that you will have*. It makes you receptive, more porous to the awakened one's energy. This is why people who had read books, seen videos and even visited didn't necessarily comprehend – *because they were not tuned into* – what was really taking place. As Osho frequently reminded us, the words were often just to keep the mind entertained; what was really happening happened within the silence. People were affected by this energy in different ways. Some became ecstatic, some just very still, while others found it scary, even alarming, and couldn't get away fast enough (because it is certainly a serious threat to your conditioned and controlling egoic mind) And for many the experience was life-changing.

My own experiences around all of this have been quite strange. For instance, I was there just shortly after Osho left his body (on January 19th 1990) and I experienced the air in the whole commune as filled with this fine kind of silvery, glittery dust. At first I thought I must be imagining it until I read something about Indian sages which described exactly that; they even had a word for it (interesting how the Indians have evolved an understanding of esoteric matters way beyond that of the West). It is apparently common to find this substance for a period of time around the place where a truly enlightened being, or holy person, has left their body.

Another powerful experience I had was with the video recordings of Osho speaking in Darshan. They started to show these on a larger-than-life screen in the evenings shortly after he had left his body, and I found that I could experience him just as though he were actually there, present in the hall. Then I found the same with his photographs – I could feel his presence as if he were there with me. You don't have to accept this, it's pretty far from what we are brought up to believe, but for me it was very moving and it gave me an understanding of why there were so many pictures of Osho around the Ashram (they have taken then down now), and why people used to wear a photo of him around their necks on a string of beads called a 'Mala' (a practice Osho dropped in 1985).

Unsurprisingly, some outsiders saw this as evidence of brainwashing and a cult. In fact, these experiences I have been describing only appear strange to a mind that has been taught to assume that people are limited to a physical body, or to a particular time. But why? The truth is that *every new discovery we make is evidence of previous ignorance,* just as every denial of ignorance is plain arrogance: this is how we miss out. Just because something can't be proved, can't be weighed, measured, explained or understood by the intellect, we reject it. What kind of *true* intelligence would limit the world in this way?

One thing that took me a while to connect with was Osho's emphasis on taking life lightly. Like so many others, I took my idea of a spiritual focus very seriously – I took myself seriously. However, after a while I began to be affected by his humour. He had the most wonderful giggle and I could see why he chose to finish Darshan with a few dirty jokes – to the horror of some of the new arrivals – this was just *so* effective in stripping people of their spiritual ego, their *idea* of how an enlightened master should behave. Something else I realised about this whole process of connecting with an enlightened teacher is that when I first visited the commune, I simply couldn't hear a lot of what Osho was actually saying – even though I could understand the words; it was as if I didn't have the space. I guess my conditioning was just so strong that I blanked things out, the way we have all learned to screen out what doesn't fit with our belief systems, so my hearing was selective.

An example of this was around sexual jealousy. I had recently been through a painful experience of my then lover sleeping with someone else, and when I first came to the Ashram, I kept hearing Osho suggesting you should have lots of lovers. I heard him talk about people needing to come free from the bondage of marriage and not be possessive and so on. For instance, he joked about how we should be monogamous from Monday to Friday and polygamous at the weekend, and this was really winding me up! Then a friend, a long-time sannyasin, quietly handed me this tape. In it, Osho is saying something like, 'why change lovers? Once you have found, why throw it away? You are only going to make the same stupid mistakes with somebody new, so why not just stay with the one?' You see how it works? I had been listening out for what it was that was upsetting me, touching a sensitive spot, and tuning out everything else. After a while I discovered this selectivity or distortion to be something that relaxes as one tunes into the energy of the speaker: it's like your receiver starts to tune in. Who or what does the tuning I don't know. Perhaps this is an automatic process, a natural ability that we don't yet recognise?

And something else: I realised that you start to hear what is for *you*. By that I mean that Osho would answer the same question from different people in different ways; he would give them an answer tailored to *them*, to where they were at. This seems to be true of all the great teachers, even though someone else may be able to relate to that answer as well. In fact, for me, Osho's tendency to contradict himself was profoundly useful. It kept throwing me back on my own resources which, I suspect, was his intention. Unlike with some teachers, it is pointless to quote Osho as an authority in the sense of 'Osho says this...' because sooner or later you will discover Osho said the opposite too!

What I know without a shadow of doubt is that those years when I visited the commune regularly, for periods of up to six months at a time, were a wonderful space of opening-up; that this supported me in attending to awareness of the mind, and having an ever-deepening experience of Being and life itself: most of which is too subtle to be neatly packaged up and described. Certainly the combination of meditation and body-inclusive therapies was supremely effective. And I remain profoundly grateful. It is clear to me that no way could such an extraordinarily powerful movement have been created and sustained by a single man who was anything less than enlightened.

Doubtless enraging those who detested him, Osho received high praise both in India and beyond. I remember one woman holding forth about how terrible he was, who looked stunned when I told her I had heard that the Dalai Lama spoke of him as 'an enlightened master working with all possibilities to help humanity overcome a difficult phase in developing consciousness'. Even more challenging, Lama Karmapa, late head of the Kargyupta, (or Red Hat) Sect of Tibetan Buddhism, apparently called him the greatest incarnation after Buddha in India: a living Buddha.

A renowned Indian poetess, Amrita Priam, is said to have commented *'Where the dance of Meera and the silence of Buddha meet, blossoms the true philosophy of Osho',* and this feels supremely true to me. Even Sting, a God of the lesser dimension of Western celebrity, said he was inspired by Osho's wisdom when he wrote the song *How fragile we are,* and that reading his books had given him hope for humanity. The truth of my own experience is that I have neither met with, nor heard of, any other profound spiritual teacher who covers the same immensity – including the religious, psychological, political, sexual and body-energies – and encourages people to meet it *all*.

Experiences with other teachers

It was some years after Osho before I found myself sitting with other teachers. There was a man called Barry Long whom I had heard about in Australia, who declared himself enlightened (even stating this on a leaflet). So when a friend invited me to a meeting of his in London I felt a bit reluctant and went as much out of curiosity as anything else. What I saw confirmed my impression. Barry spoke of one ultimate Truth in a way I couldn't relate to. I felt more comfortable with the paradoxical nature of truth: that is, truth appearing in many different and apparently opposing forms (rather like a multifaceted diamond or a strobe light – which serves to illustrates how we can *intuitively* grasp something which our mind cannot describe or explain).

With Barry, I heard a certain stridency and he failed my ultimate test for enlightenment: a sense of humour. Other people I knew loved him and found his teachings really helpful, especially around relationships, and they appreciated his making himself available so people could talk to him directly. Perhaps I was influenced by my mind's love of comparison after being round Osho, maybe there was some unconscious projection: all I can really say is that he wasn't for me. Affinity with a teacher is a mysterious force, but the love of judging and criticism and gossip are tenacious, and these happen as much around spiritual teachers as anywhere else. In fact it can be rather illuminating to witness how those drawn to spirituality are no different!

Then there was Isaac Shapiro and my first taste of Advaita. Around the mid-Nineties I was spending a few months each winter back on the East coast of Australia around Byron Bay. For those who don't know it, Byron is the California of Australia – full of the weird and wacky or of open people seeking a more meaningful lifestyle, depending on your viewpoint. The area was full of communities and free spirits and everyone seemed to be into some form of healing or psycho-spiritual activity (it's all gone disappointingly upmarket now). One evening I went with some friends to 'satsang' (an Indian term meaning 'sitting in the presence of truth'). Isaac was one of a batch of disciples of Punjaji, an Indian teacher who was himself a devotee of the well-known Indian sage Ramana Maharshi, both now dead. They taught what is known as Advaita, involving a process of self-inquiry based on asking the question 'Who am I?' (I notice I find '*what* am I?' works better for me).

What I saw was a large, energetic, South African Jew with a curly black beard and big brown eyes that had that 'look' – very direct, yet with a sort of blankness too; this sense of somebody looking out at you from a place of stillness, somebody with a big energy and a quality of presence. I also felt I detected a certain un-sureness that puzzled me, and a sense of people in the audience learning the lingo. So we would all sit there – maybe thirty or forty people in a small hall – Isaac would sit up front and someone would go up and sit on a chair facing him.

There followed a period of silent eye contact (what people call 'gazing') and then they would speak with him. Sooner or later, Isaac would ask them the question 'So who are you?' The recipient of this question is invited to look within and keep speaking what they find: and of course the mind can present many answers to this question, endlessly speculating with no way of knowing what is true. But in going deeper, beyond mind, something can be *discovered or seen*. The intention is not that you come up with the 'right' answer; rather, the question is used to provoke the *realisation* of who you are: something that cannot be put into words.

Eventually, after recognising that who they are is not their body, nor their mind, nor yet their feelings (a useful device for someone who believes that this is what they *are,* which is most of us!), they might let go. Then, from this place of surrender they might describe themselves as being emptiness, and come to the realisation that what they are is actually *nothing,* which – confusingly for the mind – can also appear as *everything.* (Don't forget these words are approximations; they do not and *cannot* truly describe what is realised. How can they when words were invented by the mind, for the mind, and realisation goes beyond mind?)

At first I found this process impressive and then I began to notice something. People would appear to realise themselves but then they would go home afterwards and, perhaps during an argument with their partner, they would say things like 'You can't be upset with me because there is no-one here to be upset'. End of story. Which felt dangerously close to 'I can do what I like because there is no-one to hurt as we are all nothing anyway'. It began to feel like people were learning a formula. It seemed to suggest that the apparent realisation of the truth of ourselves (that our separate existence is an illusion – what some people call a realisation of the Absolute) can be transitory, incomplete and maybe not quite what it seems; because it still leaves something messy in a human body behaving messily.

After a time I think Isaac realised this, because he introduced us to the work of a woman called Byron Katie, who had produced a formula for questioning the beliefs that prevent people from seeing what is real. All of this was a valuable learning around the nature of enlightenment. It showed me that just because someone had undergone a momentary realisation of truth that doesn't mean they retain this clarity. The clouds that obscure Being can return, and then someone who believes that they are free can become a real loose cannon, a danger to themselves and others, as I was to discover for myself further along the path.

Gangaji was something else. She appeared in Byron Bay amidst a great flurry of preparations; with maybe 350 people attending, it was the biggest event of its kind. It was interesting to sit with a woman for a change, and she too had been with Punjaji (or Papaji as he was known affectionately by his devotees). I remember my critical mind having a field day with her glamorous appearance with her pearls and curly white-blonde hair like a halo, until I found myself slowly dropping into the deep stillness that she radiates, from where I could appreciate her true beauty and grace – and something profound. I found her to be exceptionally articulate which gave her teaching great clarity, and I loved her ability to reach out with delicacy and precision to meet people where they actually *were*. Something about the way she put things I found easy to absorb. Maybe it's because she manages to imbue what she says with a wonderful warmth and humour that both lightens it (removing any trace of the moralism I am so allergic to) and at the same time deepens it. I noticed how this leaves more space for my own experience; how a gentle humour balances fierceness so that things that are not always comfortable to hear can be received.

The set-up was always pretty much the same. Gangaji would sit up front, either at one end of a couch or in one of two armchairs set on a platform so everyone could see, and the rest of us would sit out front. Usually she would begin by reading from a pile of letters people had written to her, with some question or a report they wanted to share. Anyone who wanted to talk with her raised their hand and some got called up. The content of what happened in the interchange varied, but the sense of intimacy didn't. So some people would just sit gazing while others were moved to tears, and I witnessed something I have referred to earlier: the power of being deeply seen and heard. Sometimes she was sharp, acute, even stern and at others very, very gentle, and often it was clear that somebody's individual question was being used to share a teaching for us all.

When I finally got to get up and sit with her and look directly into her eyes – there it was! That same black emptiness that I have come to associate with people who have really 'gone.' I felt deeply grateful to witness her embodiment of 'this'; evidence yet again of what we all are: of our innate capacity for living Being. There is a wonderful book available about Gangaji's life called *Just like you!* It's especially valuable because in reading it you get to see how an ordinary person, living an ordinary life – enduring a painful childhood, difficult parenting and partnership experiences, working out in the world and so on – can awaken: just like you!

The thing that especially drew me to John de Ruiter was that I had heard that, like Osho, he had found his own way, that he wasn't anyone's disciple (I heard later something about a Christ connection, although he made no claim to this). He is a tall, rangy Canadian with very big energy, who does have a rather Christlike appearance, with wavy blonde hair tied back in a ponytail. And I had some powerful experiences sitting with him during his meetings.

The first time he looked at me directly I felt a series of shocks, like internal shudders, ricochet through my entire body and energy system. The second time, his face seemed to keep distorting and he looked (to me) like some wild creature, some ancient god or giant roaming the land: definitely not safe! When I looked in his eyes they were like black holes in space, they went on forever – if I let myself be drawn into them I would never come back. I experienced pure terror. And then a feeling-knowing arose of 'I don't care! I don't care what happens, I *won't* look away' and then I heard this voice inside me saying 'There is only love' and everything went very quiet and still and peaceful. That was quite a testing experience!

Like Gangaji, John drew big audiences and at that time a bunch of us were following him around Europe when he came over to visit various cities – London, Bristol, Amsterdam, Copenhagen, Vienna. (These days there is a large community of his followers in Edmonton, made up of people who have moved to Canada to be with him.) During meetings he just sat there on a chair on the stage, unmoving for hours at a time; and when he spoke, he spoke very, very slowly, with long pauses between words. Sometimes I felt I could see the energy moving up into his mouth and forming a word before he spoke, and some people really didn't like this slowness, they found it irritating. For myself, I found his essentially simple teaching around being gentle with yourself, and paying attention to the little bit that you actually *know is true,* valuable. As I mentioned earlier, he taught that you have a choice every moment: to notice when you are closed and choose to open, or not. I found these basic teachings profoundly helpful. I loved his frequent use of the word 'tenderness', too, and I experienced some strong times sitting 'in the chair' facing him.

The most powerful of these sittings was on a day when he wasn't speaking (I heard afterwards that he had hurt his shoulder in a sporting accident and was in considerable pain). I felt moved to share my most deeply painful issue with him, which made me feel incredibly exposed. No words came back and then he seemed to simply dissolve: dissolve into pure unconditional love and compassion. I felt profoundly met and held in a very potent way. The space gradually filled up with what I can only describe as a kind of sweetness that seemed to have a soft pinkish glow and I moved into a space where everything was absolutely, perfectly okay *just the way it was*: a fearless space that I recognised after a potentially fatal car accident years earlier. Yet even as this was happening I knew it wouldn't last and that that was okay, too.

The next day, returning home on the train, I found myself sitting beside a small birdlike woman in a navy blue suit who looked the very epitome of somebody's secretary. Opposite us sat a bearded, middle-aged man buried behind his newspaper. Instead of that very English tendency of looking out of the window to avoid contact, I found myself engaging with this woman in just ordinary chitchat about various things happening in the world. As she got up to leave at her station she turned to me and said 'Well, I suppose nothing will really change until there is a general rise in consciousness' and the man sitting opposite folded his newspaper and smiled at me.

After a couple of years sitting with John, things started to change and I felt a certain distance opening up. He felt too big, too overpowering, and at the same time too far away from me. I felt like there was no way I could reach to where he was and began to find the formality of the meetings irritating. Also, I was uncomfortable with something that felt to me like a kind of morality, a subtle pressure to do things a certain way, to come up to scratch; something heavy around responsibility which just triggered old feelings of guilt and inadequacy. John was for while a Christian minister and maybe that does subtly colour his teachings? I don't know but I found myself reacting to his use of language; it was triggering old responses to the puritanical attitudes permeating the culture I was brought up in.

I knew a lot of this might have been projection and some people would say this was all part of the process, that I should stay with it and work through this till I stopped reacting; or maybe I just wasn't ready. Whatever the truth of that I found the connection dissolving, found myself moving away. Maybe it was a golden opportunity to deal with old issues around authority but, ironically, it felt to me like I was losing touch with my own knowing, despite being told to 'Trust the little bit that I knew'; *that I was being required to trust someone else's understanding of how things are and how to be.* I had never felt that with Osho, never felt required to surrender my own knowing, however small and impossible to articulate. In fact I had found Osho's approach so freeing and this just felt like going backwards.

And somewhere outside of my mind there wasn't a problem: I felt enormous gratitude for what I had received sitting with this powerful teacher and... life moves on. I also knew it is possible to stay with a teacher for all kinds of unhelpful reasons – such as unconscious dependency or, as I got to discover with another teacher later on, because you believe they are something they are not. At the time the feeling was to just let go and be open to sitting with whoever seems to reach where I am at the time: could be avoidance, could also be a kind of maturing, who knows?

Over the next years I sat briefly with a variety of people in England, most of them visiting the UK from somewhere else, though there were some homegrown ones too. And I continued to have differing responses. Amongst these people was Wayne Liquorman, a middle-aged, ex-alcoholic, American devotee of Ramesh Balsekar (Ramesh revered Nisagadatta, who wrote one of the best-known books on non-duality *I Am That*). Wayne positively glowed with love and warmth and I found it interesting when he shared that he still gets cross with his small son. Good to hear someone in that space sharing that sometimes they lose it too! He felt very simple and open and real.

There was Dave Oshana, with his East London cockney accent, who moved to Finland because he felt you couldn't become clear living in a polluted environment like London; and Pamela Wilson, whose wild spirit, lightness and humour I enjoyed. And there were others, including a few I felt clear were not for me, like one man I sat with whose energy felt very tight and insistent, and from whom I couldn't feel any love emanating. When I confronted him with this he turned to his wife (who was sitting beside him) and said to me 'Ask my wife if I am not a loving man!'

And there was Tony Parsons and the invincible logic of the Absolute. He is one of a couple of people I knew before they went on the teaching circuit, so it's difficult to say how much that coloured my impression. Tony had been a sannyasin and when I attended one of his meetings he seemed to be quite disparaging about Osho; and I felt troubled by what I perceived to be a lack of gratitude (he once told me how pissed-off he felt about having a tiny unskilled woman tell him what to do when he was working on a building-site at one of the communes, because of Osho's policy of putting women in charge).

The truth is, I was tired of the old 'Surrender? But who is there to surrender?' line. Tony is very, very clear that there is no-one there and that means that choice does not exist (because there is no-one there to choose). True, this realisation can bring enormous relief from guilt (because if you are not the doer, you are not responsible for your actions) and, as I have said, it can lead to a big misunderstanding. From the perspective of there being no doer, everything is seen to be just an appearance that has no meaning. And, as I saw with people sitting with Isaac Shapiro, this can be a dangerous teaching: which is exactly why spiritual teachings were kept secret in the past, because of this potential for being misunderstood and misapplied. Tony, however, clearly delights in the simplicity of his position and its apparent invincibility; because of course *from the reference point of the Absolute* this can neither be contested nor denied. I found Tony's position confusing because, despite a *mental* clarity, I sensed a lack of the deeper discernment of the heart. So my doubts remained: is this teaching the whole truth? Or is it an oversimplification? Has something essential been left out: not felt, not sensed, not seen?

This brings up the whole question as to whether someone who is not awakened can know what is true. And it seems to me that we can, that something in the intuitive heart *knows*: that Being knows. Then it's more about trusting this and following what feels true, in that moment – *for you*. So with Tony's teaching it seemed to me that there is something about wholeness that is lacking; about a relationship between two realities that are really two sides of the same coin: the Absolute and the 'Relative', this being the experience of living in a body being human. So for me, Being includes both of these and exists in that mysterious, unknowable place that is *beyond logic,* and that half the truth is not the truth at all.

Whoops – not what he seemed!

Around this time a friend mentioned someone who was awakened and living almost on my doorstep, so I went along to check him out. (Strictly speaking, there is no 'someone', no 'person' who is awakened, but for the sake of simplicity I will use this term.) I found this tall gangling youth with those unmistakable eyes standing near the door of a tiny meeting-room. He was friendly, took a small fee and made me a cup of tea and wow! that just felt so simple, so natural and just what I needed at that time. I was feeling I had had enough of sitting in big formal meetings. I wanted to see *the living of awakeness in ordinary life,* with opportunities to relate in a more casual way – and now here was someone who appeared to fulfil that role.

Over a period of about eighteen months we met in lots of different circumstances: I sat across from him in small groups of people in the meetings, where gazing and questions happened but in a small-scale, informal kind of way; I had a few individual 'sessions', I organised meetings at my home and a couple of retreats in Spain, and we sat on buses and trains and planes together; I interviewed him for a book and so on. And it was all very puzzling. What I saw for a start was that it seems to be one thing someone 'getting it', awakening, but then how that manifests appears to be restricted by their personality and maturity. I got to see how people retain their patterns to varying degrees and that *to the extent to which this is conscious* it doesn't have to be a problem – that seems to be the crux.

I used to have the idea that because someone has awakened to the truth of their Being they would be perfect, like some pure God-like being incapable of losing it, getting it wrong and having feelings and emotions like the rest of us, such as anger and fear. I have heard some people claim they no longer feel fear, but something clearly stops them walking out in front of a bus. They don't do the *Groundhog Day* film thing of walking out in front of traffic and just allowing themselves to be run over for the fun of it because they know that what they really are can never die! So perhaps accepting that teachers are also human is part of a kind of spiritual maturity? No need to worship a *person,* nor reject them because they don't match some ideal we have in our heads about what it means to be awakened. After all, we are none of us perfect – not me, not you, no-one at all. This very fallibility somehow evens things out, which in turn means that at some ultimate level of reality, we all fit together just as we are quite beautifully into the shared heart of existence. Wonderful!

Then I got to discover the difference between imperfection and self-delusion. When that happened, it came as a shock. It unglued me from a kind of trance, a gentle drifting: a space where I had decided to put any doubts into the 'too hard' basket and accept whatever appeared. So when I finally found myself on the receiving end of behaviour that made it absolutely, undeniably clear that this man was capable of a brutality, and subsequent refusal to take responsibility for his actions – an arrogance that denied honesty and had no regard for being true – that was it. What a lesson! I felt dazed and raw. It was like a veil was stripped away and I was forced to see I had been mistaken, misled. It hurt and I went through a period of feeling angry, betrayed, cheated, made a fool of and so on. I had trusted he was what he encouraged people to believe; I had accepted the role he claimed as someone who had awakened to the truth of his nature and was capable of teaching others from that space. How could I have been so blind?

I don't think it was a deliberate deception: more like the behaviour of someone who has convinced themselves that they are beyond reproach, beyond the possibility of falling back into the mind's grasp after a profound awakening; someone who doesn't recognise what is happening when the truth of this is challenged *as it surely must be*. Seeing someone in the role of spiritual teacher get caught up in delusion and act out from old, unconscious patterns, is quite something to witness. What I realised was that the only way for someone to be if this happens is to let go, to surrender – that this is the *only* thing that can allow the realisation to return; and when this fails to happen, for whatever reason, they become lost. I got to see just how tenuous this realisation can be. It also helped me see the value of some kind of conscious inner work *prior to* awakening that helps people become aware of egoic patterns and tendencies; how invaluable it is to have stood in what is painful from past circumstances, and can invoke emotions like rage and the desire to lash out, along with unmet issues around power and authority. I saw just how vital it is to gain a degree of self-awareness so we are not forced to act these patterns out – or at least if we do, we can become aware of it and move to make amends. I got to see how, in the case of someone who teaches, *this is imperative*.

I remember this man saying once, in a tone of some exasperation 'How can someone judge whether someone else is enlightened when this hasn't happened to them?' What to say to that? It may be true for the mind, but if we are all awakened – just without realising it – then surely we are all capable of insight into the truth. Ultimately, we each only have our own perception of what is real and all we can do is to respect that. Did I allow myself to be deceived? Out of wanting to be around someone who had awaked who was available? Maybe there was something of that; and I didn't trust any contraindications precisely because I felt I couldn't really know. I did know my mind could play tricks and it was confusing, because at some level something unusual and yet familiar was certainly present. I had witnessed something very gentle, loving and present with this man, an apparent innocence, and I just didn't know what to believe.

So I closed my eyes and chose to enjoy what was happening. And it was when I stopped enjoying it that I woke up to reality! By which time it had become incontrovertibly clear to me that these were not the responses of someone who was no longer identified with ego; someone who had let go of a desire for power and a need for control – that in fact *here was* a *somebody* whose guiding light was not unfailingly love and truth, not when he was feeling threatened. A great learning: amen!

Adyashanti – clean as a whistle

Some while after my experience of disillusionment I remembered the words John de Ruiter once said to me 'Just be a fool for love.' I had been moved to meet people who seemed to know who, or what they are. I had been following an intuitive pull and I trusted that, and felt profoundly grateful each time I found someone who seemed to me to be true. And now that apparent certainty had been shattered. I went through a period of feeling badly shaken – who or what to trust? The feeling was 'I want to stop this whole search and sitting with teachers and leave it all alone for now.' There was a sense of wanting to withdraw, to let my feathers settle and digest what that had all been about and where I sat now, so I felt quite bleak for a while.

It didn't last long. Maybe a few months and then one day I was browsing in Watkins, an esoteric bookshop in London, and I glimpsed a face on the cover of a book. I hadn't a clue who it was but I recognised something in that face, those eyes, that look; something I knew to be just totally, absolutely clean – no distortion, nothing wanted; there was simply no doubt. And I felt something inside me go 'Aaah!' and deeply relax. It turned out to be a man called Adyashanti, and the book was called *The Impact of Awakening*. I felt a thirst to connect with the real thing, to clarify the difference, to understand. On opening the pages I found myself drawn by words *that I could hear*, a flow that touched *where I am*; a certain lightness, a profound simplicity and a wonderful humour. However, what attracted me most was a sense that this was someone who 'walked his talk'. And it just happened: no doubts, no choosing – I simply recognised a connection already existed.

Adyashanti is a proper 'American boy', born in Silicon Valley and based in California; he doesn't do the pilgrimage-to-India thing, to visit a special place or person. After some fifteen years in Zen Buddhism, which is kind of his base (with a relatively unknown woman as his teacher, Arvis Justi), he met Gangaji and connected with the Advaita approach. He loves Nisagadatta and the true teachings of Jesus Christ, studying the Christian mystics including Meister Eckart whom he often quotes. I found an openness to his teachings – beyond any particular spiritual or religious grouping. I am not rich (by Western standards anyway) but I live simply and can usually manage to go somewhere if I really want to, at least once in a while. So I decided to do a retreat with Adya in California.

In a beautiful setting, high in the mountains overlooking Monterey Bay, what really struck me was just how powerful it is to be with several hundred people *all in silence together for a whole five days!* No chatter, no social banter, no cliques, no space for projecting stuff on to others and playing role-games: just being alone, together – what a blessing! Over the days this allows people to settle into a profound depth, the lack of distraction keeping the focus strong and clear. I felt the energy to be both intense and yet somehow freeing: rare, refreshing, wonderful. At the same time, this continuous silence can be difficult. A bit like a poultice, it draws out whatever is there, challenging you to meet what is arising; and for some people that can be just too intense. We sat silently five times a day with two 90-minute satsangs (teaching periods) morning and evening, where Adya spoke and we could ask questions or share what was going on for us. It really is an experience unlike any other, to sit with someone in such a clear and loving space surrounded by others who may be in very different places but all sharing the same intent: to uncover what is true and what is in the way of living this.

Listening to Adya helped me clarify this thing about the difference between someone having an awakening, which can be momentary or at least temporary, and what he uses the word 'enlightenment' to mean – that is, the point of no return, the complete dissolution of the ego. So here Adyashanti emphasises that even when awakening occurs, it is rarely the end of the journey, in fact, it is usually just the beginning! This was certainly his own experience: *that there is much involved in bringing this into form, into the human experience*; and that this can be a difficult, painful and confusing process, a process that appears to take time. And this contrasts with the spiritual concept many of us have, that we simply dissolve into the Absolute and live in bliss ever after: end of story!

One very powerful incident occurred when I happened to be sitting 'upfront' when Adya was just looking around and his gaze stopped at me. My experience was that he simply dissolved, leaving this pair of shiny, dark violet-grey pupils shaped like pomegranate seeds, *looking at me*. During this there was no feeling of a loving presence, in fact no *feeling* at all: just a *knowing*. I knew I was being truly seen and – at the same time – I knew I was looking at myself! Some years later, I came across a quote by Meister Eckhart where he says *'The eye with which I see God is the same eye with which God sees me';* and I have known that when I look at the pupil of any eye, human or otherwise, this is indeed all me, all one consciousness.

Something in me delights in listening to Adyashanti's teaching, these reflect truth in so many ways. It's like taking a refreshing bathe in a clear mountain stream – especially if one has been caught up in the usual convoluted 'now you see me, now you don't' games of the mind. He has a way of taking a scalpel to some popular spiritual phrase or understanding and opening it up to expose its true meaning, distinguishing the real from the false. In doing so, we see how clumsy – even dangerous – words can be, and how so many teachings can be misinterpreted or used to justify something that isn't actually true. So these clarifications are priceless.

I notice how I experience these as subtly different to the analytical information coming from mind: *I am listening from a different place.* From this place I can hear the truth dropping like clear crystal insights through the dusty shelves of accumulated knowledge. Once again, the discerning heart gains ascendancy and this arouses such a delightful feeling of 'Oh! Yes, I *see*....'. And – very occasionally – something doesn't sit with me, doesn't resonate. Like his praise of earnestness for instance (which Nisagadatta also reveres), a word I find heavy and overly serious; unlike sincerity, which feels clean and beautiful (and which Adyashanti also praises), and I do miss Osho's focus on the body and celebration.

But I have seen how each teacher retains their own personality and way of teaching, so these differences feel like mere ruffles on the surface of the water – I can still feel the true depth below. And I absolutely trust this man's dedication in support of awakening *our own knowing*, our *own* ability to listen in. Like Gangaji, Adyashanti has a very fine ability to reach out to where a questioner actually *is*, speaking to her or his present understanding, always with the utmost delicacy and respect; and this can be illuminating to watch. We so rarely get to see real, unconditional love in action. So for me, listening to Adyashanti is like listening to a skilful musician tuning a harp, combing through all the strings to remove the false notes, so you can hear the true sound. Or another analogy would be a jeweller picking out the *real* diamonds to show you, rubbing away the dust and dirt 'Here, look!': diamonds hidden within a heap of costume jewellery.

More teachers

During the first years around Adyashanti I occasionally sat with other teachers closer to home, like Mooji for instance (another Punjaji disciple). With his big, solid body and very physical presence and Rasta hair from his Jamaican heritage, he is refreshing and gives wonderful hugs. On a visit to a meeting at his tiny London flat, crammed to bursting with eager people, I learnt a valuable lesson. At the end of the meeting I had left the room and was standing out in the hall waiting for someone. Despite being asked to leave quietly, many people were (as always seems to happen) queuing to receive a hug. But then Mooji looked up and called me over. He looked at me with such profound tenderness and told me I was looking great, glowing with light (or something like that) and of course I went home feeling wonderful!

The next time I went, I was sitting squashed in on a sofa and he came in and began looking around at everyone, as he usually does. He looked in my direction but appeared to quickly look away to someone else – not a flicker of recognition. Immediately, I felt a little jerk of rejection and watched my reactive mind start buzzing away: 'What had I done wrong? Was I putting out black clouds of negativity? Had I been avoiding something? What had I done, or not done, to lose my shine?' (I have to smile as I recount this – it seems like this little 'inner child' in us never really grows up.) Later, without really wanting to, I got trapped in the queue for a hug but again, it felt like there was no energy coming from him, like he didn't want to connect. 'Perhaps he is feeling tired or not well?'. I told myself.

However inside, I noticed this horrible sinking feeling. *It was all my fault!* I just wasn't worthy. You can laugh at this, I can now, but at the time it felt terrible. My worst fear had been activated (do you know *anyone* who does not have this fear at base, if they really, honestly look? After all, the ego is only a construct, *we are identified with a construct*, so how can we feel secure if we don't know who we really are? Hence it would seem only fully enlightened people are free from this, there being no sense of ego left to experience it.)

Later, when I sat with what had happened, I recognised how my defended heart had *finally* been pierced, even though it felt like betrayal. What was so freeing was that I was able to sit with this fear, to meet it and discover that that is just what it is, *and all it is:* an emotionalised feeling provoked by an erroneous, impossible belief. I found it didn't actually crush 'me'. (I won't say there was no-one there to be crushed, that sounds too formulaic to these ears.) Let's just say somehow something was eased: stillness of Being was there, had always been there, and I was able to rest in this and accept the fear, accept these feelings; my mind went quiet.

I am not saying these emotionalised feelings won't come back — they will, they have, or at least a flicker. However I don't find myself identified with them in the same way. Something doesn't believe my mind's stance; its hold has loosened if you like. There is a feeling of 'so what?'. As to whether Mooji *intended* to snub me or whether it was all entirely my own projection, I have no idea. That's not important. What interests me is that *his response provided exactly what I needed* to touch base with this old pattern. As a great 'worthy opponent', he gave me an opportunity to discover something profound.

Someone I haven't sat with is Eckhart Tolle. His meetings now draw very big numbers and so far I haven't felt drawn to go. I read his books and watched a video and it seems clear to me that he not only comes from a beautiful place, but he has an exceptional gift for communicating: for putting into words what is so difficult to get across; to reach both mind and beyond mind in a way that doesn't threaten people, and so can act as a kind of tin-opener for a wide audience. I guess he scatters seeds that ripen in their own time because I have met many people who say, 'Oh yes, I read *The Power of Now',* but from the way they are living their lives they seem to have forgotten much of what they read.

And I guess that is always a limitation with books? And videos too, which have become a popular way of accessing spiritual teachers and teachings. They can work well to make cracks in the façade, but going deeper is where direct contact with a teacher can bring something profound. And for some people the very idea of going to see a teacher is anathema; after experiences with parents and school many, especially young people, have developed a resistance to anyone telling them how to live their lives. However, what I found is that if a teacher is *genuine* – that is beyond egoic interference – they don't do that. What they do is help you to find out for yourself. As Adyashanti frequently says: *'My job is not to answer your questions but to question your answers.'* The Chinese call teachers 'gardeners' – what a lovely way to describe this function. Then you see how, with a little of the right nourishment and support, a plant grows and brings forth flowers all by itself!

I want to add a note about women teachers here, of whom, thankfully, there seem to be a growing number. There is a book called *Ordinary Women, Extraordinary Wisdom – The Feminine Face of Awakening* by Rita Marie Robinson, in which she interviews twelve awakened women and asks them how they see the difference in the teachings of women. They mostly agree that unlike the old male tendency of focussing awakening on the Absolute (referring to the vast Nothingness which can't really be put into words), women tend to be more concerned with how to live this, here in a body, and including relationship in its many forms.

Several of the women I have mentioned are in this book: Gangaji, Pamela Wilson, and also Marlies Cocheret. There is a wonderful series of videos called 'The feminine face of God', in one of which Marlies and a woman called Ellen Emmet (the partner of another spiritual teacher, Rupert Spira) are interviewed on Conscious tv by Renata McNay. (Another woman who is interested in exploring the differences in approach of women teachers.) Marlies, who was also with Osho and Daniel Odier (the Tantric master), was asked to teach by Adyashanti. I have felt to support her work as she, unusually amongst what I call deep spiritual teachers, focusses sexuality and the body along with stillness in her teaching, which is mainly concerned with women and for which I feel there is such a great need. Here is a quote by her *'Woman so deeply knows what is possible in form, as love. That is her connectedness speaking, her feminine intuition.'*

Conclusions

So, this has been my own obviously idiosyncratic experience. I can say that sitting with all these teachers has been a blessing, a real support in my determination to look for myself. Connecting with a true teacher – that is, someone who is completely open, clear-sighted and free from egoic needs (or at least aware of these) – has an infectious quality that creates a strong pull. Shortly before he left his body Osho said *'If you need me I will be there for you until your need is fulfilled. And even if I am gone, if your love is deep enough I will be present for you. Whenever you close your eyes, you will feel me beating within your heart'* and this has been my experience – when I close my eyes I sometimes see his, closing or closed. And my sense of a loving connection with Adyashanti feels such a deep attunement that I cannot imagine it discontinuing. And yet, like any loving connection with an apparent other, on some level this really doesn't matter. After all, the heart has no boundaries. I am just thrilled to have met such clear, deep pools of reflected wisdom in human form; to commune with those beings who seem capable of meeting us on so many levels. To them I can only say 'Thank you'.

Home-play
1. I am so beautiful
- Sitting comfortably, raise both arms in front of you to just above your head, palms hanging downwards, then lift the hands up and let the arms descend in a soft, graceful movement as if you are caressing the air with your palms. Let yourself feel the energy in your hands as you do this.
- Repeat.
- On the third movement, stop with the arms, palms hanging downwards just above your head, as though you are creating an oval frame with you within it, and say the words 'I am so beautiful', noticing what happens when you do this.
- For most people there will be a struggle as the unworthy ego tries to claim this. You may feel shy, awkward or just remain at a superficial level. However you may find you connect with what is actually here as you do this, with Being. And how can Being not be beautiful?

2. Three questions to ask yourself
- What if there is no problem? (And never has been nor never will be)

- What if this life is being lived through me rather than by me?

- What if there is no such thing as a beginning or an end? (That these are concepts invented by the egoic mind to reassure itself with an idea of being in control?)

Questions are one of the best ways to go deeper, not because one expects an answer but because they can create gaps through which a realisation can appear.

Awakening through joy

'Joy is the simplest form of gratitude' ~ Karl Barth

'I don't think of all the misery, but of the beauty that still remains.' ~ Anne Frank, The Diary of a Young Girl

'I slept and dreamt that life was joy. I awoke and saw that life was service. I acted and behold, service was joy.' ~ Rabindrath Tagore

Awakening through joy – is this possible? There are so many teachings that speak of awakening happening as a result of undergoing suffering, often immense suffering. However, focussing on suffering is not the same as being willing to meet whatever is there – which might be deeply painful and even frightening – *but not needing to remain there*. So then there is space for other feelings, lighter feelings, like joy.

In my own experience it is this underground river of joy that has always been known (however fleetingly), sensed and breathed in: it is *this* that draws me towards 'this that I am.' True, in this being drawn I have to meet whatever blocks this flow and distracts from it; indeed there have been times when a desire to escape pain overrides this inner sense, times of great fear and sadness; dread, horror even and helplessness. During these times this connection with joy often got lost, buried under the anxiety and panic, guilt and all the rest. But the pull remains constant and it is felt as love. I have no idea how many people this is true for, but what I have seen is that amongst those who are not in extreme suffering, this pull towards something that is already known of love also occurs. And it increases as we begin to focus on this pull and are reminded and validated and encouraged.

This feels different to a desire to become enlightened, at least in the way we speak of this. Personally, I haven't felt that desire and neither do many of the people I see. It is happening on a different level that is far more connected – or so it feels to me – with our everyday lives; with our bodies and felt senses, and this seems not to be articulated in many of the traditional spiritual teachings. Why have I sat with so many teachers then? Because I wanted to see what could be found there. Because, within hearing the words *something can be touched, something that is alive*. With some skilful and true teachers, as you sit around them, you can feel a sense of this: this being touched beneath the words. Almost as though the glimpses of truth they reveal splash onto you and help clean away the mud of misunderstanding, the dust of old redundant 'spiritual' concepts that clutter our ability to simply be available to life.

This capacity for *availability*, for being receptive, is generally seen as feminine and is more familiar to women. We are less trained to seek and try to achieve goals. And we are generally more comfortable not just in the feeling, sensing, intuitive realms but with intimacy generally. We value relating and tend to be more practical in our spirituality. For men, spirituality can offer tantalising glimpses not only of something to gain, but also of an escape from the challenges of intimacy; and for those men who have seen through the lie of material gain, awakening can become just a higher and more prestigious goal to achieve.

For several years now there has been this sense of a constant presence of joy, which I can cover over and forget about for a while by allowing myself to get distracted into believing the nonsense of the mind. And then there it is again! I haven't done anything to deserve this, other than hold to an intention to remain as open and available to life as I can: Thy will be done – not from a sense of trying to get something, not from an idea this is a good thing to do, but from a recognition that *this is what I love.* I have *felt* joy flooding my body and am left with nothing but gratefulness.

As an energy it moves and connects and subtly changes everything. Unlike feelings of happiness, which are transitory and for most of us are dependent on outside circumstances, joy somehow recycles itself. As a natural response that connects with Being it can be felt to arise through the body; not just in the heart but arising from the base, touching us and opening us all the way up. And this includes the solar plexus which – in our time at least – is usually caught up in emotionalised feelings (along with the throat to which it connects). Then this stream of joy can even transform our anger and sadness and fear, our most basic feelings of hurt and any erroneous conclusions we made around our own culpability and worthlessness.

And... *it can only do this if we are open and available to Being*. Out in the world, living as best we can, life can seem overwhelming. If you look at the input of the various media sources and what many people talk about, it is filled with foreboding. Things to fear, reasons to be anxious, angry, upset. But if you just sit quietly *and feel and sense into what is actually here,* it looks quite different. Even if you are in the midst of dealing with something difficult and frightening, this can be underpinned with a sense of letting go into letting life handle it: in other words, surrender. Then, if it is painful and scary, you know you will just meet it as best you can. You, like me and everyone else, may get lost and forget for a while, *but you know in your essence,* in your very body-Being-ness that ultimately all is well. Then, if you reach deep enough, you inevitable encounter this well of joy. Joy that is in love – in love with life, with Being, with everything around it. There is a potential for redeeming all pain and difficulty, the alchemical potential for harvesting and transmuting suffering into joy. How can we not awaken through this?

On suffering and sacrifice

Returning to this focus on suffering which can so easily snuff out joy, where did this originate? Within both Christianity and Buddhism – or what we know about these and what is taught – there has been almost a veneration of suffering. And whilst it is true we need to allow our deepest, darkest places to open to the light, and that trying to stay happily splashing about in the shallows of positivity doesn't do it, doesn't heal or transmute anything, overly focussing on suffering can be a trap. It can so easily become a *belief* that suffering is good for the soul. Then we equate spirituality and the spiritual 'path' only with suffering; so suffering keeps us humble and bowed down and whoops! we are into martyrdom, with the whole dark, hideous history of Puritanism and practices like flagellation just around the corner. Then sacrifice is seen as a virtue. It has been used in Christianity as a measure of our spiritual attainment: saints have often suffered and sacrificed and many given their lives. But what is it that we want so much, what is it that we are giving up to attain? What are we *really* sacrificing? And who are we doing this *for*? Is it even possible to sacrifice if one is fully surrendered?

Deep questions indeed. I am no spiritual scholar. I have not read all the literature and cannot claim to know what has been said here. All I know is that joy feels like a more pure and untainted flame to me than sacrifice: a means to uplift, connect and be *real – because of its immediacy*. We have been taught and believe that only if something is hard to achieve can it be worthwhile, and this is especially true in spirituality. To the puritanical anti-lifers of history joy is dangerous, because it is en*joyed*; sacrifice, on the other hand, is not. And persuading someone to do something they find difficult to do, rather than something they love to do, provides a means for control; control through guilt and punishment or through promised reward.

I am not talking here about sacrifice in the sense of giving up your life because you know this is all you can do to be true. Jesus did not choose to die, he simply followed what he knew to be true in spite of death becoming a real possibility. He refused to back off or run away, he accepted that this was likely to happen. We can call this the ultimate sacrifice: standing by what we know to be true and even enduring torture and death for this. *It is the way this word has been used to coerce people into giving up aliveness that doesn't feel true, that feels wrong to this heart* – the active suppression of joy. Whether this is deliberate exploitation or a projection of those who created this out of their own shut-off-from-life-ness who knows? Likely a mixture of both. But it means that a man who brought a radical teaching about love was not only killed, but then had this teaching turned on its head to venerate the suppression of life and love in its true, free, all-encompassing nature.

Children know pure joy but this can be easily crushed, along with access to the spirit from which it arises: Being. So perhaps rather than focussing on awakening into the great hall of emptiness, what some call the Absolute – though not to deny its validity – we would be better served focussing on reclaiming our aliveness and joy and trusting that this, in itself, is an act of worship? Joy unites us with Being, directly, without need for any complicated knowledge or practices. It is also anarchic: it may be temporarily suppressed but ultimately it cannot be controlled. It can be experienced *through* the body and by *any*body: *because joy has no hierarchy.* It can flow through a rubbish collector, a so-called 'primitive' tribeswoman or a man on death row. I suspect it flows more rarely through a politician or an oil baron, but who knows?

Both Jesus and Buddha lived in times long past, as did Moses and Mohammed and most of the Indian gurus and sages, and surely none of them could have imagined the world we live in now and the extraordinary grip mind would take on humanity. Or how we override the wisdom of the heart and place our faith in so-called 'economics' and systems of governance based on exploiting everything for profit. They could not have envisioned the enormous worldwide reach brought about by developing air travel and the Internet and, despite the marvels, all the grim effects our clever, ego-based minds have on this world. The sheer destructive power of things like nuclear bombs wiping out whole cities and unmanned drones flying beyond our natural hearing or eyesight, capable of killing individuals and whole groups at the touch of a button, pressed by someone somewhere else across the world: all this would have been beyond their wildest imaginings. They all operated within the cultures *and cultural belief-systems* of their times.

It is curious that we seem to have few tales about those most central to our spiritual and religious images (in the West at least) – Jesus, and now the Buddha – dancing and celebrating life in pure joy. What was this about? Jesus certainly is quoted as referencing joy and it's hard to accept that he did not know about this underlying foundation when one is truly connected with life. Hard to know how much of what has been written is tainted with the various writers' own belief in the necessity of suffering. Incidentally, none of what I am saying here is to deny that suffering can be useful: that it can bring us to a place of such utter desperation that we finally let go. That suffering can ignite a desire to move beyond it and become conscious, and to let go so completely that the realisation that *we are already awake* can penetrate our awareness.

It's just that there is little evidence of a sense of valuing and celebrating life as being a form of prayer in itself. At least in the case of Jesus, something heavy and dark and ultimately untrue seems to have intruded itself into the records of this man's teachings. With the Buddha too, it all seems to be weighted with putting our attention on suffering and how to escape this. And the romantic tale of the ultra-compassionate Bodhisattva refusing to leave this Earth until every last person attains enlightenment also places this idea of sacrifice at the forefront of spiritual achievement. Yet, as Adyashanti has pointed out, as we will all ultimately awaken anyway there is no need for this sacrifice.

My own sense is that it is not sacrifice we need to value, not giving something up that is precious to us, but rather *rising in joy* (what Osho referred to as *rising* in love instead of *falling* in love). What do I mean by this? It's like a sense of *lifting up into what is already here* and adoring it, giving our all to it – not from a sense of giving something up, but rather adding ourselves *to* something: a joining (or joy(n)ing!). A subtle distinction because in moving beyond ego we give everything that we are, and this may appear as nothing because we are already one with everything anyway.

And yet... and yet somehow in the letting go of what we have been holding on to – our identification with ego and the conditioned mind – in the surrendering is also a giving: we give our hearts to this, all that we are. Another paradox if you like, something that doesn't fit into the tidy boxes of a conceptual mind. What I am talking about here is something you can only *feel,* you can't 'get' it with the mind but you can *resonate* with it. You can intuitively know exactly what I am speaking about. You can do this through Being because Being is the link to what we already are. And don't forget, nothing that I or you or anyone else says about all this is the whole truth. In these realms we go beyond words, beyond concepts, into the great mystery in which all this appears.

The importance of celebration

In terms of mysteries, I am still intrigued by the very literal way joy presented itself in my life. This happened in the early Eighties with a series of strange occurrences. First, I met a highly intuitive man who kept calling me Joy, saying that was my real name (I found this quite irritating as I have never liked the 'oi' *sound* of this name and am happy not to have been given it). We had decided to go for a walk on the beach and as we were driving there, we passed not one but *two* cars with the letters JOY on their number plates, and on arriving we found the word 'joy' already written in the sand! I realised this must have been written very recently as it was near the shoreline and the tide was going out, so there was no way this man could have somehow sneaked out and done this earlier. Nor was it the beginning of a great romance: we only met casually a few times.

So what did it mean? I have no *idea,* I have long ago given up trying to interpret life in this way and I include this because it focusses on joy, and illustrates how life has this wonderful and mysterious quality of serendipity that cannot be tamed, cannot be corralled into the domain of rational explanations to satisfy a controlling mind. For me, joy exists as a form of living celebration.

Aaah celebration! This is the natural expression of joy. So it's good to see that despite all the heavy traditional views around spirituality, where life is seen as mere Maya, or illusion – to be transcended as quickly as possible – still the pure energy of celebration breaks through. India, where these views formed and where renunciation and abstinence also have their followers, has nonetheless spawned some iconic individuals who rebelled against the accepted customs of their times to uphold and express the celebratory aspect of divine love, or Prema Bhakti as it is known there. Of these, Meera or Mirabai as she is also called, is perhaps the best known.

Living around the fifteenth century, she is still revered for her legacy of devotional poetry, her singing and dancing, which are seen as pure expressions of Bhakti. The story goes that as a very young child she was given a statue of the lord Krishna by a holy man and thereafter her life became devoted to him. Neither her royal birth nor subsequent marriage protected her from persecution by jealous relatives and, after two attempts to poison her and her refusal to leap onto the funeral pyre after her husband's death (as was expected of her), she left the palace to live as a sanyassin wandering the streets and slums of Vrindaban, where she continued to dance and sing and became a saint – a recognised flame-carrier for the divine – in her own right.

Hers is quite a story for, despite her devotion to Krishna – or perhaps because of it – she confronted the evils that still persist today (and not just in India) of deliberately enshrined poverty and misogyny. And she confronted these with her actions. Not simply by leaving her family and their royal position in society, or even the extraordinarily beautiful, yet simple and tender poetry and songs that gathered to her such an enormous and devoted following (in which she declared men and women equal in the eyes of Krishna), but by insisting on singing and dancing these in the streets. Can you imagine how that would have been received in her time? Now, she would likely be written off as just some crazy, religious feminist and maybe even locked up for continually dancing in the streets. I find both her insistence and persistence in expressing her devotion in these ways, *no matter the cost*, wonderfully heartening. She is still revered in India today and seen by many as their greatest saint. How much her presence influenced individual lives cannot be known but *joy is infectious and, as witnessed here, carries a potential for vast influence*.

There are also tales about the Indian Tantricas, couples who reputedly even lived together in one robe and danced their ecstasy in the graveyards. There are many myths and stories and for me, the clearest expression I have seen of pure, innocent joy was in the face of the Shivapuri Baba. With babies and small children too, we see this – though it is sadly far less evident in grownups. But joy itself is ageless, timeless and its presence shines out with a childlike radiance, as the Shivapuri proves.

It's high time for humanity to rediscover and celebrate joy as a central and vital expression of our being alive. To whom can we look to demonstrate this? Where are our models, especially here in the West? The Hare Krishnas dance in the streets but few people relate this to themselves. Some Christian communities, especially those with an African congregation, become ecstatic singing and speaking in tongues, but again, this doesn't feel it belongs to the rest of us. With people like Amma – who draws thousands of people on her visits to London with her incredible, joy-inspiring hugs – opportunities to focus this are arriving.

But... but we need more reminders of what some have called 'divine madness'. We have been so trained to suppress this feeling, it's seen as childlike, undignified, uncool, there are even those who are embarrassed by the free expression of joyfulness: after all, we are only supposed to show joy on falling in love, the birth of a child, at weddings or on meeting someone after a long absence. Or when we, our family or our 'team' are winning something and even then, when you watch people 'high five' each other, there is a certain brashness to this, it lacks the open spontaneity of the loving heart and has more of the excited mind about it.

This demonstrates just how far we have come from any natural state of aliveness and subsequent need to celebrate this, the spontaneous joy most of us knew as a child. And then of course there was Osho who did exactly that – who explicitly encouraged celebration as an expression of this joyful energy, where the very core, the Being-ness that we all are, is celebrated. In creating places where this was not only acceptable but actively encouraged, he has had a hugely significant impact on the lives of so many. And this has been particularly true for the German contingent (about fifty per cent when I was there), many of whom carried a heavy cultural conditioning involving guilt and reaction to the emphasis on discipline and emotional repression of their parents and grandparents time.

Amongst the Sufis too, we see this direct connection through joy, especially in their poetry (Rumi being a well-known example of this) with its capacity to aim straight for the spiritual heart, penetrating the mind's defences with ease. And their Dervishes' 'whirling': this can inspire such a sense of joy as we witness the extraordinary stillness at the centre of the movement they create, which carries something that lies beyond words. Through this, they express something profound about love, or Bhakti – the path of love. And yet despite this, in my brief time with them, I experienced the present-day Sufi teaching in the West as lacking something (remember, this is entirely subjective; other people clearly find great value within it).

My resistance to hierarchies was triggered, as it was by the rituals and secrecy (the Sufi, as the mystical branch of Islam, have long suffered persecution by orthodox Islamic authorities). All these invite a tendency to follow form, even though the majority of followers may feel something deeper and be drawn by this mystical force. For me, the form seemed to get in the way of an openness, where people can freely question and explore, connect with their bodies and confront their inner feeling, sensing, intuitive realities *and discover the truth for themselves*. Tradition – any tradition – holds a potential for the belief that others know best and for this to interfere with the freshness that comes from looking for oneself.

Joy allows the body to sing

Joy – the elixir of life – is felt directly in the body and the body's energy field. It feels like a life-giving substance that percolates through the entire energy system to become *one's direct experience of reality*; it colours everything with this sense of 'Oh *yes*!' – 'Yes' to life, 'yes' to whatever comes. To me, joy feels qualitatively different to bliss, which feels more like a state, like ecstasy. As does happiness which, although this too can radiate, lacks a sense of movement, of flow. Joy, on the other hand, is an outpouring that touches everything around us. We *seek* bliss and *pursue* happiness: these experiences can both be *attained,* temporarily at least, whether through certain practices or substances, or even purchases. But in my experience joy is not attainable: it bubbles up from within like a hidden spring, spontaneously – *it is part of our natural aliveness*. Instead of being static, a state: joy is our very essence. Delight comes close but this suggests a cause, something outside of ourselves that we delight *in,* whereas joy is cause*less* and could be described as the living essence of love celebrating itself, touching everything around us. If happiness and contentment are what we feel sitting around the fire, joy and passion are the living fire itself!

Joy has a voice. It says things like 'Hey, come on, let's celebrate! Let's dance and sing and en-joy each other and everything around us, even if this turns out to be our last moment!' – last moment in a body that is, because life doesn't care what form we take, even if that is no form: it just loves to move and change, to love and cherish all its forms. We are constantly held in the arms of existence: *there is nowhere else to be*. There is a scene in a film made a long while ago now, *Nosferatu the Vampire*, where the barge carrying Dracula's coffin, laden with plague-infested rats, comes to rest against the town's quayside and the rats scramble off. What do the inhabitants do? They bring out their tables covered with their finest linens, crystal and silverware and they dress up and dance and play music and feast. So how we perceive life and how we respond to it is entirely up to us!

If we follow our joy there also comes a deep longing to share: even if this can't be spoken, it can be felt. And there can arrive a level of acceptance of everyone *despite* what the other is believing, despite how caught up they are in the dream. The compassionate heart isn't something that belongs to 'you' or 'me': *it is the very heart of existence itself*; we just can't feel this when we are shut down and closed off in our dark little prison cells of ego. I have no idea why some of us get motivated to move – to look and find out who is really here, what life is really about.

There is a beetle called a cicada that I used to hear out in the Australian bush, where it's deafening chorus made it impossible to think. It mates and buries its eggs in the soil and these take *eighteen years* to surface. It then climbs the nearest tree, gobbles up some leaves, mates and begins the cycle all over again, leaving its brown husks to decorate the tree trunks. Who knows about the 'whys?' About time and meaning and purpose? Joy tells us something more profound. That it is just in the living, breathing, responding to what appears, without interference from conditioned mind, that we can relax and rejoice. That this is enough: amen.

What about passion?

Another word that we rarely use in its deeper meaning is 'passion.' We tend to think of passion in terms of either steamy sex or a strong interest in something, like a passion for classical music or motorbikes. The phrase 'passionate aliveness' is not something you hear people talking about, yet the capacity to feel passion – *and the suppression of this* – is surely central to everyone's life and perhaps their death too, because a body living under suppression is not a healthy body. Words like 'passion', 'desire' and 'pleasure', the no-no's of the old religious orders, are so often associated with sex that it's hard to think about them without this association. And as for 'lust'! A word with such narrow, negative connotations. But what about 'a lust for life'? What we are seeing here are the dregs of our old conditioning still clinging on, mixed in with confusing and often contradictory messages around sex in the media, our schools and society generally. And this is a real shame. Sex maintains such a powerful, instinctual pull that many people, and especially those in positions of authority, are afraid of it.

Here we see the pattern repeated – where repression forces desire to surface in all sorts of harmful and inappropriate behaviour (as the more recent revelations of the Catholic church illustrate). However if you stop a moment and connect all these words, passion and pleasure and desire, with joy and *aliveness* you see something else. You realise how *natural* these are and in consequence, as we have seen in previous chapters, how damaging the forces of repression. But more than this: you see within these words how they speak to us about venerating life and about our innate capacity for delighting in what life so freely offers: *delighting from a grateful heart*. These energies represent our nature, our *joie de vivre*. It is *life* we are making love to, making love with: there is no need for restraint when you are truly living from the body-Being.

Once again, Sufi poets like Rumi speak of this best where, within the poetical alchemy of the heart, they transform words into drops of living liquid divinity. Here is where, again speaking personally, I find Buddhist teachings too dry. Clearly it is very important to find detachment, but without the passion of the heart *connection* is lacking – connection to this sense of aliveness and Being, which can transform passion and joy into a direct form of worship. Here phrases like 'Adoration of the divine' have meaning within this often bleak and spartan land of language as it is used today. Interestingly, passion can be translated to mean suffering (from the Latin *passio*): the passion of Christ refers to this, and I find this association unfortunate. When translated to mean simply *intense feeling* this connects it with energy. Then we see passion bringing a powerful momentum within a feeling; a depth and intensification *within* connection.

And maybe this is where love and the joy of life can transmute suffering from something we cling to – as being almost a masochistic form of self-denial and evidence of the power to endure – into the recognition of and delight in the divinity in all things? *We become authentic devotees*, totally subsumed in the beauty of life: even when this carries – as it does – a terrible aspect. Then passion and compassion need not be seen as separate; they both emanate from the heart; as does joy which, ultimately, brings freedom by breaking through the limits of everyday dealings in a world dominated by the mind. In joy, life is unified through Being, unified with the ineffable, ultimate reality, the Absolute: all is both conscious *and* consciousness itself.

The joy in being an empty vessel constantly being filled with itself

Looking at the possibility that we can awaken *through* joy rather than *into* joy brings up more questions. For instance, maybe compassion requires not only ruthlessness, as the Shamballa warriors claimed, but also joyfulness? Can one have compassionate joyfulness? Does not true joy carry the seeds of compassion? Because if it is love that redeems then maybe joy is its instrument? In piercing the defences of the heart, space is made for love to enter. I don't claim to be any kind of authority here but I do have a *sense* that *something* needs to change – perhaps already has changed, *is* changing – around how we open and respond, how we open to becoming vessels that delight in being used by life. Is this awakening? Enlightenment? Seemingly not in the usual way we use these terms: as in awakened to the vast emptiness of which everything is part of the One, the 'All'. Is it self-realised? Maybe.

Perhaps this relates to what I have heard both Adyashanti and John de Ruiter distinguish as the 'awakened heart?' (As distinct from the 'awakened mind' and 'awakened gut'.) Because surely a vessel is what we all actually are? What we both long for and rediscover in the process of surrendering our egoic dream? I know now what brings me joy, what it is that I want. It is very simple and it comes down to being fully open to life – all of it – from a quiet, still but responsive place; and that what blocks the expression of love and joy is being closed off from this. I have seen that what gets in the way of this openness is my fearful, controlling mind that tries to tell me to avoid pain and uncomfortable feelings in any way that I can.

Osho comments *'Falling in love you remain a child; rising in love you mature. By and by love becomes not a relationship, it becomes a state of your being. Not that you are in love – now you are love.'* When I first heard Osho talking about rising in love, although I had a vague sense of this I never really knew what he meant: now I do. This word has associations with bread rising in the oven, with the sun rising in the morning, but I know it now because I *feel* this as rising in joy, as Being flows through my body-energy. I have the evidence, all the proof I need. And for others who don't *know* this, no amount of thinking about it and trying to work it out can find this for you – it is far too intimate. To arrive at this place requires receptivity: being open and available and letting life *enter* you. It helps if you don't try to hang on to whatever comes but just remember, there is only the one heart and this – the very centre of our Being-ness – is our home. So, to quote a line from an old, unfinished poem: 'stop flapping about in the mind: rest here in the heart and build yourself a nest.'

Home-play
1. **Three circles and inhaling: heart to cradle, cradle to earth and lastly, movements to express 'Thank you', 'Bless you' and 'Thy will be done' (See diagram)**

   This short exercise is a good one to include in your daily morning routine. It Involves splashing any perfumed oil or lotion you choose onto the wrists (Aura Soma, which is particularly refined, is great for this).
   - Raise both hands to bring palms in front of the nose and inhale; put palms together and continue to raise the hands above the head, separate and bring them down, palms facing forwards, creating a circular movement, ending with palms flat over the heart centre. Only then breathe out through the mouth, following the breath down to the cradle.
   - Repeat, this time ending the circular movement with the hands flat on the inside of hips on each the side of the cradle. Breathe out through the mouth,

following the breath down the legs and feet and into the earth.
- The last movement has three parts:

a) Repeat inhale and circular movement with the head initially tilting upwards, and feel the chest opening and expanding as you do so. Whilst saying 'Thank you", bring the hands down palms uppermost, till they almost touch at the base of the circle.

b) Turn the hands to face downwards and breathe out saying 'Bless you', while moving the hands apart following the curve back up a short way.

c) Finally, relax the hands to hang at your sides, palms facing forwards, and allow the movement of the body-reflex to let them rise up naturally, with a slight swinging movement, to about 9" (23 centimetres), whilst saying the words 'Thy will be done', with a sense of letting go. This last invites complete surrender of the personal will; a space to let go of anything one is holding on to.

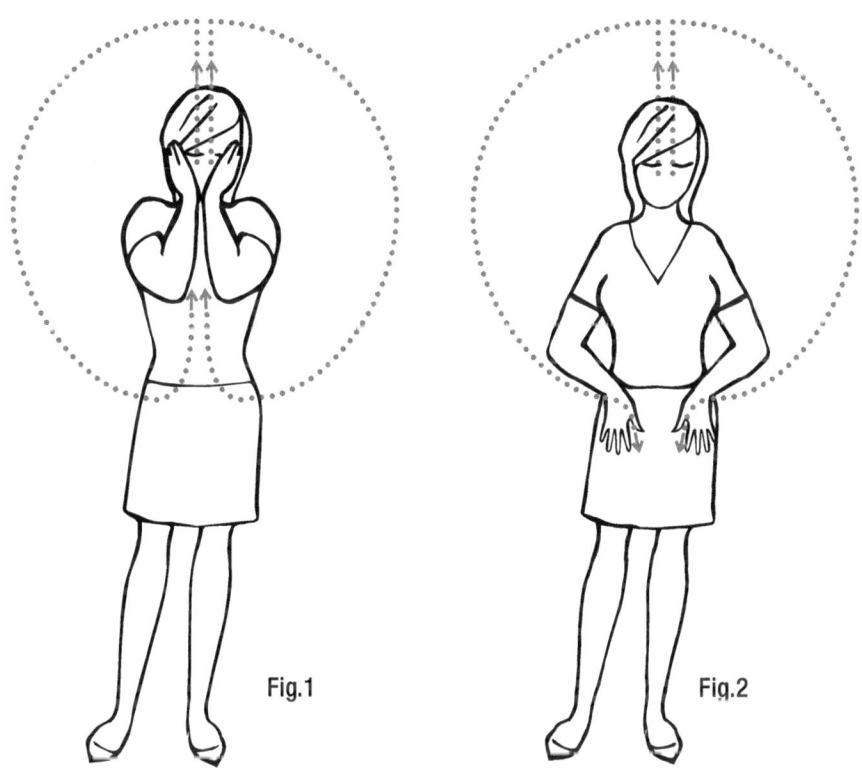

Fig.1 Fig.2

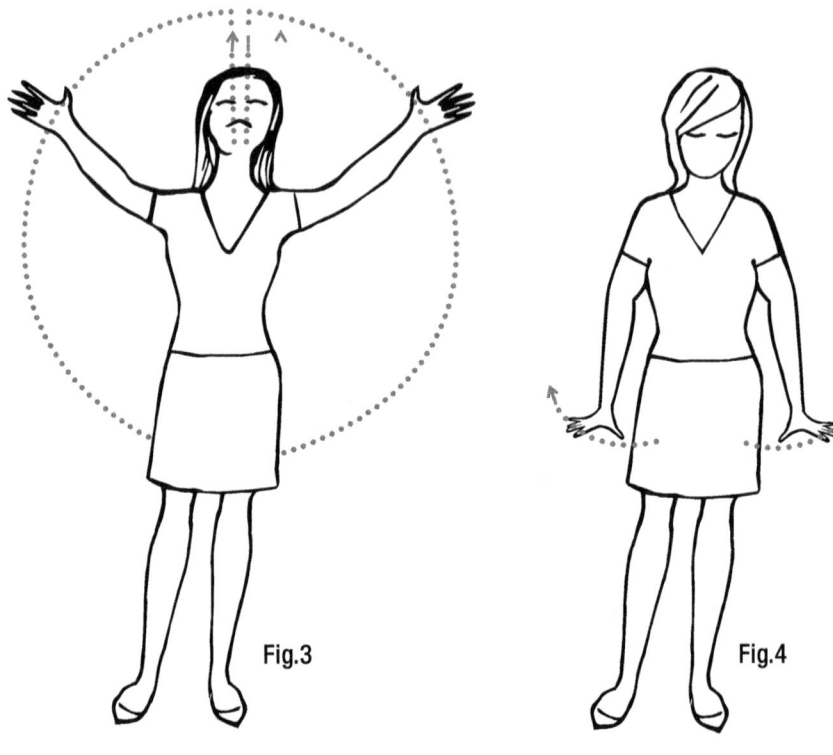

Fig.3

Fig.4

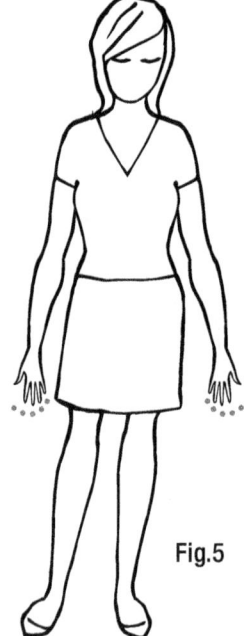

Fig.5

Interestingly, the patterns you make with your hands draw the shape of an apple cut in half (the starting place of the hands under your nose representing the core). Perhaps in biting into the apple from the tree of knowledge, man started a movement towards the domination of the head, of knowledge over knowing, mind over heart? In which case, this exercise can perhaps serve to help to restore the balance.

The politics of inner sense

'The truth is there are, on this frequency, from our human perspective, a planet, some beings, some resources; would it not be sensible to employ systems that benefit the planet, the beings and the resources?' ~ Russell Brand

'It is always easier to deny reality than to allow our worldview to be shattered' ~ Naomi Klein

'No ideology can help to create a new world or a new mind or a new human being — because ideological orientation itself is the root cause of all the conflicts and all the miseries... Now man must learn to live without ideologies religious, political or otherwise.' ~ Osho

When I started to write this book I was told I needed to identify my readers and stay within this genre. And if I were just writing for 'spiritual seekers' I would stop at that last chapter. However, I can't do that. There is something that lies within the heart of all of us humans that is trying to stir and make itself felt; and sometimes this can appear in the most surprising places. How can we speak to only a part when we seek to reclaim our wholeness; to make this visible? Wholeness can't leave anything out, including finding ways to live together as part of a conscious, loving human community.

So as we bring our focus to that which concerns the so-called 'outer' world, it should be easier by now to see how this is influenced by our subtle inner world, our essence; how these are inextricably woven together. Which brings us to the question of how becoming more consciously aware can translate into actually *living together;* into sharing this human experience of One-ness in it's apparently separate parts. So although these next two chapters are inevitably inter-twined, let's play first in the feild of politics and see what we find. For instance politics and love: 'What have they got to do with each other?' you might well ask – or politics and spirituality come to that? In fact, there is frequently a strong resistance to anything seen as religious or spiritual amongst people involved in politics, a dismissal of these as being irrelevant. And conversely, a distaste for politics amongst the religious and spiritually inclined (it seems only Jesus and Osho were prepared to include this in their teachings).

If you look at the way politics is conducted you can see why, for this appears to be almost entirely in the realm of the power-hungry egoic mind: the wisdom of the heart virtually overpowered, the divorce seemingly complete (which isn't to deny the role of feeling and *emotion* in politics, far from it). Yet politics itself has a simple remit: to find ways to govern, usually involving leaders and political parties; broadly speaking, to organise how people live together and share what we have and what needs doing to create, harvest, protect and maintain this.

Without the heart, politics naturally becomes subject to the dictates of the egoic mind. And that means – as it always does – that it will move in the directions of power and privilege for those most able to obtain and retain these; a move that includes the *emotionalisation* of politics: by which means people's emotions are used to manipulate them, to gain power and maintain control (the media being an important tool for this). So one could say bringing love into politics is radical: it means aligning politics with the heart, giving supremacy to this heart and its values anchored, as it is, in Being. It means demanding politics be reconnected with the whole. Above all, it means using our *inner* sense.

What do I mean by 'inner sense?' Inner sense is that which we know, intuitively; something that comes from the deep place of the discriminating heart. It hurts us to move away from this, we feel it when our alignment is out-of-true. It isn't a question of the rules of morality taught by religions, or ideas about ethics coming from a conditioned mind, nor is it vulnerable to the expediency and subtle deceptions of ego. Inner sense is simply *known* in that realm of feeling, sensing, intuiting reality that we come to recognise the more we access and trust in it. *And politics is no different to anything else:* when we apply our inner sense certain threads become visible, threads relating to the heart. Perhaps the most unshakeable and consistent of these, which we could extract and name as key tenets for designing a political structure based on inner sense, are the following regarding:

*Relationship between peoples: <u>Including not Excluding</u> – This is about acknowledging and living the truth that we are all one.

*Our common wealth: <u>Sharing not Hoarding</u> – In living truth there can be no 'yours' and 'mine', only an agreement to 'borrow' from the collective whole.

*This planet our home: <u>Nurturing not Plundering</u> – Recognising that what we have come to think of as a separate planet is actually our extended body.

Here, words like caring, co-operation and community come to the fore.

The lovely thing about all this is that these tenets can be *felt* once we are in touch with our Being-ness. This sees the reality that we are all one, so then we can recognise it makes perfect inner sense to respect, even to revere all beings. It's not just a nice Buddhist teaching 'practising loving kindness to all beings', it makes sense on a *felt, intuitive* level. And of course – and what is often left out in the way religions are taught – reverence for all beings has to include *us*: ourselves! That much-quoted teaching of Jesus 'Do unto others as you would have them do unto you' refers to how we treat others and how we want them to treat us. Crucially, there is no mention of *how we treat ourselves.* Of course the ego doesn't and can't love itself, no matter how many New Age workshops it attends; no matter how many positive affirmations and attitudinal ploys it uses to try to do this. How can a construct, something that doesn't actually exist, love itself?

Whereas it becomes natural to revere all beings once you recognise we are all part of the one Being: then you can't leave anything out, including yourself, as Being reveres itself. (Don't worry if the mind struggles here, just let go and relax.) Here we see how impossible revering ourselves is if we are caught up in the mind's conditioning, believing we are not only separate but somehow less than others, hence not deserving of reverence – especially if you believe in original sin. Significantly, Buddhists don't use this word 'sin', instead they speak about 'error', and Adyashanti says sin refers to 'missing the mark', both terms that are empty of guilt and shame. Could it be that 'original sin' was intended to refer to the *disconnect* we create when we lose the sense of connection with Being?

If we apply the same insights we have seen throughout this book to politics – that is, to the way we organise living together – then it is clear and easy; it really is not complicated (remember, it is mind that loves to make things complex). The true, intuitive heart operates in the same way *regardless* of what it is looking at. It is not a moral framework of the mind where we learn to try, or at least pretend to be nice to each other: *it just makes sense.* So if you translate the tenets I suggested into practical action the way becomes visible as you go along; the 'How?' of the mind becomes redundant as the intuitive heart is allowed to find its own way of reflecting these.

We have seen how the heart's approach is quite different to the dualistic and adversarial approaches of mind. The heart loves harmony and always seeks a way to flow that *includes, shares and nurtures,* and it encourages others to do the same. When these concerns are seen to be primary – how it's not about being right or wrong, or left or right, Capitalist or Communist – then however we organise living together has a natural, beautiful flow. It is automatically sustainable, automatically fair (though not necessarily as the mind would judge this), automatically of optimum value. Like a river, the movement of this flow energises the content. When everyone feels they belong, are wanted and have something to contribute, there is room for diversity, room for differences.

It's not a matter of 'shoulds' and morality: that technology is wrong, for instance, and we should all go back to living on the land in tribes. There is no correct way – there are simply ways that flow, that include change and allow for diversity. *Inner sense becomes obvious:* in the moment clarity is born. Then the movement of life itself takes over; we are in alignment with this and our joy becomes in transcribing, following, exploring and enjoying this flow: together. Any system – any way of living together that does not include and allow these priorities – is seen as redundant. Not morally wrong: just not applicable, not working, not functioning to maintain this flow.

Why does the mind love to make things complicated? Because then it can do what it knows how to do; it can present a myriad theories, systems and solutions, endless information and ways of assessing, analysing and comparing this information: it is good at this. Mind prefers adversarial activity because then it can feel powerful as it encourages us to take a position and argue and debate endlessly. Naturally, as this position becomes emotionalised and rooted in ego, we then have an investment in winning, in being seen to be right (just watch any political debate). As Osho comments *'This whole conditioning produces an inferiority complex because it wants you to become superior, superior over others. It teaches you competition, comparison; it teaches you violence, fight. It teaches you that means don't matter, what matters is the end, success is the goal.'*

This unconscious urge makes it almost impossible to see what is simple and obvious. So the thinking processes of the conditioned mind confuse and distract us, whilst keeping us believing that we are right, the other is wrong and we must, somehow, win or everything is lost. When we perceive the other to be winning we feel powerless and resentful – we may even plot revenge. And all this is a terrible waste, because the mind's wonderful talents can be used to devise *ways to implement* the knowing, movement and directions of the heart. This is it's true function. Remember, the mind judges and the heart discerns and it is this heart that we now need to trust to guide us.

At some point in this chapter the mind may come in with questions like 'And what do you know about politics? Have you studied Political Theory and Political History? Have you been trained in Economics? Are you familiar with the world of banks, business and large corporate organisations? If not, then you really have no right to comment.' This is how we have all been trained: to listen to the mind, to believe its conditioning filled with other people's 'expert' opinions and to discount the heart as being overly sentimental and basically ignorant, incapable of dealing with the harsh realities of the modern world.

However, as we pointed out earlier on, the mind has no way of measuring true value, *and living together absolutely requires this*. When this is ignored you get politics based on maximising power and profit before preservation of the Earth and the wellbeing of its peoples. Then, in order to maintain this drive the control of people becomes necessary, implemented either by indifferent bureaucracies or intrusive forms of surveillance and policing that involves threat, violence, even torture. This is exactly where you need to trust *what you intuitively know to be true*; because all but the most damaged people can learn to discriminate through the heart. The egoic mind uses fear and illusion to convince us of its policies; this is everywhere evident in the world around us – *especially in the world of politics*. So we need to counter it with trust in something deeper, something that guides us with love. We need to trust in the very heart of our Being-ness. From this arises knowing, courage and compassion: in other words, what is needed to change direction and evolve different political structures based on the politics of the heart.

Ways of the heart

We are currently seeing an almost universal wave of people feeling disempowered: evincing anger, frustration, discontent and even despair. People see for themselves that whatever the politicians, economists and those who hold power are saying and doing, it is taking away their capacity to keep themselves and their families fed, well and safe and to live in a world in which their children and grandchildren may prosper. If you look around at what is happening in politics everywhere, you see so much that simply doesn't make sense. There are some very simple questions that arise about this – about what is, essentially, a matter of how we organise living together and sharing out what we have. The very obviousness of this, contrasted with what is *actually* happening, can seem quite bizarre.

If we look at the current political processes we see they are inherently dysfunctional; mindless rhetoric covering an approach devoid of wisdom, of inner sense, lacking the intelligence of the heart. Is what we are seeing a glimpse of the dinosaurs before they became extinct? Attitudes so entrenched and turned in on themselves that they cannot adapt? 'How on Earth did this come about?' you might ask. Take a look and you will recognise something all too familiar, the same thing we have been seeing throughout this book – after all, why assume politics to be any different? Behind the questions 'What has got us into this mess?' and 'Who is really running things?' you see it! *Politics has become a forum for the egoic mind.* Not surprising then that things are organised in ways that take no account of the heart, ways that fail to prioritise taking care of everyone and the world we live in. Instead of this we see the same old drive to get (power) and to avoid (responsibility), where the most ruthless take as much as they can, leaving the rest to their fate. This is why tinkering to try to improve things can't work because of this lack of intention to serve the whole. If we back up a little, we start to get a clearer view.

When powerful feelings like fear and anger are stirred up we tend to react. How? By blaming others. This is easy. People like the Koch brothers, for instance: two sad, emotionally crippled old men who, as children, were brutally beaten into shape by their fascist father, according to Jane Meyer in her book *Dark money. The Hidden History of the Billionaires Behind the Rise of the Radical Right.* These are men who channel the billions that make them the second richest men in the world towards supporting this ideal. But that simply displaces our anger and makes us complicit in the world of violence and hatred that such extreme right-wing attitudes enflame. Donald Trump and Nigel Farrage (who advocated Brexit) epitomises this. 'Well, what can you expect of these right-wing extremists,' you might say.

But actually, the same hatred and rigidity can also be found amongst some on the Left, where there can be an almost religious sense of moral righteousness and hatred of the rich and powerful. Much of the struggle between those who have less (often a great deal less) and those with more, is played out in the scenario of 'workers' versus 'bosses', whether these are large multinational corporations or small enterprises. And these words, along with 'class struggle', 'exploitation', 'injustice' and 'greed' are loaded with *emotional reaction;* especially fear, anger, resentment and envy that can cover over the genuine seeing of a heart that seeks the good of all beings.

Out of this situation of enmity and distrust the Trade Unions were born, with mythic figures like Kier Hardy inspiring massive popular support, where workers banded together to defend their interests. Labour laws were enacted and State ownership and State health and (National) insurance provision (the so-called 'welfare state') set up in the UK by Bevan and Attlee after the second world war, to provide for the sick, the uneducated, the unemployed and those deemed too old to work. This system was then replicated in commonwealth countries such as Australia, New Zealand and Canada and all over Europe and Scandinavia (but not the US).

And then a counter movement was begun in the 80's by those who feared the loss of their power and privilege, to unpick this move towards establishing a caring and inclusive society. Emotive words like 'feckless', 'shirkers' and 'benefit scroungers' were introduced by the privately-owned popular press to encourage the public to resent and reject such State support schemes and those who use them. Labour laws have been weakened or dismantled, harsh restrictions imposed on Trade Unions and secretive (because illegal) organisations developed to counter the Unions' power by infiltrating them, monitoring Union activists and blacklisting them. Although this process of reversing protection for people was begun in the UK by Margaret Thatcher, it emulates the free-for-all, free market politics of the US – where support by the State is extremely limited – and returns power to the privileged few.

Over time, the tug-of-war between those who had managed to get more and didn't want to share this, and those with far less who wanted to be able to catch up, has evolved into a variety of political forms that, in the West at least, lie somewhere between the frightening extremes of Fascist dictatorships and Communist revolutions (that usually ended with a dictatorial group at their head, anyway). An idea borrowed from ancient Greece, something called 'Democracy' evolved where – in theory at least – everyone has a voice through elections. However *in reality,* and to varying degrees, this can be seen to be misleading, as few people's votes carry real power. In fact, rather like morality in its attempt to regulate people's behaviour, the way the term 'democracy' is used could also be seen as a way to control people by making them *believe* they are represented so they will behave and conform. Governments know their power lies not in their actions but in how they are *perceived,* hence the power of the media, which can both persuade and mislead (and why real democracy is rare).

There is a thread that runs through this picture: *the priorities of the heart versus those of the egoic mind.* Politics, ever the most likely venue, has come to be dominated by the egoic mind. As things stand, it is a quagmire of often deliberate misinformation and illusionist tricks. We rarely get to see what is really happening *or to see this with fresh eyes,* hence we have largely come to accept the more recent form of dictatorship: that is, dictatorship by the banks, multinational corporations, military-industrial complex and the super-rich, as being 'just the way things are'. One of the tools of deception is to make people believe only the 'experts' know the facts. But experts often get bogged down in the detail, along with competitive positioning, and fail to see the bigger picture. For instance, what actually *is* a multi-national corporation? And how does it function? Given the dominant role these play in our political reality, you would think this would be an obvious question, wouldn't you?

I remember reading a book that was all the rage in the 70s, *The Greening of America* by Charles A. Reich, which predicted much of what is happening today. How a corporation's essential remit, to keep growing and expanding *no matter the cost to anything in the way of this,* creates an entity that is, ultimately, programmed to destroy itself by running out of a world to exploit. Much like a cancer, it devours its host. It's like one of those nightmares where you are being pursued by something that wants to gobble you up: try getting rid of the boss and another appears in his place. There is also the small matter of how corporations have been allowed to be called 'persons' in law, meaning they are not subject to the same rules as smaller businesses. All this stands as a salient example of how, without the information, people can't see the political reality – in this case the very real threat corporations pose to humanity in an unregulated economy.

We are living in a time of severe disconnection from reality. From this place it's perhaps not surprising that as long as most people have an apparently improving 'standard of living' few question what is presented to them. It's convenient to have others make the decisions. Start to reverse this with policies like austerity however and people become more observant; particularly as the Internet now makes available so many sources of direct information and simple ways to share this. As Pablo Iglesias, the youthful leader of the Podemos party in Spain points out *'If people don't do politics, others will do it for you. And when others do it for you, they can steal your rights, your democracy and your wallet.'*

We don't know how many people, perhaps the majority, remain caught in a false but very powerful political presentation. Without some degree of conscious awareness, emotions are routinely stirred up by the media, deliberately activating the egoic mind's eternal periscope that searches for targets to instil fear and enemies to smear and attack. But this too is changing as a new clarity (and sheer desperation) – along with a heartfelt distrust of politicians and political expediency – are causing earthquakes in this cosy home for the fearful ego, in which it seeks to comfort itself with self-righteousness and blame. A growing number of people know they are being cheated, there is a longing to see something real and honest and a genuine concern for the well-being of others. Listen, and you may detect a quiet stirring of the collective heart.

Visiting an Occupy encampment in London a few years ago, I was impressed to see they were offering free classes and open discussions about alternatives. Wouldn't it be great if this was part of the curriculum in schools? As more people become interested in politics as a result of things not working for so many, there will surely come more such openings. What I am interested in focussing here is how connecting with our inner sense can not only help us see what is true, it can guide us to what is needed, when it is needed; hence the importance of being open to trying new things, experimenting and looking honestly at the results.

Because it just becomes obvious what works for the whole and what doesn't. So Communism, as practised by the State, is a doctrine that doesn't allow for diversity: of religious belief, of different abilities and interests. And Capitalism and market forces, advocated by neo-liberalism – another doctrine – doesn't allow for inclusivity and sharing. Both have led to destruction of the environment, *and both are strategies of mind.* If you bring the heart to the forefront with inner sense, things change dramatically: then we see the whole picture; meaning any actions, political or otherwise, can come from this seeing of the true heart.

Power and politics

Power is very much at the centre of the ego's concept of politics. It is all about gaining control over others for our own benefit – same old, same old: getting what we want and avoiding what we don't want. The tools of manipulation – dissembling, disguising, denying and distorting; frightening, threatening and intimidating; enticing, persuading and placating others – all are used for these ends. *This is the very opposite of innocence.* Children may use these ploys to get what they want too, but there is an innocence in this; they often learn these from the adults around them and are not necessarily aware of what they are doing. As soon as we become aware we lose our innocence; we become corrupted by ego into sacrificing our integrity and betraying others, in often very subtle ways. Here morals are waved about in an attempt to keep ego in line. A whole maze of behavioural norms and goals obscure the simple *inner knowing* that lets us know, moment to moment, what feels okay for us, and what doesn't, through maintaining connection with our intuitive heart.

Here it makes sense to ask a very basic question: 'What actually *is* power? What is *real* power? And what happens if we start to let go of this conditioned response to overpower others or allow them to overpower us?' The fear of the egoic mind is that we will lose out and either suffer in a confrontation or become helpless pawns in the desires of others. And this may well have been our actual experience, especially as we grew up.

However, the truth is that when we let go into neither *insisting* nor *resisting*, and instead surrender to Being, to being what we really *are*, we discover that this unnameable vastness that we are *cannot* be overpowered by puny little ego-mind. How could it? I am not talking apathy here, but in order to be truly powerful we need to be open and receptive; receptive to life and what is true *so that we can act from that* – which might be to take no action. Because true power is an inner thing, it has to do with connection to the presence of Being. One of my favourite Zen stories is of an old monk who is sitting in the temple garden when a Samurai warrior rushes up brandishing his sword, saying 'Why don't you run away? Don't you know I can kill you?' to which the monk replies 'And I could *let* you kill me.' Whereupon the warrior raises his sword in rage and the monk simply says 'Hell'; the warrior lowers it in amazement and the monk says 'Heaven.'

In her book *Despair and Personal Power in a Nuclear Age*, Joanna Macy talks about how cultures derive their view about what power is from their world-view. So in the West, we have for some time now assumed everything to be separate; this imbues our notion of reality. We have given far less attention to what happens *between* these separate parts, or discrete entities, because this cannot usually be seen or measured. How do you measure love or hate? We know one entity can harm another, so we give priority to protecting ourselves *from* others. Then defences get built, whether personal or within nations, and power becomes equated with invulnerability. Joanna points out how, when power is seen in terms of domination, this creates a situation where if someone gains, another loses. It creates a win-lose situation where you have got to win if you are not to lose out.

More recently, scientists have discovered what earlier peoples knew for Millenia – the crucial power of inter-relationships, how things flow and form patterns that sustain each part. Relationship and exchange are seen as fundamental to this. Such ecosystems form the bedrock of connections not only within the brain, for instance, but between a family or a society. So if an individual part of this system attempts to build a defensive wall around itself it becomes dysfunctional. It will eventually atrophy and this weakens the larger system of which it is not only a part but itself depends. We can see from this how *power is now identified as coming from our ability to be open;* to create open systems. As part of a whole, it is win-win or lose-lose. Ultimately, we come to realise, we sink or swim *together.*

So how do these what Joanna calls 'Power-over' and 'Power-with*' structures operate amongst people? (*What scientists call 'synergy'.) Some operate as separate individuals with a solid ring of defences around them, rather like a rubber tyre. This protective barrier is intended to help them maintain power by both keeping others out and holding on to what they get (thus preventing anyone else from taking this). And others operate an 'open system'. Using the neurone system of the brain to illustrate this, she shows how, within this system, participants are all interconnected. So by maintaining open channels between them, people can both give and receive from each other. Then your strength becomes my strength, and the strength of the whole is so much greater than that of separate individuals, who are both isolated and limited, each trying to keep and keep out. (The neurone system is the network of nerves that allows the brain to transmit signals – see diagram.) To quote Joanna: *'The power of a neurone lies in its capacity to open to the charge, open to the messages travelling through the larger body. From that capacity, arrive ever more intricate and appropriate responses. That is how we learn and how society learns. That is how intelligence flowers.'*

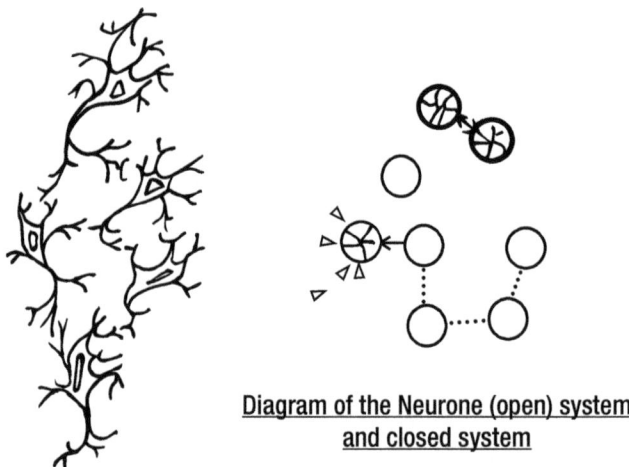

Diagram of the Neurone (open) system and closed system

These two distinct ways of operating can be likened to the approach of the egoic mind versus the heart, and it's not too hard to see how this can apply to human activity, is it? Many people try and move between the two modes of operating but most Westerners (living as we do in mainly neo-liberal, Capitalist, free-market structures) are becoming more and more unfamiliar with an open-system way of operating and its benefits for humanity. *And the trust this is based upon.* Unlike creatures such as ants and bees, for instance, where it is inarguable they function better together as part of a whole.

Humans living together in tribes, past and present, know about this because on a deep, unconscious level they recognise everything is one. This insight is a core part of their spiritual understanding that informs their actual experience, and so is woven into their view of absolutely everything. Which is not to say they too aren't conditioned and their understanding coloured by their traditions and the stories which keep these alive; so that, in spite of this wider understanding, the identification with their tribe can allow acts of violence against outsiders. So certain tribes in Borneo, for instance, practise ongoing internecine warfare between tribes, based on revenge.

Which serves to illustrate how *believing something is not the same as realising this for oneself,* with being consciously aware. Yet despite this apparent colouring by the egoic mind, one thing is evident: tribal living is fundamentally based on sharing, including and respecting all other forms of life – even when you are killing a creature to eat it – in other words, founded on the values of the heart. This, to these people, just makes such obvious sense that they don't question it. As outsiders like Jean Liedloff found when she spent time amongst tribal peoples, there exists a continuity of harmony and ease, liveliness and enjoyment of life rarely found outside of this way of living; a complete lack of the stress found in so-called 'civilised' cultures. Does this mean that we must all go back to living in tribes then? No. But what it shows us is that any changes in how we live together *that override these fundamental priorities of the heart* begin to lessen and destroy our innate capacity for living together in harmony.

Modern wo/man has forgotten this essential unity; or, more accurately, our conditioning has evolved to include a belief that we are separate individuals; so with the strengthening of this through the egoic mind, comes this increased drive to get and avoid *for ourselves,* accompanied by a suspicion of others, and the stress this induces. We have learned to prioritise this getting for ourselves and our family over the needs of others, and to avoid or deny anything that gets in the way of this, like damage to other humans and to the environment. Yet we all suffer from the loss of trust this produces. These are inconvenient truths, and the obvious direction this 'me' and 'my family' leads towards is systems of government that supposedly preserve this individual freedom (high on the U.S. list of priorities) to the detriment of the needs of others.

It really doesn't matter what you call it, it is essentially an exploitative mentality *which catastrophically overrides the heart.* Here the mind encourages us to live in a dream of hopes and fears, of getting or losing out, based on our interpretation of past experiences and future possibilities. And this leaves us wide open to being manipulated. Ironically, we then don't see the exploitation – the many small and sometimes large ways we are denied our individuality – with false choices (the choice of a dozen different shampoos or laundry detergents, for instance) and promises never intended to be kept. Donald Trump talks openly in his bestseller *The Art of the Deal,* about how he deliberately evokes people's dreams in order to sell them something.

However, when we blame politicians and big business for this what we don't see is that we are *allowing* ourselves to be duped because we want to believe false promises. We overlook our part in this. We forget our ability to be here now, in our bodies, with our full intuitive, sensing, feeling capacities functioning to tell us what is true. Which is unfortunate, as what we see when we are fully present is reality: we wake up and see through this ego-mind illusion. Then we are free to bring our love and attention to meeting whatever presents itself.

In truth, what we see around us in the field of power politics is usually its opposite: an unconscious display of the fear of *powerlessness,* and a blind, desperate and even addictive need to keep demonstrating our power to ourselves and others (here Trump provides a great illustration: an opportunity to sense and feel into what lies beneath his bluster and bravado to what is true). The belief in power as might is best illustrated by the US, with its ongoing imperialistic warfare around the world. As Barack Obama apparently insisted with some exasperation, American leadership *'is not just a matter of us bombing somebody'* and as his hero James Baldwin wrote during the futile American bombing of Indochina: *'Force does not work the way its advocates seem to think it does.'* Instead of impressing its victim, it reveals to him *'the weakness, even the panic of his adversary and this revelation invests the victim with patience'.*

The driving force for most people in positions of great power (and this is mostly men and may involve commanding vast wealth) is actually fear, *especially fear of weakness or powerlessness* – the last thing they would want you to know – hidden under a pretence of strength and invulnerability. Anyone disconnected from knowing who they are (which is most of us) is exposed to delusion. And this disconnect creates a very simple logic: 'I must get into a position of power to feel secure and stop something terrible happening to me.' Worldly power and wealth are almost always symptoms of fear (we are talking unconscious bottom-of-the-well stuff here, which doesn't mean some people don't get a kick out of gambling and winning and acquiring impressive possessions).

Seen from this perspective, we can recognise wealth and power as the visible defences, the fortress between these people and what they fear – it is a power-over attempt to keep something out, to stay safe by being in control. These are the barricades behind which they have trapped themselves. Greed is then seen as a need to keep having more, avarice as being focussed on getting what you want by any means, and both are in service to this fear of not being in control, and therefore safe. Whether it's another J. Edgar Hoover (a clear example of this mentality), a Mafia boss or some billionaire dependent on his offshore investments, the unconscious foundations are the same. How can I know this? *Because the seeds for all this are the same disconnect we see replicated everywhere.* It is this seeing through the pretences that frees us and is enabled through our connecting with Being.

The reason figureheads like Nelson Mandela, the Dalai Lama and Martin Luther King are so revered *is because they represent the heart.* In the face of a world that reveres the head – encouraging cool calculation and self-interest – they represent someone taking a stand for others, for humanity; for remembering and celebrating our brother and sisterhood. They demonstrate compassion, integrity *and a willingness to take personal risks and make enemies.* And we recognise this somewhere; it resonates with a deep longing, a knowing about who we really are.

Women like Mother Teresa and Florence Nightingale are also revered and more recently, if controversially, Camilla Batmanghelidjh, who started Kids Company, stands out. And however messed up Princess Diana may have been she also, for many people, represented the heart, and in a far more vulnerable way. She too constantly brought compassion into the foreground through her very public relationship with suffering people, especially children. (Can you imagine what she would have had to say about the refugee crisis?). However, beyond all this she stood out against those in power. She accepted the risks of being condemned for her actions and beliefs, and she rebelled against the emotionally stifling codes of behaviour demanded of her by the royal family – and she paid the ultimate price for this.

It is important to recognise here that not one of these people I have mentioned are, or were, perfect. They all have or had personalities with aspects that others could dislike or disapprove of. But it is interesting nonetheless to note the particularly cruel form of condemnation meted out by her enemies towards Diana because, of all these people, it was she who challenged the status quo most dramatically: *by ignoring the ban on exposing our inner world*, by revealing raw feelings (you can almost hear the Queen pronouncing 'We are *never* insecure!'). In fact, Diana horrified some precisely because she demonstrated vulnerability in a public domain, where those in charge often appear emotionally disabled. It seems the ordinary public understood this and perhaps that is why there was such an unexpectedly vast outpouring of grief over her death? People were touched by her and instinctively mourning the loss of the genuine qualities of the heart in public life.

The influence of mind and emotions

Do you find politics boring and off-putting? Not surprising really, the way it gets presented: politicians offering pre-rehearsed sound-bites while they scramble to avoid answering any question that would inform people of the truth, programmes and media reports that are riddled with emotion that create bias and drive people to take up antagonistic positions. So much ducking and attacking and trying to humiliate your opponent can be ugly to watch. *And nothing seems to change.* There is no life, no movement that either confronts reality or gladdens the heart. Then, disconnected from the body and Being, the realm of politics inevitably lacks both guidance and grounding: hence the messes we humans create.

So if we look through the lens of the discerning heart at what is happening as a result of our current political structures, what do we see? Okay, let's get literal: in the next paragraph are some examples of what *doesn't* make inner sense, that is sense to the compassionate, intuitive heart that knows we are all one. However, *with the influence of emotion,* this lens clouds over and loses its clarity as it becomes a vehicle for people to indulge their reactions. Then the field of politics becomes like one of those self-exposing minor celebrity programs on TV, a kind of ghastly therapy-cum-rugby scrum where 'entertainment' becomes an excuse to indulge our most unconscious selves. So can I suggest you *watch yourself* as you read on? Because politics is a great place to distinguish between a *response* of the heart and *reaction* from the egoic and conditioned mind. And how can anything really come free without some degree of conscious awareness?

Okay: so the heart doesn't leave people, including young or otherwise vulnerable people, sleeping on the streets when there are empty houses all around. Nor does it put families with children in one room in bed-and-breakfast accommodation, with no cooking facilities, often forced to share communal bathrooms with drug users. The heart doesn't require people to work long hours with no security in unsafe and unhealthy conditions, in often boring and repetitive jobs, *for no good reason other than someone else's profit.* The heart doesn't leave old people marooned helplessly in so-called 'care homes' with no dignity and no-one to actually care *about* them. The heart doesn't put children in prison because their parents came from another country without permission, nor take away the ability of the disabled to move around and access their needs. Nor does the heart drill holes deep into the earth's body and pump toxic chemicals into these, nor fill them with radioactive waste. Or grow crops that destroy the fertility of the soil, or use pesticides that kill birds, bees and insects of all kinds. The heart doesn't keep dumping its rubbish into the sea whilst taking out fish until there are none left....yes, the list is endless.

I have deliberately chosen highly emotive issues: that is, issues subject to being emotionalised by mind, so we can see that what gets in the way of a simple recognition of the heart *is the story*. The mind weaves a great story around such things filled with judgements, with 'shoulds' and 'should nots' and heavy condemnation; a story about *other people* behaving badly, being selfish and greedy or lazy and undeserving and 'It's unjust, not right, even downright disgraceful!' People take opposing positions to say all this, each pointing the finger at the other; then before you know it, you've got a fight and people hurting each other.

What I am saying here is the same as elsewhere: that seeing clearly from an intention to find solutions that work for everyone *has to include checking out our own baggage!* And this is especially important around feelings of anger and fear, which, as we keep noting, often drive these emotional reactions. It's not a question of taking a position, having an opinion: this is what the mind does;

then emotional engagement just gets in the way of a simple, clear sense of wrongness that is *known*. With the heart you feel it in the body. In the instances mentioned there is a sense of not okay-ness that can be clearly felt in the body-energy and especially in the heart. In these ways, something is known – *known beyond all argument of mind*. This knowing of the heart then needs to be valued and trusted.

Most people know intuitively that much of what is happening everywhere is out of balance with a deeper reality, out-of-true and anti-life; many of us close our hearts and allow the mind to override this knowing with the bland but ultimately false arguments of expediency, and we often feel helpless. People get upset about politics either because they are directly affected by policies they feel they have no control over, or because they have taken a position that they feel they must defend *because they have identified with this position*. Then the opposing, dualistic arguments of Right and Left serve to obscure this act of positioning and identification, along with its effects.

The movement away from the heart and towards the mind is usually driven by fear: fear of not having or of losing what we do have and not being able to go on getting more. (The values of so-called 'middle England' reflect these most clearly.) There is fear and a certain tightness and closed-ness that accompany this. Control is sought and supported, as are ways to maintain this *over any logical outcomes*. So, for example, giving people harsh prison sentences has been proven to raise levels of reoffending – 'So what! They deserve to be punished!' is a completely illogical conclusion. And scapegoating, whether of immigrants or the 'feckless' unemployed, is used to keep the focus away from the reality we have been speaking about, along with comfortable and soothing emotional attitudes like self-righteousness and bigotry.

Once you know how the egoic mind operates it is easy to see these positions are driven by beliefs and assumptions that rarely get questioned. The ego stands firmly on its turf: *the sense of oneself has to be defended at all costs*. And all the while the body and the intuitive heart and Being are overlooked and not listened to.

Injustice: the engine of all revolutions

In speaking about politics it feels necessary to look at this word 'injustice' – such an evocative word! Full of feelings and emotions, a word that lies at the heart of all political rebellions. The reality however, is that injustice is just a word, and like so many words *it depends for its significance on where it is coming from*. From the egoic-mind, it comes as a kind of childish 'It's not fair! Someone has treated me badly! I didn't deserve that' or 'I have been cheated out of what is rightfully mine!'; it is accompanied by feelings of anger and reactions of indignation, resentment and blame, along with the emotionalised attitudes of grievance and self-righteousness: 'How dare they!' and 'I'll get even!' thoughts of revenge.

All these reactions are based on the interpretations and beliefs of the conditioned egoic mind. And, as mentioned earlier, we can carry these thoughts and emotions – gelled into attitudes – for years; they have a certain unpleasantly stale smell, like an overfull ashtray. And they carry an enormous hidden cost in terms of wasted energy and tensions in the body which not only bring us problems such as ill health: like the polluting smoke from other people's cigarettes, this angry energy impacts on everyone around us.

Then there is another kind of response to perceived injustice: a response of the heart. This isn't conceptual and it doesn't necessarily stay personal, but can extend to friends, neighbours and a whole community of people and planet. We perceive something isn't right, in the sense of isn't true; we feel this in our hearts and it hurts us: *there is a kind of innocence about this feeling.* We may feel this when we see things like police harassment of people of colour, for instance, or helpless refugees abandoned to their fate. These are clear examples where we might feel to take action.

But this sense of out-of-trueness may extend in other ways. For example, by making us wonder when one human being is paid £100 or even £100,000 and another say just £7 *for the same hour of their time*, how can this be so? Or when we see a few people hoarding wealth and others starving and going without. There is a very natural response of the heart to this – even if we don't, or can't, take action: *we feel this even when we are not affected by the injustice ourselves.* When a rare politician of integrity like Bernie Sanders states *'There is something profoundly wrong when one family owns more wealth than the bottom 130 million Americans.'* he is speaking to this sense of injustice. We feel a connection with him as we sense he is speaking from his heart – which is why he touches so many ordinary people, including people who are not suffering from poverty themselves.

Folk heroes like Robin Hood and the highwayman Dick Turpin are celebrated because they robbed the rich to help the poor. This may be a romanticised image but underneath this lies a clear call and response from the heart. More recently, Che Guevara became an international symbol, especially amongst the young, of the struggle of the poor to come free from their overlords and share in the wealth of their country (that he also used violence to do this is often overlooked). More recently still, people like the whistleblower Edward Snowden are held up as an example of people who stand up and take risks to defend the interests of others. These are people who put themselves on the line; who are prepared to make the ultimate sacrifice for what they know to be true. As of course did Jesus. (Adyashanti refers to him as a revitalising force who was not afraid to speak truth to power.) 'Ah, but Jesus was preaching peace and love and bringing people to God, wasn't he? Not inciting rebellion or betraying State secrets. Really? So we see sneaky old mind again, trying to get in on the act with judgments and opinions and distorted interpretations of events.

However, what I am talking about here is on another level altogether: the level of the heart. We have a true response to something; *how we know to act on that is, however, entirely unpredictable.* So if we stay in attunement with this intuitive heart, connected with Being, whatever happens is what needs to happen. It can't be premeditated and calculated, it also can't be coerced. Once again, these are strategies of mind. As to whether the heart could direct us to kill another, even in self-defence, how could it do this if we know we are part of one whole and, therefore, what it is that we are killing?

To counter accusations of injustice, those who perpetrate this will use all the cunning arguments of mind. They accuse those who are excluded from wealth of 'envy consciousness'(!) and political extremism (whatever that is), and enact noisy character assassinations in the media. They will point out that history has always been this way, with the powerful exploiting the weaker – it's just human nature, survival of the fittest, the way things are. Is this true? Or is it simply good old egoic mind acting out again, just as it does when there is a violent revolution and soon enough a small group of people once again get to hold power and privilege over the rest.

Have you noticed that wherever we turn, we come back to the same place? We are faced with an immoveable *reality.* To be true to what we *are* means listening to the intuitive heart, trusting this, and living it as best we can; because it seems to take time for the egoic mind to be seen through and to slowly lose its hold over us, even after we have glimpsed the true nature of reality. Then eventually, as we come free, there is simply no room for the political manoeuvrings of egoic mind, that present as corruption and deceit, that foster injustice and all the painful manifestations of human beings attempting to live together in disconnection, out of touch with our Being-ness.

Values of the heart versus ideologies of the mind

When you talk about political theory, whether it's Karl Marx on communism or Friedrich von Hayek on neoliberalism or whoever, you are talking about ideologies. And where do ideologies come from? That's right, from the mind: mostly from the minds of white men. With some notable exceptions like Margaret Thatcher, who reportedly used Hayek as her bible, women tend to be less interested in political theory. And because we aren't usually trained to be aggressive, with a need to succeed and win at all cost – whether that's an argument or a fight (which doesn't mean women don't try to emulate men to compete) – we are less interested in intellectual arguments and point-scoring, which are often based on these ideologies. *Or in the assumptions these ideologies are based upon.*

Ideologies are the mind's attempt to include *values,* which are then subject to our prejudices. But, as we keep saying, the mind is not equipped to distinguish true value, this is the terrain of the heart. So when the renowned Cuban activist, José Martí, pronounced *'To the roots goes the honest man. A radical is simply this: a man who goes to the roots',* he was talking about establishing true values; about *connecting* with these as a basis for action. When the Pope condemned what he called *'the politics of exclusion'* he was referring to these values. And when Martin Luther King Jr. wrote in 1967 *'We must recognise that we can't solve our problem now until there is a radical redistribution of economic and political power ... this means a revolution of values and other things',* he was talking about exactly this.

Language is important here: it gets used to distort and deceive. Hence the terms Left and Right, which distract from basic values and confuse the political mix. It leaves the mind with a neat, abstract division. By association, left and right are of equal value; we apply them to distinguish different sides of our body, to giving directions, marching in columns, etc. *Only when used to reference politics* do they take on an emotional connotation. Imagine if you were to slander and attack one hand with the other, trying to overcome it and win the superior position. It would be absurd, wouldn't it? Yet we do this with politics all the time. Left and Right invites positioning and the old 'I am right, you are wrong' divide. Remember the mind loves division. The whole 'divide and rule' ethos is mind-manufactured. You see it in so many areas of political control *just because it works to prevent people agreeing and coming together* – whether this is to resist occupation or domination or to unite to move towards a way of living that, in benefitting everyone, takes away the egoic dream of many that is enacted by a few.

So what happens if you drop these terms? For example, the Occupy movement brought the term 'the 99%' into prominence. Suddenly, you see almost everyone becomes included; there is a sense of equality within this term. By its very nature, it says 'Look! What is going on here? What are we doing with a system that leaves *99% of humanity* struggling and a tiny 1% with so much wealth? Wealth that they then hoard and keep multiplying for themselves as they drain the resources from the planet and everyone else?' Those few that gain from our current political dogma are such a tiny minority. And it is the intuitive heart which registers this most powerfully, not the mind. When you apply values to political positions, then you can *see and sense and feel* whether the values of the heart or the egoic mind are taking prominence. Values tend to be influenced by emotion and belief, which create prejudice, making it harder to recognise them.

As we have seen in Brexit or the election of Donald Trump, feelings like fear and anger can be emotionalised to produce aggression and violence, that are in turn used towards a goal with an end-justifies-the-means argument. However, this tendency is *also* evident in many revolutions of the so-called 'Left' that spring from defending and advancing the interests of the majority. The horrendous persecutions of Stalin in Russia or the 'Cultural Revolution' in China are examples of this. And conversely, things like charity and actions to provide for those less well-off can emerge out of right-wing ideologies, especially those influenced by guilt and religion. In fact, there are many issues that have defenders in both sides of the apparent divide, such as privacy and surveillance. From this we can see how any positioning or listening to what may be claimed by either side as 'rational' arguments of mind can mislead us.

The reality is *no political parties are beyond egoic mind's ability to infiltrate them*. So-called 'class' positions invite egoic forms in different ways. So, as we noted earlier, the various forms of state protection for the poor and working class that appear so benevolent, can invite dependency and victimhood. And the left doesn't own compassion. There can be an admirable sense of self-responsibility that brings dignity in certain approaches of the right that lie outside the more obvious egoic drive towards selfishness and greed. And a sense of entitlement works both ways.

If you base any movement for change on the values of the heart, then the question becomes not 'where are we going *to*?' – as in 'what is the goal we think we want to achieve?' – but 'where are we coming *from*, inside, when we are looking at this?' Then what emerges with a sometimes painful clarity is what is true. The wonderful realisation here is that Being can be trusted to see, through the eyes of the heart, into the most sophisticated attempt to deceive; including *and especially*, deceiving ourselves. When we really get this: that it all depends where we are coming *from*; we see there is no need for any divisive positioning, any separating out into opposing groups or tribes. Because we are, quite literally, all in this together, and using the intelligence of the heart is what enables us to find what works best for everyone.

If you stop and *feel into* what is happening, you will find the heart trying to move within politics; you can recognise it in anything that carries a sense of love and compassion for one's fellows, of taking care of the whole. This was the spirit behind such schemes as the Welfare State, which unfortunately (and perhaps inevitably, given a general lack of conscious awareness in political circles) then got buried beneath enormous bureaucratic regimes; and the *spirit behind* communism too, in terms of small groups sharing in both decision-making and providing for the whole (rather than leaders and implementation of policies through the State, a central parliamentary body, a dictator, royalty, etc.). *What we are seeing here is the movement towards caring for everyone captured by ideals, devised and implemented by the mind.* Just as the insistence on unregulated markets, which was projected to create freedom and openness, has resulted in gross inequality.

It is amazing what you see when you filter actions through the discerning heart to recognise those which are driven by ego – meaning driven by the calculating mind, based on egoic goals that are often emotionalised and riddled with unchallenged beliefs. A desire for power and control *can be felt,* and also seen in the body language of people. (Both Hillary Clinton and Tony Blaire, despite his clever posturing, are examples here.) It can be heard through the sound and timbre of a voice. Humans are not stupid. We have simply been conditioned to override these intuitive, feeling, sensing and seeing functions – especially when they challenge the status quo; when they upset the current order and threaten unknown and potentially painful or frightening consequences. Clinging to security, this being largely unconscious, is what most people have learned to do. And, of course, this leaves us wide open to being manipulated by vested interests.

The heart always recognises sincerity. So when you read, or especially when you watch and listen to, someone talking about politics and related subjects, you can feel where they are coming from; a felt sense threads through their words carrying through tone, gesture and so on. Yes, a powerful speaker can exploit people's hopes and dreams and convince through charisma and craft; like a good actor, they can evoke an emotional excitement (i.e. Donald Trump) *especially if he or she is saying what we want to hear.* Whereas if you listen quietly to a Bernie Sanders or Jeremy Corbyn with your intuitive heart, you can feel a warm resonance which is quite distinct from this. There is a *felt response* in your own heart. They carry an invitation to rise up not in rage and resentment and hatred, but with love and joy and compassion; an invitation to channel indignation and anger into constructive actions. There is a sense of goodness coming through that you recognise with the heart and this inspires generosity and a concern for one's fellows, a desire to see and bring out the best in ourselves and each other, a surging hope that we can create a world that honours kindness and wisdom.

This world reflects what we intuitively long for, along with an often deeply buried knowing that love is what we all *are*, in essence. We sense something profound without any need to articulate this as part of some argument: we *know. And this is very different to the emotionalised hysteria whipped up by people like Trump and Hitler and Mussolini* to achieve their own ends. Then, when we come together to share this silent knowing there is a deep and powerful bond that connects us all.

So how can we best express these values? And here is something that stands out about recognising and naming these that rarely gets talked about, that brings us back to language and how we use this. For instance, we have plenty of language to proclaim our fury and rage about events, profane or otherwise. What we don't have – *what we have lost* – is language that allows us to express our wonder for the world, our desire for goodness, kindness, gentleness, especially amongst the young. All our soft language has been stolen and exploited: by the advertisers of trivial pursuits, via the mouths of posturing politicians and celebrities, or besmirched and belittled by the masters of cool – those insulated individuals who dare not even remember the meaning of such words, if they ever experienced them, let alone speak them out loud.

Why? Here we spot the usual culprit sitting at the controls: ego, and the fear of ridicule; of being seen as some kind of pathetic goodie two-shoes who has lost their cool, lost it. Go and become a vicar or something but don't bother us live-wires with your wishy-washy, hippy-dippy bullshit. Step a little closer and you can almost hear knees knocking, glimpse a sweaty forehead, smell the sharp tang of cowardice. High time it was challenged, time people stood up to reclaim our need to speak to, about and directly from, the heart.

Bringing feminine values into politics

So how to counter the mind-dominated, emotion manipulating, ego-centred way politics is largely conducted today? How to change a way of doing things that is subject to the negative masculine values of seeking to dominate and outmanoeuvre, using cunning, deceit and verbal aggression to do so (irrespective of the *actual* gender of those who employ these). Surely not by fighting it, becoming immersed in anger and blame and furthering a 'them' and 'us' attitude. Nor by seeking to find solutions within the same limited, emotionalised and conditioned mind. Only by returning to our true nature *and including the positive feminine* can we feel, sense and intuit what is true and in turn discover our true response to this, moment by moment. From here we are enabled to make a conscious contribution, guided by Being, anchored in stillness.

The impact of this deep and more balanced approach is rarely understood; that this impact is actually vast is not seen: that it allows a transmission – a reflection of a conscious, loving energy out into the world around us – is not recognised. This energy carries extraordinary power and it is infectious: it infects others and everything around itself, allowing a reconnection that releases us from illusion. We *feel* the one heart beating within each of us, of which we are all a part. It is from *this* place that we can support each other along the lines of a Power-with structure, so we can discover our strength is actually limitless.

NOTE: Remember, I am distinguishing between the positive and negative qualities of *both* genders because, if you examine these, you will find both carry both; much unnecessary confusion and argument arises out of failing to make this distinction. In the way of describing things I am talking about, the negative *in both genders* arises from the egoic mind, the positive from a heart guided by Being.

What becomes apparent in all this is not just a need to return politics to the values of the heart, but that it is the values associated with the feminine that are most often denied. Not so long ago, two exceptional women entered politics. One, appointed mayor of Barcelona, is Ada Colau. In her early forties, she worked as an activist helping people who were being dispossessed of their homes by the banks. The other, the mayor of Madrid, is Manuela Carmena, a retired judge in her early seventies, who has spent most of her life as a lawyer defending the poor, and including those who resisted oppression in Franco's time. Both women are Spanish, neither is a politician and they both say the same thing: that politics needs to be *feminised* (not feminist). They say it is not just about having more women in politics (as women, as we have seen with Margaret Thatcher and Hillary Clinton, can still display masculine qualities) but about *implementing feminine values*. These are based around relationship and they include caring and sharing, including and nurturing and demonstrating how co-operation works so much better than competition. (Indeed, the latest studies have concluded that our history shows man actually thrives better with co-operation than competition.)

Here is a quote by Manuela Carmena referring to public opinion just before her election: *'There are people who are entrenched in fear. That's a mistaken attitude, though it's human. Democracy is beautiful and it works because everyone feels capable of influencing the world.'* In an interview, Pablo Iglesias said he had learnt a lot from these women, especially about how the behaviour of many of those on the Left – who believe in aggressive struggle based on righteous anger – isn't productive. They had shown him that being open, listening and meeting people where they are with curtesy, was far more effective in creating dialogue and change. Speaking about the influence of recent uses of social media on politics, a man called Rick Burgess identifies a core feminine value when he concludes *'It's all about inclusion. It's important to recognise the importance of this activism and examine one's own privileges and assumptions. Inclusion is not an add-on. It is'* (I would say needs to be) *'integral to how we live.'*

Do you remember how we talked about the impact of circles and curves? Well, one way we could influence politics from a feminine perspective would be to build a round House of Parliament (as they have, in fact, done in Scotland). This would prevent the formation of opposing sides and create a space where everyone felt equal and included. And can you even *imagine* a meeting of the parliament in some country where all the different groupings are set up in ways *to support one another?* Where, instead of adversarial argument and trying to score points and put each other down (which pathetic spectacle, accompanied by jeers, can be witnessed at any parliamentary sitting in the UK), everyone pooled their resources to find the best ways of doing things that worked for the vast majority?

Where People's Representatives (which is what politicians are supposed to be) were not only trained in conflict resolution, anger management, deep listening, developing empathy and communication skills, but also how to keep their mind calm and energy fit with classes in meditation, yoga, tai chi; whatever? With individual mentoring where they can feel heard and receive help? And support groups organised to help resolve interpersonal issues? They could participate in various kinds of physical and playful activities together, too, so it isn't all just *mental* gymnastics. And what about having healthy, organic food available and a weekly massage being routine?

Are you laughing already? Could anything be further from what is happening today? But why should we not *demand* this? Why not demand the best possible representation? They could even set up a veggie garden on the lawns of Parliament! Absurd, wishful thinking? Ridiculous nonsense? Well, but what could be more absurd or ridiculous than the present set-up? After all, many forward-looking companies now have all kinds of support structures for their employees built-in. So why not our political representatives, who probably need this more than most? And, finally, why not involve children and young people in the political process? Giving them both a voice, a place to watch, learn and even participate in some way? After all, children – as free spirits – can often see the essence of something more easily than a long-conditioned adult and they have an inbuilt and heartfelt sense of fairness.

It is curious, isn't it, that the very people who are chosen to represent our interests (and whose salary we pay) are not required to do any training? Suppose any person entering public office had to be first assessed on their capacity for clear and conscious engagement? That this included training in the things we mentioned? In other words, weeding out those – and that might well be the majority of professional politicians – with a lot of unconscious, unmet baggage. One could take this even further and require anyone bent on working 'in the public interest' to be vetted to see how caught up they are in unconscious patterns and beliefs and hidden power agendas, but that gets a bit Kafkaesque. The interesting thing is, when something is set up to be *truly* open and with various support structures in place, those people stuck in old agendas of needing to have power over others, and who are unwilling to change, are likely to feel uncomfortable and de-select themselves.

The point here is, there are so many creative and exciting ways we could organise things together; replacing the existing archaic 'norms' and rituals of political life dominated, as these are, by the negative masculine and as such, highly resistant to change. Because the truth is that once you bring in the feminine values we are talking about, *everything* has to change. With an emphasis on creating healthy, supportive relations, with new respect for the intuitive, sensing, feeling realities something much softer, more open and sensitive can develop so that, whatever technological wizardry is developed in order to help our situation, this too can be integrated into a power-with, connected dynamic held within the discerning gaze of the wise heart.

However, before any of this can happen – before feminine values can be focussed and take root, in both genders – something needs to be addressed. Women (and some men) may see and try to inculcate these essentially *inclusive* values, but before this can occur men need to recover their manliness, and find their real place. What do I mean by this? Lost in the wilderness where domination and power games that involve cheating and deceiving and out-manoeuvring an opponent, many men are reduced, and reduce themselves, to possession by the ultimately destructive drive of the egoic mind. But this doesn't have to continue. Something that was demonstrated by the young white son of an ex-NATO general reversed this. He chose to represent the army veterans at Standing Rock and say sorry for all the harm the army had done to the Native Americans. This was an incredibly brave and powerful act.

Here we see *real* male strength, that can admit mistakes and say sorry. Meantime, for the first time in hundreds of years the tribes came together from across the American continent and the young men rode their horses between the police with their violence and their peacefully-protesting families. What were they doing? They were not just protecting their families, their sacred sites and their water, *but the Earth herself – for all peoples and all its inhabitants*. (We will talk more about this situation and ways of healing the divide in the next chapter).

Both events are illustrations of men finding their real place: re-connecting with their true potential, as lovers and protectors of all life; of the body of the earth that we all are a part of. *Taking their courage in ways that restore male dignity, based in heart-wisdom*. I am not saying here that all men need to be warriors, there are many other creative ways to contribute to the whole. I am saying that when men restore their sense of true purpose, based on positive *masculine* values, they can and will support the arising of feminine values in life. These values are entwined. This lays the ground for a return to balance and harmony.

NOTE: There is not space in this book to deal with this important area of gender differences and their significance.

Conflict and motivation

Perhaps before demanding politicians take courses to learn how to deal with conflict we need to look at how we approach this in ourselves? Because most people have good intentions and it's fun to indulge our dreams of how we could 'make things better', with often little awareness of how our unconscious agendas affect everything around us. For instance, we may be drawn towards putting our time and energy into saving the world from the very real peril it is in, or fighting for peace and justice or devoting our energy to helping others in some way. And although our concern may appear genuine, it's good to check out *why* we are doing these things, to look with rigorous honesty at what is *really* going on when we do this.

Then you may see there are underlying motives here that have more to do with feeling good about ourselves (a process that is *so* uncomfortable for an insecure ego to look at!). Maybe it offers a way of feeling part of something (not that there is anything wrong with that) or convincing ourselves that we are 'doing good', doing the 'right thing', being useful, even taking a stand where others are failing; and from this *we gain a sense of worthiness*. Or it may provide a means of expressing pent-up feelings of powerlessness and frustration whose origins lie in our past. But whatever the focus, whether it is *against* corruption, *against* persecution of minority groups, saving the planet or feeding the hungry, it's worth checking out what you are getting from this – in other words, worth becoming consciously aware. When you are doing these things, where are you coming *from?* Is there a sense of righteousness and hatred towards those who are doing or not doing what you think they should? Whom you perceive as causing the things you want to put right? A 'them' and 'us' positioning?

Here, once again, the body can be your guide. If your motives come from an emotionalised mind you will feel a tightness in the body, in the breath; a holding on to something, an energetic quality of pushing *against* something: qualities of resistance and insistence. You may recognise feelings of rage and frustration and a need to take action that seeks to release these. In which case by sitting quietly, just being with these feelings – or indeed with whatever is going on for you – you may sense how this has roots deep in your past. Inner conflicts that you experience in your life *now,* whether in normal daily activities or in trying to change something out in the world, may be seen to be reflections of old unresolved conflicts within oneself.

So then, instead of feeling guilty and shamed when you see these things, and allowing the mind to beat you up, you can shake yourself like a dog emerging from a swim in a pond. Shake off what has been blinding you to seeing what is true, what is really going on, and allow yourself to enjoy a sense of lightness. Ah! *Now* I see (what I couldn't see before). No blame, no self-attack; just a delighting in this seeing which can bring such a wonderful sense of relief. The breath deepens, the body relaxes, you are back in touch with what you *are*. Time to celebrate! Time to appreciate the grace that allowed you to see, and thus to come free.

Don't misunderstand me here. I am not saying don't get involved, don't become some kind of activist, if that is what draws you. Even when we are living under the influence of a conditioned mind, there will be times when we are motivated from another place, when we feel a genuine sense of wanting to share in something; to participate, to contribute our energy and take care of something; to take some action that comes from promptings of the intuitive heart. We see an elderly person sitting alone on a bench and we are moved to go sit and speak with them; we see a child being treated badly and we would like to intervene, even when we may not know how to do so usefully. Or we feel the sense of wrongness about things happening in the world which are harmful and out of harmony with the spirit of sharing and caring for all life, and we are moved to take some action.

Learning to distinguish these movements and impulses is no different to becoming conscious. It draws on the same sources that we have been talking about throughout this book. *It is the nature of Being to respond:* even if this is simply to notice and feel a connection with something – because sometimes there is no action that can or needs to be taken. Or the action may come more in the form of a transmission of empathy, a kind of prayer, a silent sending of love and concern. What can interfere with this simple response is a belief (and remember, beliefs are always of the mind) *that something should not be as it is,* which holds a quality of resistance: a fear that if we accept something is as it is, then our ability to respond would be disabled. But if our response is a true, undistorted response of the body-Being it is not subject to this belief; neither is it subject to judgements about what it sees – it simply responds.

But isn't politics unspiritual?

There can be a kind of snobbery amongst the spiritually inclined where politics is seen as a dirty word, unworthy of attention, unspiritual; a lowly playground for the ego to distract us from the serious matter of attaining enlightenment. Whereupon – we fondly believe – all such seedy machinations will abruptly cease to have an impact. But the truth is, living as humans embodying spirit in this apparent material reality *also* means meeting the issues of how we do this together. It means becoming involved in relationships with our fellow humans, and this is exactly where – to use one of Adyashanti's favourite phrases – *'The rubber hits the road.'* So we see that politics, as the collective ways we share this reality and create forms to organise ourselves that work best for such sharing, is very much a part of *living spirituality*.

Which is why it feels so important to include it in this book, because it is in cutting through the machinations and hubris of mind with clear seeing that we are able to channel love and clarity *into every area of our lives*. You can call the world Maya or Samsara – all a dream – but next time you are confronted with your child's hurt from being bullied at school, your boss's decision to sack you as part of 'downsizing', or a new airport is proposed for your neighbourhood, you may find it is not so simple; when someone you know becomes homeless or you can't have an operation because the doctors are on strike, you may find that this web of relationships exposes the most vulnerable, hidden and difficult-to-meet aspects of our being human. Here. Now. And trying to deny these and escape to a glimpse of Nirvana will not save you!

It is certainly challenging: the world of politics is full of ignorance, a visible disconnect overriding the heart in pursuit of egoic goals. The attraction of having power tends to invite some of the least sensitive and creative individuals (yes, that's a generalisation) and however idealistic the goals, these are often of the mind (as in 'idea-listic'). As we have noted, it is easy, if you are not aware of this, to engage your emotionalised mind – driven by feelings of anger about perceived injustices and a desire to take away the power of those we perceive to be controlling us and even to punish them. And politics tends to be conducted in adversarial, confrontational ways that can feel intimidating. Because of this it can feel easier to avoid it, to denounce politics as being beneath our notice, while we adjust our lotus position or chant our mantras.

And yet here we are, living in 'the world' which, just like anything else, requires to be met, along with whatever uncomfortable material this may bring up for us: *especially* fear and anger. For it is these which, when unconscious, can cause the most destruction and when suppressed and avoided, can be the most dangerous. So both politics *and* spirituality can share the pursuit of what is real and true. Then politics becomes as much a way to meet ourselves and find our inner connection with Being as anything else. And more now than ever, *politics needs connecting to a spiritual base,* and perhaps this is already beginning to happen? In which case, why avoid it? You may be familiar with the phrase 'To be *in* the world but not *of* it.' Well, connecting with politics provides a wonderful arena to see just how well we score on this!

At this point it's good to remember that what is going on in the world is a reflection of what is happening within each of us: 'As above, so below.' And this is something we are not taught at school or anywhere else – although quantum physics is beginning to suspect as much. What this means is that 'changing the world' has to involve dealing with what Jung called our 'Shadow'; the egoic force that manifests through our mind and emotions. Otherwise, how can our unresolved inner conflicts *not be* transmitted out into the world? Can we really be surprised when this creates outer conflict, reflected in power struggles and war?

Surely if spirituality is to have meaning we have to apply it to all situations. Hence it would appear that mankind's apparent pell-mell scramble towards the precipice, largely motivated by fear, *can only be altered by the acceleration of a transformative consciousness expressing itself here in the world.* And, as we keep saying, this needs to be anchored in the intuitive body. Then, beaming the light of awareness onto these difficult and often painful areas, we can dissolve the emotional entanglements, leaving an inner space; a space with a radiance that emanates a fearless clarity potentially powerful enough to return man to a state of harmony.

There have been many attempts to interpret what is happening at this time. One prediction I find interesting is the 'Second Coming of Christ' as this may refer, rather than to a return of the fellow himself, to a surge in awakening consciousness (Christ here referring to awakened Jesus 'the awakened one'). Otherwise, you can take your pick from a variety of apocalyptic, Armageddon-style, end-of-the-world scenarios; one of which predicts a dividing of worlds, where those who cannot free themselves will perish and those who can will survive ('free', as in 'liberated', perhaps being a reference to awakening?).

Meanwhile, as the mind spins its fantasies and horror stories that can fill us with dread, the heart sings its own song – calling to us in the midst of all this: the song of the body-Being asking us to refocus attention, to listen to the intuitive heart and find our way back to the presence of Being, *which never left us*. The mind, as usual, will go on asking 'But how do I do this?', to which the only answer is there is no way this can be 'done', as in 'actioned'. And yet – as Adyashanti recommends – we can *'be still and know'*.

Overcoming the fear of change

One thing that stands out when we look at politics and conflict are our beliefs, and how these limit us. Most people rarely consider this yet it often dictates our response. The main theme that emerges from Russell Brand's book, *Revolution,* is the impact of belief; how this is deliberately manipulated and why; what effect this has on people and how our beliefs either inhibit or encourage us to act – as happened in Obama's election with the use of the phrase 'We can!' (which translates as 'Podemos' in Spanish). The positive *belief* that 'We *can!'* mobilised thousands of supporters who would otherwise have remained passive bystanders, believing there was nothing they could do to affect politics. Another inhibitor is when people feel threatened; then it's harder for them to change as they can't listen. So it's a useful question to ask 'What comes up for me around things changing? Being part *of* that change?'. Watching out for fear and insecurity so we can attend to this, find ways to let this go and come back to resting in the heart; knowing that whatever happens we will respond as we respond: we can *act* but we cannot *control outcomes*.

When we recognise the fear of change is being activated, it's good to remember that love is stronger than fear. So the most powerful thing we can do in any situation – but especially around politics (because this is so often absent) – is to seek and stay connected with Being through our loving heart; empathy and compassion being part of this. And also our courage: the courage to risk, trusting the heart to inform us if action is needed. Strange, we don't often associate courage with love, do we? Yet, as any parent knows, *love gives us the courage to act*, as does anger, which can support necessary action. Beyond this we cannot know what will happen. We can only trust life to flow as it flows and accept this in each moment, aware that there are so many possibilities for fresh, creative, even joyful and playful ways of living in this world together. And that we don't need to let fear get in the way of these.

In fact, there is an extraordinary and largely unremarked educational process taking place, influenced by having access to the internet and social media. Millions of people all over the world, and especially young people, are coming free from the domination of mass media mind-control mechanisms. No longer believing what is presented to them, seeing through the deliberate lies and distortion, they can no longer be manipulated. Much that was hidden or unseen is being exposed and brought into high visibility. Writers, activists and economists such as Naomi Klein, Noam Chomsky, Yanis Varoufakis, Anne Pettifor and others are expressing alarm at our current financial and climatic trajectory.

None of these people are gods. What is interesting is *what they represent*, along with the growth of the Internet: *an unstoppable movement for change is arising*. How it will look, what it may provoke, where it will lead: these are all unknowns. Clearly there is danger, but then this has always been present. It's like the collective heart of humanity is stirring. For some this brings fear and anger, for others hope and, as I watched with some amazement a hardened US television commentator use the phrase describing people at a Bernie Sanders rally *'a sense of joyousness'!*, even awe. And at an event in Liverpool called *The World Transformed*, activists from Momentum (an organisation formed to support Jeremy Corbyn) put together perhaps the first major event to capture, express and develop this energy for change, and no doubt others will follow.

So here you and I are. Here is whatever is appearing in our lives right now, to be met as best we can. With insight into our own fears and internal conflicts and a conscious intention to open our hearts to all around us, we are in the best possible position to respond as needed – from *inner sense*. That means checking in to see what is real and what is just an old mind pattern that hooks us back into the drama (better to watch a 'soap opera' on television if it's drama you want!). It makes sense to be vigilant with our energy when we get caught up in what is *apparently* happening in the world: to not pay attention to the lies and distortion that drain us and bring in fear.

Instead, to make ourselves available to the still presence of Being that sits quietly awaiting our attention in our own backyard. As Adyashanti notes *'Beyond the known, as opposed to prior to it, lies a realm of being that pulls suffering out by its very roots and opens the door to a whole new way of experiencing life.'* Then, from this place of heart-wisdom and love, we are best placed to create and share and include and nurture political forms and directions that are in alignment with this, with life itself. Then – just maybe – the politics of inner sense can prevail.

Home-play
1. Healing conflict
Addressing 'them' and 'us'; including the politicians, bankers, big business corporations and billionaires.
- Sit somewhere comfortable, with your hands upturned on either side you.
- Now place your loved ones, friends and all those you feel care as you do, who are on the side of 'right', in one hand (choose whichever hand feels best).

- Place all those you feel are causing the problem; who are causing harm and on the 'wrong' side, in the other.
- Give time to all the feelings around this by first focussing on the one hand, then the other. Notice one hand may feel heavier than the other. Feel your lower body connected to the earth, feel the cradle in the lower belly and then move your attention up to the heart.
- Now, very slowly, bring both hands up and lay them over the heart, breathing in the pain as you do so and releasing all blame. This has nothing to do with accepting *actions* that are themselves unacceptable.

At this point it helps to notice and remember the symbolic evidence that both hands are joined to the same body. If you feel resistance to doing this exercise respect that, allow time and keep returning to the forgiving heart that, in its wisdom, knows we are *all* capable of causing harm, we can all hurt others and seek to exploit them and, ultimately, we are not separate from each other: we are all one.

2. Calling the lost souls home

The Koch brothers, Hillary Clinton, Donald Trump, Vladimir Putin, Bashar al-Assad, George Bush, Tony Blaire – whomever you can think of who symbolises for you 'wrong action' (you can include dead people like Hitler, Stalin, Margaret Thatcher, Saddam Hussein), people who deliberately do things that harm others or the world, remember: they too long to come home, they too have a heart, however buried, neglected and un-listened to. All those figureheads, those we see as responsible for creating terrible suffering, along with those who follow blindly, refusing to look into their own dark motivations; these people too are seeking love. Often unknowingly, everyone seeks what they actually *are*. The fact that they may be caught up in ignorance, arrogance, hatred and delusion doesn't change that. Who amongst us can honestly say they have never been affected by these?

- So recognising this, finding the right moment, see if you can just sit and open your arms (literally) to welcome *everyone and everything into your heart.* Nothing left out.

3. Phrases to play with

A politics for the heart - Not for me, for us - Love melts barriers, fighting makes them stronger - Bring feminine values into politics - Empathy connects - Goodness isn't owned by religion - Everyone belongs - Truth matters - Giving strengthens, taking (as distinct from accepting) weakens - Together let's imagine, create, contribute, heal and resolve differences - We are the human family - Say no to dividing, yes to uniting - Get the kindness habit - Let's bring love and politics together - What can you do? Plant seeds, water thirst, warm the heart and dance!

Creating a Community of One

'What I have believed in my whole life (is) that we are in this together. ... The truth is, at some level when you hurt, when your children hurt, I hurt. And when my kids hurt, you hurt.' ~ Bernie Sanders

'Grounded presence provides the psychic space for acknowledging the pain we carry for our world.' ~ Joanna Macy

'To feel into the wider dimension that we're all living in, where everything is completely connected to everything, matters not just to us, but to all beings that we are connected with.' ~ Adyashanti

If the reality is that we are indeed all part of one whole, then how can we live together in ways that work for this whole? How to create a community of One? From a small group, to the human community worldwide, to including all of life, this sense of community is dependent on our feeling a part of this, on a sense of *belonging*. And what grounds and strengthens this sense is when things are shared. Yet the drive to share has somehow become separated from how we live together; relegated to kindergarten dynamics where it is unacceptable to say 'That toy is *mine!*' or superimposed with corporate phrases like 'team-building'. There is an ethos of taking rather than sharing, and this attitude permeates our behaviour towards others, right down to the tiniest bug.

From the time we go to school and are encouraged to strive to 'get ahead', we have been conditioned to see ourselves as separate entities who need to put their own interests first. In sports like football, we play as a team but this team has to win against an opposing team: the ethos is the same. And parents, with their concern for the welfare of their children, along with society at large, reinforce this attitude. So how to change this? How to re-kindle the spirit of *offering*, of wanting to contribute and to include everyone? So it becomes natural to open welcoming arms to anyone who feels excluded? So we feel their pain and move to assuage this – not just with a loving heart, but out of recognition of our innate kinship?

Sharing: a means of including and levelling

The derivation of the word 'social' comes from the Latin 'socius' meaning 'to share', so this word has clear associations with company and community and participation in some kind of group activity. This has to involve us in relationship with our fellows and coming together to organise how we best do this sharing. Now, if there is one thing that gets everybody fired up it is talking about wealth and how this is shared out amongst people – who deserves and who doesn't. As we saw in the previous chapter, we in the West have become accustomed to living in a power-over world, where each seeks to get as much as they can and hold onto it. And in the doing of this varying degrees of dissembling, deceiving, lying, cheating and stealing have come to be seen as accepted norms, along with the belief that greater wealth and power bestows the right to take more.

Contrast this with an experience shared by Jean Liedloff (the woman who wrote about the importance of touch after spending time amongst tribal people) who tells an instructive story about attitudes towards sharing. One morning, she woke up with a hankering for something sweet, so the leader of the tribe took her to a neighbouring tribe to exchange something for sugarcane. As she began to take the cane, seeing the other man didn't argue or try to stop her, she took more and then more, until finally she stopped. Mortified, she realised *he was trusting her to be fair*. This illustrates how trust, which underpins sharing, is fundamental to creating a well-functioning community. And it is this trust that has been so disastrously undermined by our 'marketing' approach to everything.

The primary tool for dividing up our wealth in the modern world is money; and property of course, which represents money. Clearly, the use of money, in the form of coins or promissory notes, made it easier to exchange than actual, physical goods. However, it also makes it easier to hoard, thus encouraging a split between a person's daily *needs* and a surplus. Over time, it has led to the acquiring of money, with all its purchasing power, for its own sake. And this drives a wedge between people, encouraging a tendency to seek one's own interest before that of the community. The unspoken agreement to put the care of the whole first has been broken. It's easy to blame money for this but money itself is simply money: that is, a means of purchase and exchange. *It is how we see it and use it and what drives this that makes a difference.* Then we see how, once again, a mind out-of-control (that is, a mind not in service to the heart) becomes a vehicle for the ego; which will naturally use money to gain its programmed objectives which are – and always have been – primarily power: representing control of the means to ensure it gets what it wants and keeps itself safe.

At this point it is always useful to recognise the is-ness of something: that this just *is* how egoic mind behaves; no need for stigmatising, no need for judgement or blame. Then, seeing this, we open up the possibility for money to come free from exploitation, so it can function as it was designed to do: to allow transactions between people – so much simpler than bartering. We tend to think of money as grubby bits of paper and coins, that has no connection to the heart. But is this really so? Because money has great potential as a means for distributing love, as a tool for love in action. If you think of money as being like a great river flowing to the sea, it can bring nourishment to all it passes; creating rich, fertile valleys and bringing life to everything and everyone. *It is only when it is damned up, diverted and held in reservoirs* (like offshore tax havens) *that it loses this ability* and tends to become lifeless and even stagnant. Everything depends on how money is allowed to flow.

So much is predicated on our view of life, of reality. If we see and intuitively know everything to be part of the whole, then how we view sharing – politics, economics and money being part of this – changes radically. *It is tested against what works for this whole.* Then it's not simply that we become convinced of one way of organising ourselves as being more fair or more efficient. It just becomes obvious what is working and what isn't – as we said in the previous chapter, *it's a matter of inner sense*. Why on earth would you want to live in a system where some people can take more and leave others with less when you know that we are all one? It's like putting food into your mouth with one hand and removing it with the other: it just doesn't make sense. When you want to go out for a meal with a friend if one of you has a lot more money than the other, either that one has to pay for the other or you end up eating in the cheapest place. If this happens *every time* it starts to get uncomfortable.

It's so much more open and friendly and relaxing to be around people where everything is shared (not to mention the affect this has on reducing crime). If you have ever stayed in a community where this is the norm, you start to notice this. Amongst students it's more common, and my experience of travelling and living in different countries has shown me how sharing thrives best amongst the poorest people. As soon as some people have more than others then barriers get erected; people start to compare and exclude, the heart gets buried and forgotten. Charities are born seemingly to alleviate suffering: in fact, these often function to relieve the guilt of those who have more (and to increase people's public standing) giving those who give the questionable power to decide who gets and who doesn't. Things start to get messy.

The scientist Stephen Hawking, looking at the dire state of the world, has this to say *'...pressing issues will require us to collaborate, all of us, with a shared vision and cooperative endeavour to ensure that humanity can survive. We will need to adapt, rethink, refocus and change some of our fundamental assumptions about what we mean by wealth, by possessions, by mine and yours. Just like children, we will have to learn to share'.* You get the feeling that this man, despite his tendency to venerate the intellect (perhaps exacerbated by his physical restrictions?) is speaking from a deeper place, from the wisdom of the heart that is moved by a concern for the whole. And whatever you think about the controversial figure Fidel Castro, at his funeral a university teacher, Jorge Jorge, who had come with a group of friends said *'We have come here to share our grief and to show our determination to hold on to Fidel's ideals. He taught us how to share.'*

An example of how this drive to share can overcome situations of dire poverty occurred in Athens, after Syriza were elected and the powers that be decided to make sanctions even more severe. A public space was created by ordinary people for growing vegetables, cooking communal food, a theatre and performance space, etc. *'What we are witnessing is an explosion of social networks born of bottom-up initiatives,'* says Stavrides, who was among the activists whose spontaneous efforts stopped the lot being turned into a parking space in late 2009. *'Navarinou heralded this new culture, this new spirit of people taking their lives into their own hands. They know that they can no longer expect the state to support them and through this process, they are discovering how important it is to share.'*

It can help to have role models, because it's interesting how many people respond when they hear about someone who renounces the trappings their position entitles them to and, instead, lives a simple life. Jose Mujica, the ex-president of Uruguay, is such an example. Refusing the grand houses, big cars with chauffeurs and so on his position entitled him to, he preferred to live in a small, ramshackle old farmhouse with a bit of land for growing food – no different to his neighbours and the people he grew up with. Living in a world where opulence is the visible form of demonstrating power and position, many people respond to this chosen frugality. There is a recognition, a discernment of the heart about this; we feel warm and somehow *included* and can respect and admire someone in a true way.

There are several recent flickers of this public affirmation of the virtue of living a simple life by people in positions of power. As the head of the Catholic faith, it shouldn't come as a surprise to learn that Pope Francis chose to renounce the Papal palace in favour of living amongst visiting bishops and being able to share meals with the serving staff, and yet he is the first to do so; also to confront his bishops about corruption and their own strikingly affluent lifestyles. Jeremy Corbyn, leader of the UK Labour Party, takes a similar view. In speaking of a deceased friend he admired he recounts how, when this man was asked why he had chosen to build his house out of old recycled materials, he responded 'I live simply in order that others may simply live'. Now there's a saying for the Pope!

Gandhi was another who proclaimed simplicity as the way to live, yet despite his teachings not exactly being a religion, there is a whiff of a rigid moral crusade here, that had rules that left little space for adaptation to new possibilities. Instead of a joyful, *spontaneous* response of the heart, this kind of environment invites repression. As with everything, there are times when flexibility is needed. Hard and fast rules, whether about how we share, include or even nurture – or anything else come to that – can be obstructive.

During an experiment carried out by Osho in America called The Ranch, in which literally thousands of people spent long days transforming 6,000 acres of virtual desert in Oregon into a thriving, almost self-sufficient community, one of the edicts was sharing. With the exception of a few personal items, this meant sharing everything, including your clothes. As a friend who was there later recounted 'You can imagine the response getting up in the early hours one dark, wet, muddy morning to go on the milking roster, only to find someone else had walked off with your boots!'

The concept of ownership

Stephen Hawking goes on to ask *'Can we truly own anything, or are we just transient custodians?'*. A good question. Ownership is such a thorny and potentially explosive subject. It connects with our sense of identity as coming from possessing something, and owning land and property are fundamental to this. Here we might ask 'where did this idea come from, that *a person* could own the land? Or the water? No-one manufactured these, therefore how can anyone claim them? Or buy or sell them?' The truth is we have lived with this concept for so long that it never occurs to people to question it, or certainly not in first world countries. Not since the annexing of the commons have we even approached this subject. Indeed you are likely to provoke an outraged or curtly dismissive response if you do.

Whereas tribal people have never understood this concept. To them the land is sacred. Here, the word *custodian* holds great significance. This implies taking care of, nurturing, maintaining and protecting. I was struck by how Native Australians, according to recent research, lived together for 50,000 years without having any wars. One reason suggested for this is that they didn't farm, with all the implications involved in owning land, employing people and hoarding resources; these being seen as a big driver of war. Under communism, the land was supposed to 'belong' to the people. In fact, it 'belonged' to the state, which controlled it and its use through state sanctioned 'communes'. We could even say that the concept of ownership itself, whether private *or* by the State, is responsible for the beginning of the end, the end of the Earth's capacity to sustain everyone and everything living on her. The *belief* that everything is ours to take, to plunder, has caused so much harm and led to so many wars.

Once again you have to look at conditioning – centuries of conditioning – to see where this belief came from. Owning things is the fundamental basis of the economy we live in. Some people question the right of a few to hold large areas of land, houses and other buildings and profit from these by renting them to others. Groups like Reclaim the Land demand ownership be shared amongst everyone. *But it seems no-one questions ownership itself.* Strange, isn't it? For sure, animals lay claim to territories and defend these, but this usually applies to hunting *on* the land, not ownership of the land itself, where many other species roam freely.

We don't have space here to go into this further so I want to bring us back to the relationship with the heart. Because with the knowing that we are one comes the desire to preserve and protect everything *for the benefit of this whole*. On its own, the mind can always find ways to explain away uncomfortable truths. Beliefs like 'Science can invent solutions to any problem' are used to ignore the unpalatable. So when a prominent scientist like Hawking comes to the conclusion that unless humanity learns to drop its obsession with money and possessions and learns to share we are doomed, you can recognise the mind listening to the heart.

In talking about ownership, I am not saying that it's not okay to occupy personal space, to be able to be private and regulate who comes and goes within this. But there are ways of organising this based on agreements to become the *custodian of* a building or a parcel of land – for such things as creating a home and the growing of food – which don't need to involve either ownership or rental, where someone else profits out of this. The amazing, forgotten reality of this is that it can be enormously freeing, enormously relaxing *not to own things* like houses and land! I know, saying this to any home-owner is inherently threatening, so strong is our identification with ownership bringing security and status; talk of the importance to an Englishman of his 'castle' is real! And if you speak to any farmer, he loves the sense of the land belonging to him (if he should be so lucky, as most land is owned now by companies as an 'investment').

But that wonderful feeling of love and connection and relationship with a particular piece of land can *still* be there without needing to own it. If we treasure life and treasure each other then recognising custodianship can be a blessing. It taps directly into the energy of the heart. And this leaves the mind free to involve itself with such practical aspects as implementation: organisational strategies within a community, communal maintenance projects; details such as designing the solar plumbing for a new house, or calculating the cost of fixing the roof of an existing one. Without ownership, we are free to move as one; to care for and include each other's needs and use our creativity to do things that delight and inspire others, knowing we have valued company to support us in difficult times and to celebrate with in the good.

Work or contribution?

When you recognise everything to be One your perspective on what makes sense changes. It becomes crystal clear that the way things are organised around contributing is completely out-of-line with this insight.

During a visit to Bolivia, the Pope talked about the 'sacred rights' of people to 'labour, lodging and land' (we will look at the last two in the next section). But have you ever stopped to look at this word 'labour'? What is most often called 'work'? About what it is and where it came from? When you have the *concept* of labour, or work, you are basically talking about doing to get, doing something to get something in return. For most people, this means giving your time and abilities, unless you are self-employed, to another person or organisation, to get what you need to keep yourself and your family, if you have one: often irrespective of whether you would choose this or enjoy what you do. Nothing wrong with an exchange, but this idea of 'work' tends to override any desire to *contribute* – your time, energy, skills, creativity, wisdom and inspiration – towards taking care of the community or contributing to the whole. Though a desire to do so may be present, *this mental concept of 'work' places the emphasis on getting rather than giving*, excluding offering as being something we do outside of work, like babysitting for the neighbours or so-called 'charitable' activities.

With the concept of work comes the notion of 'rights': to days off, weekends and holidays as a break from work, and sick pay when you are ill and all the rest of it. With this *concept* come a whole lot of dynamics mixed up with moral beliefs – of which the Protestant work ethic is one – where work is seen as 'good for the soul' and people talk of the 'dignity of work.' The question 'what does the word "work" *signify*?' is not asked. Instead, we have created a peculiar situation where only the majority of able-bodied people are expected to do this; to work 'for a living', while a small minority are not; as such, rather like a parasite, these live off the work of others. As 'investors', those who have gained more than they need to live on, or have collateral to borrow against, become entitled to take money *without making a contribution*. There is no requirement to either contribute or share. Doesn't this appear a little unbalanced?

People living in tribes didn't think of dividing their time or 'income' in these ways. As we have noted, *they saw life as a whole* and their role within this, their function, as being to provide for their community, each contributing according to his or her ability. If someone was sick or elderly and otherwise unable to do this, the rest took care of them. Isn't this a more natural, intelligent and loving way to organise ourselves? I am not talking about crude, inflexible, mass-enforcement programmes like state communism (which still allows for an elite to take control and keep more for themselves anyway). This is an ideology that is still fundamentally based on the idea of 'work': people working for the state. And as with *any* ideology, it is based on the thinking mind, with all its inbuilt distortions and limitations. Nor am I saying we must return to living in tribes.

Taking a fresh look at the way things are currently organised (excepting the self-employed), we see that a person contributes an amount of their time and skills to someone else's venture, financed by that person and maybe shareholders, who have no such obligation to contribute their own time and skills, and *yet it is they, and not the community, who have control over this and stand to benefit most from it*. Once again, this feels back-to-front: not because it conflicts with a rigid moral code, but because it makes no inner sense to the heart – *it isn't in accord with including everyone and sharing both what we have and what needs to be done to provide for all of us.* Within this way of being employed by others for their individual gain, there is no space to *offer,* as happens when a friend or neighbour offers to help, nor for *exchange* (whether this is produce, skills or advice; babysitting, cups of tea or whatever). Instead, we call these 'goods and services' – such impersonal terms – which anyway have to be paid for.

In our current way of living together, everything has a monetary value and work is separated out from our social, non-working lives. So, for example, child-minding for many families means paying a large fee to a group of strangers running a crèche (and later an after-school club) to mind their children for them – safe-storage for kids till at least one parent has completed their working hours. Other people are forced to work evenings, nights and/or weekends so, while their partner works the day shift, they can look after the kids, shop, get things fixed and, if they are so lucky, have a moment to rest. All of this interferes with a *natural pattern of life* based around things like daylight, bodily rhythms, continuity of access between children and parents and so on. It sabotages our relationships by draining our patience and the natural goodwill that expresses itself as the urge to offer to help each other. And this in turn stifles love and, in a wider context, destroys the sense of community. If we want to help out, we often have to force ourselves to do so at times when we are exhausted and not in the mood.

To illustrate an absurd situation we have created around work lets look at production. Here jobs are created specifically to legitimise people earning money to pay for their needs. (Those who have no capital or assets, that is.) Doesn't that seem a little peculiar? Just stop and take look at it. People are expected to work to produce, *irrespective of what is produced, either in terms of its usefulness or any cost to the environment.* Advertising has been designed to provide the demand, and sales are reported in the media as something to celebrate. But why? Why create jobs so someone can be allowed to live? Why create goods we don't need? Not just goods that follow the latest fashion like clothes, cars and kitchens, but gadgets of all kinds? What about the *true,* full cost of these? And what about the relationship between work and time? The ability to choose free time over more goods? To live simply with minimum cost to the planet? Where is the *intelligence* amongst all this?

When you look at this with the clarity of the eyes of the heart it all appears so muddle-headed. People talk about the dignity of work, but where is the dignity in working to put money in someone else's pocket? Or to produce things where the destructive cost to the environment outweighs the need? You surely don't have to be a raging 'Leftie' to see the absurdity of this. *Any situation where you need access to money to make money brings with it the potential for division and conflict.*

One might also ask: 'What are we doing with a system of organisation that leaves numbers of our species not just redundant but trapped? With no opportunity to *offer* their skills freely without losing any income from the state – supposing they can get this – forced to spend their time going through the motions of seeking work that, if available at all, is insecure and often under poor conditions?' While others are required to work all hours, perhaps doing two or even three jobs, with no time or energy for the important things of life, like being with their family and friends, relaxing and doing things they enjoy. So many both in and out of work are increasingly unable to provide even their basic needs: like a home, food and warmth, forced to live off charity in growing insecurity; yet none of this is necessary. *There is so much available to us that could be shared, and so much potential being wasted.* This is completely out of balance, it doesn't make any kind of sense. Are those who design and implement these structures really so ignorant? Because to pretend this is necessary is to be complicit in a lie.

A culture based on sharing and the values of the heart operates in everyone's interests. So, for instance, in measuring contribution and sharing out what needs to be done, it can take into account that certain kinds of occupations are more intense and require more energy or concentration (such as a surgeon), while others (like fishing or farming) can be done over a longer, more relaxed span of time. Then time contributed can be measured proportionally. But beyond this, *there is no actual need* for any one person to be active, either mentally or physically, for excessively long periods of time on a regular basis.

In looking at all this, surely it's obvious it's not really about more jobs being needed, or higher wages and better conditions – the traditional impetus of trade unions and the Left; *it's far more fundamental.* Beneath the basic questions: 'How do we create better ways of sharing out what we already have?' and 'How do we create better ways of organising whatever activity is needed to produce and maintain this?' lie the egoic desire to get and keep more than others, opposing the heart's desire to care for everyone. And although the Left might claim to pursue the interests of the majority it too can be blinded by unconscious egoic motivations. Just as the instinct of the Right about a need for individual responsibility and initiative has relevance. For instance, in recognising how state support can create dependency and an attitude of being entitled to take without giving anything in return, we see that *within all political positions both the egoic drive to exploit and the heart's desire to recognise the truth, can be found.*

If you sit with this and sense and feel into it you come to realise a return to base is needed, beyond all political dogmas of the mind, to connect with the roots of our Being-ness and re-establish the core values of the heart. Here is where the desire to contribute originates. As long as traditional political parties avoid this they remain wilfully blind. Then, caught up in opposing ideologies, they fail to see beyond a narrow and no longer functioning (if it ever did) way of doing things. They become obsolete.

A society where everyone contributes what they can is deeply fulfilling. It provides a basis for healing the hurt of being either exploited or discarded as dignity is seen in its true light: as coming from offering your time and skills in service to the whole and taking care of this from a place of integrity. It turns everything around so life can settle back into its natural place, a place founded on love. Then it is this word 'work' that becomes redundant! Another word can take its place: to 'offer'. And although this word 'offering' may have religious associations, it is one of those words whose true beauty and significance awaits our recognition. We so easily forget the human heart *needs to both give and receive:* and that this need to give is true for children, too. This is our innate nature.

Co-operation versus competition

There is an assumption that history has always been about the 'Might is Right' conquering ethos of people like Ghengis Khan, who claimed the spoils of war for themselves and ruled with an iron fist. However in 2009 a woman called Elinor Ostrom was awarded the Nobel Prize for her work on 'common-pool' systems – societies in which resources were pooled for the good of the community, in ways at odds with our modern conception of private property. Ostrom's work demonstrated that, where conditions were favourable, these systems – such as fisheries, irrigation systems, common grazing and forests – thrived better than similar systems maintained through top-down organisation. In fact it is now believed by those who study the past that *it was co-operation rather than competition that allowed humans to progress.* This shows that even outside of tribal societies we have long been able to operate in the interests of the whole, and that any suggestion to the contrary is just a convenient narrative perpetrated by those who benefit from a top-down model (which model has also included organised religions and such things as 'tithing' to the church).

Remember how those Spanish women mayors talked about the need to demonstrate that co-operation works so much better than competition? In fact, co-operative enterprises have been operating successfully in many countries, especially in South America, for years and the Co-operative movement in the UK has a long history. There are differing models, with ownership and production costs shared amongst those who work in them (e.g. Waitrose and John Lewis) or purchase from them (e.g. The Co-operative Group), all operating in the UK. Why don't we hear more about them? Because they don't fit our current capitalist system. There is no place for people who are neither working in them nor buying from them to profit. I know someone who once tried to study co-operatives in a course on economics. First the teacher claimed no-one was interested, and when he persisted, admitted she actually knew nothing about them!

What is interesting here is the educational impact of participating in co-operatives. *Both models bring people together – in the decision-making and sharing out of any profit.* And this can be of enormous benefit to people who have grown accustomed to being passive consumers. It helps people come free from a child-like, take-care-of-me-daddy, while-giving-me-someone-to-blame attitude, based on avoiding responsibility; an attitude that becomes endemic in systems where people have little meaningful control over their lives. And at the same time, it can help wean us off the disastrous each-man-for-himself ethos of current political dogma; in other words free us from power-over structures that belong with the old 'separation' myth.

The essence of community

Including, nurturing and especially sharing, which we highlighted in the previous chapter, are generally seen as feminine traits (and thus not valued by male-dominated operating systems) which threaten any position of divide and rule. And this applies to something that affects all of our lives – our economic structures. These are purportedly based around enabling people to provide a home and food for themselves and their family, if they have one. Which would seem to support our individual endeavours. But what happens if you want to do this *directly*? For yourself? Perhaps in a way that includes the help of others? You would expect those who argue for greater personal autonomy through shrinking the state to be in support of this, wouldn't you? Yet the reality is that this is almost impossible today (unless you are stupendously rich), certainly here in Europe.

Firstly, you need land to build on, yet this is virtually unavailable to individual house-builders, held as it is by a few owners and developers, often in big blocks, as an investment. Secondly, building your own home with planning regulations designed to work for big developers, is made unnecessarily expensive and complicated for individual house-builders. And thirdly, the way work is organised most people can't take time off to build their own home, nor can their friends or neighbours get time off to help them. *So the most basic means of providing for our own survival – as we have been able to do for millennia – has become almost impossible to achieve in modern times.* (Even supposing we want to do this of course as, in a world based on producing for profit, there is no encouragement to want to do these things for ourselves.)

Similar problems apply to growing your own food, where access to land is again the main stumbling block. The reality is there is a reverse flow taking place: ordinary people are actually *losing their land* on a massive scale to international corporations and developers worldwide, and especially in poorer countries like Africa. Allotments in England were designed to help families provide for themselves in a communal setting but many are disappearing, and even if there is one nearby, and you can get a plot, this isn't enough land to keep a family. *All of this impacts on our sense of community,* with sharing and helping each other being an integral part of this (as anyone who has worked on an allotment, where exchanging seeds and tips and cups of tea is the norm, knows well).

This very fundamental provision – that we are enabled to take care of our basic needs for shelter and food in these ways and contribute to those of our neighbour, either as individuals or as part of a group – is simply not available under the current political systems of much of Europe, and a growing part of the rest of the word. *Yet this is the very basis of community, lived by humans for thousands of years.* It opens the possibility for relationships based on sharing our lives, doing things together. So different to suburban life, for instance, with its sterile dormitory towns: places where people occupy near-identical housing 'developments' and spend a large part of their time going somewhere else for work, school, shopping or various forms of entertainment.

Sadly, in many Western countries and certainly the UK, taking care of one's own basic needs in this way and sharing this with others is not recognised as important; the creativity involved in this not encouraged. Dependency is the result of having our ability to take care of ourselves removed. Which has meant that when a beautiful *concept* like taking care of everyone, and especially those who are most vulnerable, takes form it can – and often does – end up creating just that. As happens with the welfare state, we create dependency, undermining people's ability to be creative and as self-sufficient as they wish and are able to be. When bureaucracy and institutions and doing things on a large, impersonal scale are employed to 'provide' for people, this is inevitable.

Why? Because the heart functions best in small, interrelated groups; where sensitivity to individual feelings, needs and circumstances can be seen, heard *and included.* The heart respects dignity, which means that any movement to support others needs to include listening to everyone, *along with helping people to help themselves.* It is when the mind takes over from the heart and, from its disconnected perspective, fills everything with theoretical *ideas,* ideas of *what* and *how,* that things start to go wrong; when it tries to implement these – especially en masse and by brute force, and measures the results through statistical analysis – that things get messy. Hence we have evolved political dogmas and directions, even those based on good intentions, that really don't serve us.

Way back in the Seventies the economist, E.F. Schumacher, wrote the classic *Small is Beautiful: A Study of Economics as if People Mattered,* in which he talked about many things that make sense to the heart. Unfortunately (and as he predicted) modern economists became so obsessed with globalisation they ignored the wisdom his book contains. Overwhelmed by the current 'profit before people' paradigm (where fooling people for profit has almost come to be seen as a noble art) his ideas were regarded as 'romantic' and 'idealistic' when they are actually just sane.

Playing with possibilities

So how could things be different? Are there ways to organise ourselves that encourage *a willingness,* even a strong desire to share and contribute to the whole? That allow people to see the benefits and feel a gladness of heart? Before we look at these, before any real and lasting changes can take root, we need to remember about beliefs and conditioning and how the egoic mind interferes with clear seeing. We have all been taught to make assumptions and to trust these. We *assume* things have to be pretty much the way they are, and in the questioning of this we have to confront all the unconscious fears of change and inner conflicts we talked about in the previous chapter.

What I am talking about throughout this book is resurrecting the values of the heart *and placing these at the very centre of how we organise living together.* When you have a connection with a deeper reality you know that the 'hows' of this then take care of themselves. But for people who have been brought up to believe in the superiority, even the infallibility of the mind, it can be hard to envision how this might happen. Which is why it can be helpful to look at how man originally lived, if only to broaden our horizons. For instance, there is a common impression that man has always had to work from dawn to dusk just to survive. However, in Australia – and this may sound unbelievable – the indigenous people spent an average of just *two hours a day* hunting and gathering sufficient for their needs; and they frequently did this together; men, women and also children (who, unlike our own, were included in this process of providing for the community, this being a valuable part of their education).

Two hours a day? My God! What did they do the rest of the time? *They relaxed and enjoyed themselves*: they sat around the fire and sang and danced, laughed and made love; they taught skills and played games with the children, they formed secret societies to enact rituals and they loved to tell stories. Okay, they also had to repair weapons and prepare food, but they did this as part of a social situation, in the same place. Wouldn't you like to be able to live with so much time free to enjoy yourself? As part of a friendly and supportive community? Interestingly, I have met people who studied wild dolphins and they found a very similar ratio of how these highly intelligent animals spend their time. Yes, I know the world is different now: there are many more of us and things look a lot more complicated. *Nonetheless*, the current economic organisation we have bares little relationship to humanity's needs as a whole, nor those of the planet and everything on it.

At this time there are big changes on the horizon. As journalist and broadcaster Paul Mason points out about the effects of information technology in his book *PostCapitalism: A Guide to Our Future*: '*Information does more to transform work: it makes it modular, loosening the link between hours worked and wages; and it makes work possible to do outside the workplace — blurring the division between work and life.'* Clearly changes are afoot that we have barely grasped, but most people are so inured to things being the way *are* and therefore have to be – we take it so much for granted – that we fail to see that without this regimented work versus non-work system, we could simply follow our energy: being physically active when our energy is high, resting when we need to, playing when we want to, sleeping as much as we need. These are all things related to our *real* nature, based on a quite different and far more natural paradigm.

So what is preventing things changing? Here we come back to money again as we encounter one great, big, apparent stumbling block – the banks. Except that now massive unemployment is being predicted as machines take over, a factor that will require big changes in the way we organise ourselves. So an old idea is being re-discovered: the idea of money being shared out by the government to provide a baseline for people to live on. Something called 'Basic' or 'Citizens Income' is not a new idea. Way back in the 17th century Thomas More and Thomas Paine were on about it. In the 30's a man called Clifford Douglas came up with something he called 'Social Credit'. He noted that the banks dominate the economic system by means of money created out of thin air; by issuing 'bank credit', they create debt with which they effectively control prices and production through the markets, consequently controlling people's income and, through this, their lives. So he designed a system to put control of money into the hands of the government itself, who would then distribute it to the people. (This was largely discredited when it became a vehicle for an extreme right-wing agenda in Canada after the Second World War.)

Today, a more limited version is being trialled; one that doesn't affect the banks. As a means of redressing extreme inequality it is popular with the Left (it's part of the manifesto of the UK Greens', Dutch D66 and Spanish Podemos Party) *and* with the Right, as a way of removing a cumbersome and expensive benefit system (the Right-controlled Finnish government is experimenting with it). How does it work? Everyone is paid a small basic wage, enough to survive on, and (in most schemes) those who want more can work for this. There are different ways it can be implemented but all have *the capacity* to bring greater equality whilst doing away with the whole massive, complicated and hugely costly benefit system, with its vast swathes of bureaucracy, leaving no need for pensions or unemployment, disability, child or sickness benefit, or student living-allowance loans.

Essentially, it brings a potential for a shift in the way we view money and contribution. Providing for everyone out of what there is – whilst allowing those who give their time and skills to help produce and maintain this to be rewarded – could become the new norm; leaving time and energy for those who want to contribute voluntarily, to do so. It sounds hopelessly utopian and unfeasible, doesn't it? But it's not. What starts to become clear the more you look into all this, is how extreme and unbalanced are the ways we reward people under the present system; the vast amounts of waste created – wasted time, energy, food, creativity and potential, along with psychological damage (such as anxiety and depression and people taking to various forms of drugs to alleviate their misery and despair).

It is curious, isn't it, that no-one seems to question why the banks, which control money *manufactured by the government*, should be run for profit? Or they seem to quickly be removed if they do – as with Gough Whitlam, the elected prime minister of Australia who, in the 70's, proposed nationalising the banks and was promptly ejected from office by Her Majesty the Queen. The British prime minister, Harold Wilson, also tried to establish a form of public banking through the Post Office (called GIRObank) shortly before he was swept from power. But before we start talking about 'wicked bankers' and conspiracy theories like lizard men and evil blood lineages, let's stop and take a look at what is really going on.

Remember what we have seen about money and how this can function as a source of love in action? What we are seeing here is how the current banking system *acts in the identical way to the egoic mind*, to benefit itself at the expense of others. It is essentially a power-over system that carries the same agenda to control; much like a privately-owned dam, it interferes with the natural flow of money in order to maintain this control and further its interests. *This is just how it operates.* Whereas if you contrast this with the small, inter-related lending groups that usually function amongst poor communities – and are often used by women – you see the opposite effect: you see both the intention *and* the reality is to empower people. (Often referred to as 'Microfinance', an example is the Grameen banks, set up in poorer countries around the world with just this aim.) These projects operate in a power-with format that serves the heart.

Another apt analogy for the way money works is the arterial system of the heart itself. Here blood (representing money) is pumped around the body to keep it healthy and functioning. Interfere with this flow and you get weak, sluggish energy leading to disease and potentially, death of the organism. So we see money taken out of circulation, stored away in some tax haven somewhere where it continues to create profit through 'interest', leading to growing inequality; to stagnation, starvation, war and death. *Here is where the potential for change in the direction of the heart comes up against the egoic desire to control and exclude.* It is also where such schemes as 'Basic Income' could bridge this divide so that, as it becomes more obvious the old ways are not working, there is a possibility for love, based on clear seeing, to dissolve rigid resistances and move beyond them.

Does this all sound pie in the sky to you? I am aware that much of what I am writing about in this chapter can feel hopelessly far away from our actual daily reality – an impossible dream. But then this would be true for all the changes humanity has made for the people who had not yet experienced them. Imagine the confusion and sheer disbelief amongst those who believed the Earth was flat, when they were told they *couldn't* actually fall off, there *was* no terrifying 'edge of the world' to encounter. The truth is all change can be challenging, but 'going to the roots' is essential if we are to get a sense of priorities. This can help in accessing an intuitive flow that corresponds with the direction of the heart, a sense of what we love. Can you feel a resonance? Because moving with this flow brings a wonderful sense of joyousness. Something is recognised, something that has been forgotten is recovered.

Time: time to live, time to connect, time to just be

The truth is that, given the opportunity and a little encouragement, we humans are full of ingenuity. There are many possibilities for using money differently, for enhancing the way we live together by providing a resource available to everyone. Not all ways of organising ourselves address wider issues, such as the environment, but once ordinary people become involved in decision-making within their own structures, it is evident that these concerns quickly come to the fore. (As with The Co-operative Group, for example, which has a consumer-led ethical investment policy.) Then, through sharing these concerns *together*, in an atmosphere of each being valued for their contribution, miracles become possible.

Can you even imagine what could happen if enough money to live on was made freely available to all? There would be so many options. Have you ever dreamed about building your own home? Or having the time to write a book? To design clothes and have your own label? Follow up that idea for a new invention? So many creative possibilities for spending our time, and for building friendly relationships through sharing projects *together*. Perhaps you have always wanted to get together with your mates and form a band, or build a boat and go off sailing around the world? Or you might just want to have time to sit quietly, doing nothing – without all the pressures to 'get things done'. When people are occupied doing meaningful things they enjoy, surrounded by others doing the same, this brings a surge of contentment to the heart. And this is infectious; we feel naturally generous and find ourselves *wanting to participate* in things that benefit everyone. Then, whether we do this through offering our time to do the work that remains after machines take over most of it, perhaps on some kind of roster system (excepting the most specialised work), or whether we choose to reward those who take this on financially, becomes of secondary concern.

Doing things yourself can be both satisfying and cost-effective. (For instance, one can build a sustainable house for a fraction of the cost of buying from a developer.) The endless shopping, the quest to find something to make us feel better, would tend to die a natural death. As would the excess drinking and seeking to escape our troubles in harmful ways. With time for growing our own food, perhaps on communal allotments, people's health would tend to improve; there would be less need for big supermarkets (and the transport needed to get to them). Instead, we could create out own local markets, anyway more popular with users. *Because there would be no need for people to travel vast distances to 'work', life could be built, once again, around the community*; with small, local schools and classes in anything anyone, of any age, wanted to pursue. Money currently spent on new roads, rail projects and airports, could be used to build these and new communal spaces. We could expect a big drop in crime and also mental illness and this, within communities where people have *time* to care for one another, would free hospitals for other uses. It would also lead to a mushrooming of caring and creative community projects everywhere – the list of potential benefits goes on.

'Is this all just a silly, unrealistic, impossible dream?' asks a doubting mind. Why should it be? Once you examine the daft ways our lives are currently structured it becomes clear it is *this* that is crazy, and those who accept it as the only alternative who are deluded. We can recognise that not only is it enormously destructive of our capacity for aliveness – *it doesn't have to be like this*; we don't need to keep on enduring this half-life, with so many living like semi-automated, somnolent creatures in a dream.

So why not get practical? Why not put our energy into moving in the directions of the heart? Into creating time and options for everyone to contribute *and be valued for this*. Opportunities to do what the indigenous Australians did: to sing and dance and play music; to tell stories, engage with children and the elderly. These days, through sharing skills, people could make television programmes and films and run their own radio station; and use the internet in creative ways to extend genuine connections and spread a loving, caring energy. There are so many creative ways of living together, once you raise your head and look over the parapet. It can feel freeing just to know that viable alternatives exist – despite these often receiving scant publicity as they go against the dominant political philosophy of our time. There is so much creative energy that can be focussed towards positive directions, once the heart is awakened and a sense of connection restored.

Bringing consciousness into decision-making

'That's all very well' you might say 'but how do we bring changes about?' How do we get past the divisions? The power games and childlike egoic investment in 'having things my way' that tend to clutter so many attempts to organise ourselves. On a structural level, one of the most fraught areas in organising anything together involves how we make decisions.

At the Findhorn Foundation they developed something they called 'attunement' that relies in good part on intuition. So everyone would sit together – preferable in a circle which avoids hierarchies and brings a sense of unity as everyone is facing inwards, facing each other. Someone would make a proposal and then everyone would take time to sit in silent contemplation, tuning in and 'getting a feel' for what wanted to happen. Anyone who found themselves opposed to the majority response could take time to see if they could drop their objection and fall in line with the group attunement. This way of doing things avoids the usual adversarial and intellectual process of debating, inviting argument as people seek to persuade or defend a position. As a more feminine approach, it makes this whole process of decision making so much more relaxed and harmonious.

Then there are simple forms of non-verbal communication like the one I watched at an Occupy camp, that are being adopted by various groups – especially in activist circles where there is often a younger, more open energy and a willingness to experiment. This process works by people (again sitting in a circle) using their arms to make certain agreed-upon movements to indicate either interest and perhaps agreement, or dis-interest and perhaps opposition to what the person speaking is saying. That person can then read this as they are speaking to see whether to continue or not, so it cuts out any need for interruptions.

As a way of keeping things moving and the energy generated high, it works well, because everyone in the circle gets to *feel the mood* and can *tune in* to the response. This strengthen's a sense of *inclusiveness*, of a group making decisions together rather than being led by the speaker. True, it can be slow because it allows everyone who wants to, to have their say. But again, this strengthens the sense of engagement, of being an important part of something. Being a relatively new format, it often takes time for more reticent participants to speak out; on the other hand, it stops those who just want attention rabbiting on when they have nothing constructive to offer.

How can we come together to support one another in dark times?

'Climate change isn't an "issue" to add to a list of things to worry about, next to health care and taxes. It is a civilisational wake-up call. A powerful message— spoken in the language of fires, floods, droughts, and extinctions—telling us that we need an entirely new economic model and a new way of sharing this planet. Telling us that we need to evolve.' This is Naomi Klein. And in her very practical book *Active Hope* (written in conjunction with Chris Johnstone) Joanna Macy comments about the process of changing the foundations of the way we live to meet our current challenges: *'This transition is already well under way'* and *'If*

you look for it, you can find evidence that our civilisation is being re-invented all around us.' That this doesn't appear in the mainstream media is unsurprising. To those who have given up hope it may come as something of a shock. I am not saying we can save the world. I am not even sure this is the right phrase.

I have no *idea* about this but I do have a sense of *something*; a sense that I can't know what needs to happen in terms of the whole and that life involves a continual change of *forms*. Am I saying we might just as well ignore things and enjoy the ride while we can? No. Each of us has *a true response*, even when we don't know what this is. What feels important is that we honour our true nature: *what we are,* and this means acting with love and clarity, when we can. And forgiving ourselves when we can't. The form this takes will become clear as we listen *in* and move where and when an inner pull informs us. True, the evidence looks pretty much against us surviving but there is also so much that we simply do not know.

What Joanna is talking about is the largely unreported reality of thousands of groups representing untold numbers of people, who are already active in various forms, attempting to address the 'problems' – whether that comes in resisting harmful actions or processes, developing new economic and social structures or inner forms of action, such as meditation and prayer. And surely by bringing conscious awareness into everything we do? So on the level of connection with a *collective consciousness*, participating in something that involves everyone, whether they know it or admit it, it can be heartening to hear this, even as it might appear we are facing an apparently insurmountable threat.

There are numbers of people, including Jon Young and 'elders' like Joanna Macy, who have been working to address this question of how we re-connect and live together in a world made up of an enormous variety of 'beings', including us humans, of all shapes and natures. One of the things I love about Joanna's work is the way she creates processes that ordinary folk can use amongst themselves, which means no one need be excluded for lack of funds; and these involve direct, often physical and certainly *feeling connection*, rather than just cerebral information or techniques. They carry a quality of living energy which opens and invites, and they bring a powerful sense of *inclusion*.

She talks about recognising three main 'stories' we tell ourselves: 'everything is going along fine just as it is', 'everything has become so disastrous there is no point in trying to do anything about it' and, 'however bad things may seem, we will do everything we can to bring about the changes needed and heal the damage.' Towards the latter aim, she has devised something she calls *The Work That Reconnects* and a process called *The Turning*, which involves four linked stages: tuning into gratitude (the root that sustains us), feeling our pain for the world (so we can grieve for this and move on), seeing with fresh eyes (which is greatly helped by the first two) and lastly, moving out towards taking an action.

During the protests against the Dakota Access Pipeline at Standing Rock, a man called Joe Whittle at the Oceti Sakowin camp, talked about a prophesy amongst Native tribes. Here Lakota leader Crazy Horse spoke of his vision of that prophecy with the following words: *'Upon suffering beyond suffering, the Red Nation shall rise again and it shall be a blessing for a sick world. A world filled with broken promises, selfishness and separations. A world longing for light again. I see a time of seven generations when all the colours of mankind will gather under the sacred Tree of Life and the whole Earth will become one circle again. In that day there will be those among the Lakota who will carry knowledge and understanding of unity among all living things, and the young white ones will come to those of my people and ask for this wisdom.'* Indeed, visitors came from all over the world from as far away as Tibet, Japan and New Zealand, to offer support. Even the last remaining indigenous people of Europe, the Sami tribe, sent representatives. As Lakota youth Phillip Wright said *'even if we can't stop this pipeline we still won. Because we opened up everybody's eyes.'*

One of the beautiful things that can come out of difficult times is in the sharing of this *together,* including with strangers. I am absolutely *not* talking about preaching here, or getting into antagonistic positions: that's the old way. No, I am referring to genuine engagement, to listening and exchanging from a place of openness – you will quickly sense if this is wanted or even possible if you tune in. Then sharing each other's heartfelt concerns can be inspiring; sharing feelings, insights, information, passing things along can raise the energy and lift spirits.

Here is where you need to stay alert to any hidden agenda of the egoic mind, from a place of believing things 'should be' a certain way *and trying to make others think or do as you do,* or you simply introduce conflict, however unspoken this may be. In sharing, I prefer to pass on inspiring rather than worrying information, as we all know there are lots of things happening that feel upsetting, that can induce anger, fear and a sense of helplessness, about which people can get more information for themselves if they so choose. (I am not talking about avoidance here, not facing the hard stuff, but that often needs to involve *grieving* which is a sensitive matter; this is something individuals need to choose to do, along with where, when and with whom.

It is so easy to go unconscious and slide into a negative rant around authorities and the environment, a litany of complaints about others and their actions, while fooling ourselves into believing we are helping to change the world. You don't need to be part of that. In listening to others comes the opportunity to appreciate that we can *all* contribute something of value and sometimes the most surprising things happen. It can be humbling to realise you had just dismissed someone, but then they open their mouth and out comes this wonderful deep insight or words of simple kindness. Or they open up and let you see their pain.

Just sitting quietly, listening *inwards,* you may receive all kinds of input that attracts a response from you; a need, a place for itself. *Making a contribution is more than just taking an action.* Allowing the peace and joy you feel when connecting to your heart and Being and sharing this as a blessing: offering it to a conflict, a difficulty, someone who needs to find courage for something – this can be extraordinarily powerful. And remember: when darkness threatens, that means it's time to come inside, close your eyes and ears to the strident voices telling you what you should do or be concerned about, and warm yourself at the fire of remembering the goodness in all people's hearts, however buried – including your own.

Healing division

I have always loved Archbishop Desmond Tutu's work with the Truth and Reconciliation Project. This is based on the traditional African way of justice, a way which is replicated in most tribal societies. They call this 'Mata oput' and it involves confession, atonement and forgiveness. This allows for the perpetrator to acknowledge their action to the victim, to say sorry and 'give back' to them in some way. And the victim, in turn, can then forgive: thus providing a way to bring a lasting end to violence – so very different to the punitive justice systems of so many countries that often make things worse. I once watched a television documentary of this Truth and Reconciliation process being used in Northern Ireland after 'the Troubles' and it was both powerful and very moving. Sadly, there seems little evidence of it being adopted in a big way, despite it clearly being so effective in ending the cycle of revenge that we see acted out in countries across the world. Perhaps, ultimately, this might prove to be the most effective tool to use with members of extremist groups like ISIS, who are so filled with hatred and a desire for revenge that they have lost their humanity.

Talking about this makes me think about Martin Tamras, a Syrian Christian whose family were captured and endured the most hideous conditions, who said *'Much is written in books about theology; this is not theology, this is life. We have been forced to confront the worst and our role is now to be witnesses. It is a real test to believe in mercy. Of course at first I want to kill these Daesh. I want revenge on those who take my children and who kill my cousin and my friend in front of me, and who taunt me that I am next. Those who mock my wife and destroy my home, who want to buy and sell human beings. Yes, I want justice, I want them to be brought to justice, but I will not hate them, and I will not hate my Muslim neighbour... only forgiveness breeds peace. Only peace makes us comfortable. We will work together. In Syria, we are not unique. This is universal. People across the world are living in such difficulties, what is important is how we confront it.'*

One of the most divisive forms we encounter is prejudice. But what is this, really? When we look closely we see this is resistance based in fear: fear of the other and fear that others will take away or stand in the way of what we want for ourselves. It is essentially a power-over position stemming from the fearful ego. So how to approach this? There is actually a continual stream of evidence that the qualities of the heart work best to overcome prejudice.

Take empathy: this has been found to be unquestionably effective when attempting to change people's bias on transgender and homophobic issues, and it has great potential in other areas such as race too. For instance, accusing people of being racist simply re-enforces their sense of being under threat, *especially so if they feel they are themselves seen as inferior.* It hardens their resistance as they unconsciously close off to defend. Whereas through listening with empathy, asking questions that don't make others feel judged and sharing stories about our experiences, we can come together and this can open to allow receptivity and bring about change. A brave black musician, Daryl Davis, took it upon himself to approach and befriend a member of the Ku Klux Klan in his home state of Maryland. He asked the question 'How can you hate me when you don't even know me?' leading ultimately, to somewhere around 200 people leaving the KKK. (He wrote a book called *Klan-Destine Relationships* and made an award-winning documentary *Accidental Curtesy.*)

At base, everyone wants to feel included and nobody wants to be made to feel wrong. So this is love in action. We can even feel grateful for the opportunity to practise this as we seek to find common ground. This is the way of the heart, yet so often in such circumstances consciousness is avoided; fear prevails and war and the ways of the dinosaurs continue to trample the new shoots of hope as they spring up. Or so it would appear from the clatter of the printing presses and the terse, dramatic declarations of those who repeat 'the News'. So which countries is war happening in at the moment? What is the name of the latest little girl murdered or abducted? Which politician has been exposed for corruption? Who is the current celebrity cheating on his wife? Which country is currently suffering from freak weather conditions and where is the latest refugee crisis happening? When you stop and take a step back from all this, back into your body-energy – back into yourself – you can suddenly feel a whole weight falling off. 'Oh my God, I have been doing it again!', getting caught up in the daily fiction of the mind.

It makes so much more sense, instead, to look at what goes unseen in all this noise, what is not trumpeted around. That is, the millions of tiny actions of love and care and courage that are happening all over the world, everyday, amongst ordinary people – and big actions too. Just think about the extraordinary guts it must have taken those who took in the Jews during World War II. Can you imagine doing this yourself? Taking that horrific risk with your own life, and perhaps your families' lives too? Similar actions of courage amongst ordinary people, the millions of unsung heroes and heroines, are being repeated today; these are the actions that don't get brought to our attention.

So, in fact, the heart does manage to get a look in; it somehow bubbles up through the iron grip of the conditioned mind in all kinds of ways, like grass growing through concrete. Knowing this, everyone's heart is lifted; we are reminded of what we love, what our true nature *is*. And something else that is not clearly visible is an underground spread of consciousness. Nobody knows how great this is because it is still largely hidden from view, but the possibility of ignition and contamination – that is, both the cumulative effect on humanity and also the potential for jumping the gap – *this is there*.

Eckart Tolle, in his book *A New Earth,* suggests that only when mankind is pushed up against the wall will we make the jump. And it would seem that consciousness invites consciousness: meaning people who are more aware impact those around them, perhaps drawing out a corresponding consciousness, even if this is not immediately visible: this is the meaning of transmission. This is why young people, who are often more open and energised, tend to hang out with others of their own age (as always, there are the exceptions – especially amongst those older people who experienced the openness of the late Sixties and early Seventies, when there was an outburst of lively and optimistic energy and events).

Even when people are not focussed on an overtly 'spiritual' path, they can act as a catalyst. Then, like the wind on a bush fire, when a small fire starts it can spread rapidly. At this time, with varying degrees of awareness, there are prominent figures speaking the language of love and expressing concern for their fellows, speaking out against hate and greed and corruption: from older people like Manuela Carmela, Pope Francis, Bernie Sanders and Jeremy Corbyn to the more youthful such as Ada Colau and Justin Trudeau who, before losing his shine by reneging on major promises, organised local children to sing for refugees from Syria, in Arabic, a song Mohamed the Prophet sang when he himself was a refugee.

So here we all are, occupying this ball spinning in space, *together* – whether we like it or not. In fact, it can be very moving to see pictures of the Earth as this beautiful, pale blue ball suspended in space, as those who have travelled there describe seeing it firsthand. But imagine if the world was covered in tiny lights, both individual and in groups. The nearest we get to seeing something like this is the glow of flying over a city at night: lovely to see all those twinkling lights strung out like jewelled necklaces. But suppose if, instead of electrical street lights, you could see the pulsing emanations of human consciousness? Someone watching from outer space might notice this to be growing and intensifying and spreading out as it meets other groups of consciousness – even as the dark clouds appear to be gathering to smother the planet.

Who knows? Maybe this is all 'just imagination'. But what becomes clearer the deeper you dive into your Being-ness is that nothing is as it appears! And all that the egoic, conditioned mind claims to know is like an old radio broadcast:

disembodied voices recorded somewhere in the past, talking away with no relevance to the present moment.

Personal abilities that support community

For humanity, living in the world in harmony together is clearly not easy, so here are some abilities that are particularly helpful in relating to others in groups and the wider community. All those areas we have been talking about, such as intuition, sensing, feeling and being connected with your body are useful here. As is the ability to imagine, as John Lennon epitomised in his song of that name – *when this is connected with empathy*. These are valuable assets when it comes to being comfortable with differences, this being one of the major discords between humans, this fear of the 'other'.

So for instance, *imagine* and *feel* what life would be like if most people were gay and you were attracted to someone of the *opposite* sex but got maligned, insulted, threatened, beaten up and even put in jail for this. Imagine what it would be like if most of the world was black and you were discriminated against, regularly stop-and-searched, threatened and even killed (as is happening now in the US) if a policeman felt so inclined, just because you were white? Imagine if all the wealth and privilege were suddenly transferred to the working class, whose accents, manners, values and pastimes were seen as superior, and the upper classes and even some of the middle classes, were excluded from certain schools, universities and clubs, from hotels, restaurants, shops, streets, enclaves, parks, blocks of flats, private estates and gated communities; from beaches and even whole islands. Here you see how these qualities of the heart are essential in helping us relax, accept and include our fellow humans *as ourselves*.

Another asset, perhaps surprisingly, is the ability to say 'No'. A lot of our angry or defensive reactions towards others are connected with power: a desire to defend against what we perceive as an attack on, or undermining of, our authority. Or a feeling of powerlessness from not being able to *be* in our authority when confronted. Something that commonly emerges here is the difficulty in saying 'No'; yet, as we noted earlier, if you can't say 'No', how can you say a real 'Yes'? This dilemma usually comes up sooner or later with clients and it brings the potential for a big shift. In approaching this and learning to say 'No', we work with the breath and body – especially the solar plexus (see exercises at the end of this chapter). Although it's helpful to practise this with someone who knows what they are doing, you can also try this at home.

Perhaps surprisingly, you discover that a real 'No' doesn't require you to shout or even raise your voice. *It's all about your energy and what is holding that back.* At first people often feel awkward, especially when their 'No' comes out as a squeak or has a question mark at the end, as in 'No?'; but you *feel* it, you *sense* it, you absolutely *know* it, when you are finally able to speak a true 'No'. It has a simple, quiet, no-nonsense intensity that conveys the truth of your statement to others: *and they get it*. Then this can be the beginning of you feeling comfortable to be in your body, in your true authority, able to say a real 'No' and consequently, a real 'Yes': free to have all of your feelings – a fully feeling, alive human being. Wow!

Another invaluable capacity is acceptance: *real* acceptance that is. We talked about this in the chapter on feelings, but because this insight is fundamental to us living our lives in harmony together, I want to say more about it here. The ability to accept something or someone has both personal and political ramifications, yet it seems many people don't recognise this. In fact, acceptance of our fellow human beings is perhaps the most valuable asset we can develop towards maintaining good relationships in group situations.

If we are able to empathise with others and *accept them as they are,* even though we may not like them or agree with how they see things, so much of benefit to the whole becomes possible. It's easy to say 'turn the other cheek' or 'just practice loving kindness' but working with acceptance is both deep and delicate; it's not easy and it can't be forced, so maybe don't attempt this until you feel ready. A level of inner honesty is required, along with practice of conscious awareness for this to really become genuine. Essentially, it has to do with focussing the heart and letting the judging mind take a holiday.

To repeat: *the ability to let others be as they are is the most quintessential relational ability for living in the world together.* All the things we have been talking about in previous chapters contribute to this. When we are able to recognise our patterns and conditioning and not take things personally, this dissolves so much of the tension and distrust that typifies the behaviour of people who have learned to live by prioritising their own needs before those of others, before the community. Being able to recognise our 'No' and yet accept the is-ness of something allows us to be comfortable with an outcome we might not choose.

For many people, feeling seen and heard is often more important than a particular result, so listening well is a wonderful skill. Being able to sit with yourself and your energy, and just be open and sensitive to what wants to happen, to letting *in* and letting *go,* these are such valuable qualities to bring to any gathering. From this place, the movement of the heart can be trusted to guide any contribution we may feel to make. Watching the mind, you can see how it is filled with wants and desires and expectations and ideas about what and how and why; with 'shoulds' and 'can't' and all the old manoeuvrings of ego. How restful, even joyous if we can simply relax and allow life itself to be as it is!

What other qualities are useful here? Well obviously, there are many. The capacity to become conscious, to see when we are being driven by our egoic mind and emotions, to stay present in our bodies, open to all our feeling, sensing, intuiting capacities; so many aspects that we have been looking at in previous chapters can make a big difference to our ability to live and organise ways of doing this together that optimise the values of the heart. And the following is perhaps one of the most valuable.

Surrender of the personal will

Something that affects how we relate to the community at large is how we use our will – what drives this. Because of this I am including it now, rather than earlier, in the chapter on the mind where I also talk about the will. There seems to be so much misunderstanding about the use of both discipline and will. Will and wanting are connected and, as wanting is a feature of the egoic mind, then so-called *willpower* becomes its servant, focussed on getting what is wanted. Which is why it can be so destructive of harmonious relationships and organising how we all live together.

Once you have decided you want to have or do something, the will behaves like a commander of an army to enforce your doing to achieve whatever it is that you want. So if you want to run a marathon, willpower appears essential to achieving this. If you want to pass a difficult exam or finish redecorating the house to a deadline, your will is required. And if you want to meditate, you may use the will to try to make yourself do so; at least initially, you are likely to use it to overrule messages of discomfort from the body and try to control your thoughts.

In the egoic mind-driven society in which we live, the use of the will is greatly encouraged, *especially in men*: the will to get top marks in class, the will to be the best at sports, to get to the top of your profession, to make a lot of money – the *will to succeed* at whatever you do. But who *really* cares if you succeed or fail? Both are simply *experiences,* to which the mind attaches pain, pleasure, excitement or fear. We use the expression 'driven' to indicate this need to succeed and avoid failure at all costs. The will is a big part of what is seen as a masculine virtue and tends to be more used by men to get what they want, whereas women may use more subtle means (again, I am generalising as both can do both).

Essentially though, will tends to be used to coerce, force and demand; and also, to overcome. It is a distinctive energy that uses pressure: it pushes for or against to achieve what is wanted. I *will* climb that mountain or I *will not* go to school today. I *will* make you do this, I *will* stop you doing that. Will also holds on: I will never give up, let you go, etc. As in wil*ful*: will-full means full of will. In action movies, where it gets played out to extremes, words like 'gritty' and 'tough' are used in association with this, and determination is venerated – especially determination to win against all the odds. In this we can see that will is the very opposite of surrender, and so a big misunderstanding about will and power is uncovered, along with what is driving this.

In a sense will is blind: it relies on guidance to function and when used by the egoic mind it has an insistent, even ruthless quality that tends to override an inner sense that might be telling us to give way. We can see this most clearly around the will to dominate. This is one of the most common tendencies of the negative masculine that stands out. Domination is the ultimate pinnacle of the will *when it is in service to the egoic mind*: a mixture of power and control. Here, will can be seen to function like a cord that keeps us tightly bound and holds out against the process of collapsing.

My own experience of will used in this way is it has a narrow focus that is energetically very yang: felt in the body and used to achieve something I want, it has a hard, tight, pushing force that I feel in the gut. Uninhibited, it can push and push back – hence the expression that someone is being 'pushy'. I remember noticing one day, when I was trying to pull up some weeds with ginormous roots, what was happening as I used my will to do this. The world got smaller and smaller as the focus on these weeds and my determination to uproot them, took hold. I didn't care that I was cutting my hands, that my mouth was screwed into a hard, tight grimace and I was getting short of breath. I was going to get those bloody roots out no matter what it cost!

When combined with discipline, will has a stern, demanding quality that easily hooks into 'shoulds'. I see discipline as mental control over the act of will, based on an inner determination that feels like a fist; as such it can be dangerous, as it carries a purpose that is being controlled by the egoic mind, making it heart-less. And yet the will can bring great strength and fortitude and allow us to do things we would otherwise be unable to: it can allow us to triumph over our fear and resistance to achieve things of great value. It teaches us that we *can*, despite all the odds.

Pure will – as in the will to live – is a response of the instinctual body towards survival that has no mental input. So when will is guided through the intuitive heart it can serve a useful function; then it moves in response to this, which may involve such things as holding one's ground or staying focussed; then it is benign, *then* it can be both gentle yet firm. We could call this 'soft will' and it feels quite different in the body. The heart's word for will is actually 'will*ing*', and willing implies soft, open and flowing. When in service to Being, will has the quality of *moving towards what we love* – which could be described as the positive masculine principle in action (in either men or women). So one is moved to action through a pull that is free from force and comfortable in the body.

It is interesting to discover that *once the conscious capacity to listen in and follow one's flow is established*, the will itself is no longer needed, and this can be very confronting for a man, especially if this has been a major factor in the way he has come to know himself *as a man*. In fact, what I am saying around will can raise fear-laden questions like 'But without willpower how would I get up in the morning?', 'How would I get anything done?' or even 'Who would go to war to defend our country?' This is a very sticky aspect of our conditioning, tied in as it is with morality, a sense of duty and the Protestant work ethic: the idea that we need to develop will in order to achieve anything. As children know so well, this especially applies to *making ourselves do things we don't want to do*. Which is where the question 'Who or what wants this?' or 'Where is the instruction to act coming from?' is so useful.

All of this raises another, more fundamental question: what has happened to us that we have created a life where there is so little enjoyment that we need to force ourselves to do things? This question speaks not only to our collective human lives but also to the unresolved personal baggage that we lug around, that prevents us from enjoying what is already here and engaging with life willingly, joyfully. Which is, of course, what this book is about and what unpacking our baggage can allow us to reclaim. It's our lost property, if you like: our lost connection with Being. And this relates very much to surrender of the personal will. Or another way of expressing that is *recognising what we truly love*. The great Indian sage Ramana Maharshi is quoted as saying *'Surrender is complete only when you can say Thy will be done'*, but until this is seen by the heart it remains as a moral injunction of the 'should-ing' mind.

With this insight about the use of the will we can see how the masculine, action-directed way of responding, *when connected with the heart*, moves from a willingness to serve, transforming an egoic drive into a loving response. There is a relaxation of the body within which a subtle pull to act can be *felt*. We discover that, unlike mind-controlled will, this doesn't cause any tension: quite the reverse – there is a joy in following this pull of the beloved that melts away any resistances and old sticky threads of wanting for oneself. *Something* wants, in the sense of *is moved towards something*, but this is as an expression of love. What this may look like the mind has no idea. This that follows the subtle directives of the heart knows that mind does not need to know, so has no problem with this. And this initially requires trust, which grows exponentially as we glimpse who we really are and what life *actually* is. Then, being in service to Being means being in service to the whole, to the oneness in which life manifests *and of which we are an integral part*.

It is wonderful to see that with love there is no need for discipline, *because there is another way to move* that is not ego-driven. What a shame that when Jesus said 'Thy will be done' – implying surrender to the greater whole – *the way Christianity has been taught* so misunderstands and misrepresents this: creating a false hierarchy where there can be none, teaching obedience to dogma and faith in belief, and in so doing denying direct experience of God, separating action from joy, substituting duty for delight and robbing us of our innocence.

Fortunately, what can never be taken away is our capacity to listen *in*, to connect directly through our heart to Being and follow that which cannot be subjected to any of this. *When it comes from a spontaneous connection with the heart*, surrender of our will not only allows action to happen beyond the egoic drive to get for ourselves, it clears the way for Being to take charge. And then we may even become ecstatic as we recognise the true meaning of this phrase. The term 'free will' then signifies a clear choice: we are free to follow egoic mind (to eat the apple?) in all its many guises, or to surrender to the call of Being. Jesus and others say we have this choice, whereas those of the non-dual spiritual tradition say we don't (because there is no-one here to choose). Either way, the egoic mind thinks it knows best and doesn't trust anything beyond itself. It knows nothing of unity; operating in the world of duality it knows only division, and sees opposing or conquering opposition as necessary. It wants to be king of the castle (perhaps believing its rule will be benign?). And here, as we keep noting, mind cannot and was never designed to comprehend the fullness that is life: this lies beyond its abilities.

So then what surrendering to Being means is that if a movement occurs, it can only be what is needed and appropriate to that moment. For it would seem the whole has the means to resolve the 'problems' of the parts; to dissolve the illusion of division and return to unity: in other words to awaken to itself.

The longing to belong

So here we are, each with our individual experience of what we call 'reality', a reality that includes sharing this world together whether we like it or not. This vastness that some call God, has eyes everywhere and our particular viewpoint is one of them. Sooner or later we discover there is nowhere to escape to, because whatever we do, wherever we go, we take ourselves with us; we carry our own unique lens through which we see and experience what comes to us. So doesn't it just make sense to address whatever is in the way of us being *fully* here, *fully* alive, able to enjoy each moment? And as part of this, move to find ways to live together that help us love and care for one another, instead of fearing and fighting?

It's easy to believe that all we have to do is somehow wake up and everything will miraculously transform into a blissful and benign world. But what if life *itself* – and being here in a body as part of this, present to all apparent difficulty and pain – what if this is where we need to *fully be* in order to extend awakening into becoming not just a conscious part of this whole but able to respond truthfully, with love? In relationship with life *as it is*? Awakening *to* rather than *from* life? Then the most profound questions arise 'If life itself is already fully conscious, how do we humans manage to become unconscious?' and 'Where did our sense of separation come from?'

In a broadcast he called *Belonging: The Sacred Core of Community*, Adyashanti said this: *'We never feel like we completely belong until we belong to ourselves first.'* which is a truth that underlies all attempts at forming community. In fact, togetherness and community are interesting words, suggesting as they do that we *all* belong, all are part of something. But it's only when we connect with our Being-ness, *with who we really are,* that this can become a reality; as we remember that the ground of all relationships that honour our real nature is love, that this can be truly lived. Then the intuitive, sensing, feeling realms are where we best know this.

I sense that many people deeply feel this longing to re-find a sense of belonging so that, when we can unearth our courage to stop hiding and, instead, determine to live from this intuitively-felt sense of wholeness, we can finally come home. Home? Yes home: maturing beyond the child-like cry of ET, seeking a far-away place where we will be re-claimed by our family (and feel safe and looked after), to answer the song of the body-Being calling us home: *calling us to live from a different place* – as in from what we truly *are* – to live within Being, as Being.

The amazing thing about discovering you are nothing is that, simultaneously, *you realise you belong to everything.* The circle is joined; eternity is in front of your eyes. In the finding of what is true an end is put to belief: belief that has become transmuted into such a fundamental sense of separation that we fear losing ourselves in the depth of the sorrow this engenders. No wonder so few seem willing to risk going there; suppose we never find our way back? And then whoops! the mist clears and we recognise there is and never was an 'I'; there is only and ever the mystery of 'this'. And we never had to go anywhere to find it. Aaah! At last we can rest, together as One.

Home-play
1. Asserting your 'No'
- Firstly, make sure you are standing with your feet well planted on the floor, check that your knees aren't locked and that your hips are neither wedged back nor thrust forward, but positioned comfortably above your feet.
- Breathe into the Solar Plexus and connect with this centre (maybe placing a hand here) and practise saying 'No' from here. It is important that you then immediately take a breath, remembering to breath all the way out. See if you can feel the energy descending into your body on the out-breath. Crucially, this breath allows what you are doing to be integrated in the body. At first you may barely feel any strength in the solar plexus, but after a while you may notice the energy here becoming more stable and strong, or even pushing outwards.
- [a] Repeat this until you can feel a strong connection (you might want to do this in front of a mirror so you can also practise holding eye contact while you speak). Notice the timbre of your voice changing as you repeat the 'No': the loudness, and any tension in the body.

2. Asserting your 'No' while accepting the other as they are

This is how the body speaks, allowing you to integrate a subtle but very powerful internal movement for change and complete this shift within the body.

- Sitting comfortably, choose one of your arms to represent asserting your 'No' and the other to represent letting the other *be as they are*.
- Now allow the arm that is embodying acceptance to open and extend outwards in a soft, flowing movement, extending the wrist so palm opens face-up in a welcoming and accepting gesture. Repeat, allowing yourself to feel this sensation of acceptance within you each time (Remember, never fake or force this).
- Now bring attention to the other arm and, keeping the forearm in a vertical position, edge of palm facing away from you, raise and bring arm down in a clean, firm line like a guillotine (without moving the rest of the body). Repeat feeling this sensation of a clear, firm, assertive but non-aggressive 'No'.
- Then alternately express these two felt sensations, via the movement of your arms; as you do so noticing how difficult it may be to allow one, or perhaps both, of these.

Many of us live in perpetual inner conflict, continually moving from one to the other, all of this usually being unconscious. When you are able to maintain both and be aware of each at the same time, you will notice a tremendous sense of relaxation and relief. Acceptance and your 'No' can co-exist. You can have both! But in order for this to happen you have to make space within yourself, and this can take time so be patient.

3. Giving back

- Sitting somewhere or with something you find beautiful, connect with your heart. Allow your awareness to completely fill up with this sensory feast.
- Now consciously project this rich loveliness out into the world. You may choose to direct this to a particular cause or leave it general. Sense the love that (appears to) pour in and pour out of the heart as you do this.

This exercise is dependent of your capacity to fully receive and fully give, so it makes a great practice in letting go of all defences and opening into the alive heart.

4. Welcoming the world into your heart through the body

- Sitting comfortably, take a moment to ground, feel the cradle and connect with the body before focussing attention in the heart.
- Then, from this embodied place, allow a sense of inviting the Earth into your heart through the energy body, drawing it in through the breath: making space for it, receiving it, welcoming it, loving it.

- Start with the physical elements like the mountains and deserts, forests and rivers, islands, plains and seas. You can use visualisation, but this can stay quite cerebral so see if you can include *sensing* these, *feeling* these, breathing these *in* (this is very subtle).
- Return to resting your attention in your body and breath.
- Next, include the elements like the wind, rain, snow, ice and fire
- Repeat the return,
- Follow this with all the creatures that live on the earth and in the sea (a proper Noah's Ark!)
- Repeat the return,
- Next include all the peoples
- Repeat the return.
- Lastly, extend your awareness to include all the past and all the future of this world as a living entity
- Repeat the return.
- Feel the gratitude in your heart for this miraculous world, that provides your body with a home and feel the blessedness in everything.

5. The Song of Being

I open my arms to embrace all that ever has been and ever will be of myself
As the sun – I bless you with my touch
As the rivers – I weep for you with my tears
As the vastness of the sky – I welcome you
As the trees swaying in the breeze – I worship you
As the mountain peaks standing proud – I honour you
From the biggest rock to the tiniest grain of sand – I revere you
As the earth – I sustain you
As the wind – I uplift you
As the flowers – I grace you with beauty and delight
As the rainclouds – I shower you with soft, liquid balm
As the sea – I absolve you of all ignorance, and bury your sorrows in my deeps
And with the dark night I gather you into my arms once more
Nothing goes unseen, unheard, unfelt, untouched
Everything included
Nothing is excluded
Everything is welcome
Everything returns.

NOTE: The Song of Being has been set to music and is available as a download at www.moramcintyre.com (Music, singing and guitar by Hanna Burchell).

Practical suggestions for coming free

'What makes anything difficult is if you are unwilling to fully experience it. What makes anything easy is if you are willing to experience everything.' ~ Gangaji

'Courage is not the absence of fear. It is, rather, the presence of fear, with the courage to face it' ~ Osho

'What is in the way, is the way' ~ (from stoic philosophy)

Everything I am talking about in this book is intended to support this process of unravelling, but not in the ways we are conditioned to expect. We have all been trained, on identifying a problem, to ask 'how can I fix this?', when the irony is – on the inner levels anyway – the very effort of trying to fix something stops whatever needs to happen from happening, in its own way, its own time. This is an example of how we get in our own way. Instead of relaxing and being present to ourselves we try to control the process. Unravelling suggests coming free from something, so what is it that unravels? The egoic grip that has wound itself around you like a spider enveloping its prey. And the amazing thing is that as you come to recognise this and shine the light of awareness onto it, this whole illusory edifice slowly starts to crumble and, eventually, to blow away like so much dust. Time seems to be needed, courage and willingness certainly, but your own strengthening sense of connection to Being will support and sustain you. Remember, *everything you need is always available and keeps presenting itself over and over until it is seen.*

What is contained in this edifice I refer to? All our conditioned beliefs gathered from others, all the erroneous conclusions we made as a child; the patterns of behaviour and emotionalised attachments that keep us firmly treading the hamster wheel, enveloped in the confusion and suffering that results from all this. Because the bald truth is, if your are seeking your identity through the egoic mind – whether with the support of conventional therapy or counselling or your own efforts alone – you will never be free. As Osho points out *'Everybody wants freedom as far as talking is concerned, but nobody is really free and nobody really wants to be free, because freedom brings responsibility. It does not come alone. And to be dependent is simple: the responsibility is not on you, the responsibility is on the person you are dependent on.'*

So in this chapter I want to extend the content to assist this unravelling process. There is not space in one chapter, or indeed one volume, to write all that is seen that can help, but here are what seem to be the most useful insights. And, as you get more comfortable with both not knowing, and also trusting what little you *do* know, it gets easier. There seems to be a threshold over which we cross – often without knowing it – where one day we are living in this world of make-believe, fully convinced of our story about it, and the next we find our eyes have started to open, and we glimpse reality and realise we can't go back to sleep, even if we wanted to! Before that point, people carry on living with complaining and blaming, grumbling and resisting; or else we do the getting-on-with-it thing: putting up with it, lowering our expectations and trying to be cheerful. We may get excited about something, get our hopes up, even feel briefly elated, and then – crash! They get dashed again and we feel disappointed, even disillusioned and sink into a what's-the-point funk. We find distractions to keeps us going, or we switch off, shut down, get depressed, give up. This is the story of most people's lives.

Then there is struggle – struggle to survive or to get more, to keep what we have, to 'make something' of our lives and, when this doesn't work, we sit back and watch someone else doing it or getting it on television. *The truth is, living unconsciously isn't really much fun.* Of course there are moments when the sun breaks through: we fall in love, a neighbour goes out of their way to help us out, we carry our sleeping child up into bed and stop a moment to watch it's pink and tender innocence, we get together with friends and have a good laugh. There are good things that happen and surprising acts of kindness all over the place. However, because most of us are so filled with other people's judgements and our own projections towards others, along with reactive emotions and erroneous beliefs and almost no sense of what is real or indeed, how to be ourselves, then living like this just goes on creating suffering: on so many levels. And all of it needless.

Images can be powerful, and one way of describing the crucial connection with Being that can make such a difference would be to compare it to an isthmus, or a causeway that we can cross over when the tide is out. So when the waves of our conditioned, emotionalised mind have temporarily withdrawn we catch a glimpse across the pristine white sand of what lies on the other side: Being waiting patiently, forever if need be. In that moment, our intuitive body makes the leap to unite with Being – for an instant we are joined, we are one. So even when the tide returns, we have more of this connection with Being, more intuitive, sensory familiarity with what is real; we remember what we *do* know. It is *this* that draws us into love and clarity, out of illusion; *this* that keeps us moving towards what we cannot describe but sense a deep yearning for; *this* is our means, our fuel, our sustenance – this brings us all that we need.

So here are some more insights, suggestions, illustrations and further material to look into around this whole movement towards becoming conscious, fully alive – in other words, support for the process of coming undone! Putting these kind of exercises in a book is always tricky. For instance there is the issue of *timing*. Working with a 'professional' in some form allows for guidance around this; if they are fully present and tuned in to the client, they can support or suggest something that feels appropriate at that time and not before. On our own, however, because the mind is always listening in, to try and use whatever it hears for its own ends, it can interfere with this delicate process of timing.

So in doing exercises from a book, it is important to tune in to your own intuitive *felt sense* of what feels right for you *at that time*. This makes it easier to avoid doing something the body is not yet ready for. For example, when the control of the mind is still too powerful, or when you are not yet able to ground and connect with your body, you can get hooked into egoic patterns of wanting to achieve and 'make progress', and these can override subtle inner promptings to slow down or wait. This is where the old adage about not trying to learn to run before you can walk, applies. So *things that are newly seen need time to be ingested into the body.* Also, many of these exercises are extremely subtle and this makes them difficult to translate in a book. Hopefully, as you tune in and listen to your body, all this will become easier; you will *feel for yourself* what is useful and when, and adapt this if necessary.

Make a three-dimensional object representing the mind

The bringing of nebulous, abstract and conceptual material into concrete physical form is – in my experience – both extremely useful and effective. So effective that, when I ask people to do this at home (make a physical representation of something) I find they will often 'forget' or resist in some way. Because this involves *actualising* something that has been glimpsed rather than just agreeing to the *idea* of it. This actualising is far more powerful, especially when this challenges mind as a construct. So, for instance, I have spoken about how the mind gets a lot of its power by remaining hidden. In fact, so much about the mind seems intangible; we can't grasp hold of it. With the brain we have an image, we know what it looks like physically, but the mind has no size, shape, texture, colour, smell or any kind of sensory identity. So we have to give it one! To bring it into some kind of physical manifestation – if only in a representative form.

There are so many ways a concrete embodiment can be constructed. Keep it simple or make it as complicated as you like. It is not important what it is called, or how and from what constructed: anything from cardboard, cloth, clay, bone, leather, straw, foam, wire, wood, stone; it can include photographs, buttons, nails or jewels; seaweed, glitter, flowers, string, leaves, feathers, shells, etc. – get creative and enjoy the making. As you select your materials, stay alert to a *felt sense:* a pull, an inexplicable *feeling,* which may or may not carry an association. The object can be named or not, have labels or pins attached, be painted, varnished, sewn or glued together: whatever. The important thing is *you are externalising, objectifying and giving form to the inner realm.*

Pocket reminders

Okay: the following includes some more specific suggestions, along with aspects of this unravelling process that tend to cause the most difficulty. So another thing you can do is make a kind of doll or puppet that you carry around in your pocket to take out and look at, and even converse with – *if you are willing to do this* (I say this because many people find this surprisingly challenging). You can make this personification of mind out of an old sock or stocking, stuffed with the same, or with paper tissues or even newspaper; with buttons sewed on either side for eyes, loops of wool for hair, stitches for a mouth: whatever you feel to make it effective. If this feels too much for you, you can just draw these on with a felt tip pen.

This object can actually represent anything you want it to. As it is a *representation* of the mind, this process allows for it to be both solidified and externalised. Or it could represent your 'inner child' that wants to tell you something or be reassured, or a character in a pattern that you see yourself acting out, that keeps repeating, etc. By the very act of making this concrete object you are already separating out in the most subtle way and lessening the mind's power over you. Yet another thing you can do is paint or draw images of the mind – abstract or literal, whatever works for you – and pin these up somewhere. It helps too if you can bring some fun and laughter into this process, keeping it light.

Other things it is useful to carry in your pockets are pebbles or stones to hold for grounding, or perhaps a chunk of rose quartz to remind you of the heart. You can use touching these solid objects as a way of staying in contact with yourself, calm and present: of being aware of your reactions when you are in a difficult situation around others, for instance. The beauty of this is that no one need know what you are doing. With all these things, get into your creativity and remember: these simple things can be extraordinarily powerful, seemingly out of all proportion to what they actually *are.*

Do you remember the most effective way to stifle the movement towards aliveness? Ridicule! So see if you can drop your concern about what others might think, any oh-so-inhibiting conditioning. Learn to be comfortable looking foolish; turn towards yourself with gentleness when you feel embarrassed; give space to feelings of shyness and unsureness; love your vulnerability. *To be vulnerable also means to be open and available.* (Obviously, you don't just walk out onto a motorway saying 'hey, come and get me guys, I am available!'. There will be times when you do need to protect yourself, but don't let these jell into habitual reflexes.)

Preventing reengagement with the mind's story

Have you ever changed a puncture on a bicycle? As you attempt to pull the outer rubber tyre off the wheel to get at the inner tube, it reattaches itself again as you move around the wheel: so as fast as you disengage one end, the other reengages. What you do to stop this happening is you insert pieces of flat metal bent at one end, called bicycle levers, between the metal rim of the wheel and the tyre, which keeps it from reattaching again until you have got it all off. Disengaging from the mind's story is something similar, so the exercises at the end of this chapter, as well as the puppet, can all function as useful reminders: as 'levers' to stop the story regaining its control over you (through getting your attention and belief).

Keep a scorecard

Another useful practice is to get a special notebook and use this as a scorecard. So, perhaps at the end of each day, stop and take stock, giving yourself marks out of ten: 'What did I see through today? How often did I spot conditioned mind? A pattern? An emotional reaction? A projection? What was I able to let go of?', etc. Do this for a week or so until it becomes natural, then whenever you feel to. It can feel a bit arbitrary at first, a bit strange, so it's important to keep it playful. And I strongly suggest you *don't* write comments all over it, don't turn this into any kind of journal; the problem with words is they invite in the mind, with all its judgements and analysis and capacity to spin endlessly stories around the *idea* of 'you making progress': don't go there – this is a game! You could use coloured stickers instead of numbers, for instance, or stars. Remember, what is of great value with this scorecard is that while you are keeping it, *you are observing the mind*. You are, in a sense, outside, looking in – in at this mind and its behaviours; you have it under the lens of awareness so you gain a distance. In this context any process where you are *looking at the mind* is useful.

Conscious tennis

Whenever you are changing an old habitual response – like a reaction to something – there will be times you will recognise what is happening, and you may be able to catch yourself before you react: and other times you won't, or not until it's too late. So sometimes you catch the ball, sometimes you drop it, as with tennis or any ball game. Watch out here for self-attack when you don't catch it, when you fail to live up to some expectation creeping in, and drop the attack, let this go too (another item for the score card). What you can be sure of is that even when you drop the ball, another opportunity will soon come along for you to practise catching it.

What would happen, for instance, how might your life be different if you simply acted – and moved on? If someone was upset with you, or you had an uncomfortable feeling after an interaction, you looked to see if you were acting out of reaction: out of an old pattern; and if so you forgave yourself, apologised to the other person if this felt needed, and moved on? That way, life becomes a constant next, next, and next – just like fielding a ball in a game of tennis. Easily said but not so easily done, certainly, but then all changes take time; often rather longer than we would like, sometimes even years (though if we do have past lives, possibly millions of them, then making these kinds of changes within just one lifetime is truly miraculous!). It soon becomes obvious that by pulling us into thinking about the past, mind prevents us from enjoying the present. So, good to practise catching the ball!

Backstitch

Anyone who is familiar with hand-sewing will know about backstitch. You make a stitch, taking the needle through the cloth to join it together, and then you go back on it with another stitch to secure it in place. If you fail to do this it easily comes undone. So one of the things you notice after a while in this movement towards freedom is that for every step you take, it is necessary to go back and secure the 'thread', and you begin to see how you are revisiting places that seem familiar. Or we could liken this movement to a spiral where we go around the circle and appear to end up in the same place, whereas in actuality we are now on a different, deeper level.

Weebles – a useful symbol

You know how a weeble works? Those objects that have a rounded, heavy base on which they pivot? So if you push it or it falls over in any direction, it always returns to its upright position, sitting on its base. This is you in this process of coming back to yourself: to Being. So you will keep falling over (getting caught in the mind) but the more you keep returning to this base to rest, the easier it gets, until it becomes almost a reflex.

Getting to know the Grand Inquisitor

Many people are afraid of the harsh voices inside of their heads: 'Look at the mess you made!', 'You deserved that, you are such a stupid idiot', 'You are a useless (selfish, nasty, boring, cowardly – change the adjectives) person' or the more insidious 'Yes, you got that right, you are (therefore) a good (clever, nice, acceptable) person'. Nice, nasty, good, bad, right, wrong – *you* are always on the other end of this that assesses you: *just as long as you believe it*. And you will believe it until you are able to trust something else. In the meantime, it's always useful to get familiar with it and have fun! Once again images are powerful, so make an image of this tyrant and stick it on your mirror or your wall as a visible reminder of this internal character, always waiting to judge, criticise and condemn. Do you remember the child's game, 'Pin the tail on the donkey?'. Well, you don't have to blindfold yourself to just stick anything you feel like onto this character – could be a funny nose, a pair of boobs, a piece of chewing gum. Resurrect your child and get creative!

Changing attitudes

Perhaps some of the most powerful solvents we can apply to our stuck spaces come in the form of changing the ways we look at life, and at what is happening within and around us – in other words our attitudes. This can create a real shift. I am absolutely *not* talking about efforting to be positive and suppressing negative thoughts here: this is a much-advertised phoney solvent from the same makers as the conditioned mind. It may make us feel better for a while but ultimately, the ego is the ego, is the ego and it requires to be seen *through*; it can't be got rid of, it has to be lived *with* until – finally – it is no longer believed. Here it is just so useful to look at everything that you are experiencing that upsets you in others, as being about *you*. Not in terms of some sort of self-obsessed indulgence or flagellatory condemnation, but almost the opposite: recognise that what occurs in your life, and what others present to you, is often attracted *by* you, and can be used to show you where you are caught or stuck. Seen like this, everything becomes a potential gift.

Worthy Opponents and Free Workshops

Learn to see everyone you are relating with as a 'worthy opponent'. People often feel uncomfortable about using others (although the ego does this all the time, albeit below the radar), but using others to become conscious is quite different: then it is wonderful! And see all situations – especially difficult ones – as being a 'free workshop': this is another great weapon for your arsenal, another tool that can help prise you out of stuck spaces and set you on the road to freedom.

Remembering not to take minds' dictates seriously

We easily forget the mind is not who we are, so it's incredibly useful to practice reminders. Here is a very simple but powerful way to do this. It depends for its effectiveness on you being able to notice the seductive approach of a juicy judgmental thought, like 'Look at that old woman making a spectacle of herself, chatting up that young man!' or 'Of course they shouldn't have done that. I told them so at the time but they wouldn't listen to me' or 'I so wish I hadn't let my brother's wife treat me like that, I am such a coward. Next time...' – make up your own. Now stop, and simply say to your mind 'No comment'. It's funny and it works! Try it for yourself. I can't emphasise enough the importance of having fun with all this. Not getting all tense and serious. So, for example, next time you spot your egoic mind up to its tricks, you could call out, 'Yoo-hoo! I see you!' Because one of the ways egoic mind tries to keep you under control is by making you feel foolish, childish: an idiot. Don't fall for it!

Understanding the power of feelings and emotions to control us

A fundamental insight it is useful to remain constantly aware of: *we are controlled by the feelings we resist* (for 'feelings' read 'feelings and emotions'). Some people teach that we are controlled by our beliefs, but in my experience it is the feelings that underlie these that actually control us; *especially our fear of feeling uncomfortable feelings*, feelings that are awkward, painful or scary to feel, so we act on an unconscious desire to avoid these. This includes conflicting feelings that have become enmeshed – feelings we could not untangle as a child when we didn't have the resources, the insight, the support or the space.

This unconscious pattern of avoidance becomes habitual, and if we are not aware of it we can't change it. *So the seeing of this becomes the essence of our power;* ultimately, this enables us to come free from victimhood and the fear of being controlled by others. Much like an animal that has been kept in a cage for years, we will go on pacing too and fro even when the door is open. I remember watching an experiment with a chicken on a friend's farm and it was quite amazing to see what happened. If you put a length of wire mesh fencing that is only a couple of metres long in front of it, the chicken will run about half a metre each way, to and fro, to and fro trying to escape, for hours. It never realises that the fence is limited: that it could just walk around it and come free.

Accessing feelings

'Just feel your feelings': it can sound so easy to say, can't it? But people have had good reasons for suppressing these, especially if they are frightening or painful, so accessing feelings isn't always possible at first. When this happens, don't rationalise by telling yourself if you can't feel anything it must be because there is nothing there to feel. Don't try to force entry either, through some powerful breathing technique or drug, or whatever. And don't make yourself wrong. Just visit the spot from time to time. You may sense it as being like standing on the edge of a volcano, or a black tunnel; a bottomless well, an icy chasm or a sheer cliff. You don't need to do anything; just sit quietly and be patient. Make yourself comfortable: bring a deckchair and a flask of something warm to drink, take out a novel or your knitting and just hang out there – you get the picture.

When you are present in this way, without expectations, without demanding anything, it can be surprising what emerges. As you learn to trust your body's innate capacity in this way, it makes the connection *with* and integration *of* feelings so much easier. Then we see that as we are able to meet these – thereby taking care of our own baggage – so we become less reactive and more able to respond to others without taking things personally.

Cutting through drama

Through meeting our underlying feelings, becoming aware of our reactions and familiar with our patterns, we gain an opportunity to cut through drama. However, if you leave the first bit out – about meeting feelings – this will operate on a cerebral level and be disconnected from your body. Then, when you relate with another person, the resulting ambivalence is likely to be *felt* by them (whether you're communicating face-to-face, over the phone, by letter, email or text), and this will continue the drama. The ability to cut through drama relies for its effectiveness on a direct and practical use of conscious awareness, *and also on an energetic connection with your feeling body.*

To make this clearer here are a couple of examples. of how drama plays out. Daughter to mother: 'You never support me' (overt statement of accusation and blame, containing covert plea for support). Mother to daughter: 'Yes I do, look at all the money I've lent you, of course I do!' (reacting out of hurt, guilt and feeling trapped, moves into justifying and feeling unfairly treated). What would happen if the mother had done enough of her own homework so she could *recognise* her old reaction and, instead, simply respond to the covert plea with 'Would you *like* me to help you?'.

This goes to the essence of the interaction. Here, the mother, by remaining conscious and present with herself, cuts through the drama-inviting game by not going into reaction (in this case, her own hurt and aggrieved 'inner child', along with fear of her daughter's anger). It is important to see that the mother will only *be able to do this* if she has met her *own* feelings. Then, this simple reply to her daughter *requires the daughter to take responsibility for acknowledging what she wants* (acknowledging both to herself and to her mother). So this is a potential game changer for both. In stripping away the drama, it requires both mother *and* daughter to face both themselves and their relationship – the fear of doing this being the cause of the games we play in the first place! (This particular dynamic will not play out with all mothers and daughters, of course, but it is typical of many.)

In the second example, we see how drama is created by beliefs that protect us from accessing painful feelings. So, a man is talking about his parental family: 'They always criticise and undermine me, they never appreciate or value what I am doing' (expressing anger, resentment and blame). When asked the question 'Would you *like* them to appreciate and value you?', he replies 'they will *never* do that!' (the belief: they won't change). The same question is repeated. He then replies 'They are all so stupid' (blame: it's their fault). The question is repeated a third time, and this time he replies 'I don't care anyway' (denial).

Can you spot the painful feelings that lie underneath this? *The feelings these responses are protecting him from*? These are the intense pain of always *wanting* to be appreciated and valued and *never getting this* from his family, and the enormous feeling of helplessness this engendered in him. So for this man to ask them directly for what he wants, he has to face his pain (and rage) at not getting this, and his feeling of helplessness to bring about change. Up to this point, this man felt safer to continue the drama than to look at his own deep feelings. However, on recognising this, he chose to take his courage and face both feelings and family, with honesty. Here is one last provocative quote from Osho that relates to this: *'You feel good, you feel bad, and these feelings are bubbling from your own unconsciousness, from your own past. Nobody can make you angry, and nobody can make you happy'*

Expressing anger

Perhaps one of the most challenging feelings to come to terms with is anger, hence its power to keep us tightly bound. Anger can be frightening – both to express and to receive – because we are not encouraged to express our anger in healthy ways, but instead to repress it; we are afraid it may get us into trouble, we may do something we will later regret. Men, especially big men, fear they may lose it and hurt someone. So in getting to know our anger we may need to get some help (and if you are one of those people who never get angry and therefore believe you have none, take a deeper look – with care!). But whatever we do, it is important that we become familiar with anger and can accept it, instead of rejecting or denying it. Remember, anger can be our friend too, it has its place; once again, anchored in the body-Being it is safe.

It's in the explosion of old repressed anger that has become reactive to provocation, that the danger lies. So it is vital that we remain in our bodies and *breathe*. Like a kettle about to boil over, we can then hear the whistle, take a breath and release the pressure. What I have seen is that the more connected with our body-Being we are, the less we find ourselves getting angry; because anger is no longer hooking into reactive mind, where all the old grudges and resentments are stored. We are no longer sitting on it and holding back, so we can be more relaxed.

Speaking the truth to each other

Most people rarely tell each other the truth. We tell ourselves this is because we don't want to hurt the other, but if we look closely and are willing to be honest, we see this is because *we don't want their response and how this will make us feel*. We don't want to receive their hurt, rejection, anger, blame, shame – whatever this triggers in *them*. This can make *us* feel bad, *us* feel guilty; and this is uncomfortable, and we may fear losing the relationship we have with them. We likely don't tell *ourselves* the truth about our actions and non-actions either, nor the real reason for these. For instance, we may have a self-image that wants to be seen as nice and kind, that would suffer if we spoke out. Either way we are not being honest with ourselves: we don't tell the truth.

I am not talking here about going unconscious and throwing our projections around onto others, disguised as the truth. Nor am I talking about a sort of in-your-face rudeness or unnecessary criticism. Like when someone goes up to a friend at a party and says 'I must be honest, that dress really doesn't suit you!' or 'To be frank Bertie, I find your anecdotes about the war utterly boring' – truthfulness is not a licence to be unkind under the guise of honesty. But we know when this is happening, if we tune in we can *feel* where we are coming from. We are talking about self-awareness here, along with a clear intention to speak our truth. We are talking about bringing consciousness into our lives and living from this, living with others in alignment with the heart. *And this is not easily done*.

It takes courage and the willingness to be there for yourself when doing this brings up uncomfortable feelings. It helps to recognise that, when you are able to come from a true space (i.e. not motivated by ego), however much other people may resist this or become upset, it's actually *always what they need*. The beautiful thing about all this is it begins to bring a sense of openness and – ultimately – trust, and an opportunity to go deeper. Because truth is connected with openness and sincerity, and sincerity is infectious: it can transform apparently limited and banal situations into something fresh and of potential value to everyone present.

Getting up close and personal with fear

Next time you feel fear, turn to face it. Stop and take a really good look, using all your senses to check it out. Where in the body do you feel it? What colour is it? Does it have a smell? A taste? A shape? Is it warm or cold? Smooth or prickly? Hard or soft? Notice any related feelings of panic, how it affects your body. Is there trembling? Tightness somewhere? A clenching? Maybe holding the breath? Keep investigating: How big is the fear? Does it feel overwhelming or is it more of a slight nervousness? Is there anything it wants to tell you? When you can't find an answer to any of these questions, don't push it or make yourself wrong. We are just exploring something here, getting to know a visitor, usually a regular one. So take your time and notice how, when you examine fear like this, it likely changes in some way; it's ability to affect you, your relationship with it may change too. But remember, this is not about trying to get rid of fear or control it. If you can just let go of all expectations what needs to happen can happen, and this can be very subtle; it may appear as a chink or a shift in this energy of fear some while afterwards – maybe a very long while.

The importance of breathing

The breath and fully breathing are crucial to unravelling, and there are so many options to remember to breathe and be still. For me, this happens when I have to catch a flight in the early hours of the morning (I set two, even sometimes three, alarms or I can't sleep) or dealing with some form of technology, when my body quickly becomes tense. So in order to relax again I have to remember to breathe, deep and slow; to stop and be still, bringing my attention to the presence or stillness of Being *that is already here.* Nothing else works, so a great practice! In interactions with others where they or I behave in ways I find difficult, again I have to stop and breathe and take a moment to connect with stillness. In fact life itself continually provides reminders to practise this and, when I am relaxed, to enjoy it, to appreciate all the little things. We are given so much, every moment: then gratitude becomes a constant response of the heart, a moment to stop and just watch what comes next.

When challenging situations, big and small, present themselves – such as a need to catch a plane – these all become moments to breathe and let go, secure in the knowledge that being present is all we can do. Life will do what it does.

The attempt to control with habits formed over years is not helpful: nothing to do but watch and be grateful. There is something around death that relates to this. I have talked about my fear of flying: once in the air, my body just cannot believe that sitting in an armchair, sealed in a tin tube hurtling through space at 600 mph, 37,000 feet above the ground, is a good idea. It is convinced at every jolt it will come back to earth with a bang. So I breath, consciously, and use this to practise letting go – and as dying is perhaps the ultimate let-go, it makes sense to get in some practice!

Fuck-it land and accepting disconnection, accepting this is how it is

Something that can happen along the way, as we start to use these various suggestions, is that they can seem to stop working; we feel disconnected and can't seem to find our way back again. I have mentioned the profound value of being able to rest in the reality of what simply *is*, to accept it. This is resting in Being, which can be recognised to be not only *where* we are, but also *what* we are. (That is why death really does have no dominion, because what I am always *is*.) It can feel so good as we begin to move in our lives from this place of connection: able to watch the mind, listen *in*, sense our energy, connect with our body and feelings; able to be more relaxed and present in a whole new way. A flow starts, we see changes in how we relate to ourselves and others, and what is reflected back as a result of this.

Then one day we notice that things have changed – seemingly gone backwards – and we don't understand why. 'So how come I can't *be* present?' we ask ourselves. 'How come I'm not finding the time to be alone and nurture myself? That I feel grumpy all the time? That I am treating others I care about badly?'. We start to resist what is happening: 'I don't like it like this', 'I don't want this'. Essentially, we are saying 'I want this to be different'. We don't accept reality: that this *is* what is happening *regardless of how we feel about it*. We ask ourselves 'why am I doing this? What's wrong with me? I was doing so great! I have all these tools, so what am I doing wrong?'. We start to analyse, then we stop that, as we realise we are in our head; then more self attack, then we realise we are doing this, and on and on, around and around – it's totally exhausting. The simple truth is, we are into resistance to what is. We are refusing to accept what is happening. We don't like it, we feel it *shouldn't be* like this. We likely either go in a funk and retreat or we start to get pissed off with ourselves and everyone around us.

This is where it can help to *name* this state we are in: I call it 'Fuck-it land'. I find that using four-letter words help's to keep this real, grounded. 'Fairyland' for instance doesn't quite do it, doesn't express the frustrated energy of this state.

So then with a name this can have a ground. No matter what is going on and how you feel about it, here you are! In Fuck-it land. So *now you can accept the truth of this* and drop down out of the clouds of mind to land with your feet firmly on the ground. 'I know this place. Here I am'. Back in accepting what *is* again, where you are – *which is where you belong.*

Compassion for yourself and others

If you stop and look back on your life, it can be disconcerting to realise that – unless you are truly exceptional – you too have felt, thought and acted out of the same negative spaces as everyone else: like there is one vast pool of collective negativity into which we all dip our toes, into which the Hitlers and others who initiated our historical horror stories, also dipped (or, in their case, maybe plunged). You too have surely felt the desire to outdo someone, to put someone down or to hurt someone; you have felt or thought or acted out of petty spite, jealousy, revenge ('Who, me?'); been motivated by a desire to get something for yourself at another's expense – just like everyone else! You too have betrayed and rejected and tried to pretend that you are something you are not, tried to avoid responsibility for something you did; you have lied, even if that was by omission.

It can be oh-so embarrassing and uncomfortable to admit these things. We feel bad about ourselves, it invites in all that guilt and shame – at least at first. And then, as you see more, you begin to realise that this is the *inevitable* consequence of believing conditioned, egoic mind; you start to get it, you see it: 'Oh, of course! This is what egos *do!*' Then you recognise that you were just being unconscious; you were lost inside that tangled web of conditioning, you just forgot and went on automatic – *just like everyone else*. Except that it would seem that few have the balls to look for ourselves to see what is true; it feels way too scary.

We have all been raised to protect our self-image, our comfortable picture of ourselves; to be the one who knows how things *really* are, who is on the 'right' side, who is basically a 'nice' person (however much we may feel inadequate and unworthy underneath); someone who doesn't think or feel or do bad or harmful things to others. (And of course there are some whose self-image is negative, the ones who are mean or stupid.) But the wonderful outcome of all this is that when you can *finally* face this, you discover you can feel compassion for all those other souls who are acting out *their* unconscious patterns with no knowledge of any alternative. You can see how blame keeps everyone stuck in pretending, and how judgement and comparison are just the poor defences of egoic mind that hasn't a clue about truth and reality.

Feeling our love

We are not taught about love, by which I mean to know ourselves *as* love, but this is what we all actually *are*, at our core. So spending time tuning into this can bring a profound change: feeling into it, sensing it, intuiting it, remembering it. Yes, we have all evolved this sense of ego, this that wants to get and avoid; it is useful – *no, essential* – that we come to recognise this as being so, and give it our conscious attention. But we also need to spend time getting to know our love, intimately: feeling into this every day, getting to know it and trust it. The more you do this, the more the connection with Being comes alive within you. Make this a practice (if you want to have a practice, this is a very powerful one): to remember and know the truth of this core of love at your centre, to remember to honour and spend time with this gentle focus of love, that is actually vast. You cannot plumb the depth of this loving heart, it is beyond what can be known; you *can* acknowledge its presence in your life *as your nature.* What this then provides is a strong and reliable foundation for the process of unravelling.

Something that can help here is noticing what happens when you open your heart to others. For instance, you sit next to a stranger on a bus and as they move to leave you find yourself saying 'I love that scarf you are wearing, it's such a beautiful colour', and they light up as they turn to you and you smile at one another. In this moment you are meeting, connecting hearts; you are responding from your love, you are expressing what you are. Notice how light and lovely that feels, to share this. It needs to be spontaneous to be real but being aware of your heart and your ability to impact others is part of this whole relational energy that allows this to happen. We have such a big impact on each other so in doing this we are responding from our knowing that we are all connected, all one. With no mental thinking about this, we affirm the truth of ourselves.

Meeting doubt

When you feel disturbed, anxious, sad or just uneasy, stop for a moment and remember: this moment, here, is where you can find solace. Allow yourself to be embraced by, and to rest in, presence of Being. The more you start to focus on Being – the more you feel into it, get a sense of it – the more available it becomes. It is, if you like, *a major shift in attention:* a shift that subtly alters our priorities and begins the process of turning us inside-out. In the previous chapters of this book we have talked about becoming aware of the conditioned mind, of how this distorts and attempts to control our every waking moment, until we begin to see through this and reconnect with the wholeness of ourselves; and how this wholeness essentially includes the body. I have talked about ways to support this process and how these can help us come free. In this, the frequent remembering of Being that I keep talking about, remembering what you know – even if this is only a tiny, weeny, tentative awareness of Being – is both essential to this process and extremely powerful. Because the more attention you give to it, the more it exerts a pull, like a magnetic attraction – which is hardly surprising as this is where you truly belong, as Being is what you essentially *are*. So make this your mantra.

Yet still, for many of us, this can seem a long way away from where we experience ourselves to be, a long way from our apparent everyday reality. As long as the conditioned mind holds sway, with its powerful belief systems and sticky emotional patterns inlaid from childhood, the more coming free can seem a far-off dream. There are so many influences waiting in the wings to pull us back: people who don't get it and have an unconscious investment in undermining our new and tender explorations; we may have friends or family or workmates who are sceptical of our new-found insights and realisations, who fear we are going a little bit crazy, or that the people who are helping us are crazy, even fraudulent. They may worry that what we are doing will in some way cause us harm.

So, for instance, as our priorities shift we are likely to be less and less interested in achieving goals, like wealth and possessions and prestigious positions; and this can make these people (and at times us too!) anxious we will lose out, that we may even end up penniless on the street. Other people can feel subtly threatened by what we are focussed on because it challenges their own attachment to the dream, and they may use sarcasm and other means to put us down and discourage us. So then it helps to take time out to just be with ourselves, and, if we can, to find others who honour this that we are valuing, too. This is where connecting with spiritual teachings and teachers can help. Or consciously feeling into that subtle sense of 'something' we have always known and, if we can't find that, remembering that, however things may appear and strange as this may sound, *our lives know exactly what they are doing!*

Awakening without true understanding

We have mentioned how some spiritual teachings and teachers, especially those from the non-dual approach, see therapy as being unnecessary: that all that's needed is to *realise* who we are. But seeing beyond illusion, beyond the *apparent* reality we have learned to accept, in one huge flash of realisation – *before* what needs to be met has been attended to – can bring trouble: trouble in the form of delusion, a not uncommon occurrence in spiritual circles. It is natural to want to avoid fear and pain; to avoid certain thoughts and feelings that feel threatening, like rage or impotence, and that are conflicted with beliefs that make it difficult to approach or admit to them.

Sooner or later, in my experience anyway, what has not been met will re-present and then there can be a split, where one part sees clearly whilst the other is still caught up in the egoic morass. Then, lacking conscious awareness, feelings and emotions get denied and acted out. This seeing of something before we are prepared can make everything very confusing, especially energy-wise. We may have lots of new *experiences* – of peace and bliss and far-out insights and sensations and movements of energy. We may come to feel we are almost omnipotent and, for instance, interpret an insight (such as there being nobody here doing anything) to mean we can do no harm.

Then, as we saw in the chapter on teachers, if people don't see deeper they can act pretty unconsciously, in the belief that there is no-one there to *be* responsible. Of course, when ego hears that you don't need to address this, it pounces on what it sees as clear permission to go on the rampage: to get and avoid and deny, without consequence. But, again in my experience (and as in any other stage along the way to full consciousness), *it is not possible to hear certain truths at their deeper level until a space is created to receive these*. And if what some teachers say is true – that we awaken in stages and at different levels (as in mind, heart and gut) – then it's not hard to see how this state of being out-of-alignment with a deeper truth can have dire consequences, is it?

Facing darkness

It can be scary opening Pandora's Box – we don't know what will emerge. When we allow what has been repressed in the body to surface, it can seem very dark. Some of what I am writing about can seem too much, too depressing, if you don't also remember that what we are doing is letting in the sunlight and fresh air. The murky floor of this box is littered with spent beliefs, like after a fireworks' party when some of the fireworks still have powder in them while others just smell bad; or like devils and demons that get their power from our believing in them but actually have no real substance. The *really* scary thing is that *whole societies* can carry a belief that repressing feelings is a good and necessary part of living together. Such societies are dangerous places to live (as Hitler's Germany proved), ripe for manipulation by those who seek power. As we have seen, the very act of repression forces what is being repressed to find another outlet, and this can be cloaked in self-righteousness.

I don't know the psychological history of Anders Breivik, the man who shot all those teenagers on an island off Norway, but it seems clear he was sitting on a powder-keg of unmet personal baggage. And now we have another example that illustrates this potential for violence erupting from repressed feelings of fear, frustration and anger – the racism and misogyny raising its ugly head in response to Donald Trump's invitation. This response cuts us off from the humanity in us that would otherwise seek to help refugees and other suffering people (Brexit in the UK has a similar base). This dark repressed energy of the unconscious doesn't respect national boundaries: in some countries it is overt and visible and in others more hidden and unseen, but both can lead to participating (albeit passively) in acts of disturbing violence.

But no matter what your own personal hell realms are, how dark and deep (and who is to measure this?) and frightening, opening to let in the light of Being – that is also love – allows for an enormous lightening of the load. Then flashes of insight, new found recognition, fresh clarity about old wounds, all bring movement and change and a softening around old feelings and memories that were unendurable at the time. Rather like greeting a bunch of starving miners trapped underground for an age, as they slowly begin to surface there can be a real feeling of welcoming and joy. We may even discover nuggets of acceptance and a forgiveness *that has already taken place*, leaving space for new possibilities. *This* is what changes the world, *this is* what takes true courage. And this applies to all of us, even if we don't know it yet.

One thing you can be sure of is that your time will come; because, ultimately, anyone can do this, anyone can face themselves. It's like discovering you can transmit healing energy: *you find you can do this once you let go of the belief that you can't* – preferably with a little support, and necessarily in your own time. In fact, it's heartening to realise that any one of us, anywhere, can contribute to this meeting with, and opening up to what appears so dark and difficult: and that this impacts everyone. By bringing the light of consciousness in to meet our own repressed darkness, and seeing through an egoic mind that insists on continuing this repression, we act to redeem all pain and all misunderstanding. Isn't that incredible?

Grieving fully

There is much happening around us that is painful to watch, to acknowledge, to feel. It's not all constant bliss at all, which can be hugely disappointing if this was your idea, your goal. This is where we get to know the heart is not simply a vehicle for joy. It can also feel the full range of pain and sadness, loss and grieving for this. Seeing this home we call the Earth and all living creatures under threat from human actions stretches our capacity to *let in*. The pain and horror so many people, especially innocent children, and animals and all sentient beings are experiencing can seem too vast. And yet to do anything else would be denial. *Suffering is absolutely real for those that are suffering,* in whatever form; even when this comes from a belief that isn't actually true.

Even when it's personal, people resist fully grieving. Why? Like jumping into Niagara Falls, we fear being sucked under and pounded by the sheer volume of grief crashing down on us. Also, opening to our feelings risks revealing anything we are holding onto, such as old issues that are painful and unresolved. Like velcro these cling on, tending to stifle the heart which, when free of this, behaves rather like the seashore: waves of grief can come in and then depart again, leaving us empty and washed clean. We discover it didn't destroy us, and this helps us to trust, to find our courage and be ready for more of this beautiful but unpredictable life.

Seeing from joy

As we begin to unravel the threads that our unconscious conditioning has tangled us up in, seeing becomes joyful and inspiring. It gives us back the energy to face what is difficult and painful, and even turn fear into delight. This soothes the tension we hold in our bodies and helps us to relax. We start to experience a lightness of being that we come to recognise and value. As we are drawn into trusting this indescribable reality of Being, so we are able to rest more and more in simple presence. Conflict begins to dissolve, moments of supreme ease arise by themselves. There is a sense of the rightness of things; that, despite all appearances, on the level where true reality is seen, all is well. And this has a powerful influence on the energy we transmit that affects everything around us. Then we cannot help but change the world – even as, on a deeper level, we recognise that nothing needs to be changed.

The hidden power of reverence

What if all the trees that are raising their branches to the sky are standing in silent worship? If all the flowers are offering themselves to divinity? If all the natural world exists in constant prayer? If it is, in fact, a living, breathing means of life celebrating itself? Praying, singing, enjoying, laughing, dancing, revering, adoring? Growing deeper into love? Then you see that we are, truly, living in Heaven! Or Hell. Ours to choose what we see, how we see what we see and what we focus our attention on as we walk by – so often lost in our thoughts, in our mind, entangled in our self-absorbed inner world. Where *are* you? Where do you belong? What about here, where there is only ever *now?* There is nothing *you lack, you already know everything you need to know.* Being is everywhere, touching everything. Adyashanti comments *'When we relinquish trying to get somewhere, we naturally start to arrive fully where we are. Have trust in your own way. There's something in the unfolding of your own life that is your greatest teacher.'*

A flash of sun lights up the rooftops – you *know;* the smooth feel of an egg in your hand – you *know,* a child's voice calling – you *know;* the smell of a rose or of roasting coffee as you pass – you *know.* You have always known. It is not complicated. You don't need to study or acquire any more knowledge. There are no gilded cups or degrees or public accolades of any kind. You just quietly let Being swallow you whole. What is stopping you? Reach out a hand and touch a tree with reverence, and *feel* the life pulsing through you – are you so sure that you are 'you'? A separate 'person'? Who or what or even where is this 'you'? Can you find it, this separate entity?

When you touch Being, to stay in connection and maintain this, you will need to see and sense and feel and discover whatever works for you to come free from the seductive but fatal embrace of your egoic mind and its conditioned beliefs. But you can *always* return, again and again and again, until there is no more pull to leave. You just remain here. Present. Living what you are – open and *being,* open and *knowing,* open and *knowing* your*self* as Being. It's as simple as that! Watching bubbles rise in a pot of boiling water – open; staring at the reflection on a passing car – open; sitting gazing out of the window – open. Watching your child playing with a ball – open, your cat curled up in front of the fire – open, a lake dappled by the wind – open. seeing the reflection of tree branches making a moving pattern on the water – open, clouds appearing behind these reflections – open. You *know.* Sun reappearing – you *know: absolutely.* Beyond the shadow of any doubt.

Home-play (a continuation of!)
1. Asserting your 'No!'
- Firstly, make sure you are standing with your feet well planted on the floor, check that your knees aren't locked and that your hips are neither wedged back nor thrust forward, but positioned comfortably above your feet.
- Breathe into the Solar Plexus and connect with this centre (maybe placing a hand here) and practise saying 'No' from here. It is important that you then immediately take a breath, remembering to breath all the way out. See if you can feel the energy descending into your body on the out-breath. Crucially, this breath allows what you are doing to be integrated in the body. At first you may barely feel any strength in the solar plexus, but after a while you may notice the energy here becoming more stable and strong, or even pushing outwards.
- Repeat this until you can feel a strong connection (you might want to do this in front of a mirror so you can also practise holding eye contact while you speak). Notice the timbre of your voice changing as you repeat the 'No': the loudness, and any tension in the body.

2. Slowing down

Make all movements slow. Notice how you speed up automatically and deliberately slow down again. This is one of the simplest, most powerful, transformational acts you can do.

3. Letting go of all blame

- Stand with your legs your under hips, knees unlocked, and feel the connection through the feet with the ground. Raise your arms to about shoulder height, palms uppermost, breathing in as you do so. Visualise as you do this, that you are holding all the blame you have ever attached to yourself, anyone or anything, in your hands; feel the unbearable weight of this for several seconds, holding your breath.
- Now let go, allowing your arms to swing downwards, bending the knees and letting the arms swing between these, breathing out forcefully as you do so. Really *feel* the sense of letting go of this enormous burden and the relief of this. Shake out your hands and feet.
- You can include the words 'I let go of all blame' as you do this. If visualisations strengthen this for you, you can try imaging a huge hairy spider at the centre of its web and it has you trapped through thousands of tiny sticky threads, each attached to someone you have blamed. As you let go these threads break; the spider shrivels into dust and blows away on a gentle cool breeze. Or invent your own scenario.

4. Gathering what is yours

- First, sit and sense the cradle. Keeping your elbows against the body, extend your forearms out in front of you with palms upturned.
- Now extend arms out to their full reach in front of the body, and draw them back in, with the finger tips curling towards you. Feel the energy as you do this, as if you are gathering it back towards yourself, stopping about 4 cm from the cradle. Repeat several times.
- Next, allow your hands to come together, fingers slightly linked, palms facing towards the cradle in a relaxed manner. Sense this as creating a container, a kind of basket in which the outer part is formed by your wrists and hands, the inner curve being internal and linking the cradle. Feel the dense energy-field you are creating as you bring all your energy to this place.
- Finally, with one arm remaining still, as part of this 'basket', allow the other to reach out and, using your finger and thumb, pluck something that belongs to you and bring it back and place it in this basket. Continue this as long you are able to identify items that belong to you.

All this can be repeated whenever you feel like it. With the last part, it is as though you are giving a physical, energetic recognition and acceptance to what you have seen: owning it and restoring it, instead of leaving it as a concept stored in the mind. This is a way of concretising and using the body as both repository and reclaim box.

5. Giving back to others what is theirs (and therefore not yours)
- Place two chairs facing each other. Find a cushion, the heavier the better.
- Now, sit on one chair and place the cushion on your knees, feeling the weight of it pressing down on you. This cushion represents someone else's baggage that has been given to you to carry. It could be someone close, in your family, or just a friend, workmate or acquaintance.
- Now, breathing fully, lift the cushion and *place it down with firm emphasis* on the other chair. There may be words that go with this like 'I don't want to receive your upset. Please take care of it yourself' or, more concisely, 'This belongs to you!'; or whatever words affirm this for you.
- Immediately take a deep breath (this is extremely important), knowing that with the out breath you are integrating the experience into your body. Also, try placing the chairs in front of a mirror so you can maintain eye contact while you say this. Or, if you have a suitable 'buddy' who will role-play for you, *without commenting*, get them to sit in the opposite chair and first place the cushion firmly on your knees. Then receive the cushion back from you. This can make it more real.
- Feel the lighter-ness in your body after doing this a few times, and any relief. Give space to any feelings that come up during this exercise.

6. Playing with projection
- Put on a pair of sunglasses and notice how these change the way you see everything.
- Now remove them to give yourself a sense about how projection works, how it colours what we see. Observe the way we project out onto others and then react to these projections; they relate to issues that often have little to do with the other. Perhaps the other person looks like your mother? Or they have a way of moving that reminds you of someone familiar? Or of someone who played a significant role in your life? It's highly valuable when you can see that you are doing this and take the projection back to where it belongs: with you.

7. Bringing yourself here
You know how people try to train a dog to walk beside them by calling out 'heel!'? You can do this with yourself as a playful way of reminding yourself to come back here into present-time reality. You may get some funny looks if you do this walking down the street, but again, if you choose to, you can *even use that* as a way to be with your fears of other people's judgements and reactions. And remember to smile!

8. Sing 'I bless what comes – (pause) – and I bless what goes'

Tune into the heart and let yourself *feel* this; feel the willingness to let in the new and unknown and let go of the old, grieving if this comes up. Any simple tune that has the sense of swinging one way with the first line and then the other with the second, will do. This is a lovely exercise to do with a partner, where you hold hands and swing them first to the right (letting come) and then to the left (letting go).

Here is a brief summary of the most useful things you can do in support of your own unravelling

* **Breathe** fully: Check that you are breathing fully and naturally. This allows you to stay connected with your body and feelings.

* **Listen** *in*: Do this frequently: listening to your feelings, sensings, intuitions; how your body is feeling and anything it wants to say to you. Make sure you are grounded while you do this.

* **Relax** into just being here: Know that you will always meet whatever comes as best you can, so you can stop worrying about the future.

* **Enjoy** what you can and watch what you can't.

* **Allow** expression of feelings: Give regular space and permission for the expression of feelings, including movement, sound, colour and shape. *Avoid thinking about feelings.*

* **Stop** trusting the emotionalised, conditioned mind: Remember that the mind is unable to tell you about life and what is true. Be wary of rationalisations, logical explanations and justifications.

* **Witness** your thoughts, don't try to control them: Simply notice when your thoughts are active and pulling your attention. Remember that what is noticing this is awareness, not your mind.

* **Realise** that the world is not as you have learned to see it. Give yourself permission to return to a state of innocence.

* **Be willing** to not know: Even when this makes you feel vulnerable and exposed.

* **Trust** your own knowing before that of anyone else: It's better to make your own 'mistakes'. If what someone else says reminds you of and resonates with what you know then there is no problem.

* **Be aware** of the mind's tendency to turn all information into fixed views and then take a position on these.

* **Remember** egoic mind always wants to get or avoid. This creates the drama, the fear and the hurt; it is not real and is not who you *are*.

* **Question** beliefs: Recognise when something is being believed and question if this belief is really true. Be with any emotions that are gluing the belief in place.

* **Recognise** how memory is controlled by emotions: Remember that memory is selective and becomes distorted by its emotional content.

* **Watch** emotional reactions and patterns playing out: Take a pause. This gives you the opportunity to stop reacting. Forgive yourself when you can't do this. Take a moment to be with what is triggering this reaction but don't start analysing.
* **Notice** when you are in resistance: Feel the subtle pressure; pause, open and relax.
* **Invite** don't fight: Instead of trying to *make* yourself do something, *invite* yourself to do it. Feel the difference in your energy. I *could* do this (no shoulds).
* **Pause** when you feel anxious or uneasy: Stop and meet whatever is there to be felt. Embrace yourself and allow the body to rock or make movements or any sounds.
* **Welcome** uncomfortable feelings: Give regular time to just being present with your feelings, without having to do anything about them.
* **Pay attention** to the flow: Notice in your body how this feels when you do this.
* **Look** for the heart and connection to Being in everyone: Remember, no matter what the appearance, everyone has a heart and Being resides everywhere.
* **Risk** everything to come fully alive: Be willing to risk others' negative opinions and reactions.
* **Rest** in the cradle: Relax, let go, let be and deeply rest. Make this a habit.
* **Find** something of beauty and something to be thankful for everyday.
* **Sense *into*** Being-ness: Sense, feel, intuit and *know* presence as Being, outside of time. Know that all is well, always.
* **Let go**: in times of extreme stress and turmoil, <u>surrender:</u> Nothing to do but lay yourself down in the cradle of life, suspended in the sky of emptiness and be gently rocked back into Being.

(Observe the key words here) Breathe, listen *in*, relax, enjoy, allow, stop, witness, realise, be willing, trust, be aware, remember, question, recognise, watch, notice, welcome, pause, invite, pay attention, look, risk, let go, rest, find, sense *into*, surrender.

And a few helpful things to remember
* We are controlled by what we resist
* You can't change what you are not aware of.
* It's *always* all about us.
* Our 'story' is like airtight sticking-plaster covering an old wound: it stops it healing.
* Don't take others' reactions personally (let others pick up their own baggage).
* Life is a Free Workshop and everyone your Worthy Opponent (so use everyone and everything to become conscious).
* Watch your mind, participate in everything else.
* Only ego can feel unworthy

* What comes is always what you need, and what goes is no longer needed.
* Dedicating your life to unravelling is the greatest gift you can give yourself, those you love (including your children and grandchildren, if you have any) and the planet.
* Being is *always* listening.

There are so many ways you can support yourself, including those I have described in other chapters – these just appear as constants no matter what the individual make-up.

And here are some phrases to play with: to enjoy, soothe and inspire
Don't read them all at once, spread them out over weeks or months and allow time for each one to be digested. Pick out your favourites and discard what doesn't work for you: even better, invite, invent or intuit your own!

Aaaaahhh 'thisss...' (as in smelling divine perfume) – Absorbing beauty – Acceptance instead of resignation – Acceptance of helplessness – Ageless grace – A human being natural – Always arriving – Always and never alone – Appreciating uncertainty – A time to move into living from the Heart – Awareness is not of the mind – Be a fool for love – Belonging to truth – Body as truth speaker – Breathing to return – Caressing what comes – Celebrating being here – Celebrating sorrow – Clean and fresh – Close up with reality – Compassion opens, judgement closes – Consciousness equals awareness of what is – 'Could' frees, 'should' binds – Dancing foliage – Deep listening – Delighting instead of worrying – Divine flesh – Devotion is a living force – Disintegration and re-integration – Dissolving defences – Dissolving into 'this' – Docking – Dying to live – Dying to every moment – Embodying spirit – Embracing the miracle – Empathic response – Endless becoming – Enjoying ambiguity – Everyone is family – Eyes of the heart – Faith in the unfathomable – Faithful to truth – Falling into Being – Feeling reality – Feelings are like a river; always flowing, always changing – Flowing from stillness – Following the feminine – Freedom calling – Freedom *to* – From aridity to nurturing – Free from fear and stagnation – Grateful for every moment – 'Grocking' equals absorbing, taking-in, digesting reality – Grounding in the miraculous – Hidden language: a bird's wing stroking the sky – Humanity unfolding – I am moved – Infinity is here now – Intimacy, the ultimate exposure – Intimate responsiveness – Intuition: knowing without mind – Keeping faith – Keep coming *here* – Knowing nothing is knowing everything – Laughter out of nowhere – Life never-ending – Liquid divinity endlessly pouring – Listening in – Living values – Looking freely – Loving what is here – Melting into 'this' – Mindless existence – Money is like a river – Moving closer – Moving in and out of emptiness – Moving in stillness – Moving in truth – Nature as teacher – Never doubt your own true love – Never trust justifications – No escape, nowhere to run – No strangers here – Nothing more is ever needed – Nowhere else to go – Only 'this' – Overwhelmed by beauty – Overwhelmed by love – Penetrated by love – Playing with everything – Presence is enough – Rebelling *for* – Receiving 'this' – Recognising truth – Regret can be healing, guilt enslaves – Remembering the already known – Resistance melting away like snow in the morning – Resting in the unknown – Returning to 'this' – Reverence for the other – Risking exposure – Safety as part of the whole – Satisfaction without end – Saying Yes to your No – Seeing beauty everywhere – Seeing through distortion – Seeing what is already here – Sensory connectedness – Settling into yourself – Sharing is our nature – Shifting down – Silent communion – Silliness is lovely – S l o w n e s s grows on you – Smiling at life – Softly, softly – Standing in clarity – Stepping lightly – Stop and live – Stopping right here – Sun and cloud – Tasting everything – The courage to do nothing – The end of time as we know it – The intelligent heart – The invincible logic of the Absolute – The limitation of words – The moving heart – The power of tenderness – There are no outsiders – There is only love – The smell of a rose – The such-ness of everything – Touching stillness – Touching 'this' – True freedom – True grieving equals loving what was even as you let it go – Trusting what cannot be spoken – Trust simplicity, beware complexity – Turning towards – Unconsciousness is blind – Value what cannot be weighed or measured – Violence is love distorted – Volcanoes of rage, oceans of tears – Warm aloneness – Warm silence – Wisdom is always available – Witness to the inevitable – Wordless understanding – Yearning to come home – Yes to life! – Zorba and the Buddha.

EPILOGUE

At the beginning of this book I talked about what I get to *see*. So what is this? What do I see in those who come to work with me? What do I notice in myself? I see an ongoing movement towards awake-ness and full aliveness; they belong together, the becoming more available, less constricted, with less attachment to something that isn't real. I watch the withering of the power of the egoic mind to pull attention as this is *seen through*; the melting away of beliefs as these are held up to the light of truth and revealed to be the illusions that they are. So then emotions can return to being simply *feelings* – feelings being a wonderful and important part of a natural flowing response to life. I *sense* the movement of energy down into the body from the mind, to where the eyes and ears of the heart lie waiting and the cradle, as anchor, resource and refuge.

Then, like one of those weebles I mentioned with a weight at its base, when we fall over we quickly come back up again. There is a lessening of the power of fear, as the ability to let go and rest in not-needing-to-know becomes established. And a growing ability to *speak the truth* to ourselves and others. More *energy* can become available, with less need to repress this and maintain defences. Maybe not for a while, but eventually, I see a lighter-ness, an expanded-ness, a certain ease and relaxation: an inner joy and sense of playfulness, along with something solid, present and quietly at home with itself.

I notice how outer lives change to reflect this inner dynamic, including relationships with family and friends, where there is an easing up of old fixed positions and sometimes surprising changes. For all of us there is so much joy and validation in letting go into this living intuitive reality that we are, and which appears to have two faces – the two faces of Being: the Absolute and the Relative. One is experienced, the other is *known*, two aspects of the same thing: the grounding in this earthy physical reality that allows us to be fully present in our bodies *and* – simultaneously – connected with that which is within and beneath and beyond everything: the silent, pregnant stillness that seems to contain a powerful magnetic force of its own.

What do I mean by this? I am referring to what it is that pulls us to return, what has been described as God breathing out and breathing in again. I like the simple analogy of waves in the ocean, always and perpetually returning to source. I know this slow 'process' I am talking about, that I sense as a kind of melting down, appears to diverge from the approach of those who teach that awakening is instantaneous; that there can be no gradual process – but then if time is not as it appears? Perhaps both are true.

Something around this whole deal of awakening I feel to share. I don't know why, but I have never been able to get excited about having what often seems to be painted as a great big fat revelation (whatever name you give to it): a clap of thunder, a flash of lightening, a moment where everything is revealed and transformed. Does this sound contradictory to you? Maybe this is a female thing, as women tend to be more connected with our bodily experience of carrying and later nurturing children. But whatever it is it just doesn't excite me. I am aware that in some spiritual circles saying this can sound almost blasphemous. Yet I am drawn to this that feels more of a gradual melting into true reality. Not that insights and shifts don't occur, but I am somehow comfortable with this weaving in and out of clarity doing its own thing, in its own way; its own time.

Am I just lazy? Subconsciously afraid of what instantaneous awakening might mean? I don't know. I don't know why this is so, I only know it's what I find when I look at this. I find no attraction to a kind of instant crossing-over; I just know there is something I know and love and it is *here*: always present, everywhere – *even when I can't connect with it* – and that the living *as* this 'I am' is enough. It reminds me of a short poem that arrived in the night by itself, unannounced: *'I am drowning in the river of am-ness, not yet arrived at the sea. I tremble as I begin to lose sight of my mind. Don't pull me out, don't teach me to swim. Just touch me as I pass – it is enough to feel the tenderness in your fingertips.'*

I see that despite any 'inner' knowing, I still have attachments; I feel pain, fear can arise and the doubts of the mind take over. I remain aware that there is much suffering in the world, on every level, and that this is very real for those who experience it; being alive we witness and experience a whole range of feelings and some of these are certainly not comfortable. It is, after all, our human nature to be feeling, sensing, intuiting bodies-Being. But I don't seem to claim these feelings in the same way, they are not held on to as tightly. As for what comes next, I can't get too interested in that as I know I can't be sure – what I *can* be sure of is that I will find out! What is clear is that the nature of what we call 'life' involves constant change and movement, and that this little 'I' does not and cannot control this. We can only bring our attention back to the present and the voice of the intuitive heart.

In writing in this way, in sharing these personal experiences, insights and questions, I offer you what *I* see. You, dear reader, may see some things more clearly yourself. There are no 'experts' – although I have found some who reflect and express what I recognise to be true exceptionally clearly and beautifully. So I would hope to invite you to look for yourself rather than looking to others for answers. In these deepest of questions trust your own intuitive knowing, and join me in direct investigation through these realms of feeling and sensing and looking and discerning and seeking to know the face of the divine: as others have said before me, your very own face! For how can there be a difference?

Just resting here, quietly listening in, with no effort; open to what comes, willing to engage, enjoying the feel of ourselves: stretching, wriggling, yawning, humming; whatever way the body wants to move and express is totally fine, resting in the knowing that all is well. Because the reality seems to be that when you can say, truthfully, 'I am all here', there is nothing left to say; nothing to acquire, nothing to search for except enjoying searching itself, adventuring into the dark, playing in the unknown.

The closer we get to this that we are – the further Being reels us in – the more we encounter simplicity. And with this, a strange sense of familiarity: *we have known this all along!* This is what I see time and again. No matter the apparent complexities of what presents, however seemingly multilayered and complicated things might appear, what is actually found to be there, what is seen and realised within the field of love – that provides a sense of holding and cherishing no matter what – is just *this*. So here we are, this is it! Nowhere to go but *here*.

ACKNOWLEDGEMENTS

I would like to express my deep gratitude to the following people for their interest, support and faith in this project which has been such a great blessing: for professional services Shantam Chalkley (proofreading and advice) and Barbara Doherty (who generously put her graphic design expertise in service of improving my amateur drawings and cover design to create the overall book design); to Anne, Debs, Ingrid, Pia and Thor for various input and ongoing support; Anthony, Nisha, Satyo and Trish for comments; Anita and Wendy for reading; and the proofing gang: Adam, Alex, Antonio, Dave, Ilaria, Laura, Miriam, Muna, Paola, Rosaria, Sophie and Sue.

REFERENCES

With sincere gratitude to those many people and publishers who have freely granted permission for quotes to be used in this book.

1. **Adyashanti** - (www.adyashanti.org) Open Gate Sangha, California, US (Quoted widely throughout book).
2. **Krishnamurti** (1895-1986)
3. **Breytenbach, Anna** - Excerpts from Animal Spirit (www.animalspirit.org).
4. **Young, Jon** - Program Community, Mentoring and Nature Connection, California, US.
5. **Osho** (1931-1990) - (www.osho.com) Quotes reprinted by permission of Osho International Foundation, Switzerland (Quoted widely throughout book).
6. **Katie, Byron** - Excerpt from *A Thousand Names For Joy: How To Live In Harmony With The Way things Are*, published in 2007.
7. **Shakespeare William** (1564-1616)
8. **Einstein, Albert** (1879-1955)
9. **Razzaque, Russell** - Independent, 21st August 2015 (www.independent.co.uk/voices/as-a-psychiatrist-i-find-the-emotional-reactions-of-the-anyone-but-corbyn-camp-interesting-10465279.html).
10. **Klein, Naomi** - Excerpt from *This Changes Everything*, published in 2014.
11. **Karantzakis, Nikos** (1883-1957) - Excerpt from *Zorba the Greek*, published in 1946.
12. **de Ruiter, John** - College of Integrated Philosophy, Edmonton, Canada.
13. **Pope Francis** - Christmas Day, 2014.
14. **Moreland, Doris** (1927-2008) - Excerpt *Gods Gift of Anger* (permissions@chalicepress.com).
15. **Rumi** (1207-1273)
16. **Lund, Jeb** - The Guardian (www.theguardian.com/commentisfree/2016/feb/24/donald-trump-victory-nevada-caucus-voter-anger).
17. **Alvarez, Ali** - The Guardian (www.theguardian.com/lifeandstyle/2016/oct/29/ali-alvarez-monarch-butterflies-mexico-bereavement-mother?CMP=share_btn_link).
18. **Wilson, Tim** - Quote from his Film *Griefwalker*, National Film Board of Canada.
19. **Jenkinson, Stephen** - Quoted by Tim Wilson talking about the film *Griefwalker* (www.orphanwisdom.com/contact), 29th April 2013.
20. **Macy, Joanna** - (www.joannamacy.net) Books *Despair and Personal Power in a Nuclear age* and *Active Hope* (with Chris Johnstone).
21. **Kobayashi, Nobuyuki** - The Guardian (www.theguardian.com/artanddesign/gallery/2017/mar/22/nature-photography-nobuyuki-kobayashi-japan?CMP=share_btn link).
22. **Caddy, Eileen** - Excerpt from *Opening the Doors Within*, © Eileen Caddy 1986, 2010. Published by the Findhorn Press, Scotland.

Zephaniah, Benjamin - Rastafarian poet (www.benjaminzephaniah.com).

24. **Lavater, Joseph Kasper** (1741–1801) - 17th century Swiss poet, philosopher and theologian.
25. **Phillpotts, Eden** (1862-1999) - Excerpt from *A shadow passes*, published in 1919.
26. **St Maarten, Anthon** - www.anthonstmaarten.com/contact.html.
27. **Wilson, Pamela** - Fellowship of the Heart, N. California, US. Excerpt from *Ordinary Women, Extraordinary Wisdom - The Feminine Face of Awakening* by Rita Marie Robinson, published in 2007. Quotes reprinted with permission of John Hunt Publishing.
28. **Rylance, Mark** - The Guardian (www.theguardian.com/culture/2015/mar/15/mark-rylance-wolf-hall-interview-the-gunman).
29. **Aron, Elaine** - Book *The Highly Sensitive Person,* published in 1996.
30. **Diodge, Norman** - The Guardian (www.theguardian.com/science/2015/feb/08/norman-doidge-brain healing-neuroplasticity-interview).
31. **Octopus Experiment** - Desmond Ramirez and Todd Oakley, University of California, US (www.theguardian.com/science/neurophilosophy/2015/may/20/octopus-skin-contains-light-sensors).
32. **Whitman, Walt** (1819-1892) - Excerpts from *Leaves of Grass.* Originally published in 1855.
33. **Mukti** - Open Gate Sangha, California, US (www.adyashanti.org/index.php?file=mukti_main).
34. **Thích Nhät Hanh** - Excerpt from *Peace in Every Step*, published by Rider in 1991. Quotes reprinted with permission of the Random House Publishing Group Ltd.
35. **Liedloff, Jean** - *The Continuum Concept,* published in 1977, revised edition 1985.
36. **London, Jack** (1876-1916) - Excerpt from *The call of the Wild,* first published in 1903.
37. **Penn, Robert** - The Guardian (www.theguardian.com/books/2015/nov/15/the-man-who-made-things-out-of-trees-review-robert-penn).
38. **Rostrum, Lief** - The Guardian (www.theguardian.com/science/2016/oct/25/bio-inspiration-thrilling-new-science-could-transform-medicine?CMP=share_btn_link).
39. **Monbiot, George** - The Guardian (www.theguardian.com/commentisfree/2017/feb/28/greatest-peril-screening-reality-4chan-pewdiepie-nothing-matters-fascism?CMP=share_btn_link).
40. **Manning, Richard** - Excerpt from *Against the grain: How agriculture has hijacked civilisation,* published in 2014.
41. **Caeiro, Alberto** (1888-1935) - Excerpt from *O Guardador de Rebanhos (The Keeper of Sheep)*, part of Poemas Completos de Alberto Caeiro. Published in 2015 by Fernando Pessoa.
42. **Hendy, David** - Excerpt from *Noise: A Human History of Sound and Listening* (©D.J.Hendy@sussex.ac.uk), published in 2013.
43. **Santana, Carlos** - The Guardian (www.theguardian.com/music/2016/jul/16/carlos-santana-you-can-get-high-on-whats-within-you).

44. **Netherlands Institute of Ecology (Students)** - The Guardian (www.theguardian.com/science/grrlscientist/2015/aug/26/urban-song-birds-stress-hormones-light-pollution).
45. **Jacobsen, Abdiel Cedric** - The Guardian (www.theguardian.com/stage/gallery/2016/oct/26/dancers-the-art-of-movement-in-pictures?CMP=share_btn_link).
46. **Godfrey-Smith, Peter** - The Guardian (www.theguardian.com/environment/2017/mar/28/alien-intelligence-the-extraordinary-minds-of-octopuses-and-other-cephalopods?CMP=share_btn_link).
47. **Wohlleben, Peter** - The Guardian (www.theguardian.com/environment/2016/sep/12/peter-wohlleben-man-who-believes-trees-talk-to-each-other?CMP=share_btn_link).
48. **Abhinavagupta** (950–1016 AD) - 10th century Kashmiri philosopher (quoted by Tantric master Daniel Odier).
49. **Payne, Roman** - Excerpt from *The Wanderess,* published in 2013.
50. **Brenot, Philippe** - The Guardian (www.theguardian.com/lifeandstyle/2016/oct/29/a-graphic-history-of-sex-there-is-no-gene-that-drives-sexuality-all-sexuality-is-learned?CMP=share_btn_link).
51 **Cocheret, Marlies** - www.marliescocheret.com
52. **Kennedy, Anne** (1953-2016)
53. **Brand, Russell** - Excerpt from *Revolution,* published in 2014 by Century. Quotes reprinted by permission of the Random House Group Ltd.
54. **Field, Rechad** (1934-2016) - Sheik of the Sufi Order International with Per Vilayat Inayat Khan.
55. **Gangaji** - The Gangaji Foundation, Ashland, Oregon, US. Excerpt from *You Are That,* published in 1995.
56. **Barth, Karl** (1886-1968) - Swiss Protestant theologian.
57. **Frank, Anne** - *The Dairy of Anne Frank,* published posthumously in 1947.
58. **Tagore, Rabindrath** (1861-1941)
59. **Obama, Barack** - The Guardian (www.theguardian.com/us-news/2015/dec/18/obama-year-end-press-conference-american-leadership-syria-paris-iran-tpp-cuba-guantanamo-bay).
60. **Baldwin, James** (1927-1984) - The Guardian (www.theguardian.com/commentisfree/2016/jan/01/generation-failed-politicians-elite-liberal-values).
61. **Sanders, Bernie** - Senator. Quoted from CNN Town Hall, S. Carolina with Jimmy Kimmel Live on 23rd February 2016, and from Twitter (twitter.com/berniesanders/status/810262550361145345) on 17th December 2016.
62. **Marti, Jose** (1853-1895) - Cuban activist.
63. **Meyer, Jane** - The Guardian (www.theguardian.com/us-news/2016/jan/17/dark-money-review-nazi-oil-the-koch-brothers-and-a-rightwing-revolution)
64. **Luther King, Martin** (1929-1968) - Excerpt from the Report to SCLC Staff, May 1967.
65. **Corbyn, Jeremy** - Rt. Hon. MP (www.jeremycorbyn.org.uk)
66. **Carmela, Manuela** - Bloomberg (www.bloomberg.com/news/articles/2015-05-26/madrid-s-next-mayor-may-be-a-social-activist-grandmother).
67. **Burgess, Rick** - Morning Star, 21st January 2016 (www.morningstaronline.co.uk/a-6904-Is-social-media-a-recipe-for-real-change#.WKgem4wNi4s.email.

68. **Hawking, Stephen** - The Guardian (www.theguardian.com/commentisfree/2016/jul/29/stephen-hawking-brexit-wealth-resources).
69. **Jorge, Jorge** - The Guardian (www.theguardian.com/world/2016/nov/28/fidel-castro-cubans-last-respects?CMP=share_btn_link).
70. **Stavrides, Stavros** - The Guardian (www.theguardian.com/cities/2016/sep/21/athens-unofficial-community-hope-government-failures?CMP=share_btn_link).
71. **Ostrom, Elinor** - Nobel Laureate (1933-2012). The Guardian (www.theguardian.com/global-development/poverty-matters/2012/jun/14/elinor-ostrom-commons-rio20).
72. **Mason, Paul** - Excerpt from keynote speech at Barcelona Initiative for Technological Sovereignty, 18th November 2015, Mosquito Ridge.
73. **Whittle, Joe** and **Wright, Phillip** (Lakota) - The Guardian (www.theguardian.com/us-news/2016/nov/30/standing-rock-indigenous-people-history-north-dakota-access-pipeline-protest?CMP=share_btn_link).
74. **Tamras, Martin** - The Guardian (www.theguardian.com/world/2016/nov/06/from-isis-jail-to-audience-with-pope?CMP=share_btn_link).
75. **Davis, Daryl** - Al Jazeera (www.aljazeera.com/.../kkk-members-leave-clan-befriending-black-musician-1701081).

Lightning Source UK Ltd.
Milton Keynes UK
UKHW011816301118
333254UK00011B/936/P